ADO.NET Examples
and Best Practices
for C# Programmers

WILLIAM R. VAUGHN WITH PETER BLACKBURN

ADO.NET Examples and Best Practices for C# Programmers
Copyright © 2002 by Beta V Corporation and Boost Data Limited

ISBN (pbk): 1-59059-012-0
Printed and bound in the United States of America 12345678910

Trademarked names may appear in this book. Rather than use a trademark symbol with every occurrence of a trademarked name, we use the names only in an editorial fashion and to the benefit of the trademark owner, with no intention of infringement of the trademark.

Editorial Directors: Dan Appleman, Peter Blackburn, Gary Cornell, Jason Gilmore, Karen Watterson, John Zukowski
Managing Editor: Grace Wong
Copy Editor: Christina Vaughn
Production Editor: Kari Brooks
Compositor: Diana Van Winkle, Van Winkle Design Group
Artist: Kurt Krames, Kurt Krames Design
Indexer: Carol Burbo
Cover Designer: Tom Debolski
Marketing Manager: Stephanie Rodriguez

Distributed to the book trade in the United States by Springer-Verlag New York, Inc., 175 Fifth Avenue, New York, NY, 10010
and outside the United States by Springer-Verlag GmbH & Co. KG, Tiergartenstr. 17, 69112 Heidelberg, Germany.

In the United States, phone 1-800-SPRINGER, email orders@springer-ny.com, or visit http://www.springer-ny.com.
Outside the United States, fax +49 6221 345229, email orders@springer.de, or visit http://www.springer.de.

For information on translations, please contact Apress directly at 2560 Ninth St., Suite 219, Berkeley, CA 94710.
Email info@apress.com or visit http://www.apress.com.

*This book is dedicated to those people in uniform who risk
more than their careers every time they go to work. We are all indebted to them.*

*And to Charles Victor Heintzelman:
Veteran, Father, Grandfather, and Great Grandfather. He will be missed.*

Contents at a Glance

Contents

Acknowledgments

Bill's Acknowledgments

This book has taken longer to create than any of my previous books, due in part to the fundamental differences between Visual Basic 6.0 and its version of ADO and the new .NET paradigm. Throughout this process, I asked for and received lots of help. While some contributed more than others, all were generous with their time, talents, guidance, patience, and inside information. Microsoft was very helpful in many ways and should be proud of their Visual Studio .NET and SQL Server 2000 teams as represented by (in alphabetical order) Andrew Jenks, Ann Morris, Ari Bixhorn, Brad Merrill, Brian Henry, Chris Dias, Dave Mendlen, David Sceppa, David Schleifer, Drew Fletcher, Ed Robinson, Edward Jezierski, Jonathan Hawkins, Michael Pizzo, Mike Iem, Omri Gazitt, Paul Vick, Richard Waymire, Rick Nasci, Rob Copeland, Rob Howard, Robert Green, Sean Draine, Sidney Higa, and Stacey Giard. Microsoft provided training sessions, beta software, and code reviews that made the process of getting accurate information (not always favorable to Microsoft) in the book. This is a departure from Microsoft's prior approach to new versions of Visual Studio—and we authors really appreciate it. Others outside of Microsoft were also helpful—most of all Kimberly Tripp Simonnet and the Aces team, including Charles Carroll.

I would also like to mention the cadre of technical editors I enlisted to take on the challenges of learning an entirely new language, learning a basically new development suite, working with pre-beta and beta code, and doing so at great distances. Early on, David Jezak, an old friend and co-worker from the Visual Basic development team at Microsoft, took on the monumental task of building the example CD. He was able to reorganize it and repeatedly test the examples on each version of .NET as they emerged. Carl Prothman and Pamela Fanstill also provided repeated in-depth technical reviews of the .NET code and the prose. As the project was nearing completion, Peter Blackburn made another pass at the prose and the examples as he converted the Visual Basic edition to work in C#. All of these folks added significant value to the book because they made sure the words were right and that the examples did what they were intended to do. Thanks to all of you.

Since writing the first edition of *ADO Examples and Best Practices*, I have set up my own company to manage the business side of being an author and trainer. My wife, Marilyn, has been instrumental in keeping the company books and business in the black and on the right side of the (rather complex) tax laws. She has also been able to let me live and work in the same house with her, which is quite an accomplishment in and of itself given my grumpy nature when I'm working—but if she comes in here again with the vacuum . . .

This is the eighth book I've written and each time I've had to work with publisher-provided copy editors. Sometimes these folks were very good and sometimes . . . well, not as good. For this book, I was fortunate enough to be able to hire my own daughter, Christina (Fred), to do the copy edit. Having her work with me on a daily basis has been a challenge for both of us, but a prideful joy for me. I think she did very well, but I'll let you, the reader, be the judge of her skill and dedication. Throughout the project, Chrissy also kept me on schedule and working on the correct files (no small task). More importantly, she made sure the words made sense and the jokes were funny (at least the ones she understood). Without her, I don't know that this book would have been written on time—if at all. Thanks, Fred. It's been a kick.

Peter's Acknowledgments

On the surface, rewriting the code samples in C# and then repurposing the prose ("leveraging") for C# sounds like an easy task—a breeze, a walk in the park. The reality was certainly much more demanding than I anticipated when Gary Cornell, Apress' publisher, first mentioned this project. I think the words Gary left out were "Your mission should you choose to accept it is to…" and the terminal phrase of "This will self-destruct in fifteen seconds."

My mission was made a little easier by the support and assistance of a few people I'll identify. Ildikó Blackburn, my technical wife (not that I have a nontechnical one), took much pleasure in reading the proofs and identifying my mistakes—or things that I'd let slip. Thank you, Ildikó! (Grrrr).

(Stuart) Godding, my butler, who very efficiently runs my English household, always makes my life so much easier by always anticipating and attending to my needs, in addition to the requirements of my guests, by ensuring that they feel welcome and especially inebriated. I am particularly indebted to Godding who, given that he is completely nontechnical, successfully reconfigured my household VPN while I was recently meeting up with Bill in San Francisco—at the same time that my ISP (un)helpfully decided to reconfigure and brownout parts of their network. Thank you, Godding. I would not have been able to continue working on this project as easily without your obsequious attentions.

Of course I should mention and thank Bill and Chrissy for their attentiveness. They have been and are great fun to work with. Also, thank you to the production team and all the folks behind the scenes at Apress, especially Tom Debolski and Grace Wong, who kept this all together and performed miracles with the schedule when I slipped behind.

About the Authors

About Bill Vaughn

I've been working in the computer industry since 1972. My first job was teaching FORTRAN and COBOL labs at Central Texas College in Killeen, Texas. After graduating, I worked in the mainframe industry for about seven years—desperately trying to stay sane. During this time I designed and implemented a number of DBMS systems, some of which might still be in use today. When I built my first microcomputer (while working for EDS in Dallas), Ross Perot found out and ended up hiring me to work for him in the Business Systems Division. I worked in the BSD for several years in the very early days of the PC industry. When this division folded, I surfed the industry for many years, working for companies large and small. These included Mostek (integrated circuits and systems manufacturer), Challenge Systems (a PC startup), Digital Research, and finally CPT Corporation. All of these companies were successful for awhile, and then succumbed to the heavy waves of competition and innovation. I worked in systems design, architecture and integration, marketing, training, and customer support. I supported, designed, and coded systems software, applications, and operating systems. I also managed two- to twenty-person teams of developers, mentored hundreds, but also spent quite a bit of time answering the phone to support PC novices and experts alike.

In 1986 I joined Microsoft and started by supporting Windows 1.0 developers. About a year later I started writing courses, training, and managing trainers at Microsoft University. There I met and mentored developers from all over the industry and learned a great deal about DBMS implementations. After Microsoft University folded, I wrote my first book on Visual Basic and data access, *The Hitchhiker's Guide to VBSQL,* and published it myself. This first book helped me get my next job on the Visual Basic documentation team at Microsoft. I wrote data access content for them for five years and wrote five more editions of my book. Before long I was "promoted" to work in the marketing group. After a couple of years of speaking, writing, and marketing Visual Basic 5.0 and 6.0, I moved to the MSTE internal training group where I worked for two years before my retirement in August of 2000. Since then I have earned an honorary Ph.D. from the University of Advancing Computer Technology in Tempe, Arizona.

I married in 1968 while at flight school—just before I went to Vietnam to fly helicopters. My wife Marilyn earned her bachelor of science in education and taught math for many years before she got her master of science degree in mathematical science. She is currently the treasurer of Beta V Corporation and does a great job managing the business side of my book and training business.

My younger daughter, Christina (a.k.a. Fred), graduated cum laude from Whitman College with an English and classics degree. She is currently working as an editor for Beta V Corporation; she copy edited this book. Her interests include indoor and outdoor soccer; she's playing on and coaching several teams.

My older daughter, Victoria (a.k.a. George), graduated from the University of Washington with a bachelor's degree in chemical engineering. I had to send her back to the Civil Engineering school at the University of Washington because her chemical engineering degree left her far from "civil." In March 2001, Victoria and her husband, 1st Lt. Michael Ballard (USAF), gave birth to my first granddaughter, Mary Anne Ballard.

My other interests include digital photography, home automation, and travel. I'm currently developing a CD of Windows wallpaper pictures that illustrates the best of the places my lectures have taken me.

About Peter Blackburn

Peter (Zebedee to his friends) was born in the north of England in 1967, and now lives in the center of Huntingdon in England—in fact, it's the same town where Oliver Cromwell was born, and Peter lives on the same street where the diarist Samuel Pepys went to school. He is looked after by his (IT contractor) wife, Ildikó, as he forgets to feed himself when left to his own devices. It took just a little over eleven years for him to boot up, but since 1979, Peter has been more or less continually connected as a peripheral coding device to one computer system or another. He becomes strangely agitated and irritable if deprived of his coding fix for more than a few hours at a time.

He left secondary school in 1985 before completing his A' Levels (roughly equivalent to high school graduation in the U.S.), so that he could to teach and prepare himself for the Cambridge University entrance examinations, and he subsequently also taught and prepared himself for A' Levels, too. (During this time, he also found time to run a small publishing company and to program). Once at Cambridge University, Peter (occasionally—oops!) studied Computer Science at St. Catharine's College and graduated in 1989. Those who knew him well at the time knew that his attentions were a little more focused toward his publishing activities.

Over the last thirteen years, since graduating from Cambridge, Peter has contracted his services to corporations, local governments, and other development teams, working as Lead Consultant Project Developer on many large database developments. He enjoys receiving the mantle of a challenge and gets called upon to parachute into a number of wayward developments to turn them around.

His knowledge of client/server databases extended to building his own client/server databases (in the early '90s) from the ground up. Peter has also created travel reservation databases operating under Unix and programmed in C, and has utilized D-ISAM libraries (which were custom-built systems capable of maintaining 200+ connected sessions on minimal hardware through TCP/IP streams) and X25 networks. All were a very good grounding to get an in-depth, instinctive idea of the issues and design decisions that face the vendors of today's client/server DBMSs.

At the moment his burning passion is for disconnected distributed databases utilizing various smart devices.

In addition to being the CEO of Boost Data Ltd., CTO of International Network Technologies Organization Ltd., and his obvious involvement with Peter Blackburn Ltd., Peter is the editorial director at Apress with authoring, book commissioning responsibilities, and a special responsibility toward quality control of all Apress products.

When contracting on client sites, Peter often wears a bowtie (with teddy bears on it), waistcoat, and suspenders. (For the U.K. readers, "suspenders" are what Americans call "braces," whereas "suspenders" in the U.K. are called "garter belts" in the U.S.) Peter is very quick to add that he doesn't wear garter belts!

You can visit Peter's Web site at http://www.boost.net.

Introduction

FOR THOSE OF YOU NEW to my earlier book, *ADO Examples and Best Practices*, it was originally written as an update to my popular *Hitchhiker's Guide to Visual Basic and SQL Server,* Sixth Edition. Happily, the first edition of *ADO Examples and Best Practices* received glowing praise from a variety of reviewers, trainers, and developers all over the world. The first edition was not designed as a tutorial on basic ADO; it assumed you had at least some experience with ADO (there are lots of elementary ADO books). In contrast, the Visual Basic version of this new edition adds quite a bit more introductory material to fill in some of the spaces not covered by the introductory books. It also leads the way for developers contemplating the process of converting existing COM-based ADO code to ADO.NET.

ADO.NET and ADO Examples and Best Practices for VB Programmers, Second Edition, focuses on ways to make your applications more efficient and at the same time help you write more efficient code in less time. These efficiencies can make the difference between a successful application (or component or Web page) and having to spend your weekends fixing its problems.

It's been several years since the first edition was published and what Microsoft was going to call "Visual Basic 7.0" is still not released to manufacturing—and it's probably never going to be. Instead, Microsoft has decided to forego any further changes to Visual Basic 6.0 in favor of creating an entirely new product—Visual Studio .NET. While I expect that some of you are looking forward to the innovations introduced in the Visual Studio .NET tools and languages, I was not so anxious to start learning a new language. I'm like the old carpenter who's used to his tried-and-true hammer. When a new-fangled tool comes to the local hardware store, I'll be one of the first to try it out, but one of the last to trust it. I've had too many hair-pulling, gut-wrenching, marriage-threatening experiences with version 1 tools to depend on them.

Yes, .NET eliminates a whole set of serious issues that have "bugged" Visual Basic developers. I expect, however, that we'll see an entirely new and yet-to-be-discovered set of issues that will make our work even more challenging—at least until version 3. I also expect that ASP (Visual Basic Script) developers will be far more inclined to jump on the .NET bandwagon because it directly addresses many more of their language and architecture issues. But, to tell the truth, they never really programmed in "Visual Basic" in the first place.

About six months ago, I suggested to Apress that we clone this book and rework it for C# programmers. They thought this was a great idea and got right on it. Before long, Apress asked Peter Blackburn, a dynamite developer and writer from the U.K., to do the conversion. He's done a great job of adapting my Visual Basic point of view to C#.

As the title suggests, *ADO.NET Examples and Best Practices for C# Programmers,* is totally focused on ADO.NET. Unlike the Visual Basic version that starts with a discussion on COM-based ADO, the ADO.NET section begins at a more elementary level because I can't assume many developers out there are that familiar with this new technology. Peter and I have written the C# version with both experienced and novice ADO developers in mind. Throughout the book you'll find comparisons to COM-based ADO that can help make your transition to Visual Basic .NET and ADO.NET less daunting.

I see this conversion process from two points of view. First, you, your co-workers, and your managers have to learn new ways of creating solutions using basically new architectures. No, your business problems haven't really changed that much, but you'll find that the .NET Framework provides a number of new approaches to addressing these problems. The next phase of the conversion process is to consider what parts of your existing code can be brought forward into your new .NET applications. I expect that there are many applications, components, controls, forms and reports that won't be easy (or even possible) to convert. On the other hand, .NET does know how to access COM components through its COM interop technology. How well this works and what new issues this raises is an underlying thread in many of the chapters. Frankly, I would not rely on the conversion process working particularly well at first. Keep in mind that COM DLL hell is, well, hell.

Over the past year, I've come up with and learned a number of new "best practices" when working with .NET. Unfortunately, some of these (but not nearly all) contradict best practices espoused in the first section of the VB .NET book. To make things easy, I begin with a focus on transitions from COM-based ADO and design alternatives that can't help but improve performance and scalability. I've also gleaned a number of excellent suggestions for good designs and the answers to typical questions based on my own testing, literally thousands of e-mail threads, and a number of .NET conference sessions. Microsoft was more than helpful as well; without their support, this book would never have been published and I would have taken up a new career by now.

Obviously, *ADO.NET Examples and Best Practices for C# Programmers* focuses on the most evolved form of ADO—namely, ADO.NET, but in a way that reflects what countless developers, trainers, and support engineers have passed on to me over the years. Yes, it's these people that provide the pathway to what I write in these books. I have made a living over the last fifteen years by writing, training, and documenting code—not by writing or supporting applications (as I did the first twelve years of my career). Because of this, I must constantly work with others who do. When I can, I help them solve problems encountered in the "real world," but just as often, the developer community provides me with innovative and tried-and-true ways of using the tools and languages. These examples and "best practices" are techniques discussed, refined, and used by hundreds (or thousands) of the most talented developers in the world. And yes, many of the ideas come from "international" developers outside of the U.S. While some of the ideas come from inside Microsoft—where I used to be bound to a certain level of confidentiality—many come from off-campus, where developers often have to make do with what the folks on-campus produce and shove out (and under) the door. I also communicate on a regular basis with the product managers, developers, and product support teams at Microsoft, trying to get the tools and interfaces to work better—based on your requests (and mine).

This book assumes that most Web developers will want to migrate to .NET, so it does not spend a lot of time dwelling on ASP development. While the book covers ADO.NET features, it also discusses other technologies, such as XML and MSXML, whenever it makes sense to do so. While this book is not a "programmer's reference," it does detail many of the individual objects, properties, and methods similar to my strategy in writing the *Guide*. Despite the Web hype out there, this book fully discusses client/server and middle tier, along with Web-based, ADO architectures, and the code development, deployment, and performance analysis issues associated with each paradigm. Why do I keep focusing on client/server? Well, at each conference I attend, I ask the developers there what they're working on and what type of architectures they are implementing. The vast majority are (still) working with client/server architectures.

Performance is another binding thread in this and all of my books. But to me, "performance" means more than writing code that runs fast. It means writing code that helps developers perform more efficiently—write more solutions in less time and at a lower cost, not necessarily more code. This is especially important for developers who work in teams. All too often now-a-days the programs we write were originally designed and implemented by others—or at least parts of them. This means you have to deal with other developer's designs, techniques, and documentation—assuming the latter exists. And others have to deal with what you write. We are constantly challenged to create code that can be passed on to others to integrate, support, or debug. There are a lot of techniques you can use to make this process easy—easy for you and for the people who have to deal with what you write.

This book, like my others, also discusses team development philosophy and how to best manage these teams. For example, in later chapters I mention that the development process requires what many programming shops, even the ones at Microsoft, sometimes don't have: discipline. No, I'm not talking about having a person walking the halls in leather and studs, cracking a whip (or at least I hope not)! I'm talking about establishing standards within the organization and sticking to them. It means writing specs and coding to spec. It means curbing your desire to code outside the spec because you know how to do something better than the toads that created the spec. That might be the case, but unless you get your co-workers and managers to help change the spec, what you're creating is counterproductive. If you don't code to spec, your innovative code is not likely to work with other developers' code now or in the future. Discipline also means curbing your arrogance. Deciding that the consumer of your code can take it or lump it is hardly a productive attitude—but it is not an uncommon mindset in some shops. Of course, if you are paid by the line, you are free to ignore these suggestions. Just don't look for repeat business.

I also look at ways to reduce COM overhead, reduce load time in your applications, and ways to better utilize the LAN, WAN, and Web, as well as RAM, disk space, and other system resources. I examine the newest .NET technology and show ways to make it work for you, instead of making more work for your server and staff. Most importantly, I look at how to write programs that *other* developers can understand and support—without you having to interrupt your Saturday afternoon barbecue.

The next few years are going to be very challenging for all of us. We're all going to have to learn a new language and new design paradigms to stay competitive. If we don't, we had better start looking for another way to earn a living. We're going to discover that the new .NET Framework and the languages and tools that depend on it are full of new issues and challenges. Frankly, I'm excited about these challenges. I really like working with the new Visual Studio .NET and Visual Basic .NET. That's the good news. The bad news is that once you've gotten over the initial shock and get used to the new features you, like I, will have trouble going back to Visual Basic 6.0, Visual InterDev, or Visual Basic Script. It's like owning a Porsche and having to take a Ford Escort as your loaner car when your car is in the shop.

CHAPTER 1

Introducing ADO.NET

Hijacked by Bill Vaughn's Inquisitor Peter Blackburn

Ahem! Perhaps I should mention that I needed to tie up Bill Vaughn in order to distill his world-class excellence on ADO.NET for the C# community. I am presently helping with Bill's rehabilitation. ...Now repeat after me, Bill, "C# is the bee's knees!" ... "Hmmmmph! Hmmmmph!" Ah! well yes I can see that we need just a little more assistance; I do hope I'll be able to remove the gag eventually...Wind the rack up a notch, Anders, would you please! ...

This book is all about using ADO.NET with C# (pronounced C sharp), .NET Framework,[1] and to some extent about how Visual Studio .NET helps you build ADO.NET-based applications. The concepts and code discussed and illustrated here apply (in most cases) to .NET Windows Forms and ASP Web Services and other ADO.NET platforms.

To make the transition to .NET easier for you and to clarify how I view this new technology, I start by helping you get familiar with .NET, its new terminology, and the new ways it allows you to access your data. There are many tutorials on .NET, most of which clearly describe the technology, albeit each from a unique and distinct point of view. In this book, my intended target audience is the experienced COM-based ADO developer. I focus strictly on my personal area of .NET expertise: data access and especially, data access with SQL Server. You might sense a bias in favor of Microsoft SQL Server (guilty) and the SqlClient namespace. Perhaps that's because I've had more experience coding, designing, implementing, testing, and teaching SQL Server than any other DBMS system. Again, in most cases, the OleDb and Odbc namespaces implement the System.Data classes (Microsoft.Data classes in the case of Odbc) in much the same way.

---

1. For an in-depth analysis of the .NET Framework check out Dan Appleman's *Moving to VB .NET: Strategies, Concepts and Code*, (Apress) ISBN: 1893115-97-6.

The Odbc .NET Data Provider is not a part of the Visual Studio .NET initial release—you'll need to download it directly from Microsoft's Web site. My informal tests show that the Odbc data provider, which uses Platform Invoke (PI), is faster than the OleDb data provider, which uses COM, although it is roughly twenty percent slower than the SqlClient data provider, which uses Tabular Data Stream (TDS). I talk a little more about this later. Before you decide to close your ears to the OleDb data provider for being the tortoise of the pack, just note that at present this is the *only* data provider that directly supports importing good ol' ADO Recordsets.

For differences and issues, check our Web sites or the Apress Web site[2] for updates sometime after this book hits the streets.

How We Got Here

A number of years ago, Microsoft found itself in yet another tough spot. Overnight (or so it seemed), the Internet had become far more popular than expected and Microsoft was caught without a viable development strategy for this new paradigm. Developers all over the world clamored for ways to get their existing code and skills to leverage Web technology. Even Microsoft's own internal developers wanted better tools to create cutting-edge Web content and server-side executables. These same developers also found that component object model (COM) architectures didn't work very well with or over the Internet—they were never designed to. Sun Microsystems' virtual stranglehold on Java and the ensuing fight over this language made it imperative that Microsoft come up with another way to create fast, light, language-neutral, portable, and scalable server-side executables.

Microsoft's initial solution to this challenge was to reconfigure their popular and well-known Visual Basic interpreter in an attempt to provide server-side (IIS) functionality to the tool-hungry developer community. To this end, VB Scripting Edition sprung to life, aimed at a subset of the four million Visual Basic developers trying to create logic-driven Web content for this new beast called "eCommerce." As many of these developers discovered, an Active Server Page (ASP) created with Visual Basic Script (VBScript) was relatively clunky when compared to "real" Windows-based Visual Basic applications and components. The VBScript language was confined to the oft-maligned Variant datatypes, copious late-binding issues, and interminable recompiles. Despite these issues, a flood of Web sites were built around this technology—probably because they were (loosely) based on a form of a familiar language: Visual Basic.

---

2. http://www.betav.com, http://www.boost.net, and http://www.apress.com.

Ahem! For those developers who had grown up using C and then its object layer abstraction C++ (these are the scary, awkward languages to the VB community—the ones with the curly braces {}, pointer things ->, and semicolons ;, and in the case of C++, OOP),[3] Microsoft offered JScript—a version of ECMAScript, which from a syntactical viewpoint is closer to C++ and JavaScript than Visual Basic. There were some advantages to be gained by using JScript over VBScript in client-side code, one of which being that, in theory, many other browsers, other than just those Microsoft offered, supported JScript, thereby potentially enabling the code to be browser neutral.

However, Microsoft sought some better way to satiate the needs of millions of Visual Basic developers and their ever-growing interest in the Web without compromising performance or functionality, perhaps providing them, maybe forcing them, to a new world of OOP without the need to learn JScript (or any other curly-brace language)!

It wasn't long before it became clear that Microsoft needed something new—no less than a whole new paradigm, a landslide shift, a new reality with some old familiar concepts, some new concepts, and some borrowed or adapted concepts—in order to accomplish this goal. This was the birth of the .NET platform.

Anders Hejlsberg, a Microsoft Distinguished Engineer,[4] crafted a brand new programming language for this new world reality. This language is C#, which fits with .NET hand in glove, horse and carriage, love and marriage, so to speak. Okay, so I like C#, but it isn't the only language that is now supported in .NET. Syntactically, C# is an OOP, curly-brace language, with semicolons, and thus a language with which C++ and Java developers will quickly feel comfortable and "at home."[5]

You see, Visual Basic just didn't cut it when compared to the heavily object-oriented Java applications with which it was competing. Before this, each new version of VB had inherited language and user interface (UI) supported functionality features from its predecessor. Yes, each new version usually left some unworkable functionality behind, but generally, these "forgotten" features were minor—most developers learned to live without them. When designing VB .NET, however, the Microsoft development team felt that too many of these "legacy" features hobbled Visual Basic's potential by preventing, or at least complicating, easy implementation of more sophisticated features. Thus, the advent of VB .NET.

---

3. OOP: Object-Oriented Programming—IPHO: Many of those who develop without it (as in totally unplanned and unstructured) tend to find that they have lots of places in their code at which they frequently have to exclaim "OOPs!" or other expletives as their code falls over.

4. Not to be confused with "Microsoft Drudge Engineers" who do less theoretical thinking and more real work trying to implement what the "Distinguished" engineers dream up.

5. Gary Cornell, co-founder of Apress and author (with Cay Horstmann) of the two-volume set, *Core Java 2* (Prentice Hall, ISBN: 0-13-089468-0), has been overheard saying that any Java programmer who cannot program proficiently in C# within half an hour of starting C# was probably not a Java programmer to begin with.

Unfortunately, as I see it, more than a few BASIC and Visual Basic developers really expect continued support for much of this "obsolete" functionality. Over the years, VB developers have learned (for better or worse) to depend on a forgiving language and an IDE that supports default properties, unstructured code, automatic instantiation, morphing datatypes, wizards, designers, drag-and-drop binding, and many more automatic or behind-the-scenes operations. More importantly, VB developers pioneered and depended on "edit and continue" development, which permitted developers to change their code after a breakpoint and continue testing with the new code. This was a radical departure from other development language interfaces and, for a decade, put Visual Basic in a class by itself.

IPHO *Microsoft's top engineers tried to move heaven and earth to get "edit and continue" functionality into Visual Basic .NET, but in the end, they just could not get it to work properly; so, it was dropped from the language. I expect that edit and continue is such a core part of the development methodologies used by so many Visual Basic 6.0 developers that Microsoft will be including it—just as soon as they can work out how to do it in a Garbage Collected world.*

Microsoft expects "professional" Visual Basic developers (whoever they are) to wholeheartedly embrace Microsoft's new languages—including the new "Visual Basic"—and (eventually) step away from Visual Basic as we know it today. Consider that a Visual Basic "developer" can be as sophisticated as a front-line professional who writes and supports thousands of lines of DNA code or as challenged as an elementary school student or part-time accountant creating a small application against an Access database. Some of these developers will be skilled enough and motivated enough to adapt to a new language—some will not. Some have the formal training that permits them to easily step from language to language—many (I would venture the majority) do not. Some professional developers, faced with this magnitude of change, will opt to find another language or another seemingly simpler occupation, such as brain surgery.

IMHO *Microsoft continues to complicate the situation by insisting that VB .NET is **really** just another version of Visual Basic 6.0 and that ADO.NET is just another version of COM-based ADO. They clearly aren't the same—not even close.*

IPHO *Those "professional" Visual Basic developers might very well go just that tiny bit further and take the opportunity to learn and then use C# as their language of choice. The way I look at it, Visual Basic .NET is almost a case-insensitive version of C# without the braces and semi-colons (and an inbuilt default of go-slow…); and for me, alas not Bill (yet), C# "feels" cleaner (more syntactically correct), the block structures of the language are clearer, and I really like the cool automated self-documentation of comments in the code to HTML Web pages.*

I tested the performance of examples in Visual Basic .NET against similar C# examples. If in Visual Basic .NET you remember to set "Option Strict On" (that means take the go-slow default Off), then the MSIL (Microsoft Intermediate Language) produced by the compilers for either language is very, very similar—almost identical, but not quite. If you don't set "Option Strict On" and you leave Visual Basic .NET to its default of loose type checking, then C# is always much faster. In my friendly sparring fights with Dan Appleman, he was able to convince me that Visual Basic could usually get very close to C# performance—at least in our tests to within the region of "noise" (single figures of ticks apart over millions of repetitions). I always found that there was always more "noise" affecting Visual Basic .NET tests than C#.

I think the new Visual Basic .NET language is just that: new. (*Ahem!* V sharp?) While it emulates the Visual Basic language in many respects, it's really not the same. As many of you have heard, I wanted to call it something else—anything else—but my daughter, Fred, told me to keep my mouth shut to prevent her from further embarrassment. I complied, as I don't want to give anyone at Microsoft apoplexy—again.

What Do These Changes Mean?

The Microsoft .NET Framework's system of language(s), tools, interfaces, and volumes of supporting code has been constructed from the ground up with an entirely new architecture. For those of you who remember IBM 3270 technology, you'll find that the .NET Framework tracks many of the same wheel ruts laid into the road during the 1960s. IBM 3270 systems were central processor (mainframe)–driven "smart" (or "dumb") terminal designs. They relied on a user-interface terminal which supported very sparse functionality. The terminal's only function was to display characters at an x-y coordinate and return characters entered into "fields." There were no mice or graphics to complicate things, but a dozen different keyboard layouts made life interesting.

While the industry's current browser technology includes far more intelligence and flexibility at the client, the general design is very similar to the 3270 approach. .NET applications now expect code similar to a browser to render the forms and frames and capture user input, even when creating a Windows Forms application. This means .NET applications will behave and interact differently (at least to some extent) than "traditional" Windows applications.

What's new for server-side executables is the concept of a Web Service. I discuss and illustrate Web Services in Chapter 10, "ADO.NET and XML." This new paradigm finds its roots in Visual Basic 6.0's so-called IIS Applications—better known as Web Classes. Web Services place executable code on your IIS server to be referenced as ASP pages or from other executables such as WinForm applications just as you would reference a COM component running in the middle tier. The big difference is that Web Services do not require COM or DCOM to expose their objects, methods, properties, or events—they are all exposed through SOAP.[6] I explain what this means in Chapter 10.

For the C++ developer moving to C#, these .NET innovations mean that the huge Rapid Application Development (RAD) advantages that Visual Basic developers had over C++ developers are no more, no longer, gone, zip; there is now a level playing field. Previously, C++ Windows Application developers had to do battle fighting with the Microsoft Foundation Classes (MFC), while their Visual Basic developer cousins needed only to tinker with the facile "Ruby" Windows Form Engine. They rarely bothered, cared, or needed to know what a Windows handle or a device context was, but were by far more visibly productive. This leveling of the playing field has been achieved in part by replacing Visual Basic's "Ruby" forms engine and the accompanying run-time library (VBRUN.DLL) with a new run-time platform and forms engine, as well as a new user interface and development IDE. (If I can use the word "replaced" to mean that the new version does not implement the same functionality.) Saying the Visual Basic run time has been replaced is like saying the diesel engine in a semi-tractor-trailer rig was replaced with a cross-galaxy transport mechanism.

The Visual Basic 6.0 IDE, the Visual InterDev 6.0 IDE, and the Visual C++ 6.0 IDE have been replaced with a new "combined" system that integrates all of the language front ends into one. From the looks of it, Microsoft used the Visual Studio 6.0–era Visual InterDev shell as a base. These changes mean that Visual Basic .NET is *not* just the newest version of Visual Basic. While Visual Basic .NET is similar in some respects to Visual Basic 6.0, it's really a lot more like C# (pronounced C sharp) or C++ (pronounced C hard-to-learn). For the professional, school-trained veterans out there, VB .NET and C# are just other languages. For many, though, they're a big, scary step away from their comfort zone.

---

6.   Simple Object Access Protocol. See http://www.w3.org/TR/SOAP/#_Toc478383486.

ADO.NET—A New Beginning

This section of the book introduces something Microsoft calls ADO.NET. Don't confuse this new .NET data access interface with what we have grown to know and understand as ADO—I think it's really very different. Yes, ADO.NET and ADOc both open connections and fetch data, however, they do so in different ways using different objects and with different limitations. No, they aren't the same—no matter what Microsoft names them. Yes, ADO.NET has a Connection object, Command object, and Parameter objects (actually implemented by the SqlClient, OleDb, and Odbc .NET Data Providers), however, they don't have the same properties, methods, or behaviors as their ADOc counterparts. IMHO, this name similarity does not help to reduce the confusion you're likely to encounter when transitioning from ADOc to ADO.NET.

 NOTE *To avoid confusion, I've coined a new term to help you distinguish the two paradigms; henceforth "ADOc" refers to the existing COM-based ADO implementation and "ADO.NET" refers to the new .NET Framework implementation.*

Actually, the name ADO.NET was not Microsoft's first choice (nor is it mine) for their new data access paradigm. Early in the development cycle (over three years ago),[7] their new data access object library was referred to as XDO (among other things). To me, this made[8] a lot of sense because ADO.NET is based on XML persistence and transport—thus "XML Data Objects" seemed a good choice. Because developers advised Microsoft to avoid the creation of yet another TLA (three-letter acronym)–based data access interface, they were hesitant to use the XDO moniker. I suspect there were other reasons too—mostly concerning the loss of market product name recognition. So, XDO remains one of those words you aren't supposed to mention in the local bar. Later in the development cycle, XDO evolved into ADO+ to match the new ASP+ technology then under construction. It was not until early in 2001 that the name settled on ADO.NET to fit in with the new naming scheme for Windows XP (Whistler) and the newly dubbed .NET Framework.

Microsoft also feels that ADO.NET is close enough to ADOc to permit leveraging the name and making developers feel that ADO.NET is just another version of ADOc. That's where Microsoft and I differ in opinion. The documentation

---

7. Circa AD 1999.

8. I was opposed to another TLA at the time—for some reason that now escapes me.

included ever since the first .NET betas assures developers that ADO.NET is designed to "…leverage current ADO knowledge." While the connection strings used to establish connections are similar (even these are not *exactly* the same as those used in ADOc), the object hierarchy, properties, methods, and base techniques to access data are all very different. Over the past year I often struggled with ADO.NET because I tried to approach solutions to my data access problems using ADOc concepts and techniques. It took quite some time to get over this habit (I joined a twelve-step program that worked wonders). Now my problem is that when someone asks me an ADOc question, I have to flush my RAM and reload all of the old concepts and approaches. I'm getting too old for this.

No matter what you call it, I think you'll also discover that even though ADO.NET is different from ADOc in many respects, it's based on many (many) years of development experience at Microsoft. It's not *really* built from scratch. If you look under the hood you'll find that ADO.NET is a product of many (but not all) of the lessons Microsoft has learned over the last decade in their designing, creating, testing, and supporting of DB-Library, DAO, RDO, ODBCDirect, and ADO, as well as ODBC and OLE DB. You'll also find remnants of the FoxPro and Jet data engines, shards from the Crystal report writer, as well as code leveraged from the ADO Shape, ADOX, and ADOMD providers. Unfortunately, you'll also find that ADO.NET's genes have inherited some of the same issues caused by these technologies—it also suffers from a few "DNA" problems; I discuss these as I go. Most of these issues, however, are just growing pains. I expect there will be a lot of lights left on at night trying to work them out—unless the energy crisis has us working by candlelight by then.

That said, don't assume that this "new" ADO.NET data access paradigm implements all of the functionality you're used to seeing in ADOc. Based on what I've seen so far, there are lots of features—among them many important ones—left behind. I discuss these further in the following chapters.

Comparing ADOc and ADO.NET

Data access developers who have waded into the (generally pretty good) MSDN .NET documentation might have come across a topic that compares ADOc with ADO.NET. IMHO, this topic leaves a lot to be desired; it slams ADOc pretty hard. Generally, it ignores or glosses over features such as support for the Shape provider (which exposes hierarchical data management), pooled connections and intelligent connection management, disconnected Recordsets, serialization, XML functionality, ADOMD, and ADOX. Yes, ADO.NET is a new and innovative data access paradigm, but so is ADOc. In its defense, the documentation does say there are still a number of situations where ADOc is the (only) solution. I suspect that the Microsoft .NET developers will make ADOc redundant over time—just not right away.

Later in this and subsequent chapters I visit the concept of porting ADOc code over to .NET applications. It's a complex subject full of promise and some serious issues—a few with no apparent resolution. Stay tuned.

 IMHO *The job of a technical writer at Microsoft is considerably challenging. I worked on the Visual Basic user education team for about five years and, while some changes have been made, there are still many issues that make life tough for writers, editors, and developers alike—all over the world. One of the problems is that when working with a product as new as .NET, there are few "reliable" sources of information besides the product itself. Unfortunately, the product is a moving target—morphing and evolving from week to week, sometimes subtly, but just as often in radical ways as entire concepts are lopped off or jammed in at the last minute for one reason or another. This problem is especially frustrating when outsiders work with beta versions. To add to Microsoft's problems, they have to "freeze" the documentation months (sometimes six or more) in advance, so it can be passed to the "localizers." These folks take the documentation and translate into French, German, Texan, and a number of other foreign languages. A lot can (and does) happen in the last six months before the product ships. If the product doesn't ship—this has happened on more than one occasion—it is also difficult to keep the documentation in sync.*

Another factor you need to consider is your investment in ADOc training and skills. Frankly, quite a bit of this will be left behind if you choose ADO.NET as your data access interface. Why? Because ADO.NET is that different. This issue will be clearer by the time you finish this book.

Understanding ADO.NET Infrastructure

Microsoft characterizes ADO.NET as being designed for a "loosely coupled, highly distributed" application environment. I'm not sure that I wholly agree with this characterization. I'll accept the "loosely coupled" part, as ADO.NET depends on XML—not proprietary binary Recordsets or user-defined structures—as its persistence model and transport layer. No, ADO.NET does not store its in-memory DataTable objects as XML, but it does expose or transport them as XML on demand. As I see it, XML is one of ADO.NET's greatest strengths, but also one of its weaknesses. XML gives ADO.NET (and the entire .NET Framework) significant flexibility, which Visual Basic 6.0 applications have to go a long way to implement in code—and C++ applications a little further still. However, XML is far more verbose and more costly to store and transmit than binary Recordsets; granted, with very small data sets, the difference isn't that great. By passing XML instead of binary, ADO.NET can pass *intelligent* information—data and schema and extended properties, or any other attribute you desire—and pass it safely (and securely) through firewalls. The only requirement on the receiving end is an ability to parse XML—and that's now built into the Windows OS.

Understanding ADO.NET's Distributed Architecture

As far as the "highly distributed" part of the preceding ADO.NET characterization, I think Microsoft means that your code for .NET applications is supposed to work in a stand-alone fashion without requiring a persistent connection to the server. While this is true, I expect the best applications for .NET will be on *centralized* Web servers where the "client" is launched, constructed, and fed through a browser pointing to a logic-driven Web page. I think that Microsoft intended to say that ADO.NET is designed primarily for Web architectures.

On the other hand, ADO.NET (in its current implementation) falls short of a universal data access solution—one of ADOc's (and ODBC's) major selling points. The ODBC provider (Microsoft.Data.Odbc) is not included in the .NET Framework but is to be made available through a Web update sometime after .NET is initially released. I don't think one can really interpret this as a policy to back away from the universal data access paradigm—but it would not be hard to jump to that conclusion. I'm disappointed that ODBC is not part of the initial release. But better late than never.

In my opinion, the most important difference between ADO.NET and any other Microsoft data access interface to date is the fact that ADO.NET is multidimensional from the ground up. That is, ADO.NET:

- **Is prepared to handle—with equal acuity—either single or multiple related resultsets along with their relationships and constraints.**

- **Does not try to conjure the intratable relationships—it expects you to define them in code.** But it's up to you to make sure these coded relationships match those defined by your DBA in the database. It might be nice if Visual Studio .NET could read these definitions from the server, but then again, that would take another round trip. Be careful what you ask for…

- **Permits you to (expects you to) define constraints in your application to ensure referential integrity.** But again, it's up to you to keep these in sync with the database constraints.

- **Does not depend on its own devices for the construction of appropriate SQL statements to select or perform updates to the data—it expects you to provide these.** You (or the IDE) can write ad hoc queries or stored procedures to fetch and update the data.

In some ways, this hierarchical data approach makes the ADO.NET disconnected architecture far more flexible and powerful than ADOc—even when including use of the Shape provider in ADOc. In other ways, you might find it difficult to keep component-size relationships and constraints synchronized with their equivalents in the database.

A Brief Look at XML

No, I'm not going to launch into a tutorial on XML, just as I found it unnecessary to bury you in detail about the binary layout of the Recordset (not that I know anything about it). I do, however, want to fill in some gaps in terminology so that you can impress your friends when you start discussing ADO.NET.

XML is used behind the scenes throughout ADO.NET and you ordinarily won't have to worry about how it's constructed until ADO.NET, or an application passing XML to you, gets it wrong. Just remember that the ADO.NET DataSet object can be constructed directly from XML; this includes XML generated by any application that knows how to do it (correctly). The .NET architecture contains root services that let you manage XML documents using familiar programming constructs.

As I said, when you transport your data from place to place (middle tier to client, Web Service to browser), ADO.NET passes the data as XML. However, XML does not describe the database schema by itself—at least not formally. ADO.NET and the .NET IDE know how to define and persist your data's schema using another (relatively new) technology called Extensible Schema Definition (XSD). Accepted as a standard by the W3C[9] standards organization, XSD describes XML data the same way database schemas describe the structure of database objects such as tables. XSD provides a way to not only understand the data contained within a document, but also to validate it. XSD definitions can include datatype, length, minlength, maxlength, enumeration, pattern, and whitespace.[10] Until recently, XML schemas have been typically created in the form of Document Type Definitions (DTDs), but Visual Studio .NET introduces XSD, which has the advantage of using XML syntax to define a schema, meaning that the same parsers can process both data and schemas.

---

9.   See http://www.w3.org for more information.

10.   I expect this list to change (expand, contract) as XSD is nailed down.

IIRC,[11] XSD has been W3C final recommendation status for several months. Visual Studio .NET can generate XSD schemas automatically, based on an XML document. You can then use it to edit the schema graphically to add additional features such as constraints and datatypes. There are also .NET tools that can help construct XSD from a variety of forms including Recordsets, XML data structures, and others.

Later in the book (Chapter 10) I discuss how you can use the XML tools in .NET to manage your data.

ADO.NET—The Fundamentals

For those developers familiar with ADOc and the disconnected Recordset, ADO.NET's approach to data access should be vaguely familiar. The way in which you establish an initial connection to the database is very similar to the technique you used in ADOc—at least on the surface. After that, the similarity pretty much ends.

There are several base objects in ADO.NET. These objects are outlined and briefly described several times in this chapter and discussed in depth in subsequent chapters. Each of the following objects are implemented from base classes in the System.Data namespace by each of the .NET Data Providers:

- **The Connection object**: This works very much like the ADOc Connection object. It's not created in the same way nor is the ConnectionString property exactly the same, but it's close.

- **The Command object**: This works very much like an ADOc Command object. It holds a SQL SELECT or action query and points to a specific Connection object. The Command object exposes a Parameters collection that works something like the ADOc Command object's Parameters collection.

- **The DataReader object**: This is used to provide raw data I/O to and from the Connection object. It returns a bindable data stream for WebForm applications and is invoked by the DataAdapter to execute a specific Command.

- **The DataAdapter object**: There is no exact equivalent to this in ADOc; the closest thing is the IDE-driven Visual Basic 6.0 Data Environment Designer. The DataAdapter manages a set of Command objects used to fetch, update, add, and delete rows through the Connection object.

---

11. IIRC: If I recall correctly.

- **The DataTable object**: Again, there is not an ADOc equivalent, but it's similar in some respects to the Recordset. The DataTable object contains a Rows collection to manage the data and a Columns collection to manage the schema. No, DataTables do not necessarily (and should not) be thought of as base tables in the database.

- **The DataSet object**: This is a set of (possibly) related DataTable objects. This interface is bindable in Windows Forms or WebForms. The DataSet also contains Relations and Constraints collections used to define the interrelationships between its member DataTable objects.

A Typical Implementation of the ADO.NET Classes

One approach (there are several) calls for your application to extract some (or all) of the rows from your database table(s) and create an ADO.NET DataTable. To accomplish this, you create a Connection object and a DataAdapter object with its SelectCommand set to an SQL query returning data from a single table (or from several tables using separate SELECT statements in a single Command).

The DataAdapter object's Fill method opens the connection, runs the query through a DataReader (behind the scenes), constructs the DataTable objects, and closes the connection. If you use individual queries, this process is repeated for any related tables—each requiring a round trip, separate queries, and separate DataTable objects. However, if you're clever, you can combine the SELECT operations into a single query. ADO.NET is smart enough to build each resultset of a multiple-resultset query as its own DataTable object. I show an example of this in Chapter 5, "Using the DataTable and DataSet."

After the DataTable objects are in place, your code can disconnect from the data source. Actually, this was already done for you; ADO.NET opens and closes the Connection object for you when you use the Fill method. Next, your code can define the primary key/foreign key (PK/FK) relationships and any constraints you want ADO.NET to manage for you. All work on the data takes place in client memory (which could be in a middle-tier component, ASP, or distributed client's workstation).

When working with related (hierarchical) data, you can write a SELECT query to extract all or a subset of the customer's table rows into a DataTable object. You can also create queries and code to construct additional DataTable objects that contain rows in the related Orders and Items database tables. Code a single bindable DataSet object to manage all of these DataTable objects and the relationships between them. Behind the scenes, ADO.NET "joins" these DataTable objects in memory based on *your* coded relationships. This joining of DataTable objects permits ADO.NET to navigate, display, manage, and update the DataSet object, the DataTable objects, and ultimately, the database tables behind them when you use the Update method. After ADO.NET fetches the queried rows to construct the DataSet, ADO.NET (or your code) closes the connection and no longer depends on the database for any further information about the data or its schema.

When called upon to update the database, ADO.NET reopens the connection and performs any needed UPDATE, INSERT, or DELETE operations defined in the DataAdapter as separate Command objects. Your code handles any collisions or problems with reconciliation.

The Visual Studio .NET IDE lets you use drag-and-drop and a number of wizards to construct much of the code to accomplish this. As I discuss in later chapters (see Chapter 4, "ADO.NET DataReader Strategies") you might not choose to avail yourself of this code—it's kinda clunky. As with ADOc's Shape provider, ADO.NET can manage intertable relationships and construct a hierarchical data structure that you can navigate and update at will—assuming you added code to define the relationships and constraints. I show you how to do this in Chapter 5 and in Chapter 8, "ADO.NET Constraint Strategies."

Based on my work with ADO.NET so far, I have a number of concerns regarding the disconnected DataSet approach:

- **The overhead involved in downloading high volumes of data and the number of locks placed on the server-side data rows is problematic at best.** The ADO.NET disconnected DataSet approach might work for smaller databases with few users, but you must be careful to reduce the number of rows returned from each query when dealing with high volumes of data. Sure, it's fast when you test your stand-alone application, but does this approach scale?

- **Assumes that the base tables are exposed by the DBA; in many shops, this is not the case, for security and stability reasons.** While you can (and should) construct DataSet objects from stored procedures, you also need to provide stored procedures to do the UPDATE, DELETE, and INSERT operations. It's not clear if this approach will permit ADO.NET to expose the same functionality afforded to direct table queries—it does not appear to. I have found, however, that it is possible to perform updates against complex table hierarchies, but it requires more planning and work than the simplistic table-based queries often illustrated in the documentation.

- **The Visual Studio .NET drag-and-drop and wizards used to facilitate ADO.NET operations generate (copious) source code.** That's the good news. The bad news is that this source code has to change when the data structures, relationships, or stored procedures used to manage the data change—and this does not happen automatically. This means that you want to make sure your schema is nailed down before you start generating a lot of source code against it. Once inserted, it's often tough to remove this code in its entirety if you change your mind or the schema.

- **The disconnected approach makes no attempt to maintain a connection to the data source.** This means that you won't be able to depend on persisted server-side state. For example, server-side cursors, pessimistic locks, temporary tables, or other connection-persisted objects are not supported.

- **When compared to ADOc, ADO.NET class implementation is fairly limited in respect to update strategies.** As you'll see in Chapter 3, "ADO.NET Command Strategies," and Chapter 7, "ADO.NET Update Strategies," the options available to you are nowhere near those exposed by ADOc—especially in regard to Update Criteria.

ADO.NET .NET Data Providers

A fundamental difference between ADOc and ADO.NET is the latter's use of .NET Data Providers. A .NET Data Provider implements the base System.Data classes to expose the objects, properties, methods, and events. Each provider is responsible for ADO.NET operations that require a working connection with the data source. The .NET Data Providers are your direct portals to existing OLE DB providers (System.Data.OleDb), ODBC drivers (Microsoft.Data.Odbc), or to Microsoft SQL Server (System.Data.SqlClient). ADO.NET (currently) ships with two .NET Data Providers:

- **System.Data.OleDb**: Used to access existing Jet 4.0 and Oracle OLE DB providers via COM interop, but notably not the ODBC (MSDASQL) provider—the default provider in ADOc.[12]

- **System.Data.SqlClient**: Used to access Microsoft (and just Microsoft) SQL Server versions 7.0 and later.

NOTE *The System.Data.SqlClient provider is designed to access Microsoft SQL Server 7.0 or later. If you have an earlier version of SQL Server, you should either upgrade (a great idea),or use the OleDb .NET Data Provider with the SQLOLEDB provider or simply stick with ADOc.*

---

12. I expect that other .NET Data Providers will appear very soon after .NET ships.

As I said earlier, the Microsoft.Data.Odbc provider was made available via Web download not long after .NET was released to the public. It is used to access most ODBC data sources. No, it's not clear that all ODBC data sources will work with ADO.NET. Initial tests show, however, that this new Odbc .NET Data Provider is twenty percent faster than its COM interop brother, the OleDb .NET Data Provider. This is to be expected because COM is very "chatty," requiring more server round trips than ODBC to get the same data. The Odbc .NET Data Provider uses the more efficient Platform Invoke.

As I said, the ADO.NET OleDb provider uses COM interop to access most existing OLE DB providers—but this does *not* include the ODBC provider (MSDASQL). This also does not mean you can use any existing OLE DB providers with System.Data.OleDb. Only the SQLOLEDB (Microsoft SQL Server), MSDAORA (Oracle), and Microsoft Jet OLEDB.4.0 (Jet 4.0) providers are supported at RTM.[13] Notably missing from this list is MSDASQL—the once-default ODBC provider. In addition, none of the OLE DB 2.5 interfaces are supported, which means that OLE DB providers for Exchange and Internet Publishing are also not (yet) supported in .NET. But, remember that the .NET architecture lends itself to adding additional functionality; I would not be surprised if additional providers appeared before too long.

However, consider that these data access interfaces are very different from the OLE DB or ODBC providers with which you might be accustomed. ADO.NET and the .NET Data Providers implemented so far know nothing about keyset, dynamic, or static cursors, or pessimistic locking as supported in ADOc. Sure, the ADO.NET DataTable object looks something like a static cursor, but it does not share any of the same ADOc adOpenStatic properties or behaviors with which you're familiar. They don't leverage server-side state or cursors—regardless of the data source. ADO.NET has its own hierarchical JOIN engine so it doesn't need the server to do anything except run simple (single-table) SELECT queries. Whether it makes sense to let ADO.NET do these JOIN operations for you is another question.

A .NET Data Provider is responsible for far more functionality than the low-level ODBC or more sophisticated (and complex/bulky/slow/troublesome) OLE DB data providers in ADOc. A .NET Data Provider implements the System.Data objects I described earlier that are fundamental in the implementation of your ADO.NET application. For example:

- **The Command object**: SqlCommand, OleDbCommand, OdbcCommand

- **The Connection object**: SqlConnection, OleDbConnection, OdbcConnection

---

13.   RTM: Release to manufacturing.

- **The DataAdapter object**: SqlDataAdapter, OleDbDataAdapter, OdbcDataAdapter

- **The DataReader object**: SqlDataReader, OleDbDataReader, OdbcDataReader

.NET Data Providers also directly support and implement code to generate Commands, and control the connection pool, procedure parameters, and exceptions. It's clear that .NET Data Providers bear far more responsibility than their ADOc predecessors did. I expect that this also means that the features exposed by one provider might not be supported in the same way or with the same issues (bugs) as another. Of course, this has always been the case with ADOc and its predecessors. Anyone who's worked with ODBC and transitioned to OLE DB in ADOc can bore you with war stories about how "stuff" changed from one implementation to the next. I'm sure we'll see some of the same in ADO.NET.

I think the fact that the .NET Data Provider for SQL Server speaks Tabular Data Stream (TDS) is a *very* important innovation. Not only do I think this will help performance (it will), but it also means Microsoft is not afraid of creating a Microsoft SQL Server–specific interface (no, it does not work with Sybase SQL Server). This opens the door for better, more intimate control of Microsoft SQL Server systems from your code without having to resort to SQLDMO. It also implies that native Oracle, Sybase, and other high-performance native .NET Data Providers are possible. Your guess is as good as mine as to when these will actually appear; for those players who want to stay in the game, I expect sooner rather than later.

Leveraging Existing COM-based ADO Code

The .NET Framework is flexible enough to support more than just the three .NET Data Providers I've mentioned. This adaptability is especially important in light of ADO.NET's architecture, which leaves out a number of data access paradigms that you might find essential to your design. But up to this point, all of you have invested many (many) hours/months/years of work on ADOc code imbedded in all types of applications, middle-tier components, and Web-based executables. The burning question most of you have is "Can I leverage this investment in ADOc in my .NET executables?" The answer is not particularly clear. First, you'll find that you can imbed ADOc code in a .NET executable—while it might not behave the same, .NET applications, components, and Web Services can execute most (but not all) COM-based code.

NOTE *Visual Studio .NET includes an (excellent) conversion utility to take existing ADOc code and convert it. However, it does not convert it to ADO.NET code—it's converted to COM interop-wrapped ADOc code designed to run in a .NET application. While this utility converts the code, it does not convert the architecture or query strategy. These might not be appropriate for your new .NET application.*

Fundamentally, there are two approaches to access existing ADOc objects from .NET executables. First, you can simply reference adodb (the COM interop wrapper around MSADO15.DLL) and include "using adodb;" in your solution. In this approach, you access the objects and their properties and methods directly. The problem is that each and every time you reference an ADOc object (or any COM object), property method, or event, the Common Language Runtime (CLR) has to make the reference to and from the COM interop layer. This will slow down the references to some degree and if the interop does not behave, it might impair functionality. We already know this is the case when it comes to executing stored procedures as methods of the ADODB.Connection object—it's no longer supported. There are other issues as well, as I discuss in Chapter 2, "ADO.NET— Getting Connected."

Another approach for accessing existing ADOc objects from .NET executables is to encapsulate your ADOc (or other COM object reference) code in its own wrapper. With this approach, you only access specific methods of the wrapper object, which execute blocks of ADOc code. Few if any properties are exposed. This approach resembles what you do to implement a middle-tier COM component. It also means that you spend far less time in the interop layer—once when you enter the wrapper DLL and once when you return. The problem here is that you often have to reengineer your ADOc code, resulting in some loss of flexibility in coding directly to the ADOc objects.

When importing ADOc code you have to instantiate your objects differently. I walk through several ADOc examples in Chapter 2. There you'll discover that some of the methods work differently—for example, you can't use the GetRows method to return a Variant array, and your simple constants must now be fully qualified—but for the most part, ADOc codes about the same, after all it's just another COM object with properties, methods, and events, and those remain just the same. However, as I said before, you might notice a drop in performance or somewhat different behavior due to COM interop.

Creating DataSets from ADOc Recordset Objects

The .NET developers knew that some of you would want to import ADOc
Recordsets from existing COM components and create ADO.NET DataSets;
fortunately, this is easy in ADO.NET. The OleDbDataAdapter Fill method directly
recognizes ADOc Recordset and Record objects to populate a DataTable in a
DataSet. This functionality enables .NET developers to use existing COM objects
that return ADO objects without having to rewrite new objects using the .NET
Framework. But as of the release of Visual Studio .NET, *only* the OleDb .NET Data
Provider supports filling a DataSet from an ADO Recordset or Record object.
I illustrate this with an example in Chapter 4.

How COM Interop Affects .NET Applications

As I said before, all "unmanaged" code executed by the CLR must be handled
differently from "managed" code. Because of this stipulation between managed
and unmanaged code, all of the ADOc and the ADO.NET OleDb .NET Data
Provider data I/O operations are processed through a COM interop "wrapper."
(The ADO.NET SqlClient .NET Data Provider does not use COM interop.) This
extra layer on legacy COM components makes the .NET application think it's
communicating to a .NET component and the COM-based code thinks that it's
communicating to a COM-based host. Figure 1-1 illustrates this extra layer of
protection wrapped around all COM components.

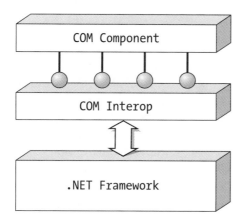

**All COM object, property, method, and event
references pass through the COM interop layer.**

Figure 1-1. COM components access .NET via the COM interop layer.

I suspect we'll see a few side effects caused by this additional translation layer that can't help but hurt performance. COM interop is something like ordering a hamburger from a Spanish-speaking clerk at your local burger palace through a speakerphone. If you don't speak Spanish, the result might have *un poco más cebolla*[14] than you planned on—but for me, that's okay!

One of the major (that should be MAJOR) differences in the .NET Framework is that your .NET application assembly is built using a *specific* version of ADOc DLLs (msado15.dll) and all of the other COM DLLs and components it references. In fact, these DLLs can be (should be?) copied from their common location to the assembly's disk directory. This means you could have the ADO run-time DLLs installed any number of times on your disk—*n* copies of the same ADO DLLs or *n* different versions of the ADO DLLs.

When you start a .NET application, the DLLs used and referenced at design/test/debug/compile time are referenced at run time. This means your application behaves (or misbehaves) the same way it did when you wrote and tested it. Imagine that. If the version of ADO (or any other dependent DLL) gets updated (or deprecated) later, or you deploy to a system with different DLLs, your existing applications still install and load the "right" (older, newer, or the same) version of ADO and your other DLLs. This means that "DLL hell" as we know it has become a specter of the past—at least when all of your applications are based on .NET. I expect DLL hell applications will still be haunting us for decades to come—rattling their chains in the back corridors of our systems and playing evil tricks on unsuspecting tourists.

I walk you through converting and accessing ADOc objects in the next chapter.

ADO.NET and Disconnected Data Structures

ADO.NET constructs and manages DataSet and DataTable objects without the benefit of server-side cursors or persisted state. These objects roughly parallel the disconnected Recordset approach used in ADOc. Remember, ADO.NET provides no support for pessimistic (or any other kind of) locking cursors—all changes to the database are done via optimistic updates. ADO.NET does not include the entire "connected" paradigm supported by every data access interface since DB-Library. Microsoft suggests that developers simply use existing ADOc code wrapped in a COM interop layer for these designs—or stick with Visual Basic 6.0 *(Ahem! or Visual C++—especially for MTS/COM+ ADOc components that use object pooling)*.

---

14. A little more onion.

Behind the scenes, ADO.NET's architecture is (apparently) built around its own version of ADOc's Shape provider. It expects the developer to download separate resultsets (Tables) one at a time (or at least in sets). This can be done by using separate round trips to the data source or through multiple-resultset queries. After the DataTable is constructed, you're responsible for hard coding the parent/child relationships between these tables—that is, if you want ADO.NET to navigate, join, manage, display, and update hierarchical data and eventually post batches of updates to the back-end server. All of this is done in RAM with no further need of the connection or the source database. I'm not sure what happens when the amount of available RAM and swap space is exhausted using this approach. There is some evidence to suggest that your system might try to order more from the Web. Just don't be surprised to get a package in the mail addressed to your CPU. I expect that performance and functionality will also suffer to some degree—to say the least. This "in-memory database" approach means that you developers will have to be even more careful about designs and queries that extract too many rows from the data source. But this is not a new rule; the same has always applied to DAO, RDO, and ADOc as well, most especially in client/server circumstances.

The System.Data Namespace

Before I start burrowing any deeper into the details of the .NET System.Data object hierarchy, I'll define a term or two. For those of you who live and breathe object-oriented (OO) concepts, skip on down. For the rest of you, I try to make this as clear as I can despite being a person who's been programming for three decades without using "true" OO.

The .NET Framework is really a set of classes organized into related groups called namespaces. See "Introduction to the .NET Framework Class Library" in .NET Help for the long-winded definition. When you address the specific classes in a namespace you use dot (.) notation—just as you do in COM and did in pre-COM versions of Visual Basic. Thus, "System" is a namespace that has a number of subordinate namespaces associated with it. System.Data.OleDb defines a specific "type" within the System.Data namespace. Basically, everything up to the right-most dot is a namespace—the final name is a type. The System.Data namespace contains the classes, properties, methods, and events (what .NET calls "members") used to implement the ADO.NET architecture. When I refer to an "object," it means an instantiation of a class. For example, when I declare a new OleDbConnection object, I do so by using the new constructor on the OleDbConnection class.

```
System.Data.OleDbConnection myConnection = new System.Data.OleDbConnection();
```

Clear? Don't worry about it. I try to stay focused on the stuff you *need* to know and leave the OO purists to bore you with the behind-the-scenes details. See MSDN .NET[15] for more detailed information on the System.Data namespace.

The ADO.NET DataSet Object

The System.Data.DataSet object sits at the center of the ADO.NET architecture. While very different from an ADOc Recordset, it's about as close as you're going to get with ADO.NET. As with the ADOc Recordset, the DataSet is a bindable object supporting a wealth of properties, methods, and events. While an ADOc Recordset can be derived from a resultset returned from a query referencing several database tables, it's really a "flat" structure. All of the hierarchal information that defines how one data table is related to another is left in the database or in your head. Yes, you can use the ADOc Shape provider to extract data from several related tables and manage them in related ADOc-managed (Shape provider–managed) Recordsets. Anyone familiar with the Shape provider will feel comfortable with ADO.NET's DataSet approach. I would characterize the DataSet as a combination of an ActiveX Data Source control,[16] due to its ability to bind data with controls; a multidimensional Recordset, due to its ability to manage several resultsets (DataTable objects) at one time; and the Data Environment Designer or Data Object wizard, in that the DataSet can manage several Command objects used to manage the SELECT and action queries.

In contrast to the ADO Recordset, the ADO.NET System.Data.DataSet object is an in-memory data store that can manage *multiple* resultsets, each exposed as separate DataTable objects. Each DataTable contains data from a single data source—a single data query. No, the DataTable objects do not have to contain entire database tables—as you know, that simply won't work for larger databases (or for smaller ones either if you ever expect to upscale). I suggest you code your queries to contain a parameter-driven subset of rows that draw their data from one or more related tables.

Each DataTable object contains a DataColumnCollection (Columns)—a collection of DataColumn objects—that reflects or determines the schema of each DataTable; and a DataRowCollection (Rows) that contains the row data. This is a radical departure from DAO, RDO, and ADOc, where the data and schema information are encapsulated in the same Recordset (or Resultset) object. Consider, however, that the data in the DataTable is managed in XML and the schema in XSD. I discuss and illustrate this layout in Chapter 2.

---

15. http://www.msdn.microsoft.com/library/en-us/cpref/html/cpref_start.asp

16. The ADO Data Control, the Jet Data Control, and your hard-coded data source controls fall into this category.

You can construct your own DataTable objects by query or by code—defining each DataColumn object one-by-one and appending them to the DataColumn-Collection, just as you appended Field objects to an unopened Recordset in ADOc. The DataType property determines or reflects the type of data held by the DataColumn. The ReadOnly and AllowNull properties help to ensure data integrity, just as the Expression property enables you to build columns based on computed expressions. The DataSet is designed to be data agnostic—not caring where or how (or if) the data is sourced or retrieved; it leaves all of the data I/O responsibilities up to the .NET Data Provider.

In cases where your DataSet contains *related* resultsets, ADO.NET can manage these relationships for you—assuming you add code to define the relationships. For example, in the Biblio (or Pubs) database, the Authors table is related to the TitleAuthor and Titles tables. When you build a DataSet against resultsets based on these base (and many-to-many relationship) tables, and you construct the appropriate DataRelation objects; at that point you can navigate between authors and the titles they have written—all under control of ADO.NET. I illustrate and explain this in detail in Chapters 4 and 8.

DataTable objects can manage resultsets drawn directly from base tables or subset queries executed against base tables. The PK/FK relationships between the DataTable objects are managed through the DataRelation object—stored in the DataRelationCollection (Relations) collection. (Is there an echo in here?) When you construct these relationships (and you must—ADO.NET won't do it on its own; but, you can get the Visual Studio IDE to do it for you), UniqueConstraint and ForeignKeyConstraint objects are both automatically created depending on the parameter settings for the constructor. The UniqueConstraint ensures that values contained in a DataColumn are unique. The ForeignKeyConstraint determines what action is taken when a PK value is changed or deleted. I touch on these details again in Chapter 8. No, ADO.NET and the .NET IDE do not provide any mechanisms to construct these PK/FK relationships for you, despite supporting functionality to graphically define these relationships.

The following diagram (Figure 1-2) provides a simplified view of how the DataSet object is populated from a SqlClient .NET Data Provider. It illustrates the role of the bindable DataSet object and the important role of the .NET Data Provider. In this case, the diagram shows use of the Microsoft SQL Server–specific SqlClient .NET Data Provider, which contains objects to connect to the data source (SqlConnection), query the data (SqlDataAdapter), and retrieve a data stream (DataReader). The DataSet object's DataTable objects (Tables) are populated by a single call to the DataSet Fill method.

The DataAdapter also plays a key role here. It contains from one to four Command objects to (at least) fetch the data (SelectCommand) and (optionally) change it (UpdateCommand, InsertCommand, and DeleteCommand). Each of these Command objects are tied to specific Connection objects. When you execute the DataSet.Update method, the associated DataAdapter executes the appropriate DataAdapter Command objects for each added, changed, or deleted row in each of the DataTable objects.

Once constructed, the DataSet need not remain connected to the data source because all data is persisted locally in memory—changes and all. I drill deeper into DataSet topics in Chapter 4.

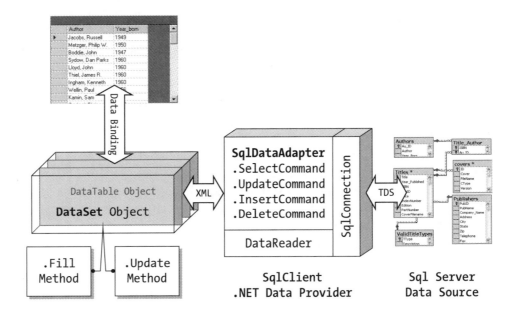

Figure 1-2. ADO.NET Data Access using the DataSet object.

The DataSet object supports a DataTableCollection (Tables) collection of DataTable objects, which contain a DataRowCollection (Rows) collection of DataRow objects. Each DataRow object contains the DataColumnCollection (Columns) of DataColumn objects, which contain the data and all of the DDL properties. Remember that, like the ADOc Recordset, the DataTable object can be bound by assigning it to the DataSource property of data-aware (bindable) controls.

Figure 1-3 illustrates the look of the System.Data.DataSet in a hierarchical diagram. Note the difference in the .NET naming convention. In COM, we expect a collection of objects to be named using the plural form of the object. For example, a collection of Cat objects would be stored in the Cats collection. In .NET, most (but not all) collections are named using the singular object name followed by "Collection," as in DataTableCollection. I found this very confusing until I started to code. It did not take long to discover that ADO.NET uses *different* names for each of these collections. These "real" names are shown in parentheses in the preceding paragraph and in Figure 1-3. I'm sure there's a good OO reason for this—I just have no idea what it is.

I explore each of these objects in more detail in subsequent chapters.

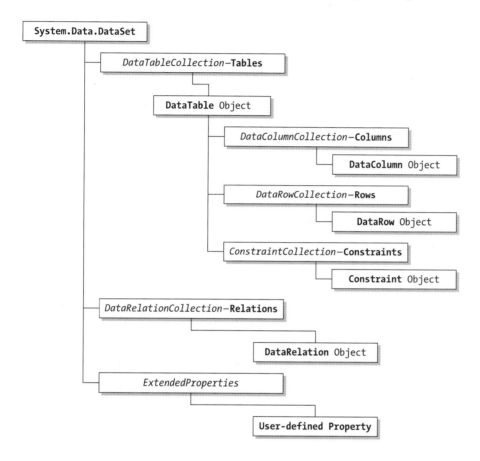

Figure 1-3. DataSet object hierarchy.

So, what should you know about this new ADO.NET structure? The DataSet:

- **Is a memory-resident structure constructed by the DataAdapter Fill method.**

- **Contains zero or more DataTable objects.**

- **Is logically tied to a DataAdapter object used to fetch and perform action queries as needed.**

- **Contains Constraints and Relations collections to manage inter-DataTable relationships.**

- **Is data-source agnostic, stateless, and can function independently from the data source.** All data, schema, constraints, and relationships to other tables in the DataSet are contained therein.

- **Is transported through XML documents via HTTP.** This means a DataSet can be passed through firewalls and used by any application capable of dealing with XML.

- **Can be saved to XML or constructed from properly formatted XML.**

- **Can be created programmatically**. DataTable by DataTable and DataColumn by DataColumn—along with DataRelation objects and Constraints.

It's clear that the DataSet was designed to transport "smart" data (and schema) between a Web host (possibly implemented as a Web Service) and a client. In this scenario, a client application queries the Web Service for specific information, such as the number of available rooms in hotels given a specific city. The Web Service queries the database using parameters passed from the client application and constructs a DataSet, which might contain a single DataTable object or multiple DataTable objects. If more than one table is returned, the DataSet can also specify the relationships between the tables to permit the client to navigate the room selections from city to city. The client can display and modify the data—possibly selecting one or more rooms—and pass back the DataSet to the Web Service, which uses a DataAdapter to reconcile the changes with the existing database.

Descending the System.Data Namespace Tree

I think pictures and drawings often make a subject easier to understand—especially for subjects like object hierarchies. So, I'm going to begin this section with a series of diagrams that illustrate the layout of the System.Data namespace.

ADOc has a relatively easy-to-understand and easily diagrammed object hierarchy. ADO.NET's System.Data namespace, however, is far more complex. As it currently stands, there are dozens upon dozens[17] of classes and members in the .NET Framework. Few of the complexities of the OO interfaces have been hidden—at least not in the documentation. Fortunately, there is a fairly easy way to climb through the object trees and get a good visual understanding of the hierarchies—basically what goes where and with what: Use the object browser in Visual Studio .NET. You can launch it from the **View | Other Windows** submenu. Figure 1-4 illustrates how the object browser depicts the System.Data namespace (unexploded). Throughout this section of the book, I walk through these object trees one at a time. By the time I'm done, you should either be thoroughly familiar with the System.Data namespace or thoroughly sick of it.

Figure 1-4. The System.Data namespace.

System.Data Namespace Exploded

The exploded System.Data namespace has over forty members—the top dozen or so are shown in Figure 1-5. I hope that we won't have to learn and remember how to use *all* of these objects, properties, methods, and events to become productive ADO.NET developers. Table 1-1 lists and describes the most important of these objects—the ones you'll use most often (at least at first).

---

17. I tried to count all of the objects in System.Data but lost count … sorry.

Figure 1-5. System.Data objects.

Table 1-1. Selected Members of the System.Data Namespace

Object	Description
Constraint and ConstraintCollection (Constraints), ForeignKeyConstraint, UniqueConstraint	Represents referential integrity constraints. Used to specify unique keys or PK/FK constraints and what to do when they change. Used to prevent duplicate rows from being added to the current dataset. No equivalent in ADOc. Hard coded by your application.
DataColumn and DataColumnCollection (Columns)	Represents a single data column schema associated with a DataTable object and the collection used to manage the columns. Similar to the ADOc Field object and Fields collection—but without the Value property. Automatically generated from the resultset.
DataException (and various other exception objects)	Represents the various exceptions thrown when an ADO.NET error is triggered. Similar to the ADOc Error object.

(continued)

Table 1-1. Selected Members of the System.Data Namespace (continued)

Object	Description
DataRelation and DataRelationCollection (Relations)	Represents table/column/table relations. Hard coded by your application. Specifies the tables and columns used to interrelate parent/child tables. No equivalent in ADOc.
DataRow and DataRowCollection (Rows)	Represents the *data* in a table row. Generated automatically.
DataRowView	Permits customized views of data rows based on changes applied during editing. Original, Proposed, and Current versions of a data row are exposed.
DataSet	Represents an in-memory data store consisting of DataTable, DataRelation, and Constraint objects.
DescriptionAttribute	Permits definition of code-specified properties for properties, events, or extenders.
DataTable and DataTableCollection (Tables)	Represents in-memory rows and columns of data returned from a data source or generated in code.
DataView, DataViewManager, DataViewSetting, DataViewSettingCollection (DataViewSettings)	Permits viewing one or more subsets of a DataTable. Similar to ADOc Recordsets after the Filter property is applied. Several DataView objects can be created against the same DataTable.
PropertyCollection (Properties)	Permits definition and retrieval of code-defined properties.
(and several others)	There are several other objects, event enumerations, and support objects exposed by the System.Data namespace.

Instantiating System.Data Objects

Your .NET application should be fairly specific about the libraries it expects to reference. In .NET, the ADO.NET .NET Data Providers (roughly equivalent to the ODBC and OLE DB providers accessed by ADOc) are built into the System.Data namespace so you don't have to add an explicit reference to use them. An exception is the Odbc .NET Data Provider that must be installed and registered separately—and so it is not part of System.Data namespace, rather it's part of the Microsoft.Data namespace. The Solution Explorer is a handy way to see what namespaces are already referenced for your application's assembly, as shown in Figure 1-6.

Figure 1-6. The Solution Explorer showing a newly created WinForm application.

Depending on the ADO.NET data access provider you choose, you'll want to use the using[18] directive with either System.Data.OleDb or System.Data.SqlClient (or in unusual situations, both), or Microsoft.Data.Odbc to make sure your code correctly references these libraries. Actually, the CLR, which sits at the core of .NET, won't permit name collisions, but adding a namespace to the using list makes coding easier by providing "shorthand" syntax for commonly used objects. Although not required for ADO.NET, the using directive signals the compiler to

---

18. For Visual Basic developers converting from Visual Basic .NET, the using directive is equivalent to the Imports directive in Visual Basic .NET and (very) loosely similar to the inclusion of header files in C and C++.

search the specified namespace referenced in your code to resolve any ambiguous object names. Basically, using helps the compiler resolve namespace references more easily. The using statement should be positioned first in your code—above all other declarations. For example, to add the OleDb .NET Data Provider namespace, place the following at the start of your code module:

```
using System.Data.OleDb;
```

Similarly for the SqlClient .NET Data Provider namespace, add the following to your code module:

```
using System.Data.SqlClient;
```

Because you used the using directive with the System.Data.SqlClient .NET Data Provider, you can code

```
SqlConnection cn = new SqlConnection();
```

However, the downside to this approach is potential object collisions and failed compiles. Again, some pundits feel that it's best to explicitly reference declared objects. You can also reference your ADO.NET objects explicitly if you don't mind typing a lot (or if you are paid by the word). For example, you can create a new ADO.NET Connection object this way:

```
System.Data.SqlClient.SqlConnection cn =
            new System.Data.SqlClient.SqlConnection();
```

However, I try not to use this approach in my examples or sample code. I provide more examples of object and variable declarations as I go—and there is a long way yet to travel.

Introducing the ADO.NET DataAdapter

Think of the DataAdapter as a "bridge" object that links the data source (your database) and a Connection object with the ADO.NET-managed DataSet object through its SELECT and action query Commands. All of the .NET Data Providers implement their version (instance) of the System.Data.DataAdapter class; OleDbDataAdapter, OdbcDataAdapter, and SqlClientDataAdapter all inherit from the base System.Data class. Each .NET Data Provider exposes a SelectCommand property that contains a query that returns rows when the DataSet Fill method is executed. The SelectCommand is typically a SELECT query or the name of a stored procedure. Each Command object managed by the DataAdapter references a Connection[19] object to manage the database connection through the Command object's Connection property. I discuss the Connection object in Chapter 2.

The invocation of the DataSet Update method triggers the execution of the DataAdapter object's UpdateCommand, InsertCommand, or DeleteCommand to post changes made to the DataSet object. I discuss updating in Chapter 7. The figure shown earlier (Figure 1-2) also illustrates the working relationship between the DataSet and the DataAdapter.

Constructing DataAdapter Command Queries

If the query set in the SelectCommand is simple enough (references a single table and not a stored procedure), you can (usually) ask ADO.NET to generate the appropriate action queries for the DataAdapter UpdateCommand, InsertCommand, and DeleteCommand using the CommandBuilder object. If this does not produce suitable SQL syntax, you can manually fill in the action queries using queries of your own design—even calling stored procedures to perform the operations. I discuss the construction of these commands in Chapter 3.

Coding the DataAdapter

I expect you'd like to see some code that demonstrates how all of this is implemented. Because I haven't discussed the Connection object yet, this will be a little tough, but let's assume for a minute that you know how to get connected in ADO.NET. Let me walk you through a small example.[20] (Don't worry about the code I don't explain here—I discuss many of these points again in the next chapter.)

First, make sure that your application can see the SqlClient namespace. It's already part of the .NET Framework, but not part of your application's namespace.

```
using System.Data.SqlClient;
```

Next, within the address range of your Form's[21] class, define the objects and variables to be used.

---

19. Actually, the name of the Connection object is SqlConnection, OleDbConnection, OdbcConnection, or <ProviderSpecific>Connection in the case of other vendors' .NET Data Provider namespace's Connection object.

20. Located in the "\Examples\Chapter 01\Data Adapter" folder on the CD.

21. The default architecture in most examples (before I get to Chapter 10) is Windows Forms.

NOTE *In C#, objects and variables have private scope by default. I will have a little more to say on constructors later on—like where and how best to deal with them—but those familiar with VB .NET should just note here that* strConnect *is declared here as a* const. *This means that it is effectively a read-only field—a constant. Why? Well, we use this string in the constructor argument for the new SqlConnection object. So what? Well in C#, non-static instance fields cannot be used to initialize other instance fields outside of a method, and this is quite different from VB .NET.*

```
public class Form1 : System.Windows.Forms.Form
{
    const string strConnect = "data source=.;database=biblio;uid=admin;pwd=pw";
    string strQuery   =
        "Select Title, Price from Titles where Title like 'Hit%'";
    SqlConnection cn = new SqlConnection(strConnect);
    SqlDataAdapter da = new SqlDataAdapter();
    DataSet ds = new DataSet();
......
}
```

In the Form1_Load event handler, you set the DataAdapter object's SelectCommand string to a SELECT query that returns a few rows from the Titles table. Actually, you shouldn't have to open the connection explicitly, because, if the connection is not already open, the Fill method automatically opens it and then closes it again. If you use this auto-open technique, you need to be prepared for connection errors when you execute the Command. I'm using this approach because it's more familiar to ADOc developers. I illustrate how to get the Fill method to manage connections in the next chapter and a simpler, more ADO.NET-centric approach later in this chapter.

Notice the use of C#'s try and catch error handler.[22] In the catch statement, you reference the System.Data.SqlClient.SqlException object simply as SqlException (remember that you placed the using System.Data.SqlClient; statement in earlier so that you could make these "shorthand" references). SqlException exposes a Message and Error number (and more) that can be used to figure out what went wrong. The simplest way to provide **all** of the SqlException object information to a developer during debugging is to cast it to a string with a call to the ToString() method, sending this to the Debug output window via the

---

22. Error handling is discussed in Chapter 9, "ADO.NET Error Management Strategies." The ADO.NET concepts I use apply universally in most cases.

`Debug.WriteLine()` method. To use the Debug object, you must reference the System.Diagnostics namespace by `using System.Diagnostics`. This is helpful when the intended recipient of an exception message is a developer, but not necessarily so useful for your program to spew it all out to a user while committing hari-kari. Fortunately, the Debug object is automatically stripped from release builds. Your user doesn't care much for which line in your code triggered the self-disembowelment—but more on exceptions in Chapter 9.

So here, if the `cn.Open();` statement does not work, the next statement is never executed and the catch block will deal with the exception, depositing its remains to the console/debug output window.

```
...
using System.Diagnostics;
...
private void Form1_Load(object sender, System.EventArgs e)
{
    try
    {
        cn.Open();
        da.SelectCommand = new SqlCommand(strQuery, cn);
    }
    catch(SqlException ex)
    {
        Debug.WriteLine(ex.ToString());
    }
}
```

In the Button click-event (did I say there are both DataGrid and Button controls on the form?) you use the DataAdapter Fill method to "run" the SelectCommand query in the specified DataAdapter. The results are fed to the DataSet object. By default, the Fill method names the DataSet "Table" (for some reason). I would have preferred "Data" or "DataSet" to discourage confusion with database tables. The Fill method is very (very) flexible as it can be invoked in a bevy of ways, as I describe in Chapter 4. The options I chose in this example name the resulting DataTable "TitlesandPrice." In the next statement, I bind the DataSet to the DataGrid control.

```
private void Button1_Click(object sender, System.EventArgs e)
{
        da.Fill(ds, "Titles and Price"); // Defaults to "Table"
        DataGrid1.DataSource = ds.Tables["Titles and Price"];
}
```

The result? Well, this code opens a connection, runs a query, and fills a grid with the resulting rows; but what's missing? To start with: error handlers. This code does not deal with bad connections (except to print a debug message), bad queries, empty queries, or the fact that most applications will want to create a parameter-based query instead of a hard-coded SELECT statement. However, baby steps come before running—especially in *this* neighborhood.

As I wrote this example, I was reminded of a few lessons:

- **The** using System.Data.SqlClient **directive helps.** Statement completion did not show the objects I was referencing nearly as quickly (if at all) until I added the using directive.

- **The DataSet object is suitable for binding.** That is, it can be assigned to the DataGrid or any bindable control for display. In my example, I bind the DataSet to a DataGrid control's DataSource property.

- **It helps to bind to a specific DataTable.** If you bind to the DataSet, the data in the DataGrid isn't immediately shown. This requires the user to drill down into a selected DataTable. It's better to bind to a specific DataTable in the DataSet Tables collection.

- **Use the form's constructor method to initialize instance variables**. It is not a good idea to initialize instance variables at class level declaration since they can't be encapsulated in try/catch blocks to deal with any exceptions arising in the initialization.

TIP *This is a practice I picked up years ago: Install crude error handlers from the very beginning. I encourage you to do the same. The crudest, of course, is a simple catch and casting of the exception object to a string that is sent to the debug output window. This can save you an extra ten minutes as you try to figure out what went wrong.*

A Simpler Example

Okay, now that I have shown you an example based on how an ADOc developer might code, take a look at the same problem using the new ADO.NET approach. You should notice that there is no explicit call to open the connection—that is taken care of here silently by the Fill() method; I talk more about this later.

Also, I am specifying properties for the class' constructors to use when instantiating. Most .NET classes have one or several constructors used to set different combinations of properties as the objects are being instantiated. After you understand these, you'll really appreciate how they make your code easier to write.

```
private void btnRunQuery_Click(object sender, System.EventArgs e)
{
    try
    {
        SqlConnection cn =
            new SqlConnection("data source=.;database=biblio;uid=admin;pwd=pw");
        SqlDataAdapter da =
            new SqlDataAdapter(
            "Select Title, Price from Titles where Title like 'Hit%'", cn);
        DataSet ds = new DataSet();
        da.Fill(ds, "Titles and Price");
        DataGrid1.DataSource = ds.Tables["Titles and Price"];
    }
    catch (SqlException ex)
    {
        Debug.WriteLine(ex.ToString());
    }
}
```

ADO.NET's Low-Level Data Stream

By this time you know that by default, ADOc Recordsets are created as RO/FO[23] firehose data structures. This low-level data stream permits data providers to return resultsets to the client as quickly as the LAN can carry them. While fast, the default firehose ADOc Recordset does not support record count, cursors, scrolling, updatability, caching, filters, sorting, or any costly overhead mechanism that could slow down the process of getting data back to the client.

ADO.NET also supports this firehose functionality, but in a different way. After you establish a connection, you can stream data back to your application using the ADO.NET .NET Data Provider's DataReader class (SqlDataReader, OdbcDataReader, or OleDbDataReader) through the provider's Command class (SqlCommand, OleDbCommand, or OdbcCommand).

---

23. RO/FO: read-only/forward-only

Although the ADO.NET data stream is RO/FO, the fundamental data access technique is different from ADOc in a number of respects. Let's walk through a simple example[24] as an illustration. The following section of code declares Connection, DataAdapter, DataReader, and Command objects using the SqlClient .NET Data Provider. As you'll see throughout this section, C# permits you to declare and initialize selected properties of the declared objects in a single line of code; although, as I said earlier, departing from VB .NET, C# does not permit you to initialize selected properties with other non-static instance fields outside of a method.

If you look carefully at this code snippet you'll notice that the SqlCommand cmd object is declared in the Form1 class outside of a method. By default this gives the cmd object private scope, ensuring that it is accessible to all methods within the class. I have, however, placed the constructor code

```
cmd = new SqlCommand(strSQL, cn);
```

for the cmd object within Form1's constructor method Form1() after the call to InitializeComponent(); since this depends on other non-static instance fields strSQL and cn.[25]

```
...
using System.Data.SqlClient;
...
public class Form1 : System.Windows.Forms.Form
{
    ...
    SqlConnection cn =
        new SqlConnection("data source=.;database=biblio;uid=admin;pwd=pw");
    SqlDataAdapter da = new SqlDataAdapter();
    string strSQL = "Select Title, PubID from Titles where Title like ";
    SqlDataReader Dr;
    SqlCommand cmd;
    ...
public Form1()
{
    ...
    InitializeComponent();
    ...
    cmd = new SqlCommand(strSQL, cn);
}
    ...
```

---

24. Located in the "\Examples\Chapter 01\Data Stream" folder on the CD.

25. Well I suppose we could declare strSQL and cn as static but then that would force them to be common across **all** concurrent instances of Form1.

This next routine is fired when a button is clicked on the form. The ExecuteReader method is executed—instantiating a SqlClient.DataReader. When first opened, the DataReader does *not* expose a row of the resultset because its current row pointer is positioned before any rows (as in a Recordset when BOF = True). To activate the first and each subsequent row one at a time, you have to use the DataReader object's Read method, which returns False when there are no (additional) rows available. Once read, you can't scroll back to previously read rows—just as in the FO resultset in ADOc.

As each row is read, the code moves data from the columns exposed by the DataReader to a ListBox control. Note that you have to use the Add() method to add members to any collection—including the ListBox and ComboBox controls' Items collections. You also have to be very careful about moving the data out of the DataReader columns; each column must be specifically cast as you go—converting each to a datatype suitable for the target. In order to code these conversions correctly, your code will have to know what datatypes are being returned by the resultset or use the GetValue method. .NET is pretty unforgiving when it comes to automatically morphing datatypes.

TIP *I use the ListBox BeginUpdate and EndUpdate methods to prevent needless painting while I'm filling it.*

```
private void Button1_Click(object sender, System.EventArgs e)
{
    cn.Open(); //The connect string was defined when the object was created
    cmd.CommandText = strSQL + "'" + TextBox1.Text + "%'";
    Dr = cmd.ExecuteReader();
    ListBox1.Items.Clear();  // clear the listbox
    ListBox1.BeginUpdate();  // Prevent the listbox from painting

    while (Dr.Read()) // get the first (or next) row
    {
        ListBox1.Items.Add(Dr.GetString(0) + " - " + Dr.GetInt32(1).ToString());
    }

    ListBox1.EndUpdate();  // Let the listbox paint again

    Dr.Close();   // close the data reader.
}
```

CHAPTER 2

ADO.NET—Getting Connected

WHILE IT'S POSSIBLE to create stand-alone data structures using ADO.NET without the benefit of a back-end data source—such as SQL Server, Access, Oracle, or other DBMS data sources—most developers must depend on ADO.NET and a database engine to construct objects reflecting the data *and* its schema. This chapter discusses how to establish a connection in .NET using three different .NET Data Providers as well as the "traditional" ADOc Connection object:

1. Via the ADO.NET OleDb .NET Data Provider—System.Data.OleDb.

2. Via the ADO.NET Tabular Data Stream (TDS) or SqlClient .NET Data Provider—System.Data.SqlClient.

3. Via the ADO.NET Odbc .NET Data Provider—Microsoft.Data.Odbc

4. Via ADOc. (*Remember that ADOc refers to traditional COM-based ADO.*)

As ADO.NET and the .NET Framework mature, more and more providers will come on line. I expect that the techniques discussed in this and subsequent chapters will apply (at least for the most part) to these evolving .NET Data Providers. That said, be prepared for differences. Consider that many of these new providers will be written by non-Microsoft coders who might not under-stand (or agree with) the subtleties of provider coding—especially on a brand new platform. Many of these provider developers will want to take advantage of the features of their target data source—who would blame them? Hopefully, they will also document these extensions and their implementation of the "base" features so that your use of their new provider will be painless.

The Odbc .NET Data Provider was not ready in time to meet deadlines so it is not a part of the initial Visual Studio .NET setup. It can, however, be downloaded from the Web. I have also seen evidence of other providers; see http://www.msdn.microsoft.com/downloads/ for details.

Like ADOc and OLE DB, ADO.NET depends on connection pooling to reduce the overhead of establishing and tearing down connections. Unlike ADOc, ADO.NET includes methods, properties, and events used to enable, disable, and tune the connection pooling mechanism. I visit this technology in some detail later in this chapter.

ADO.NET .NET Data Providers

As I discussed in Chapter 1, ADO.NET is designed around a "disconnected" approach to data access. This applies to all of the .NET Data Providers just described. A .NET Data Provider is simply a block of low-level data access code written for the .NET Framework and ADO.NET designed to access a particular type or class of data source. For the bulk of the beta test cycle, .NET Data Providers were referred to as "managed" providers. They were called "managed" because they know how to behave themselves in the .NET Framework.

The first two of these data providers (SqlClient and OleDb) are included in the System.Data namespace to which all .NET applications have access. The Odbc .NET Data Provider can be downloaded from the Web[1] and added to your application's namespace through the IDE. After you have downloaded and installed it on your development system, simply click the **Project | Add References** menu and select **Microsoft.Data.Odbc** from the .NET tab. If the Odbc .NET Data Provider is not listed (and you have installed it), then select **Browse** and navigate to "\Program Files\Microsoft.NET\Odbc.Net" and select the **Microsoft.Data.Odbc.dll** assembly. From there on onwards you should be able to add a reference to the Odbc .NET Data Provider from the **Project | Add References** menu.

As I also discussed in Chapter 1, the .NET Data Providers are your direct portals to many (not all) existing OLE DB COM-based providers (System.Data.OleDb), ODBC drivers (Microsoft.Data.Odbc), or to Microsoft SQL Server TDS (System.Data.SqlClient). ADO.NET expects the .NET Data Provider to connect (sometimes automatically) to the data source, query data, return any rowset(s), and then (possibly) disconnect. The .NET Data Provider (usually automatically) reconnects when it's told (or needs) to get fresh data or to post updates. As I discuss more completely later, you'll find it's *essential* to close your database connections after you're done with them—.NET *won't* do it for you—at least not in a reasonable length of time. The OleDb documentation says that the OleDb provider does not even attempt to close an OleDbConnection object that falls out of scope. I expect this is universally true with all providers. This is very different from the behavior you've encountered when working with COM-based components and ADOc.

Later on (in Chapters 4, "ADO.NET DataReader Strategies" and 7, "ADO.NET Update Strategies") I describe how the DataAdapter Fill and the SqlCommand Execute methods include an optional `CommandBehavior` argument that tells ADO.NET to close the connection after the resultset is populated—assuming the

---

1.   The Odbc .NET Data Provider should be a part of the .NET SDK after its second release.

methods didn't automatically open the connection in the first place. If the executed method opens the connection, it also automatically closes it.

WARNING *I can't stress this enough: You* must *close any Connection object you explicitly open. If you don't, you'll leak connections in the connection pool and the memory associated with these connections.*

Behind the scenes, ADO.NET and the .NET Data Providers use XML to manage the data and schema. This permits .NET applications to easily transport your resultsets from application to application or tier to tier with the only common factor being knowledge of XML (on the part of the code sending or receiving the data). You can also open DataSet objects directly from XML data sources such as FOR XML queries or other XML data sources. I discuss the XML aspects of ADO.NET in Chapter 10, "ADO.NET and XML."

ADO.NET and the .NET Data Providers implemented so far know nothing about keyset, dynamic, or static cursors, or pessimistic locking as supported in ADOc. They don't leverage server-side state or cursors of any kind—regardless of the data source. ADO.NET has its own hierarchical JOIN engine so it doesn't need the server to do anything but run simple (single-table) SELECT queries. I expect we'll see ADO.NET mature before long and add native support for server-side cursors and pessimistic locking.

IMHO *This client-side data crunching leaves quite a bit of power idling on the server—a server designed and tuned to provide high-speed JOINs and other functionality not needed or replicated in ADO.NET. You can still run a complex query on the server, but the resultset might not be manageable by ADO.NET. I'll be experimenting with this in the near future.*

Choosing the Right Provider

When you're ready to use the ADO.NET approach to data access, you need to decide which of the .NET Data Providers is best for your situation. One choice is to use the generic OleDb .NET Data Provider—System.Data.OleDb. This name reflects what it is—a generic OLE DB interface to data that has little resemblance to ADO as we've known it in the past. You must use the System.Data.OleDb .NET Data Provider if your data source is accessed through a native OLE DB provider—even for SQL Server. However, not all of the OLE DB providers are supported. For example, there is no support for Exchange and many other OLE DB providers.

While there is another .NET Data Provider designed specifically for Microsoft SQL Server (System.Data.SqlClient), you don't *have* to use it. As a matter of fact, you *can't* use SqlClient if you are still running a version of SQL Server prior to 7.0. In situations where you want to write a generic front end or component that can connect to any selected back end, you might choose to forgo the features, speed, and functionality of the TDS SqlClient .NET Data Provider in favor of the generic (one-size-fits-all (OSFA)) OleDb .NET Data Provider. My recommendation? If you're running SQL Server 7.0 or later, use the SqlClient .NET Data Provider. If you're not, then you can't, so don't.

The newest (albeit late) addition to the list is the Odbc .NET Data Provider. It's designed to connect to existing ODBC drivers used for older, more obscure, or simply unsupported (by Microsoft) data sources.

Creating ADO.NET Connection Objects

I think you'll find that the Connection object in ADO.NET is very similar to the ADOc Connection object in many respects. There are differences, however, in the ConnectionString property and in the Open method. Also, when it comes to getting access to a DBMS, each of these ADO.NET .NET Data Providers does very similar things; they each establish a connection to a back-end data source so you can run queries and return rowsets or perform updates. A significant difference in the ADO.NET Connection object is that you don't have to use the Open or Close methods—not as long as you use the Fill and Update methods. This is because ADO.NET will open and close the Connection object automatically. However, if you use the (faster) DataReader to return data, you will have to use the Open method—but the DataReader can be programmed to automatically close the Connection object when it's done.

Let's take a closer look at the Connection object. Just as in ADOc, the .NET Data Providers establish connections, validate users, and set ADO.NET options by passing some or all of the following values to the provider:

- A server name or database filename

- A provider name

- A UserID and password (one way or another)

- Possibly a default database

- Other information to assist in getting connected or to manage the connection pool

If the connection is established, ADO.NET hooks your application to the chosen data source. Each of the .NET Data Providers and ADOc uses a different code path to get you connected to your data. All are viable, but each has its own limitations and benefits. I clear up the nitty-gritty details on those differences later, but let's look at the fundamental variations before going on.

Using Constructors in Declarations

When you declare a variable in C#, you have the option of instantiating the object using one of the object's constructor methods. The following will create a new instance ds of type DataSet, with the default constructor method DataSet():

```
DataSet ds = new DataSet();
```

Some objects have overloaded constructors. That is, they can call different constructor methods (with the same name), but with a different set of parameters to use for instantiation. For example, an instance field ds of type DataSet can also be constructed to initialize the DataSetName property of the DataSet to dsEmployees with the following:

```
DataSet ds = new DataSet("dsEmpolyees");
```

However, consider that if you have an instance field strDataSetname of type string and an instance field ds of type DataSet, then the following will give a compiler error (assuming that you are trying to do this outside of any method):

```
string strDataSetName = "dsEmployees";
DataSet ds = new DataSet(strDataSetName);
```

This is very different from the behavior of Visual Basic .NET, which will permit you to initialize instance objects (Dim), based on other instance objects outside of methods.

So what do you do about it? Well, all it means is that you must place instance field constructor code into the class's (form's[2]) own constructor method(s).

 NOTE *The plural is very important to recognize here! A class can have more than one constructor, and if you have instance field initialization code, then you may need to ensure that it is fired for all the instances of the class's construction.*

---

2.   A form is really just a special class.

Of course this means that you can instantiate and initialize your class's instance fields differently for each of a class's constructors—sometimes the very reason why you want a class to have different constructor signatures.[3]

Visual Basic .NET will let you instantiate your instance fields differently in each of the overloaded New( ) methods—but then you might also have initialization code outside of a method.

> **WARNING**   *Irrespective of the ability of C# to instantiate (some) instance fields outside of methods (e.g.,* DataSet ds = new DataSet( ); *) at class level, as above, it is IPHO still best to do this only inside constructor methods inside of a* try/catch *exception handler so that any exceptions arising can be dealt with.*

Building an ADO.NET ConnectionString

At this point, I'm ready to discuss construction of the ConnectionString property (and argument) which is used by all of the providers in one way or another. It won't take long before you discover that the ConnectionString is no longer passed to the Open method (it takes no arguments), so you must code it as a constructor argument when you declare the Connection object or you must directly set the Connection.ConnectionString property.

You might have noticed that the ADO.NET ConnectionString is easier for you (the human) to read and its syntax is very (very) flexible. It seems that every ODBC and OLE DB operator is supported in the string and they're accepted in almost any combination. Thank you Microsoft. This means you can call the default database "database" instead of "initial catalog" (unless you *really* like "initial catalog"). It's about time. Each of the arguments in the ConnectionString is identified and passed to appropriate properties of the Connection object, but, unlike ADOc providers, any unknown arguments trip a trappable error. This means you had better learn how to spell, space, and format your connection strings correctly—or leverage someone else's.

Nope, sorry, your ADOc ConnectionString won't always work with the ADO.NET .NET Data Providers. You can, however, strip off the Provider=xxxx; argument when using the SqlClient provider—you might get lucky. Note that the Connection.Open method does not accept *any* arguments. This means that you can't expect to pass in the UserID and password separately during the Open.

---

3.   A method signature is just a way of referring to the set of argument types a method call accepts.

And no, there are no UserID or password arguments in the Connection object (sigh). This means you must include the UserID and password arguments in the ConnectionString or use NT (domain/SSPI) authentication where available.

For those of you who used the ADOc Connection.Properties collection, you'll discover that the ADO.NET Connection object has no equivalent collection. Fortunately, the ADO.NET ConnectionString can accept the arguments you used to code as extended properties. Appendix C lists these properties for the primary ADOc providers. You should be able to use these properties in your ConnectionString property—assuming you know how the enumeration is exposed. That is, you can't code `Prompt=adPromptNever` in the ConnectionString. You have to look up the property (unless it's shown below) and use the enumerated constant instead of the named enumeration. For example, to change the prompting behavior of ADO.NET connections using the OleDb ConnectionString, you could code:

```
cn.ConnectionString = "Provider=SqlOleDb;Prompt=1;";
```

Okay, folks, this is just an example of using ADOc properties in a ConnectionString. Don't go off using the Prompt argument to launch the OLE DB provider's dialog to capture the UserID, password, and default database. For one thing, it won't work in a Web page or a middle-tier component—it's not supported (in addition to not being very smart). This particular property can lead to a nasty security breach because it permits the user to guess the UserID and password until they get it right and even select from any visible database after they correctly guess.

The real question is: How did I figure out that the enumeration I wanted was "1"? Well, I had to do some digging in the MDAC SDK to discover this value. No, this SDK is not installed when you install Visual Studio .NET; you have to install it from the Web or your MSDN CDs. I located these enumerations in "ADO Enumerated Constants" in the SDK.

Remember that you can't change the ConnectionString after the connection is open. Also, unlike ADOc, the "post open" ConnectionString does not contain all of the default properties—it does not change post open. Check the SqlConnection.State property to verify that the connection is closed before trying to access the ConnectionString property.

```
if (cn.State == ConnectionState.Closed)
{
    cn.ConnectionString = strConnect;
}
```

Setting the ConnectionString in code (as in an assignment statement) or in a constructor statement tells ADO.NET to immediately parse the ConnectionString and move its arguments into associated properties. This is different from ADOc which simply passed the ConnectionString to the provider for processing.

Most ConnectionString arguments don't have equivalent Connection object properties (such as the UserID and Password) so they *must* be set in the initial ConnectionString. If the process of parsing the ConnectionString fails for any reason, none of the properties are set and you get a trappable error (SqlException), which might point the way to your problem. Of course, even if all of the arguments are successfully copied to properties, there's no guarantee that the Open will succeed.

The ADO.NET ConnectionString itself is basically identical in format—with a few notable exceptions—to the one you constructed for ADOc. One significant difference is that the SqlClient provider does not accept the `Provider=` argument—so don't include it. Also, the OleDb provider now *requires* a `Provider` argument; you can't simply default to MSDASQL (the ODBC "Kagera" provider). As with ADOc, setting Connection object properties (SqlConnection, OdbcConnection, and OleDbConnection) also changes the ConnectionString property. This is the string used to manage the connection pool. See Connection Pooling later in this chapter for details.

When you build your ConnectionString, you specify name/value pairs just as in ADOc. In ADO.NET these can be delimited by single or double quotes, (for example, `name='value'` or `name=\"value\"`)—but more commonly you would simply place them all in a single string literal. No escape sequences are supported and the name argument is not case sensitive.

This means that if in SQL Server you have a database called "Peter's DB" which is quite legal (although perhaps not advisable), then you cannot (presently) build a ConnectionString to connect directly to the database. The ConnectionString

```
cn.ConnectionString = "data source=.;database=Peter's DB;uid=admin;pwd=pw;";
```

or

```
cn.ConnectionString = "data source=.;database=Peter\'s DB;uid=admin;pwd=pw;";
```

will throw a run-time exception of "`Invalid delimiter ' found in the connection option value.`"

There is, however, a workaround of sorts to this particular problem: Use the Connection object's `ChangeDatabase()` method after the connection has been opened.

```
cn.ConnectionString = "data source=.;database=Master;uid=admin;pwd=pw;";
cn.Open();
cn.ChangeDatabase("Peter'sDB");
```

 WARNING *I have not found a satisfactory workaround to UserID or passwords that contain escaped character sequences; they are legal in SQL Server and I suppose in the case of passwords might have even been considered favorable. The problem is that the UserID and the password, if using SQL Server Authentication, MUST be submitted in the ConnectionString; there are no separate UserID or Password properties on the Connection object.*

If a given name occurs more than once in the ConnectionString, the value associated with the last occurrence is used—just as in ADOc.

 WARNING *The fact that ConnectionString operands can over-ride existing operands is dangerous—especially if you blindly concatenate strings to the ConnectionString from outside sources. Malicious users could add or override operators and potentially gain access to your data sources. Be sure to screen incoming user-generated (or any) strings before tacking them on to the ConnectionString. Any incoming string that contains a ";" is suspect.*

The following table (Table 2-1) lists the valid "name" arguments, and how they are used. Note those arguments marked ✔ are new for ADO.NET .NET Data Providers. Notably missing are "Remote Provider, Remote Server, and URL." These are (currently) not supported. Remember, you can also add all of the connection properties listed in Appendix D to this list—assuming you determine the correct enumeration to use.

Table 2-1. Connection String Arguments

New	Name	Default	Description
	Application Name		The name of the application.
	AttachDBFilename, extended properties, or Initial File Name		The name of the primary file, including the full path name, of an attachable database. The database name must be specified with the keyword 'database'.
	Connect Timeout or Connection Timeout	15	The length of time (in seconds) to wait for a connection to the server before terminating the attempt and generating an error.
✓	Connection Lifetime (SqlClient)[4]	0	How long (in seconds) a connection should be left in the pool after that connection is closed.
✓	Connection Reset	'True'	Determines whether the database connection is reset when being removed from the pool.
	Current Language		The SQL Server Language record name.
	DSN= (Odbc only)		Points to registered data source name.
	Database (SqlClient only)		Name of the default database.
	Data Source, Server Addr, Address, or Network Address		The name or network address of the instance of SQL Server to which to connect.
✓	Enlist (SqlClient only)	'True'	When True, connection pooling automatically enlists the connection in the creation thread's current transaction context.
	File name= (OleDb only)		Points to UDL file containing the ConnectionString.
	Initial Catalog (OleDb and SqlClient only)		Name of the default database.
	Integrated Security or Trusted_Connection	'False'	Use Windows-based security or not. Recognized values are 'true', 'false', and 'sspi', which is equivalent to 'true'.

(continued)

4.　SqlClient keywords are designed for the SqlClient provider.

Table 2-1. Connection String Arguments (continued)

New	Name	Default	Description
✓	Isolation Level (OleDb only)	ReadCommitted	The transaction isolation level for the connection. Can be one of the following values: ReadCommitted, ReadUncommitted, RepeatableRead, or Serializable.
✓	Max Pool Size (SqlClient only)	100	Maximum number of connections allowed in the pool.
✓	Min Pool Size (SqlClient only)	0	Minimum number of connections allowed in the pool.
	Network Library or Net	'dbmssocn'	Network library used to establish a connection to an instance of the data source. The default value, dbnssocn, specifies TCP/IP sockets.[5] Other values include dbnmpntw (Named Pipes), dbmsrpcn (Multiprotocol), dbmsadsn (Apple Talk), dbmsgnet (VIA), dbmsipcn (Shared Memory), and dbmsspxn (IPX/SPX). The corresponding network DLL must be installed on the system to which you connect.
	Packet Size	8192	Size in bytes of the network packets used to communicate with the data source. PacketSize may be a value in the range of 512 and 32767 bytes. An exception is generated if the value is outside of this range.
	Password, or Pwd[6]		The password matching the UserID provided.
	Persist Security Info	'False'	When set to 'false', security-sensitive information, such as the password, is not returned as part of the connection if the connection is open or has ever been in an open State. Resetting the connection string resets all connection string values including the password.

(continued)

---

5. This default changed in MDAC 2.6. It used to be dbnmpntw (Named Pipes) in earlier versions.
6. Note that these keywords must be spelled correctly (even if they aren't in your Webster's dictionary)—but case is *not* significant.

Table 2-1. Connection String Arguments (continued)

New	Name	Default	Description
✓	Pooling (SqlClient only)	'True'	When True, the connection object is drawn from the appropriate pool, or if necessary, is created and added to the appropriate pool.
✓	Prompt (OleDb only)	4	Specifies whether a dialog box should be displayed to prompt for missing parameters when opening a connection to a data source. 1: Prompts always; 2: Prompts if more information is required 3: Prompts if more information is required but optional parameters are not allowed; 4: Never prompts.
	Provider (OleDb only)	(no default)	Required for OleDb connections. Sets the name of the OLE DB provider. See the text for supported providers.
	UserID or UID		The login account.
	Workstation ID		The local computer name. The name of the workstation connecting to SQL Server.

When setting Boolean properties, you can use 'yes' instead of 'true', and 'no' instead of 'false'. Integer values are represented as strings.

TIP *You might be able to reduce round trips by tuning the packet size property. If an application performs bulk copy operations, or sends or receives large amounts of text or image data, a packet size larger than the default may improve efficiency because it results in fewer network read and write operations. If an application sends and receives small amounts of information, you can set the packet size to 512 bytes (using the Packet Size value in the ConnectionString), which is sufficient for most data transfer operations. For most applications, however, the default packet size is best.*

It's clear that the .NET team is moving in the right direction as far as ConnectionString arguments are concerned. The arguments enable developers to carefully tune the connection pool—either by enabling it or turning it off—quite easily (at least in the SqlClient provider). However, it seems that there is something missing here: Where is the Connection object's Properties collection? In ADOc, each of the objects had a Properties collection that maintained an expandable set of properties enabled by the OLE DB or ODBC provider. After some research, I discovered that you can expose these properties by including the named property in the ConnectionString along with its enumerated value (not the enumerated keyword, but its value). I discuss this in more detail a little later.

 WARNING *The default setting for Net or Network Library has changed. It used to be "dbnmpntw" (Named Pipes) but it's now "dbmssocn" (TCP/IP sockets). If you notice your server struggling to establish connections, you might consider changing the Net setting back to named pipes.*

Connecting via the SqlClient .NET Data Provider

.NET includes a new "native" ADO.NET provider for SQL Server—the first of its kind. It's not based on OLE DB or ODBC in any way; it's designed around SQL Server's native tongue: Tabular Data Stream (TDS). Other database vendors are bound to follow suit with their own native providers—I expect Oracle, DB2, and others to be available by the time you read this. This section walks you through opening connections with this new TDS .NET Data Provider—System.Data.SQLClient.

Introducing System.Data.SQLClient

For those of you who have been developing applications for SQL Server (Sybase or Microsoft) for some time, you might remember that the low-level language used by SQL Server is Tabular Data Stream (TDS), not DB-Library or ODBC API. Because there has never been (and never will be) a TDS SDK, we've always had to use DB-Library or one of the ODBC or OLE DB providers to translate to and from TDS when connecting to and communicating with SQL Server. This has now changed; ADO.NET ships with a new "SqlClient" .NET Data Provider (System.Data.SqlClient). As I mentioned before, this .NET Data Provider exposes objects similar (but not identical) to the OleDb and Odbc .NET Data Providers. However, Sybase SQL Server developers should not get too excited. The SqlClient .NET Data Provider *only* works against Microsoft-based TDS and then only with versions 7.0 and later. The Sybase and Microsoft versions of TDS diverged not long after the two companies parted ways years ago. Sybase developers will have to locate an OleDb or Odbc .NET Data Provider to access their data sources.

The SqlClient .NET Data Provider promises to be far (far) faster than the OleDb or Odbc .NET Data Providers. A few reasons for this better performance could be that it does *not*:

- **Translate from a common OleDb interface to TDS.** All data I/O to and from the SQL Server is done in the server's native tongue (TDS).

- **Include functionality unsupported in Microsoft SQL Server.** Thus there is no additional overhead carried to support nonexistent features.

- **Use COM interop.** This is the first (of many) providers written to the new .NET specification. It does not depend on legacy COM-based providers or drivers as do the OleDb and Odbc .NET Data Providers.

Thus, the SqlClient .NET Data Provider can be a much better choice for those applications and components targeting Microsoft SQL Server.

In the future, I expect we'll see SQLDMO functions added to the SqlClient .NET Data Provider. This means you'll be able to start, stop, pause, and perform many administrative functions against the server without resorting to the COM interop version of SQLDMO. Cool. These features are sorely needed for those of you working with MSDE. In these situations, you need to be able to tell programmatically if the server is started, start it if it's not, and stop it when you are done. It would also be nice to be able to back up and restore a database programmatically, as well as perform periodic maintenance and bulk loads without having to resort to TSQL or external utilities.

NOTE *I expect the appearance of both "OracleClient" and "DB2Client" namespaces supporting "native" Oracle and DB2 data stores before too long. Although I haven't heard a single word from Microsoft about these, it seems to me the industry and the success of .NET will depend on them. Of course, both of these data sources are supported via existing OLE DB and ODBC providers so ADO.NET developers can access them through ADOc. However, native providers promise to be faster, expose more native functionality, and be more stable than generic OSFA providers.*

For the most part (at least as far as your code is concerned), the SqlClient .NET Data Provider is similar in structure to the OleDb .NET Data Provider, so converting a SQL Server-specific or an OleDb class from one to the other should be fairly painless. However, the namespaces have diverged so there are some differences here and there. Just remember that these two providers are likely to diverge even more over time as additional features added to one are not mirrored in the other.

Watch out for how the ConnectionString is constructed because this is a specific difference between the SqlClient and OleDb .NET Data Providers. SqlClient only knows how to connect to SQL Server, so there's no need for a `Provider=` argument (it's not permitted). Otherwise, the ConnectionString syntax follows the same conventions as the ADOc OLE DB provider syntax you're used to, as well as the OleDb syntax used in ADO.NET.

You can't use a UDL or DSN to persist your connect string with SqlClient, so you either have to use integrated security or your own caching scheme until the .NET folks come up with another strategy. I provide some examples of coding SqlClient connections a little later in this chapter. The ADOc techniques—constructing a ConnectionString and pasting it into your code, as described in the first half of this book—won't work with SqlClient.

IMHO   *The name of the TDS SqlClient .NET Data Provider includes the word "client." To me this implies that Microsoft is considering development of a "server" provider. This might support the now-missing server-side state management, as well as pessimistic cursors and other features not supported by the client-only approach now implemented. Of course, I also might be hallucinating again. Actually, I expect this dream to become reality sometime in 2002.*

Examining the Connection Object Properties

There are a few new Connection object properties to which you will probably relate immediately, but there are also a few newcomers that need a little clarification. Table 2-2 lays out these properties for you. Note that many of them are set in the ConnectionString and can't be changed like they can in ADOc. Dem's da breaks. The ADO.NET folks are considering changing this, but they're concerned about security and want to keep these bound to the ConnectionString for now.

Table 2-2. ADO.NET Connection Object Properties

Property	OleDb	Odbc	SqlClient	Purpose
ConnectionString	✓	✓	✓	Holds connection string. If you don't know what this is by now . . .
ConnectionTimeout	✓	✓	✓	How long the provider waits until giving up its attempt to make a connection. Same caveats as the ADOc ConnectionTimeout property. Something like the time you spend in a bar trying to get connected.
Database	✓	✓	✓	The default database as specified by the ConnectionString or based on the UID account. It's read-only but you can change the default database with the ChangeDatabase method.
DataSource	✓	✓	✓	Points to the SQL Server or data source as set in the ConnectionString Server or DataSource keywords.
Driver		✓		Indicates ODBC driver selected in ConnectionString (RO).
PacketSize			✓	Determines the number of bytes used to transmit network data for this connection. Useful when tuning high-traffic components.
Provider	✓			Indicates OLE DB provider selected in ConnectionString (RO).
ServerVersion	✓	✓	✓	Reports the version of DBMS server. This way you can tune your application based on version.
State	✓	✓	✓	As with ADOc, indicates Open, Closed, Connecting, Executing, or Fetching state. No, this does not indicate if the server is running in Ohio or not.
WorkstationID			✓	Corresponds to the Workstation ID ConnectionString keyword (RO).

Examining Connection Object Methods

The Connection object also supports a few new methods that you haven't seen in ADOc. Table 2-3 lists and briefly explains these methods.

Table 2-3. Connection Object Methods

Method	OleDb	Odbc	SqlClient	Purpose
BeginTransaction	✓	✓	✓	Returns a Transaction (OleDbTransaction, SqlTransaction, OdbcTransaction) object used to manage transactions on the connection and begins a transaction on the connection. See "Managing Transactions" later in this chapter.
ChangeDatabase	✓	✓	✓	Changes the current default database.
Close	✓	✓	✓	Closes the database. Duhh.
CreateCommand	✓	✓	✓	Creates a Command object to be used against the Connection object.
Dispose	✓	✓	✓	Releases resources used by the Connection object. See "Closing Connections" later in this chapter.
Open	✓		✓	Opens the Connection object based on the ConnectionString property. If you open it, close it!

No, most of these methods don't take arguments, with the exception of the BeginTransaction and ChangeDatabase methods. It's a whole new world out there folks.

TIP *One of the unresolved issues with .NET is how (and when) it performs object cleanup—called "garbage collection." .NET does not immediately discard objects that have fallen out of scope, it simply marks them for eventual deletion. Apparently, .NET might not get around to freeing these resources for some time—perhaps several minutes or longer. Just be aware of this issue when declaring variables— and tearing them down.*

Sinking Connection Object Events

There are two events fired on the Connection object. The first, InfoMessage event, works pretty much as it does in ADOc. The new event here is ChangeState. It fires when the connection is opened or when you close the connection, the connection pooling routine closes it, when you execute a query, or when the Connection State property is Fetching—in other words whenever the Connection State property changes. Table 2-4 lists and explains these events.

Table 2-4. Connection Object Events

Event	OleDb	Odbc	SqlClient	Purpose
InfoMessage	✓	✓	✓	Returns an error collection containing any warnings returned from the server.
ChangeState	✓	✓	✓	Fires when the database State property changes.

Here's an example[7] to demonstrate the triggering of these events and to see the values returned from them when making a normal connection. Start by creating a new C# Windows Application Project and drag and drop[8] a SqlConnection object from the toolbox **Data** tab onto the default project form; rename the Connection object cn. (The reason that I'm using drag-and-drop in this example is that this is the only way I have found to automatically create the event stubs and subscriptions in the IDE.)

You can then review the event properties of the Connection object: just double-click on each of the event names (see Figure 2-1) and the IDE will drop you directly into an event stub that it creates. Behind your back, the IDE will also initialize any of the Connection object properties that you place in the Forms Designer and set up the event handler subscriptions placing code into the InitializeComponent() method. However, this is the very reason NOT to use drag-and-drop for ADO.NET data objects because the initialization of the objects is not performed with a try/catch code block that the enables you to handle exceptions. Take a look at the InitilizeComponent() method. If you are like me, you'll probably leverage the code created—moving to your own methods where you can adequately manage exceptions from the #region code block that is marked with the "do not modify" caveat:

---

7. See the "\Examples\Chapter02\Connecting\ConnectionString Test" folder on the CD.
8. Read on; I explain in just a moment why not to use drag-and-drop.

```
#region Windows Form Designer generated code
/// <summary>
/// Required method for Designer support - do not modify
/// the contents of this method with the code editor.
/// </summary>
```

Figure 2-1. Connection property events

> **WARNING**   *Don't go thinking that you can modify the* InitializeComponent() *method and place* try/catch *exception handling into it—you will confuse the Forms Designer.*

This is what the Forms Designer placed into the InitializeComponent() method:

```
private void InitializeComponent()
{
    this.cn = new System.Data.SqlClient.SqlConnection();
    //
    // cn
    //
    this.cn.InfoMessage += new
        System.Data.SqlClient.SqlInfoMessageEventHandler(this.cn_InfoMessage);
    this.cn.StateChange += new
        System.Data.StateChangeEventHandler(this.cn_StateChange);
```

So now let's take a look at the rest of the sample code to demonstrate sinking Connection object events.

```
private void Form1_Load(object sender, System.EventArgs e)
{
    try
    {
        cn.ConnectionString = "data source=.;database=pubs;uid=admin;pwd=pw;";9
        cn.Open();
        cn.ChangeDatabase("Biblio");
        cn.Close();
    }
    catch (Exception ex)
    {
        Debug.WriteLine(ex.Message);
    }
}
private void cn_InfoMessage(object sender, SqlInfoMessageEventArgs e)
{
    Console.WriteLine(e.ToString());
}
private void cn_StateChange(object sender, StateChangeEventArgs e)
{
    Debug.WriteLine("Original State: " + e.OriginalState +"\rCurrent State: " +
        e.CurrentState.ToString());
}
```

When the preceding code executed, the following event handlers returned:

```
Original State: Closed
Current State: Open
Changed database context to 'biblio'.
Original State: Open
Current State: ClosedClosedOpen
```

Without the ToString coercion, these states return an InfoMessage event that triggers when ADO.NET informs you of RAISEERROR messages passed from the server.

---

9. Yes, I could have set the Connection property in Windows Form Designer Property
    dialog. If I had done that the Forms Designer would have put even more code inside
    InitializeComponent(). Don't do it in the Forms Designer because you can't encapsulate it
    in a try/catch block if you do.

Managing Transactions

If you want to manage transactions from your ADO.NET application, you're in for a bit of work. Unlike every data access interface since DAO, ADO.NET has chosen to reinvent the way programs manage transactions. Basically, you have to use the BeginTransaction method of the Connection object to create a Transaction object. Yes, you can create several of these if you have a note from your mom and she agrees that you know what you're doing.

The process of creating the Transaction object specifies one or both the IsolationLevel and the transaction name. Frankly, any option that can be set to "Chaos" sounds pretty scary.[10] After you've created a Transaction object, you can use its methods to Commit, Rollback, or Save the transaction.

Because I don't really endorse client-managed transactions, if you choose this path I'm going to leave you to your own devices. There are plenty of working examples in the MSDN Help topics. Good luck—you'll need it. Just don't come crying to me when you see little ripples in the puddles of melted lead around the base of your server.

Connecting with the Odbc .NET Data Provider

IPHO *Odbc .NET Data Provider is better late than never and is the most important Data Provider after the vendor-specific Data Providers (that have been platform optimized—like the Microsoft SqlClient Data Provider) that we will no doubt see. Many folks will wonder why get excited about Odbc .NET? I mean, after all, OleDb provides pretty much ubiquitous data access these days doesn't it? Well, yes it does, but the OleDb Data Provider is based on COM—and COM is very chatty. This talkative nature means that it takes many more round-trip exchanges before it gets down to the business of moving data or executing commands as it negotiates it way through COM, meaning it is slower—much MUCH slower in fact—than the Odbc Data Provider, which uses Platform Invoke (PI). So, there is now a very good reason to blow the dust off and freshen up your knowledge of ODBC.*

---

10. Didn't that Ph.D. in *Jurassic Park* discuss chaos theory just before the dinosaurs took over the park and tried to eat him for dinner?

Late in the development cycle, the folks at Microsoft released the first of many "add-on" .NET Data Providers. The Odbc .NET Data Provider is an add-on component to the .NET Framework SDK. It provides access to ODBC drivers in the same way that the OleDb .NET Data Provider exposes native OLE DB providers. The following existing ODBC drivers are compatible with the Odbc .NET Data Provider:

- **Microsoft SQL ODBC Driver**: For use with versions of SQL Server prior to SQL Server 7.0. For more recent versions, I recommend use of the SqlClient provider.

- **Microsoft ODBC Driver for Oracle**: For versions of Oracle that are not supported by the OleDb provider.

- **Microsoft Jet ODBC Driver**: For versions of Jet (Access) that are not supported by the OleDb provider.[11]

The Odbc .NET Data Provider also requires the installation of MDAC 2.7 (if you have it you should have ADO 2.7). If the right version of the MDAC stack is not installed on the machine where the Web release will be downloaded, you can install it from `http://www.microsoft.com/data`.

Tracing and connection pooling are handled by the ODBC Driver Manager utility, which is installed as part of MDAC 2.7.

Eventually, the Odbc .NET data provider is expected to be incorporated into the .NET Framework so you should not have to install it separately. As part of Visual Studio .NET Setup, the Gacutil.exe tool adds the Microsoft.Data.Odbc namespace to the Global Assembly Cache. Gacutil.exe is installed as part of the .NET Framework SDK.

Using the Odbc .NET Data Provider

The Microsoft.Data.Odbc namespace contains the Odbc .NET data provider. The core objects that make up a .NET data provider are identical to the objects associated with the other .NET Data Providers. Table 2-5 explains this in more detail.

---

11. IPHO: The Odbc .NET Data Provider is still useful for those versions of Jet that are compatible with OleDb because it is FASTER! Vroom! Vroom!

Table 2-5. Objects Supported by the Odbc .NET Data Provider

Object	Description
OdbcConnection	Establishes a connection to a specific data source.
OdbcCommand	Executes a command at a data source. Exposes Parameters and can enlist a Transaction from a Connection object.
OdbcDataReader	Reads a forward-only stream of data from a data source.
OdbcDataAdapter	Populates a DataSet and resolves updates with the data source.

To use the Odbc .NET Data Provider, you should set up a `using` directive for the Microsoft.Data.Odbc namespace in your DLL application, as the following code illustrates:

```
using Microsoft.Data.Odbc;
```

Managing the Odbc.Connection Object[12]

As with the ADOc and ADO.NET Connection objects, an OdbcConnection object represents a unique connection to a data source using a connection string or DSN. Yes, this means you have to manage a data source name or connection string. In the case of a client/server database system, the OdbcConnection object is equivalent to a network connection to the server. Depending on the functionality supported by the native ODBC driver, some collections, methods, or properties of an OdbcConnection object may not be available. In other words, if the ODBC driver does not support certain functionality, it won't be exposed in ADO.NET. In addition, some ADO.NET methods, properties, and events are not implemented or supported by the Odbc .NET Data Provider. I'll try to note these as I go.

When you create an instance of OdbcConnection, all of its properties are set to their initial values. For a list of these values, see the `OdbcConnection()` constructor (the method that builds or initializes the OdbcConnection object) in online Help.

The OdbcConnection object manages its own native resources, such as ODBC environment and connection handles. As with the other .NET Data Providers, you should *always* explicitly close any open OdbcConnection objects by calling `Close()` or `Dispose()` before the OdbcConnection object goes out of scope. Not doing so passes the job of freeing these native resources to garbage collection,

---

12. Sample code is located in the "\Examples\Chapter 02\ODBCTest " folder on the CD.

which may not free them immediately, if at all. Unreleased Connection object resources may eventually cause the underlying driver to run out of resources or reach a maximum limit, resulting in sporadic failures. For example, you might encounter Maximum Connections-related errors while a number of Connection objects and the database connections they are holding are waiting to be deleted and released by the garbage collector. Explicitly closing the Connection objects by calling Close or Dispose allows a more efficient use of native resources, enhancing scalability and improving overall application performance.

TIP   *If one of the Execute methods of the OdbcCommand class results in a fatal OdbcException (for example, a SQL Server severity level of 20 or greater), the OdbcConnection may close. However, you might be able to reopen the Connection object and continue.*

An application that creates an instance of the OdbcConnection object can require all direct and indirect callers to have adequate permission to the code by setting declarative or imperative security demands. OdbcConnection creates security demands by using the OdbcPermission object. Users can verify that their code has adequate permissions by using the OdbcPermissionAttribute object. Users and administrators can also use the Code Access Security Policy Tool (Caspol.exe) to modify security policy at the machine, user, and enterprise levels. For more information, see "Securing Your Application" in online Help.

NOTE   *To deploy high-performance applications, you often need to use connection pooling. However, when you use the Odbc .NET data provider you don't need to enable connection pooling because the ODBC Driver Manager manages this automatically. For more information about enabling and disabling connection pooling, see the Microsoft Open Database Connectivity (ODBC) documentation.*

The following example creates an OdbcConnection, OdbcCommand, OdbcDataAdapter, and an OdbcDataSet. The OdbcConnection is opened and set as the Connection property for the OdbcCommand. The Fill() method is used to create the DataSet. The code subsequently closes the OdbcConnection object.

First, I declare an OdbcConnection instance object variable; I do this because I want to close the OdbcConnection object in a `finally{}` block. This is really important because if you don't close the Connection object, the connection pool fills up and you run out of connections. I close in a `finally{}` block to ensure that I will have always forced the connection closed no matter which exceptions occur.

```
private OdbcConnection cn;
```

```
private void button1_Click(object sender, System.EventArgs e)
{
    try
    {
```

I am using a DSN-less ConnectionString; this means that I must specify the DRIVER and then the parameters required by the driver. In this case, I'm using the SQL Server Driver, so I must supply SERVER, UID (the User Account), and PWD (the User Password). I don't need to specify the database as the default database because the admin user on my server is set to be the biblio database—but it's still a good idea to set it. In the case that I change the admin user's default database on the server, this code will still work. I say a little more on the ConnectionString property in a moment. I open the Connection object following its instantiation.

```
cn = new OdbcConnection(
        "DRIVER={SQL Server};SERVER=.;uid=admin;pwd=pw;database=biblio");
cn.Open();
```

Assuming that I have not tripped an exception (like the server being down or password being changed), I can press on and create a `SelectCommand` for use in a DataAdapter—everything is just the same as you've seen before.

```
OdbcCommand sc = new OdbcCommand(
        "SELECT title, price FROM titles WHERE title LIKE 'Hi%'", cn);

// SelectCommand property
OdbcDataAdapter da =new OdbcDataAdapter(sc);

// Create a DataSet called "TitlesDS"
DataSet ds =new DataSet("TitlesDS");
```

```
                // Populate the DataSet from the DataAdaptor
                da.Fill(ds);

                // Populate a dataGrid from the default DataTable in the DataSet
                dataGrid1.DataSource = ds.Tables[0];


        }
        catch (Exception ex)
        {
                Console.WriteLine(ex.ToString());
        }
        finally
        {
                cn.Close();
        }
}
```

ODBC Connection Strings

I'll take just a moment to give some examples here of valid connection strings
(to jog your memory back to the good ole days of ODBC). Those of you coming
from a Visual Basic background be aware that if the driver you are specifying
includes a file path, then you need to escape any backslash characters.

```
"DRIVER={Microsoft ODBC for Oracle};SERVER=ORACLE8i7;UID=admin;PWD=pw"
"DRIVER={SQL Server};SERVER=.;UID=admin;PWD=pw;DATABASE=biblio"
"DRIVER={Microsoft Access Driver (*.mdb)};DBQ=c:\\NorthWind.mdb"
"DRIVER={Microsoft Excel Driver (*.xls)};DBQ=c:\\Mybook1.xls"
"DRIVER={Microsoft Text Driver (*.txt; *.csv)};DBQ=c:\\bin"
"DSN=dsnname"
```

If you are using another vendor's ODBC driver, you might need to include
other attributes in the ConnectionString as well.

WARNING   *The Odbc .NET Data Provider does not support the
Persist Security Info Parameter, which means that the whole
connection string you use—including any User Accounts (UID)
and Passwords (PWD) embedded in a ConnectionString—can
be read back. This might be a security problem for you, in
which case I suggest you use the DSN approach.*

Opening ADO.NET Connections in Code

Okay, let's look at some code to establish a connection. One of the special aspects of the OleDb and SqlClient namespaces is that they can both use the same connection string arguments—except for the `Provider=` string when using SqlClient. The Odbc namespace needs its own style of connection strings. Those of you who have been connecting to your mainstream or obscure (as in the ODBC driver for the database used on the B1 bomber) already know how to build your ConnectionString. For the most part, expect it will continue to work with the Odbc .NET Data Provider. I illustrate use of the OleDb and SqlClient .NET Data Providers later.

 NOTE *The notation used to address a named SQL Server 2000 instance (SS2K) is new for some of you. For example,* `Data source=betav10\ss2K` *references the "ss2k" instance of SQL Server running on the server "betav10". This particular server runs both SQL Server 7.0 and SQL Server 2000 at the same time. If you are running multiple instances, you must change this string to reference your own server instance.*

The following example constructs a separate connection string and uses it with both the SqlClient and OleDb .NET Data Providers to open a Connection object.

```
SqlConnection cnSqlClient;
OleDbConnection cnOleDb;
string strConnect = "data source=.;database=biblio;uid=admin;pwd=pw";

    private void Form1_Load(object sender, System.EventArgs e){
        try{
            cnSqlClient = new SqlConnection(strConnect);
            cnOleDb= new OleDbConnection("Provider=SQLOleDB;" + strConnect);
            cnSqlClient.Open();
            cnOleDb.Open();
            TextBox1.Text = cnSqlClient.ConnectionString;
            TextBox2.Text = cnOleDb.ConnectionString;
    ...
            cnSqlClient.Close();
            cnOleDb.Close();
        }
        catch (Exception ex){
            Console.WriteLine(ex.ToString());
        }
    }
```

Okay, this code seems simple enough, but consider that it's not necessary. When I get to Chapter 3, "ADO.NET Command Strategies," you'll see that the Connection object's Open and Close methods are used infrequently, if at all. Virtually all of the examples in subsequent chapters depend on ADO.NET to open the Connection object automatically and close it immediately after it's no longer needed. Because ADO.NET uses connection pooling by default, the performance impact of this approach is minimal for the component but yields more availability for other components attempting to get connected. The DataSet Fill and Update methods both provide this "auto-connect" feature. I think their use constitutes one of ADO.NET's best practices.

Using the IDE to Get Connected

As I discussed earlier, I'm not a great fan of drag-and-drop (D&D)[13] connections. Every time I see a new implementation of this approach I shudder and remember the UserConnection designer, the DataEnvironment designer, and all of their predecessors. I remember what countless developers tell me about the wasted time trying to get D&D applications to work. In each case, the numerous issues involved with these "features" often made them more trouble than they were worth. I suspect that Microsoft keeps including these tools to make entry-level programming easier. I also suspect that Microsoft has a lot of ground to make up before most experienced developers will trust them for production applications.

The .NET IDE offers another set of these D&D tools. Swell. It's clear that they use code leveraged from Visual InterDev 6.0 and Visual Basic 6.0. .NET exposes the same MDAC connection dialog to capture the connection parameters—despite the issues raised over the last few years. Okay, the issues notwithstanding, let's take a look at the differences.

TIP *The .NET Help documentation includes several walk-through examples that illustrate how to construct queries, parameter queries, and more. I heartily suggest you step through these before venturing further. I don't repeat what those examples illustrate.*

Adding Connections

To add a connection to your project, you first need to add a connection to the IDE Server Explorer if you haven't already. The Server Explorer is a new offshoot of the Visual Studio 6.0 DataView window. Open the Server Explorer window by

---

13. With apologies to *Dungeons and Dragons.*™

pressing CTRL+ALT+5 or by clicking the **View | Server Explorer** menu. You should see a window something like Figure 2-2.

Figure 2-2. The .NET Server Explorer window

I've already created several data connections to my test databases (biblio and pubs). Also, the connection to the BETAV10\SS2K.biblio.admin database is open while the BETAV3.pubs.dbo connection is not open. Apparently, the .NET IDE uses connections a little less extravagantly than the Visual Basic 6.0 and Visual Studio InterDev 6.0 IDE. Frankly, I wish I had the time to devote an entire chapter to the Server Explorer. It's really matured and exposes a number of cool new features. Remember that Visual Studio is *not* a V1.0 product; this is its second or third major revision.

The process used to create .NET data connections is virtually identical to the procedure for working with the Visual Studio InterDev 6.0 and Visual Basic 6.0 IDE Data View window—just start by right-clicking the **Data Connections** icon and fill in the dialogs. Make sure to create a Data Connection to connect to your working database because many of the subsequent wizards depend on a functional connection. The Server Explorer window is "dockable" and "pinable" so you can easily manage it in the new .NET IDE. You can also create a Data Connection by using the **Tools | Connect To Database** menu.

Yes, you can "leverage" the connection string from the Server Explorer window if you have trouble writing a working connection string. This is a best practice technique to reduce errors made when creating new ConnectionStrings. Follow these steps to extract a known-working ConnectionString from the Server Explorer:

1. Simply use the Server Explorer to construct a working data connection to your data source. Right-click on **Data Connections**, then choose **Add Connection**.

2. Fill in the usual OLE DB dialogs to capture the server name, default DB, UserID, and password.

3. Select the new data source and press F4 to expose the property page.

4. Select the ConnectionString property and right-click.

5. Click **Select All** and **Copy**. The clipboard now contains the "post-open" connection string that will be able to open your data source at run time.

6. Simply paste this value into your code and you're in business.

Closing Connections

It's more important than ever to close the connections you open or get ADO.NET to close them for you—but make sure the job gets done. *Connections do not get closed* after the Connection object falls out of scope—at least according to the documentation. Even if they do, this behavior is not guaranteed to work. It's always essential to explicitly call {Sql, OleDb, Odbc}Connection.Close() or .Dispose() when you are done with your connection. If you're using a DataReader (see Chapter 4) you can ask ADO.NET to close the Connection object for you, but this is not done until you close the DataReader in code—it's not done automatically as some other sources have said.

As I have discussed before, the implication of not doing this could be disastrous. If you're using connection pooling, your pool might grow to exhaust the space and resources allocated for connections. This occurs when the CLR garbage collector doesn't kick in fast enough to clean up the connections properly. In extreme cases, you might even run out of sessions to your target database. It's always better to close connections explicitly.

Managing the ADO.NET Garbage Collector

As I've said before in many other ways, the .NET Framework uses new technology to address everything from painting forms to allocating memory. Memory management is now implemented in the CLR and so is the garbage collector routine that the CLR uses to release unused or unreferenced resources. However, the .NET garbage collector (GC) works very differently from the equivalent in the Visual Basic 6.0 run time; of course in Visual C++ 6.0 it was even easier to leak memory. Depending on how much free memory is available, and the load on the system, the GC might not get around to freeing up memory for a long (very long) time.

The SDK says:

The only potential disadvantage of traced garbage collection is the interval between the release of the last reference that can be reached by running code, and the moment when the garbage collector detects this condition. On a lightly loaded system with a great deal of memory, considerable time may elapse before your component's destructor is called.

By "considerable" they really mean seconds to minutes to days or longer. I also know that if an object was referenced many times in its lifetime (as a Connection object might be), it is marked by the memory manager as an object that is not freed in the initial pass of the GC, thus it might not be released for an even longer period of time. That's one (among several) really good reason to be diligent about closing your database connections, your DataReaders, and other objects as soon as you can and without fail.

The use of manual methods—Finalize, Dispose, and Close—to destroy unused (and released) objects can be another safeguard for ensuring that your objects are released more expeditiously. The GC calls the Finalize method when it's cleaning up memory. You might choose to add your own custom method that overrides the Finalize method to your class to deal with issues that the GC might not handle. The downside to this approach is loss of security (if not done correctly) and loss of performance because the GC will have to sweep twice instead of just once. Because of these effects, use the Overriding Finalize method with caution.

The Dispose method is an Overriding or Protected method that your code can invoke or that the GC calls during the destructor process. You need to use this method when you call unmanaged resources from your class—such as system objects, database connections, or other finite stores. This approach enables a user to immediately discard resources if you feel that the GC won't do the job soon enough for your taste. You use the IDisposable interface to implement the Dispose method so that it assumes the special Dispose method properties within the class. The Dispose method incurs no discernible performance costs.

There are lots of examples of the use of these .NET language features on the Web and in recent magazine articles. I defer to those sources for more specific information.

Connection Information and Security

Because opening a connection involves getting access to an important resource—your company's data—there are often security issues in configuring and working with a connection. If your information has already been broadcast all over the Web by hackers, don't bother with security—your data is already compromised. However, if you haven't had your MasterCard numbers show up on the billboards on Times Square, you're probably going to want to take as many steps as possible to secure what data you have left.

As you've probably guessed by now, the technique you choose to secure the application and its access to your data depends on the architecture of your system. For example, in a Web-based application (which is where ADO.NET is targeted), users typically get anonymous access to IIS and therefore do not provide security credentials. In such a case, your application maintains its own logon information and uses it (rather than any specific user information) to open the connection and access the database. This means that the component (ASP page) that makes the connection logs on with its own UserID and password— a UserID that has permission to do *nothing* but execute a specific subset of your stored procedures or access *nothing* except a few chosen tables. The UserID and password can either be directly compiled into the application as properties you set at design time, or they can be specified as dynamic properties you set in the ASP.NET Web application's configuration file. Other alternatives to hard coding these sensitive security strings include using a UDL file (but this is only supported by the OleDb provider), using a custom file in the Windows Registry, or using construction strings in the COM+ catalog (for serviced components only).

The ASP.NET Web application binary files and configuration file are secured from Web access by the inherent ASP.NET security model, which prevents access to these files using any Internet protocol (HTTP, FTP, etc.). To prevent access to the Web server computer itself via other methods—for example, from within your internal network—use the Windows security features. You might also want to consider security measures to prevent access by your own team. There's often no need for all of your developers to have access to the keys for the data vault.

In intranet or two-tier applications, you can take advantage of the integrated security option provided by Windows, IIS, and SQL Server, or anywhere that the component is running on the same server as the data source. In this model, a user's authentication credentials for the local network are also used to access database resources, and no explicit UserIDs or passwords are used in the connection string. (Typically, permissions are established on the database server computer via groups, so that you do not need to establish individual permissions for every user who might access the database.) In this model, you do not need to store logon information for the connection at all, and there are no extra steps required to protect connection string information. Again, the various providers deal with integrated security differently. I've found, however, that if you don't specify any logon name in an Odbc connection string and you have a SQL Server account set up for the Windows user (or the group to which they belong), you'll be granted access to the database resources permitted by the database SA. This means the Windows Administrator role becomes a vital link in database security. If he or she adds a user to a role already granted access to sensitive data, that user also gains access to that data.

If you want to use one of the older (read more-understood, experienced) technologies to persist your connection string—such as a registered ODBC DSN or an OLE DB UDL file—these are still supported (but only in specific providers). For example, the OleDb provider supports the `File name=My.UDL` connect string, but SqlClient and Odbc do not. The Odbc provider supports familiar DSN-less connection connect strings and the `DSN=MyDSN` syntax as well—but the others do not.

It's clear that the .NET architects were concerned about Web and data source security when constructing the new framework. They removed (at least for a time) the UserID and Password properties from the ConnectionString property and made it RO to prevent some (imagined?) threat. Of course, if you capture a UserID and don't filter for additional arguments, you could open your database to a number of pretty ugly issues—especially because the ConnectionString property now accepts so many more arguments.

ADO.NET Connection Pooling

Connection pooling is an integral part of the ADO.NET .NET Data Providers—it's on by default. If you don't turn it off—and you can via the ConnectionString property—before your database connection can be reused, you must close or call `Dispose()` on the Connection object. In C#, the new "using" clause automatically calls `Dispose()` when the block using the Connection object is exited; in other languages, or when not placing the Connection object reference in a `using` statement, you should explicitly call `Close()`.

SqlClient Connection Pooling

The SqlClient .NET Data Provider depends on the operating system to provide connection pooling through Windows 2000 Component Services. It's on by default so turn it off if the need arises (it shouldn't). You can manage how Win2K manages the connection pool for the SqlClient .NET Data Provider by including keywords in the ConnectionString property. For example, to disable connection pooling for this connection, use `Pooling=False` in the ConnectionString. These keywords are shown in Table 2-6 in the "SqlClient ConnectionString Keywords" section later in this chapter.

You might already know that there are really several connection pools—one for each unique "post-open" ConnectionString and transaction context. The provider generates a post-open ConnectionString based on the arguments you include in the ConnectionString property plus the default settings. If the requested connection's ConnectionString property does not match one of the pooled connection strings, a new pool is started. This means that if you change the ConnectionString property for any reason—such as changing the UserID, transaction scope, or default database—a new pool must be started.

When your application or ADO.NET closes a connection, the associated pooled connection is made dormant, but the connected link to the database is left open. With SQL Server 2000, if you don't override the Connection Reset argument in the ConnectionString property, the server is notified that the connection has been released by the application and that it should clear any connection-owned objects (such as temp tables, server-side cursors, or SET state values).

When your application opens a connection and a matching pooled connection is dormant, the connection is reenabled and its handle is passed back to the application. If there is no matching dormant connection, a new connection is established to the server; the ConnectionString is added to the pool and its handle is returned to the application.

This process is repeated for each new connection requested until the pool is filled. No, you can't tell when the pool is full by looking under the server to see if the connections are pouring out on the floor—although some have tried. After the pool is full—Max Pool Size is met—applications are blocked and the request is queued until ConnectionTimeout (property) or Connect Timeout (ConnectionString argument) seconds have passed. You can also set the Min Pool Size in order to set a lower limit on the number of connections in the pool.

TIP   *If, for some reason, the password for your connection's UserID is changed or if the UserID itself is dropped, the connection will remain viable as long as it's in the pool.*

Once created, connection pools are not destroyed until the active process ends. Maintenance of inactive or empty pools involves minimal system overhead.

Cleaning the Connection Pool

After a dormant connection's lifetime has expired (you can set this period of time), the connection pool closes the connection and removes the entry from the pool. If for some reason the server closes the connection at its end, the connection pool discards the connection from the pool. No, the connection pool mechanism does not poll the server to see if the connection is still viable, it can only tell if a connection is broken if an operation requested by your application fails to complete because the connection was dropped by the server.

It is possible for an apparently valid connection to be drawn from the pool although the associated server has disappeared from the net or was stolen in the night. When this occurs, an exception is generated but the police are not called automatically—that's up to you. However, the user must still close the connection to release it back into the pool. The user is not responsible for calling the authorities either.

Transaction Support

Connections are drawn from the pool and assigned based on transaction context. The context of the requesting thread and the assigned connection must match. Therefore, each connection pool is actually subdivided into connections with no transaction context associated with them. Each pool is also separated into *n* subdivisions, each containing connections with a particular transaction context. This means you can close the connection without generating an error, even though a distributed transaction is still pending. This allows you to commit or abort the distributed transaction at a later time.

SqlClient ConnectionString Keywords

The SqlClient SqlConnection object knows how to manage the connection pool using specific keywords (name/value pairs) as described in Table 2-6.

Table 2-6. ConnectionString Keywords for the SqlClient.SqlConnection Object

Name	Default	Description
Connection Lifetime	0	When a connection is returned to the pool, its creation time is compared with the current time, and the connection is destroyed if that time span (in seconds) exceeds the value specified by connection lifetime. This is useful in clustered configurations to force load balancing between a running server and a server just brought online. A value of zero (0) will cause pooled connections to never time out.
Connection Reset	'True'	Determines whether the server-side database connection is reset when being removed from the pool. Setting to False avoids making an additional server round trip when closing a connection, but you must be aware that the connection state—such as database context—is not being reset.
Enlist	'True'	When True, the connection pool mechanism automatically enlists the connection in the current transaction context of the creation thread if a transaction context exists.
Max Pool Size	100	The maximum number of connections allowed in the pool.

(continued)

Table 2-6. ConnectionString Keywords for the SqlClient.SqlConnection Object (continued)

Name	Default	Description
Min Pool Size	0	The minimum number of connections maintained in the pool.
Pooling	'True'	When True, the SqlConnection object is drawn from the appropriate pool, or if necessary, created and added to the appropriate pool.

Monitoring the Connection Pool Using Performance Counters

In situations where you need to keep a close eye on your SQL Server connection pool you can access a number of performance counters returned by the SqlClient provider. These performance counters make it easy to fine tune the connection pooling mechanism, help improve performance, discover failed attempts to connect, and determine why connection requests are timing out.

To access these counters, you have to use the Windows 2000 Performance Monitor and choose one or more of the counters from the .NET CLR Data performance object. See Table 2-7 for a list of these performance counters and their descriptions.

Table 2-7. Performance Counters to Monitor the Connection Pool

Counter	Description
SqlClient: Current #\ of pooled and non pooled connections	Current number of connections, pooled or not.
SqlClient: Current #\ pooled connections	Current number of connections in all pools associated with the process.
SqlClient: Current #\ connection pools	Current number of pools associated with the process.
SqlClient: Peak #\ pooled connections	The highest number of connections in all pools since the process started.
SqlClient: Total #\ failed connects	The total number of connection open attempts that have failed for any reason.

OleDb and Odbc Connection Pooling

The Odbc .NET Data Provider depends on the same techniques used to manage ODBC connection pools. In both cases, the connection pool is on by default. Be aware that the OleDb and Odbc .NET Data Providers don't provide the same degree of control over connections pool as SqlClient provider.

Debugging the Connection Pool

If your pool starts to fill up faster than your user load or if the pool overflows, there's obviously something wrong. In a high-traffic system, your connections should not stay open very long—milliseconds to seconds. If you believe that your application is closing connections properly and the pool is still filling up, try turning off connection pooling and use the Windows performance monitor to watch the server's connection load. If the number continues to build beyond the number of active operations, some component is not releasing the connection objects properly or not closing connections. Increasing the Max Pool size won't help if you exhaust the number of licensed or allocated connections on the server. Perhaps new connections are being created because they are in different uncommitted transactions or you're somehow changing the ConnectionString property for each operation.

COM-based ADO as a .NET Data Provider

While your existing ADOc logic has to be recoded (and sometimes rearchitected) to run in .NET, the basic functionality should work (about) the same. With some notable exceptions, you should be able to use the same flow, similar (not the same) error handlers, and most of the same methods, properties, and events as you did in Visual Basic 6.0—at least that's the goal for the Microsoft .NET development team. Here are a few issues to consider:

- **You have to instantiate your objects differently.** I show you how to do this in the next section.

- **Some of the methods work differently.** For example, you can't use the GetRows method to return a Variant array.

- **Your ADODB enumerations and constants must now be fully qualified**.

- **The controls to which you bind to don't expose the same properties and they don't interact or bind as they did in Visual Basic 6.0.** For example, the MSHFlexGrid control no longer exposes a property that accepts an Open Recordset.

You also might notice a drop in performance. Remember that ADOc, like all legacy COM components, is wrapped in an additional COM interop code layer so it can interoperate in the .NET Framework. This means that every reference to your ADOc objects, their properties, and methods must travel through a code layer that converts from .NET to COM and back. But, then again, so does the .NET OleDb .NET Data Provider System.Data.OleDb. At this point, only the System.Data.SqlClient .NET Data Provider uses a direct "native" protocol (TDS in this case) to access Microsoft SQL Server.

TIP *One approach you might take is to reduce these interop round trips by building ADOc classes that perform all or most of the ADOc code in encapsulated code modules. This way you make one interop COM call that performs the ADOc work and returns to your .NET code with the result (hopefully in a form the .NET application can understand). Converting class property reference to method calls can also help performance by reducing the COM interop calls.*

Instantiating Your ADOc Namespace

If you want to use ADOc in your .NET application, you have to use the **Project | Add Reference** menu or the Project Explorer window and select **adodb** under the .NET tab. This is a .NET wrapper around ADOc. Once referenced, your Project Explorer window will list "adodb" as a known reference and you can start instantiating ADOc objects in your project. If you look at the **Reference Properties** you will see that you can set a property called **Copy Local**. If you set Copy Local to True, then the DLL will be copied to the target system's program folder when you deploy your assembly. Then, even if the underlying DLLs change, it won't matter because your assembly will still reference this specific version of ADO since it has its own copy of this library. This is partially how the "Gates of DLL hell" have been conquered.

Okay, so you want to write code against your newly referenced ADOc DLL? Well, as with the ADO.NET .NET Data Provider namespaces, you can either declare the objects explicitly or make life a little easier with a `using` directive to shorthand the references. You can also wrap the component using Tlblmp.exe.

```
using ADODB;
```

After the ADODB library is referenced, you can code:

```
Connection cn;
```

Accessing ADOc Objects from Visual Basic .NET

The cool part about the ADOc approach in .NET is that much of it actually works just as it did in Visual Studio 6.0—well, for the most part. You'll find that the ADOc object model and its properties and methods are the same but you have to remember to use "full" object references; the .NET language does not like you to code using default properties. Without the IDE's statement completion option, we would all be looking for another language or another way to earn a living.

If you are trying to convert a Visual Basic 6.0 ADOc application for use in ADO.NET, you'll have fun converting `On Error` handlers to C#'s `try/catch` exception handling. I think I'd rather take up crocheting with barbed wire.

CHAPTER 3

ADO.NET Command Strategies

AFTER YOU GET YOUR ADO.NET Connection[1] object instantiated, you're ready to start running queries. No, your code doesn't necessarily have to explicitly open the connection to run a query, but you do need a well-written SQL SELECT statement. For the last twenty years, it's been clear that improving poorly written queries plays a bigger role in best practice designs than any other single issue. The impact of a 100,000 row query on an ADO.NET application is no less serious than in an ADOc application. This chapter shows how to get Visual Studio to construct that optimal SQL query and pass it on to ADO.NET for execution.

I start with tips and tutorials about how to manage ad hoc queries (queries you hard code as SELECT statements). In some cases, you might want to have ADO.NET provide parent/child navigation between the rows of related resultsets. To enable this functionality, you can build a number of DataTable objects and append them to the DataSet—or get ADO.NET to do it for you. This chapter provides several examples of these techniques.

This chapter also walks you through several typical ADO.NET Command strategies—at least as far as queries used for returning rows. Chapter 7, "ADO.NET Update Strategies," covers the code for handling changes to your data. I've also devoted separate chapters to the DataReader object (Chapter 4, "ADO.NET DataReader Strategies"), and to DataSet and DataTable objects (Chapter 5, "Using the DataTable and DataSet"). Chapter 6, "Filtering, Sorting, and Finding," discusses, you guessed it, filtering, sorting, and finding data after the Command has executed.

Understanding ADO.NET Commands

ADO.NET supports several ways to execute SQL SELECT and action queries to ask questions about the data and to post changes to the database. ADO.NET is similar to ADOc in this respect—both return rowsets, Return Value, and OUTPUT

---

1. When I refer to a "Connection" object, consider that in ADO.NET this can be SqlConnection, OleDbConnection, OdbcConnection, or any of the implementations of the "Connection" classes. They all share the same properties—when they're different, I'll explain why.

parameters, as well as other operational feedback from the server. How you go about constructing and executing the queries is, however, very different. Well, it's not as different as apples and bicycles, but it's different. While you're still executing queries, you won't find Recordset Open—mostly because there isn't a "Recordset" object in ADO.NET and the only Open method is on the Connection object.

Remember, the ADO.NET DataAdapter is the bridge between the Connection object and your ADO.NET resultsets. The DataAdapter includes several Command objects (not unlike ADOc Command objects) to fetch and update the data. You should grasp this aspect of ADO.NET fairly easily. The difference is that you now have four Command objects to define—one for each type of SQL operation (listed in Table 3-1). They are as follows:

Table 3-1. DataAdapter Commands

DataAdapter Command Property	Contains . . .
SelectCommand	SELECT query
UpdateCommand	UPDATE action query
InsertCommand	INSERT action query
DeleteCommand	DELETE action query

TIP *If you've ever worked with the Data Object wizard, you'll notice a striking similarity to the DataAdapter and its four Command objects.*

To get started building a query, create a SelectCommand object to manage the initial SELECT and (optionally) separate Command objects to execute the UPDATE, INSERT, and DELETE commands. Later in this section I discuss ways to get Visual Studio to create these for you, as well as how to use the CommandBuilder to construct all but the SelectCommand.

Each Command object points to a Connection object or ConnectionString—for example, SqlCommand.Connection—and can contain a collection of Parameters. You can encourage Visual Studio to set these up for you, but I'm going to defer discussion of the issues associated with this approach until later in this chapter. Setting up Commands in code is also easy—the following Command constructor helps quite a bit:

```
SqlConnection cn=
    new SqlConnection("data source=.;database=biblio;uid=admin; pwd=pw;");
SqlCommand cmdSelect = new SqlCommand("SELECT Title, Price FROM Titles", cn);
```

After you set up the `SelectCommand` you can execute it using one of the Execute methods to populate a DataReader. On the other hand, you can execute the DataAdapter Fill method to run the query. After you make changes to the data, you can use the Update method to execute the `UpdateCommand`, `InsertCommand`, and `DeleteCommand` queries. I show you how to do this in Chapter 7.

When working with ADO.NET Command objects,[2] start by writing the SELECT or row-fetch part of the query as previously shown . After this is done, you can either hard code the action queries by hand or use the ADO.NET CommandBuilder to construct the UPDATE, DELETE, and INSERT SQL commands—almost like ADOc did behind the scenes. Remember that ADO.NET is no better at figuring out these action queries than ADOc—especially if you don't help by keeping things simple. Later in this section, I suggest a number of ways to give ADO.NET a fighting chance in the construction of these action queries—if that's what you *really* want to do. I also revisit action queries again in Chapter 7.

The `SelectCommand` query returns data and the DDL associated with the columns, but remember that ADO.NET is capable of managing several result-sets at once in separate DataTable objects. Because ADO.NET is incapable of determining inter-resultset (inter-DataTable) relationships on its own, your code should provide that information as well—at least for multidimensional DataSet objects. One technique for providing the schema is to include an XSD schema description of your data. This chapter discusses how to do just that and a lot more. Chapter 10, "ADO.NET and XML," goes even deeper into ADO.NET XML functionality.

After you work with ADO.NET for awhile, you'll see that the architecture is heavily slanted toward "just-in-time" operations. While it's possible to open a Connection object, construct a Command object, run a query, and leave the Connection and Command in place for use later, most of the strategies illustrated in online Help construct objects on the fly each time they are needed—Connection and Command objects alike. This "stateless" approach is typically used in Web applications and Web Services—the intended target platform for .NET applications.

Regardless of the technique you use to execute your ADO.NET query, most performance benefits can be reaped from efficient SQL. Fortunately, the .NET IDE also includes a new version of the Da Vinci Tools (first seen in Visual Studio 5.0) to help construct SQL queries using drag-and-drop GUI windows. I discussed these tools in Chapter 12 of *ADO.NET and ADO Examples and Best Practices for VB Programmers—2nd Edition*. I also discussed the importance of queries that make sense. That is, if you expect to create a scalable application, you need to consider the impact your query has on the entire system. Generally,

---

2. Again, the term "Command" object can refer to either the SqlCommand, OleDbCommand, or the OdbcCommand objects.

these guidelines boil down to fetching just the rows and columns you need and reducing round trips to the server.

 WARNING   *Many of the .NET documentation examples still include queries that return **all** of the rows from one or more tables. One reason (excuse) for this is that the documentation authors apparently don't want to complicate these examples with complex WHERE clauses or specific column selections.* SELECT * FROM authors *queries, while easy to include in an example, do little to help an application's scalability or over-all performance. I discussed the impact of this book's suggestions before and frankly, some of them won't help in any noticeable way with single-user or five thousand-row databases. However, when your Web site or client/server application gets successful and you need to scale up, poor initial design won't get you very far.*

One of the interesting and underdocumented features that ADO.NET supports is its ability to construct DataSet objects directly from FOR XML queries executed against SQL Server 2000. The new SQLXML provider was released for better support for this feature. Very cool, but of uncertain value performance-wise due to the extra expense of constructing, parsing, and transmitting a Unicode data stream that has to be parsed and deconstructed on the other end. I discuss the more subtle aspects of XML in Chapter 10.

Introducing ADO.NET Parameter Queries

When you want to return a subset of the rows from one or more database tables (at least not all of the rows at once), you should set up and execute parameter queries to narrow the scope of the query. These parameters usually get inserted into arguments in the WHERE clause. For example:

```
SELECT Title, Price, Pub_ID FROM Publishers
WHERE Price BETWEEN @Low AND @High
```

Yes, ADO.NET supports parameter queries, but the familiar ? parameter marker is not universally supported. The SqlClient provider only supports *named* parameters, but the OleDb and Odbc providers do not—both require ? parameter markers. This means when using SqlClient, you must provide a marker such as

@StateWanted in your SQL query at the point where you want to insert a parameterized value.

The SqlClient provider also supports "sparse" parameter lists. This means that you don't have to pass any parameters defined in the stored procedure with a default value. This is not the case for the OleDb provider. Later in this chapter I walk you through setting up the parameters collection and building intelligent parameter-driven queries—see "Managing Parameter Queries." You'll even be able to use these queries to feed DataTable objects and get ADO.NET to provide parent/child navigation.

When constructing and executing parameter queries, the trick is to construct queries that return *related* child rows for the subset of parents selected by scoping parameters. Most of the documentation examples use individual SELECT * from <table> (with no WHERE clause) for the parent and child tables. There's a general consensus that applications that depend on SELECT * queries do not scale for reasons I discussed earlier. Some of the documentation examples lead you into executing two, three, or more round trips to the server to get the data— another time-consuming bottleneck. It turns out that you might be able to execute the queries in a single batch[3] or even by executing a single stored procedure that returns the related rows in multiple resultset form. ADO.NET knows how to construct a DataSet with multiple DataTable objects from these batches. However, you must make a number of changes to the DataSet and DataAdapter to fill in the missing pieces before using or binding to the newly constructed DataSet. I discuss these points in Chapter 5.

As your DBA and SA might have already informed you, there is a distinct possibility that you don't have permission to access to the base tables—in most cases you've probably only been granted permission to call stored procedures. Well, you're in luck. The Visual Studio .NET IDE knows how to construct Command objects using direct table access,[4] ad hoc SQL queries, or stored procedures. This chapter also discusses how to get Visual Studio to construct stored procedure-based queries—with or without parameters. While the stored procedures are crude (and sometimes less than useful), at least they are a step in the right direction.

NOTE *While Visual Studio supports creation of databases through the Server Explorer (a new feature), there is no mechanism in the Visual Studio IDE to manage permissions—so you're on your own. Send your SA some flowers or candy to get on his/her good side or learn to use SQL Enterprise Manager or your target database's SA tools.*

---

3. Assuming your provider supports the feature. Not all providers or servers support multiple resultsets or batched queries.
4. Direct table access queries are not supported in the SqlClient provider.

This chapter also discusses how to execute more-sophisticated queries—those that return multiple resultsets. Many stored procedures are famous for returning rows-affected values, OUTPUT parameters, the Return Value, as well as interim rowsets that have to be dealt with at the client. I point out how to manage each of these values and rowsets extruded from the DBMS's back end—see "Managing Multiple-Resultset Queries."

Executing Ad Hoc Queries Using ADO.NET

So, you want to execute a query? That's no surprise if you're reading a book on ADO. Before you go amuck writing SQL and code, I recommend you try to figure out which ADO.NET strategy makes the most sense for your application. Do you want to create and execute a query the "old-fashioned" way, as in ADOc (and all of the previous data access interfaces)? If so, submit a query that instructs the DBMS to select from a single table, or more typically, JOIN two or more tables and return a SQL product. One dramatic difference between ADOc and ADO.NET is that the latter really expects to do the relational JOIN *in memory*—at the client[5]—not on the server. While ADO.NET can manage the product of a server-side JOIN (what you've been developing up until now), it's tuned to construct stand-alone DataSet objects that include multiple DataTable objects and the criteria used to define their relationships.

On the other hand, do you want to create and execute a query using *new* ADO.NET technology? In this scenario, write individual SELECT queries against a number of tables and get ADO.NET to JOIN the resultsets and manage the parent/child relationships for you. This new approach uses many of the same techniques described earlier in this book, but the SELECT statements are far simpler and don't require the server-side DBMS engine to JOIN the tables and produce a SQL product—it just returns one or more simple rowset.

TIP *No, you don't have to use the "disconnected" strategy with ADO.NET if you don't want to. There are perfectly good scenarios that leave the database connection open while you work on the data. However, since ADO.NET defers all of its updates until you commit them as a batch, any advantage of keeping the DBMS connection open is pretty thin.*

---

5. Consider that a "client" can be another system connected via a network or simply a middle-tier component setting up and executing queries.

You can also use ADO.NET's ability to import DataSet objects directly from ADOc Recordset objects, directly from FOR XML queries executed against Microsoft SQL Server 2000, or from XML generated by another application. While ADO.NET does not implement many of the ADOc data access paradigms with which you might be familiar, it is by no means inflexible. It's just stretching out in a new direction.

All of these and several other approaches are available to you in ADO.NET. Yes, you can still use ADOc to execute your queries—but you should already know how to do that by now.

Constructing SQL for your Query

Don't worry, the new version of .NET did not change the basic Structured Query Language (SQL) query syntax—it couldn't, thank goodness. The SQL you use is still dictated by the SQL engine to which you're connecting—with a few exceptions as I highlight as I go.

As I mentioned earlier, the SqlClient .NET Data Provider does not support the ? character as a parameter marker—you must use named parameters. Named parameters can be defined in any order—at least for those providers that support this functionality.

The familiar ? parameter marker *is* still available for use in the OleDb and Odbc providers that you use with Oracle and Jet data sources, as well as the various ODBC data sources. But, remember that the ? parameter marker is positional, so all of the members of the Parameters collection *must* be defined in the order in which they appear in the stored procedure—just as in ADO 2.5.

The fact that the SQL has not changed means that most of your existing SQL training, books, articles, and experience can still be applied to create both SELECT and action[6] queries against your database. In addition, .NET exposes its Query Builder in ways that are far more intuitive than Visual Basic 6.0—and still better than Visual InterDev 6.0, which was a prototype for the new IDE.

 TIP *Keep in mind that the performance of your application depends more on how well you write your SQL queries than any other factor and ADO.NET does not* wait *any faster or slower than ADOc.*

---

6. Action queries: UPDATE, INSERT, DELETE, or other queries that affect the database.

One of the flashier features of the Visual Studio .NET IDE is the Query Builder that helps you construct SQL queries and DataAdapter objects in the process. The Query Builder is not new—you've seen it before in Visual Studio 6.0—but it's now easier to use and you no longer have to drag tables from the Data View window or set up the (ugh) Data Environment Designer.

> **NOTE** *See "Data Walkthroughs" in Visual Studio .NET online Help for several tutorials on this subject.*

Using the DataAdapter Configuration Wizard[7]

Use the DataAdapter configuration wizard (DACW) to get the .NET IDE to construct the code needed to instantiate and configure an ADO.NET DataAdapter (either an OdbcDataAdapter, OleDbDataAdapter, or SqlDataAdapter). While you don't need to construct your DataAdapter with the wizard, it can help you build a pretty verbose block of code to implement the DataAdapter. The DataAdapter contains the SelectCommand object used to return your rowset data. When I get to Chapter 7, I revisit the DACW again to discuss how to create and manage the action queries used to change a DataSet.

The DACW inserts a boatload of code into the hidden regions of your application based on the SELECT statement and other arguments you provide to the wizard at design time. While some of this generated code is fairly intuitive, some is constructed rather crudely and is hard to read—especially the constructed SQL statements. It seems that the query parser doesn't know how to detect whitespace very well. That said, this code is *not* generated with the CommandBuilder—it's done using another very similar function found in the Da Vinci tools. This means that the code generated by the IDE is different from that generated by the CommandBuilder and is, in many cases, more suitable. For one thing, the Visual Studio-generated code knows how to deal with imbedded spaces in the arguments. That is, if a database table name or column name has an imbedded space,[8] Visual Studio knows how to delimit the names (with quotes or brackets) so the SQL query can compile. The CommandBuilder does not know how to do this without setting the QuotePrefix and QuoteSuffix properties.

Let's take a walk through setting up a typical query using the DACW with a Windows Form application. First, open the **Data** tab of the Visual Studio .NET

---

7.   Sample DACW code is located in the "\Examples\Chapter 03\DACW Example" folder on the CD.

8.   This adds to the total number of reasons not to imbed spaces in your object names—the total number is now 7,546.

Toolbox. You might have to expose the **Toolbox** pane using the **View | Toolbars** menu. The Data tab is shown in Figure 3-1. Try right-clicking on the **Toolbox** and selecting **Show All Tabs** if the Data tab doesn't appear. Select one of the DataAdapter icons (either **OleDbDataAdapter** or **SqlDataAdapter**) and drag it to your form. This installs code to construct the DataAdapter in your Form, places an icon for the DataAdapter in the Form's "tray" area, and launches the DACW. Dragging a base table to your Windows Form form also generates a DataAdapter and Connection on your form. You can right-click the **DataAdapter** and choose **Configure Data Adapter . . .** to launch the DACW.

The Data tray is a new pane on the Visual Studio .NET IDE design surface used to hold any type of control that has no visible manifestation—such as

Figure 3-1. The Data tab of the Visual Studio .NET Toolbox

a Timer control, Connection, or DataAdapter as in this case. You might have to activate it in Visual Studio by right-clicking on the **Toolbox** and selecting it or by choosing **Show All Tabs**.

The DACW needs to know the answers to the following questions in order to generate the code needed to construct the DataAdapter:

- **What's the name of the connection?** If you've already created a Visual Studio connection using the process just described (Adding Connections), you can select it or any connection already known to the Visual Studio IDE by choosing from a drop-down menu. You can also click the **New Connection** button to create a new connection and add it to the Data Connections window so you won't have to repeat this process.

- **What type of query is used to fill the DataSet?** This question is posed by the following dialog (Figure 3-2):

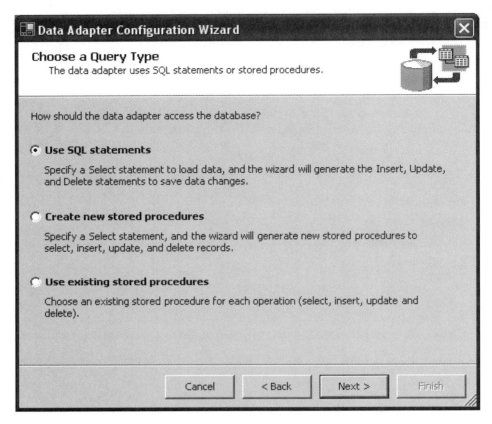

Figure 3-2. The DataAdapter configuration wizard captures query type

When choosing a query type with the DACW, the choices seem fairly intuitive; however, there are side-effects to each choice. If you expect to create an updatable DataSet, you have to use a *simple* SQL SELECT statement (with or without parameters to limit row count). The wizard will warn you if it can't create the action queries needed to make changes to your DataSet. If this happens, you have to use the Query Builder to do so, or give up updatability—at least via automatically generated SQL statements. You can always use stored procedures to do the updates if you behave yourself. As I said, I discuss the update issues in Chapter 7. Let's step through each of these query type options.

Using SQL Statements with the DACW

If you want to enter an ad hoc SELECT query or get the wizard to create one for you to return the initial rowset,[9] click **Use SQL statements** in the DACW. This launches the next dialog (shown in Figure 3-3) that solicits the SQL text for the SELECT query. You must enter this query or click **Query Builder** to launch the SQL generation tool we've used since Visual Basic version 5.0. The Query Builder is somewhat easier to use (it was pretty easy already) in that it provides a list of tables exposed by the current connection (you chose the connection when you entered the DACW). See Chapter 12 of *ADO.NET and ADO Examples and Best Practices for VB Programmers—2nd Edition* for details on how to use the new Visual Studio .NET Query Builder. Remember, fewer is faster—if you fetch fewer rows the whole system runs faster.

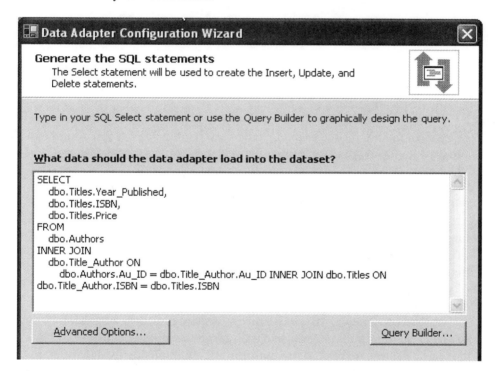

Figure 3-3. DACW generates SQL dialog

As you construct your SELECT statement, consider the strategy you expect ADO.NET to use when managing the DataSet. If the SELECT statement is too

---

9. Folks there are many situations where it's totally unnecessary to construct a rowset to get a question answered. ADO.NET supports the ability to execute a query that simply returns OUTPUT parameters or simply the Return Value from an action query or stored procedure.

complex—as when you JOIN several tables—ADO.NET won't be able to construct the action queries to make changes to the data. Don't worry about including the primary key column(s) in your query. If you don't include a PK as one of the selected columns in your SELECT statement, the wizard will add it for you. The PK is essential in identifying the specific row to UPDATE or DELETE or when creating new rows. As before, it's usually a bad idea to simply code SELECT * queries—but you already know that.

Another consideration here has to do with the construction of hierarchical resultsets. There are several approaches you can use—here are two likely candidates:

- **Construct individual DataAdapters—one for each rowset (DataTable) to be managed and provide the relational schema later.** Consider that these rowsets can be drawn from a variety of data sources and don't necessarily have to come from the same database or same connection.

- **Write the SQL query to include several resultsets (several SELECT statements) that provide stand-alone parent and child resultsets.** Again, you provide the relational schema later.

Consider that each DataAdapter created will require one or more round trips to the data source to populate its member DataTable objects. While ADO.NET might end up reusing the Connection object, each trip to and from the server is expensive. Work toward tactics that eliminate as many of these trips as possible.

If you click the **Advanced Options . . .** button on the Generate the SQL statements dialog, the DACW exposes another dialog (see Figure 3-4) that lets you change the way Visual Studio .NET constructs the action query SQL statements. No, there's no way to adjust the action queries to parallel the ADOc Update Criteria property. It's expected that a later release of ADO.NET will support the ability to alter the generated command SQL based on selected columns, just changed columns, time stamps, and other criteria.

If you uncheck the first (**Generate Insert, Update . . .**) checkbox in the Advanced SQL Generations Options dialog, the wizard does not insert the code into your application to fill in the action commands. In this case you have to do that yourself. For example, if you leave **Generate Insert, Update . . .** checked, the UpdateCommand looks like this:[10]

---

10. Actually, the code does not look like this. The routine to break the lines into 80-column segments is pretty "challenged." I cleaned it up to make it far more readable.

```
this.sqlUpdateCommand1.CommandText = @"UPDATE dbo.Authors"
 + @"SET Author = @Author, Year_Born = @Year_Born"
 + @" WHERE (Au_ID = @Original_Au_ID)"
 + @" AND "
 + @"(Author = @Original_Author OR @Original_Author IS NULL AND Author IS NULL)"
 + @" AND (Year_Born = @Original_Year_Born"
 + @" OR @Original_Year_Born IS NULL AND Year_Born IS NULL);"
 + @" SELECT Author, Year_Born, Au_ID FROM dbo.Authors WHERE (Au_ID = @Au_ID)";
```

However, if you leave it unchecked, the SqlUpdateCommand is left set to null, so you're on your own when it comes time to update. I discuss this more completely in Chapter 7.

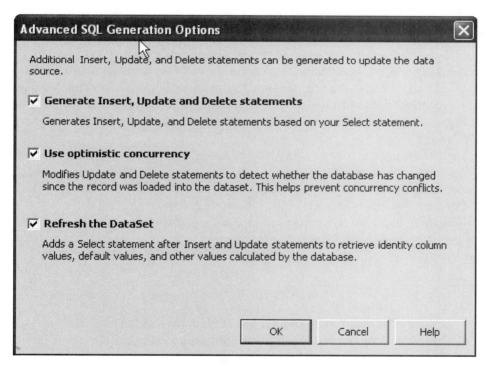

Figure 3-4. Advanced SQL Generation Options

 IMHO *The .NET developers could have spent another five minutes working on the string parsing routine to break up these long SQL statements. As it is, the parser seems to have forgotten how to break on whitespace or commas. Fortunately, there is no performance penalty when using the + operator in .NET.*

Notice that the UPDATE statement is coded to function only if the current row values match the row values as originally fetched from the database and if the primary key (the Au_ID column in this case) matches the existing Au_ID. However, if you uncheck the **Use optimistic concurrency** checkbox, the UpdateCommand is coded to force the UPDATE to complete regardless of the current state of the row. The column-by-column checks are not made, but the UPDATE WHERE clause (as shown following[11]) includes a reference to the existing row based on the primary key:

```
this.sqlUpdateCommand1.CommandText = "UPDATE dbo.Authors SET Author = @Author,
Year_Born = @Year_Born WHERE (Au_ID = @O" +
"riginal_Au_ID); SELECT Au_ID, Author, Year_Born FROM dbo.Authors WHERE (Au_ID =
" +
"@Au_ID)";
```

If you uncheck the **Refresh the DataSet** checkbox, the code generated in your application does not include the final SELECT statement that returns the current data values of the row updated. In this case, the controls bound to your DataSet might not reflect the current state of the row(s) being updated. This particular feature is not present in the action queries generated by the CommandBuilder.

All of the code generated by the wizard is added to your Form's code in the "Windows Form Designer generated code" region. As I said in the last chapter, it's not a good idea to modify any code in this section because doing so might cripple the DACW or the other IDE-driven code generators in Visual Studio .NET. In addition, if you remove the DataAdapter icon from your project or simply rerun the DACW, the code is replaced—your changes are discarded without mercy or notice.

TIP   *If you want to change the DataAdapter created by the DACW, simply right-click on the DataAdapter (**SqlDataAdapter, OdbcDataAdapter**, or **OleDbDataAdapter**) in the tray and choose **Configure Data Adapter.** The wizard will then restart using the settings you used last time and replace the previously generated code.*

---

11.   I didn't clean up this DACW-generated code. Notice the strange line breaks.

IPHO *I prefer to leverage the code that the DACW generates and move it out of* InitializeComponent() *method so that I can try/catch exceptions more cleanly.*

The action commands defined here don't run as you change rows or add new rows. These commands are executed when and only when you explicitly commit the changes to the DataSet using the DataAdapter Update method. All changes to the DataSet are managed in *memory* and persisted there until the power fails and all of the changes are lost or until you tell ADO.NET to reconnect and post the updates by using the Update method. I discuss when and how this happens in Chapter 7.

Using Stored Procedures with the DACW

Most shops will probably want to use stored procedures to fetch and update data. As with the Data Object wizards in Visual Studio 6.0 components, the DACW can capture the names of the SELECT and action query (UPDATE, DELETE, and INSERT) stored procedures—but only if they already exist.

A new .NET IDE feature takes the next step: It automatically creates the stored procedures—very cool. But this feature is only available on selected providers and against selected data sources. For example, it's available on the SqlClient provider against SQL Server, but not on the OleDb provider when connecting to an Access (Jet 4.0) database, but it does work with the OleDb provider when connecting to SQL Server. Regardless of your provider, be sure to check the code generated by the DACW to make sure it makes sense. Good code does more than just compile.

Let's walk through both of these options to get a better understanding of what's being done for you (and to your code). First, let's get the DACW to generate new stored procedures based on a SELECT statement.

Generating Stored Procedures with the DACW

Begin by starting the DACW and choosing a (compatible) data source. The DACW works with both the SqlClient and OleDb providers. Next, enter a valid SQL statement to fetch the PK and any *required* columns from a single table (let's keep it simple for now). Next, you're confronted with a dialog used to name the individual SELECT and action query stored procedures—see Figure 3-5.

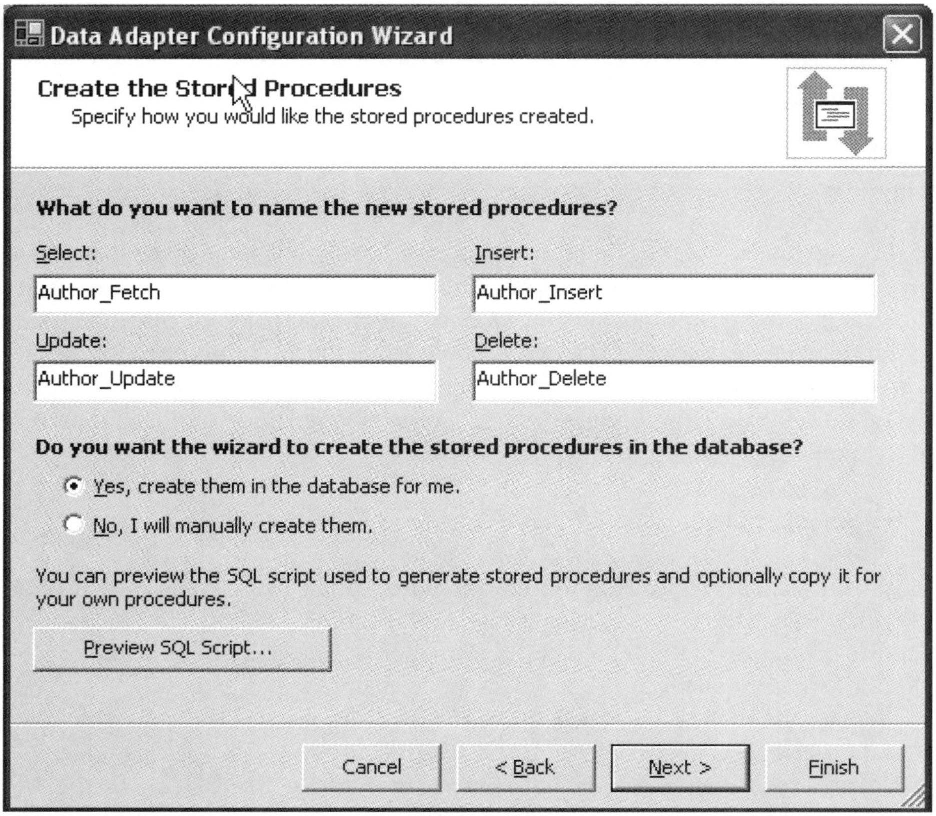

Figure 3-5. Name the stored procedures to be created

The wizard also lets you preview the script to be used in creating the stored procedures—as shown in Figure 3-6. Notice what's missing from this script? Where are the permissions settings for these stored procedures? Fortunately, you can simply save this script to a file and give it to your DBA with a box of candy— perhaps he or she will run it for you and grant you permission to use the stored procedures. If you try to create the stored procedures in the database (you don't check the **No, I will manually create them** option), you had better have permission to do so. No, that does not mean you have to raise your hand first— you'll have to get the SA or DBO to grant "create stored procedure" permissions for the account you're using to work with this database.

The SQL in the stored procedures is very similar to the SQL generated for your application when you had the DACW generate ad hoc SQL; therefore, your application should behave more or less the same regardless of the technique you choose.

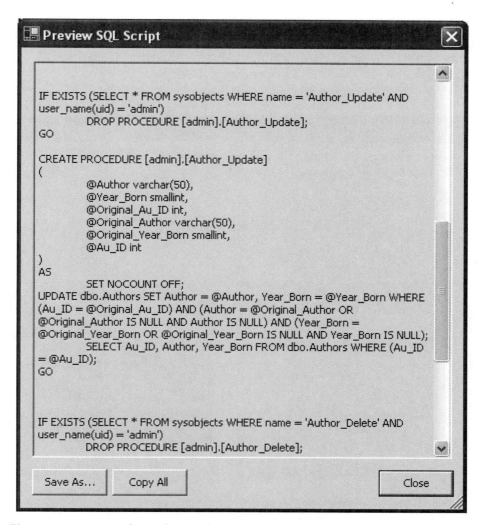

```
IF EXISTS (SELECT * FROM sysobjects WHERE name = 'Author_Update' AND
user_name(uid) = 'admin')
        DROP PROCEDURE [admin].[Author_Update];
GO

CREATE PROCEDURE [admin].[Author_Update]
(
        @Author varchar(50),
        @Year_Born smallint,
        @Original_Au_ID int,
        @Original_Author varchar(50),
        @Original_Year_Born smallint,
        @Au_ID int
)
AS
        SET NOCOUNT OFF;
UPDATE dbo.Authors SET Author = @Author, Year_Born = @Year_Born WHERE
(Au_ID = @Original_Au_ID) AND (Author = @Original_Author OR
@Original_Author IS NULL AND Author IS NULL) AND (Year_Born =
@Original_Year_Born OR @Original_Year_Born IS NULL AND Year_Born IS NULL);
        SELECT Au_ID, Author, Year_Born FROM dbo.Authors WHERE (Au_ID
= @Au_ID);
GO



IF EXISTS (SELECT * FROM sysobjects WHERE name = 'Author_Delete' AND
user_name(uid) = 'admin')
        DROP PROCEDURE [admin].[Author_Delete];
```

Figure 3-6. Preview of stored procedure command scripts

That's it. After you define the first SELECT statement, the DACW does most of the rest. You still might (should) add triggers and other referential integrity constraints, but I talk about constraints in Chapter 8, "ADO.NET Constraint Strategies."

Using Existing Stored Procedures with the DACW

The third option in the initial DACW dialog is to **Use existing stored procedures**. This process is also similar to that used in the Data Object wizard in Visual

Basic 6.0. Just select the appropriate stored procedures for each of the SELECT, INSERT, UPDATE, and DELETE operations; you get to select these procedures from simple-to-use drop-down lists. It couldn't be easier. And, the best part is that you don't have to use the Data Environment Designer. Now *that's* cool. Check out Figure 3-7.

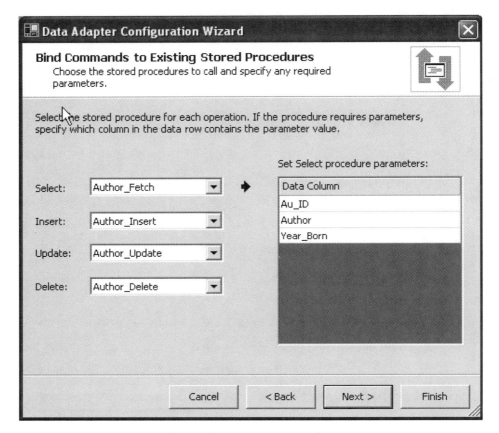

Figure 3-7. Selecting stored procedures for SELECT *and action queries*

When you choose the INSERT, UPDATE, and DELETE stored procedures, you should verify that the DACW chose the right columns to source the parameter. This is pretty intuitive, as shown in the dialog in Figure 3-8. This mapping ties a column in the DataTable resultset to the appropriate parameter generated to pass the value when the action query is executed.

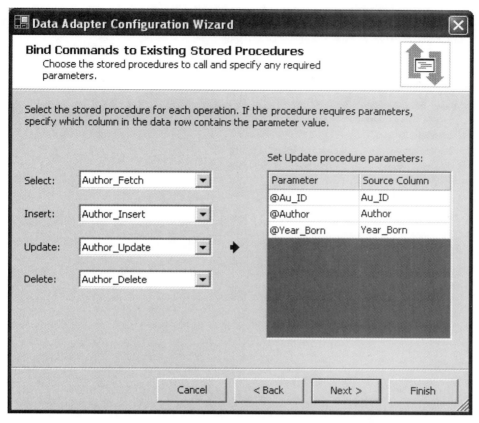

Figure 3-8. DACW Update mapping of parameter to source column

No, you don't get to name the DataAdapter or the Command objects created by the DACW. By default these are simply named after the objects. In this case (because I used the SqlClient provider), the DACW created SqlConnection1 and SqlDataAdapter1. It might be helpful to rename these before going on. If you feel the need to do this, simply right-click on the object in the IDE tool tray and choose **Properties.** You can use this property page—as seen in Figure 3-9—to change the names and other properties of the DataAdapter. I discuss the use (and importance) of the ContinueUpdateOnError property in Chapter 7. If you change the name of one or more of the objects referenced in the Property Page, the code generated by the DACW is also changed for you.

Figure 3-9. SqlDataAdapter1 Properties page

Creating a DataSet with the IDE

After the stored procedures are selected, the DACW proceeds to add code (as described earlier) to the hidden regions of your application. At this point you need to add a DataSet to your project to hold the results of the SelectCommand. This can be done in code or better yet through the .NET IDE. If you create a DataSet with the IDE, .NET creates the files and code needed to strongly type the members of your DataTable.

WARNING *No, it's not easy to remove an incorrectly constructed DataSet. You can't simply delete it from the project and expect the IDE to rip it out. Okay, I kinda expected it to—but you should not make that assumption because it does not work.*

It's not difficult to create a DataSet if you can find the right menus. If you're working with a Windows Form application, make sure the Form design pane has the focus, otherwise the Data menu is hidden and really tough to find. Look for the Data menu as shown in Figure 3-10.

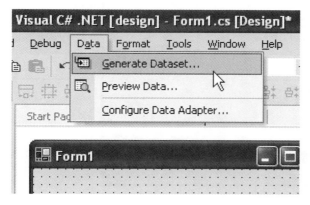

Figure 3-10. ***Data | Generate DataSet*** *menu*

After the **Generate DataSet** dialog appears, the trick is to rename the DataSet so it makes sense for your application. The default is DataSet1. On first inspection, this seems reasonable, but for some really important OO reason, the DataSet you reference in code will be DataSet11. Don't worry, this is easy to fix; simply rename the DataSet being created to some more meaningful name that does not end in "1". Figure 3-11 shows this dialog.

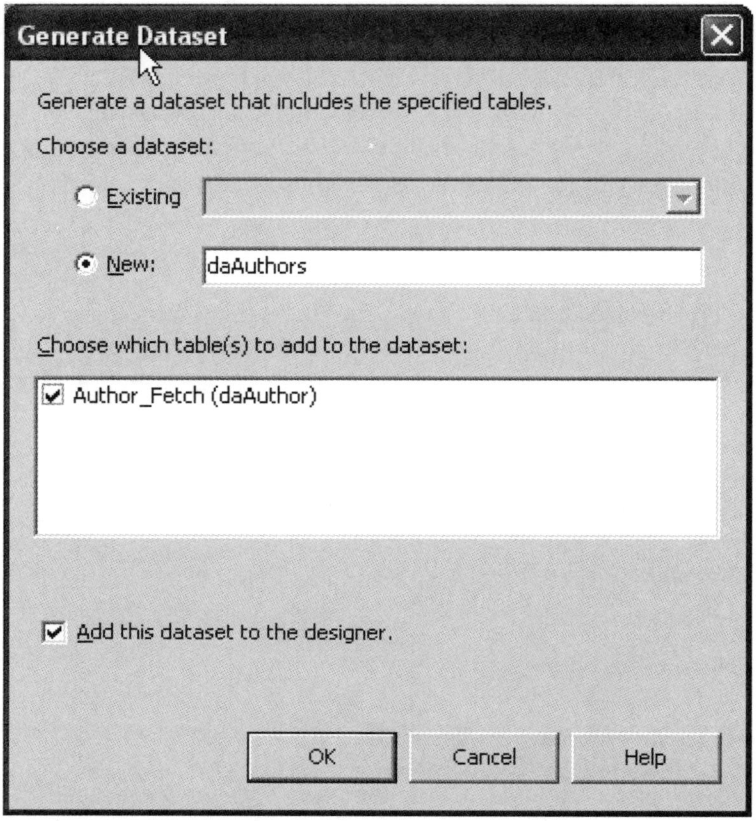

Figure 3-11. Generate DataSet dialog

Because the earlier DACW steps have only built a single DataAdapter, only the Author_Fetch (named SqlDataAdapter1 by default) is exposed. Clicking **OK** generates appropriate code in your application to instantiate the DataSet, but you still have to add code (somewhere) to fill it. The IDE also adds a new file to your solution—dsAuthors.xsd—as well as creating a new class for the DataAdapter. If you click the **Class View** (in the same tab set as the Solution Explorer), you can drill down to this automatically generated code (as shown in Figure 3-12). This code permits you to reference the objects in the DataSet as you would any other class. Although this process generates a lot of code, it does considerably improve object referencing performance. In Chapter 6 I start a discussion about strongly-typed DataSet objects.

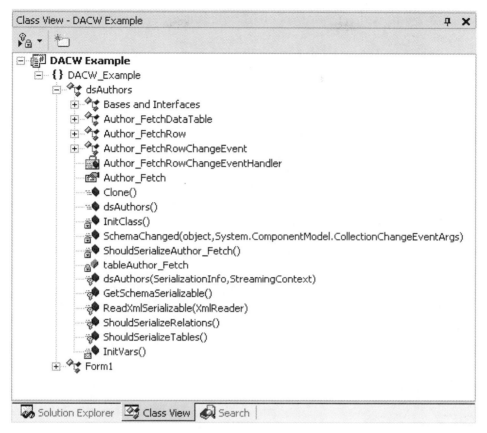

Figure 3-12. Class View of generated DataSet

Okay, the DACW is done and I'm (finally) ready to add some code to fill
the DataSet by executing the DataAdapter object's SelectCommand. Because the
SelectCommand has a parameter, I need to set it first; the following code does
just that. It also binds the constructed DataTable to a DataGrid so you can see the
initial resultset.

```
daAuthor.SelectCommand.Parameters["@Year_Born"].Value = "1947";
daAuthor.Fill(dsAuthors1);
dataGrid1.DataSource = dsAuthors1.Tables[0];
```

I discuss how to manage the DataSet and DataTable objects it contains in
Chapter 5.

Using Drag-and-Drop with the IDE

If you haven't had enough D&D up to this point, you can also generate code to build DataAdapter and Connection objects by using the IDE to drag and drop a Table or View from your Server Explorer to the Form. This approach can be used with WebForms or Windows Forms. To use a selected Server Explorer's Data Connection and its associated tables (or views) in your application, you can expand the Tables tab and drag one of these tables to your application's form. This adds both a Connection and a DataAdapter icon to your form's "tray" area. If you right-click either of these icons, the IDE takes you to the appropriate configuration wizard or simply exposes dialogs to change their properties. Any changes are reflected in source code included in the hidden regions of your form.

Dragging a data table icon to your application's tray causes .NET to add considerable code to your form (in the hidden region). I suggest you open your form's code window and expand the region "Windows Form Designer generated code." There you'll notice that .NET has created four Command objects, a Connection object, and DataAdapter. For example, if you use the SqlClient provider, SqlSelectCommand, SqlUpdateCommand, SqlDeleteCommand, and SqlInsertCommand objects are all created, as well as SqlConnection and SqlDataAdapter objects. Even if you don't use D&D to generate your code, you can use this generated code as a template for your own code. Notice how each of the commands is set up. Shown following is the code used to set up the SqlSelectCommand, the SqlUpdateCommand, as well as the SqlConnection and SqlDataAdapter.

```
private void InitializeComponent() {
this.sqlSelectCommand1 = new System.Data.SqlClient.SqlCommand();
this.sqlInsertCommand1 = new System.Data.SqlClient.SqlCommand();
this.sqlUpdateCommand1 = new System.Data.SqlClient.SqlCommand();
this.sqlDeleteCommand1 = new System.Data.SqlClient.SqlCommand();
this.sqlConnection1 = new System.Data.SqlClient.SqlConnection();
this.sqlDataAdapter1 = new System.Data.SqlClient.SqlDataAdapter();
//
// sqlSelectCommand1
//
this.sqlSelectCommand1.CommandText = "SELECT Au_ID, Author, Year_Born FROM
Authors";
this.sqlSelectCommand1.Connection = this.sqlConnection1;
//
// sqlInsertCommand1
//
this.sqlInsertCommand1.CommandText = "INSERT INTO Authors(Author, Year_Born)
VALUES (@Author, @Year_Born); SELECT Au_ID" +
```

```
      ", Author, Year_Born FROM Authors WHERE (Au_ID = @@IDENTITY)";
this.sqlInsertCommand1.Connection = this.sqlConnection1;
this.sqlInsertCommand1.Parameters.Add(new
System.Data.SqlClient.SqlParameter("@Author", System.Data.SqlDbType.VarChar, 50,
"Author"));
this.sqlInsertCommand1.Parameters.Add(new
System.Data.SqlClient.SqlParameter("@Year_Born", System.Data.SqlDbType.SmallInt,
2, "Year_Born"));
//
// sqlUpdateCommand1
//
this.sqlUpdateCommand1.CommandText = @"UPDATE Authors SET Author = @Author,
Year_Born = @Year_Born WHERE (Au_ID = @Original_Au_ID) AND (Author =
@Original_Author OR @Original_Author IS NULL AND Author IS NULL) AND (Year_Born
= @Original_Year_Born OR @Original_Year_Born IS NULL AND Year_Born IS NULL);
SELECT Au_ID, Author, Year_Born FROM Authors WHERE (Au_ID = @Au_ID)";
this.sqlUpdateCommand1.Connection = this.sqlConnection1;
this.sqlUpdateCommand1.Parameters.Add(new
System.Data.SqlClient.SqlParameter("@Author", System.Data.SqlDbType.VarChar, 50,
"Author"));
this.sqlUpdateCommand1.Parameters.Add(new
System.Data.SqlClient.SqlParameter("@Year_Born", System.Data.SqlDbType.SmallInt,
2, "Year_Born"));
this.sqlUpdateCommand1.Parameters.Add(new
System.Data.SqlClient.SqlParameter("@Original_Au_ID", System.Data.SqlDbType.Int,
4, System.Data.ParameterDirection.Input, false, ((System.Byte)(0)),
((System.Byte)(0)), "Au_ID", System.Data.DataRowVersion.Original, null));
this.sqlUpdateCommand1.Parameters.Add(new
System.Data.SqlClient.SqlParameter("@Original_Author",
System.Data.SqlDbType.VarChar, 50, System.Data.ParameterDirection.Input, false,
((System.Byte)(0)), ((System.Byte)(0)), "Author",
System.Data.DataRowVersion.Original, null));
this.sqlUpdateCommand1.Parameters.Add(new
System.Data.SqlClient.SqlParameter("@Original_Year_Born",
System.Data.SqlDbType.SmallInt, 2, System.Data.ParameterDirection.Input, false,
((System.Byte)(0)), ((System.Byte)(0)), "Year_Born",
System.Data.DataRowVersion.Original, null));
this.sqlUpdateCommand1.Parameters.Add(new
System.Data.SqlClient.SqlParameter("@Au_ID", System.Data.SqlDbType.Int, 4,
"Au_ID"));
//
// sqlDeleteCommand1
//
```

```
this.sqlDeleteCommand1.CommandText = "DELETE FROM Authors WHERE (Au_ID =
@Original_Au_ID) AND (Author = @Original_Autho" +
    "r OR @Original_Author IS NULL AND Author IS NULL) AND (Year_Born =
@Original_Yea" +
    "r_Born OR @Original_Year_Born IS NULL AND Year_Born IS NULL)";
this.sqlDeleteCommand1.Connection = this.sqlConnection1;
this.sqlDeleteCommand1.Parameters.Add(new
System.Data.SqlClient.SqlParameter("@Original_Au_ID", System.Data.SqlDbType.Int,
4, System.Data.ParameterDirection.Input, false, ((System.Byte)(0)),
((System.Byte)(0)), "Au_ID", System.Data.DataRowVersion.Original, null));
this.sqlDeleteCommand1.Parameters.Add(new
System.Data.SqlClient.SqlParameter("@Original_Author",
System.Data.SqlDbType.VarChar, 50, System.Data.ParameterDirection.Input, false,
((System.Byte)(0)), ((System.Byte)(0)), "Author",
System.Data.DataRowVersion.Original, null));
this.sqlDeleteCommand1.Parameters.Add(new
System.Data.SqlClient.SqlParameter("@Original_Year_Born",
System.Data.SqlDbType.SmallInt, 2, System.Data.ParameterDirection.Input, false,
((System.Byte)(0)), ((System.Byte)(0)), "Year_Born",
System.Data.DataRowVersion.Original, null));
//
// sqlConnection1
//
this.sqlConnection1.ConnectionString = "data source=.;initial
catalog=biblio;persist security info=False;user id=sa;work" +
    "station id=D1;packet size=4096";
//
// sqlDataAdapter1
//
this.sqlDataAdapter1.DeleteCommand = this.sqlDeleteCommand1;
this.sqlDataAdapter1.InsertCommand = this.sqlInsertCommand1;
this.sqlDataAdapter1.SelectCommand = this.sqlSelectCommand1;
this.sqlDataAdapter1.TableMappings.AddRange(new
System.Data.Common.DataTableMapping[] {new
System.Data.Common.DataTableMapping("Table", "Authors", new
System.Data.Common.DataColumnMapping[] {
new System.Data.Common.DataColumnMapping("Au_ID", "Au_ID"),
new System.Data.Common.DataColumnMapping("Author", "Author"),
new System.Data.Common.DataColumnMapping("Year_Born", "Year_Born")})});
this.sqlDataAdapter1.UpdateCommand = this.sqlUpdateCommand1;
 . . .
}
```

After you have dropped one (or more) Table(s) on your form, the Data menu is activated and you can click **Data | Generate DataSet**. This menu launches a dialog that captures options and properties used to generate queries—as shown in Figure 3-13. This process creates a "strongly typed" DataSet. I discuss this in Chapter 5, but basically, a typed DataSet exposes the resultset's metadata (the Table and its Column names) as a class. This way you can reference Tables and the columns in them as objects. Strongly typed DataSet object references are considerably faster than the "late-binding" techniques shown in most examples.

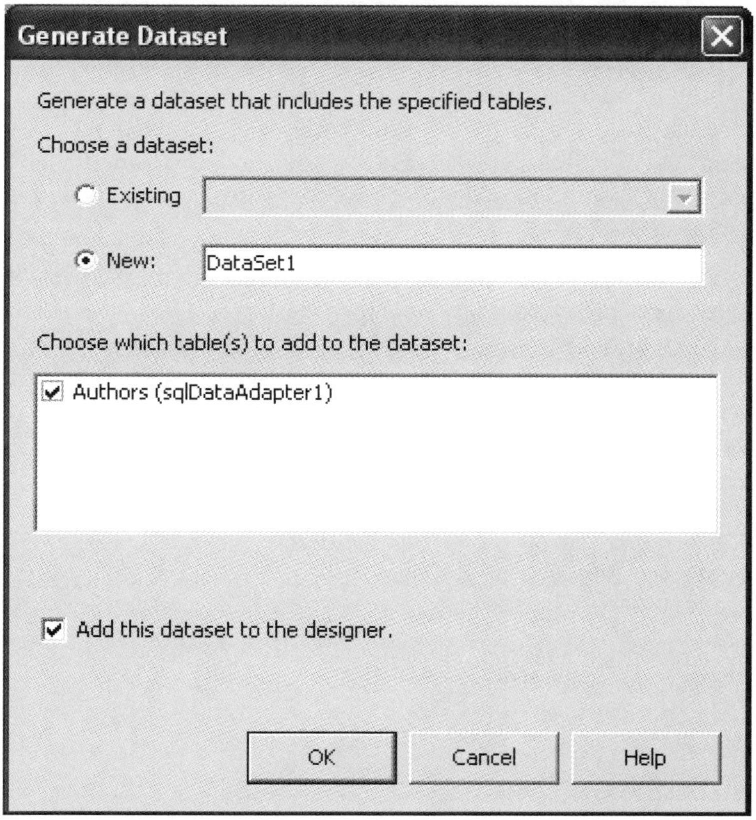

Figure 3-13. Generating a DataSet with the IDE—naming the DataSet

Executing "Traditional" Queries

If you decide to execute a query that either returns rows from a single table or returns the product of a multiple-table JOIN executed on the server, read on. This section discusses how to set up the type of query you're probably most used to executing.

For those ADO developers who are set in their ways and just want to execute a query using ADO.NET, you're in luck: You don't have to use any wizards or magic OO dust to get this to work. Let's walk through a simple sample that executes a SELECT query and displays the rows in a DataGrid. I did this in about four lines in ADOc; ADO.NET is not that easy, but it's not *that* hard. Let's step through a hand-written code sample. I start with code to shortcut the namespace and to declare the working objects I'll need to open the connection and run the query. These include: Connection, DataAdapter, Command, and DataSet objects. The first thing you may notice about my code is that while I could instantiate the instance objects at their time of declaration—for example, private SqlConnection cn = new SqlConnection();—I don't. I choose to instantiate my instance objects within the class constructor—in this case, the form constructor—so that I can courteously deal with exceptions within a try/catch block. Also, if I subsequently overload the class constructor, I don't have to hunt down all of the instance objects' instantiation code—I know they are all encapsulated in the class constructor(s).

NOTE *All of the following examples use the DataSet Fill method to extract the rows from the data source. Nowhere in this code will you find use of the Connection Open method; the connection is opened just-in-time (when the Fill method is invoked) and closed immediately—or at least released to the connection pool as soon as rowset population is complete.*

```
using System.Diagnostics;
using System.Data.SqlClient;
    . . .
    public class Form1 : System.Windows.Forms.Form {
    . . .
        private SqlConnection cn;
        private SqlDataAdapter da;
        private SqlCommand sc;
        private DataSet ds;
    . . .
        public Form1() {
            try
            {
                InitializeComponent();

                cn = new SqlConnection();
                da = new SqlDataAdapter();
                sc = new SqlCommand();
                ds = new DataSet();
```

```
    }
    catch (Exception ex) {
        Debug.WriteLine( ex.ToString() );
    }


}
```

Let's pause a moment and consider the nature of the typical way that ADO.NET will be employed. I think we can agree that it's not likely to be a traditional client/server application. In many (if not most) cases, I expect ADO.NET to be used in middle-tier components, embedded in Web applications, or in a new Web Service. With this in mind, consider that the following examples don't always follow the model where a globally declared Connection object is opened during the Form's construction and closed when the application is done. This is because when connections are made in the middle tier (and in Web pages), the connection is opened, the query is executed, and the connection is closed (released to the pool) almost immediately. The following examples will illustrate several techniques including just-in-time connections.

In this code, I construct and assign a ConnectionString to the SqlConnection object. Yes, I could have used a constructor to specify the ConnectionString property, but because .NET does not permit `Try/Catch` blocks outside of functions, this was not an option. Because declarations (with a constructor) can fail, it's foolhardy to use this technique without a safety net.

Note that I don't *open* the Connection object in code; this is done automatically by the Fill method. Fill closes it too. Interesting. This means you might not want to use the Fill method to fetch more rows than you need because your code will block while the connection is opened, the rows are fetched, and the DataSet is constructed. Don't be mislead by the response times you witness during development. The delays you'll see during single-user testing are exacerbated as additional users are added. I discuss these subtleties in the next chapter.

Okay, let's take a look at another example. This code could appear in Form_Load and it would certainly be framed in a `try/catch` exception handler block.

```
cn.ConnectionString = "data source=.;database=biblio;uid=admin;pwd=pw";
```

The next section sets up the SelectCommand SqlCommand object's properties. I also set the DataAdapter's SelectCommand property to this newly configured Command object.

```
cn.ConnectionString = "data source=.;database=biblio;uid=admin;pwd=pw";


sc.CommandText = "SELECT pubid, pubname, city, state " +
                 " FROM publishers" +
```

```
                                         " WHERE state = '"   +
                                         strStateWanted.ToString() + "'";

                     sc.CommandType = CommandType.Text;
                     sc.Connection = cn;

                     da.SelectCommand = sc;
```

When it's time to run the query, I clear any previous contents of the DataSet and then use the Fill method to open the connection, run the query, and return all of the rows. The concatenation operation in the Fill method arguments sets the newly created DataSet table name to PublishersIn plus the name of the state wanted. That's so when I display the DataSet in a bound control, the heading reflects the parameter used to narrow the query.

```
try {
    ds.Clear();
    da.Fill(ds, "PublishersIn" + strStateWanted.ToString());
 . . .
}
```

This meager error handler simply dumps any exceptions that occur during these operations.

```
catch (Exception ex) {
    Console.WriteLine(ex.ToString());
}
```

All that's left to do is set up the DataGrid control to bind to the resultset and force its columns to be set based on incoming data—automatically.

```
dataGrid1.DataSource = ds.Tables[0];
```

Using .NET Constructors to Initialize Variables

I have discussed several times in the preceding chapters the ability to initialize objects as they are being declared:

```
private string strMyString = "This is the initial Value";
```

This technique has its advantages because it reduces the number of lines of code and clearly sets an initial value for a variable; but, it also has a number of side-effects that have to be (must be) dealt with. For instance, you must trap errors that might be caused by the instantiation; this means that if the expression passed to an object's constructor is incorrect, .NET throws an exception.

When using constructors to initialize ADO.NET objects (as I am about to do), consider that you are passing one or more values (strings, numbers, etc.) that are applied to the underlying object's properties. This means that the values have to be correct on several levels. For example, a connection string has to be syntactically correct before you assign it to the ConnectionString property or you'll trip an exception. If a Connection property must be a string or a specific value and this value is incorrect, the property assignment operation in the constructor will fail and throw the exception. It is for this reason that you must cradle such declaration statements (that contain constructors) in try/catch blocks that can sink any resulting exception.

The problem with this approach is that try/catch blocks can't be coded in the "global" areas where instance object variables are declared; they (try/catch blocks) can only be coded *within* Function blocks. Therefore, this means you should only use the technique of instantiating when declaring your variables if these variables have local Function scope—to be used and then immediately discarded. It seems the whole .NET philosophy is built around this just-in-time object creation strategy.

IMHO   *another issue with this strategy is performance. Using this technique, objects are created each and every time they are declared. If the combined variable declaration and instantiation statements are in click-events, the objects are constructed and torn down each time the button is pressed. In the past, I've tried to avoid needless creation of objects as a way to improve performance. I expect we'll have to focus our attention elsewhere for our performance gains—that is, if we follow the lead of these OO gurus.*[12]

The following example shows how to execute the preceding query using this just-in-time paradigm. Notice that the example has only one "global" variable: strStateWanted.

```
string strStateWanted "CA";
```

---

12. Of course, if each instantiation of such an object takes a huge performance hit, then this object is probably best instance object declared atdecat class level and instantiated (within a try/catch block) in a class constructor.

All ADO.NET operations are done here in the Find button click-event. Using declaration statement constructors, I can build the variables and initialize them in one step. Notice that these declaration statements are framed in a try/catch block so if something goes wrong (doesn't it always?), I can deal with the error. In this case I am creating all of the required ADO.NET objects *each time* the button is clicked. Because they are constructed in the event handler, these objects are marked for disposal by the garbage collector after the handler ends.

```
private void btnFind_Click(object sender, System.EventArgs e) {
    try {
        string strSelectQuery = "select pubid, pubname, city, state"
            + " from publishers where state = '"
            + txtStateWanted.Text.ToString() + "'";
        string strConnectString =
            "data source=.;database=biblio;uid=admin;pwd=pw";
        SqlDataAdapter da =
            new SqlDataAdapter(strSelectQuery, strConnectString);
        DataSet ds = new DataSet();

        da.Fill(ds, "PublishersIn" + txtStateWanted.Text.ToString());
        dataGrid1.DataSource = ds.Tables[0];
    }
    catch (SqlException sex) {
        Debug.WriteLine(sex.Message);
    }
}
```

Which of these techniques should you choose? Well, IMHO, I expect that will depend on whether or not you can benefit from persisted objects or not. I'm not really in favor of going to the expense of creating objects just to have them tossed out a moment later when they are no longer in scope. I think strategies that construct objects early in globally referenceable scope and set their properties just before execution are a better idea. However, that said, this option is often not available to ASP or middle-tier developers whose code lives for only a few hundred milliseconds.

TIP *At least that's until I heard about the .NET Cache object. While this book does not have the bandwidth to get into the Cache object, consider its use to cache DataSet or DataTable objects for use from session to session in Web apps.*

Managing Parameter Queries[13]

As you might have noticed in the preceding examples, I basically hard coded the scoping parameter to limit the number of rows returned from the Publishers table. This technique isn't particularly useful because most queries need to be flexible enough to let scoping parameters be set at run time. ADO.NET supports parameter queries in a fashion similar to ADOc, but the SQL syntax and the code to construct the Parameters collection are both new and different in a number of ways. The following example accepts a parameter value from a TextBox control and passes this value to the Parameters collection. Yes, you can use either the persisted property or just-in-time techniques to implement this code, but this example uses the latter.

Note that this code does not create a Connection object—it just passes a ConnectionString to the DataAdapter which constructs the Connection object behind the scenes. This means the errors you get from this routine might include exceptions returned from failed connection attempts. I also pass the SQL query to the DataAdapter. Notice that because I'm using the SqlClient .NET Data Provider, I can't use the ADOc-type ? parameter marker—I have to use named parameters. I named our parameter @State. This is a step in the right direction as far as I'm concerned. The SQL is more readable and should play better with back-end databases.

```
private void btnFind_Click(object sender, System.EventArgs e) {
    try {
        DataSet ds = new DataSet();
        SqlDataAdapter da = new SqlDataAdapter("SELECT pubid, pubname, city,"+
            state FROM publishers where state = @State",
            "datasource=.;database=biblio;uid=admin;pwd=pw");
```

Construction of the Parameters collection is also (very) different from ADOc. The Parameters collection already exists as an integral part of the DataAdapter object's SelectCommand object—but it starts out empty. As I discussed earlier, the DataAdapter object also contains the InsertCommand, UpdateCommand, and DeleteCommand classes which can all be instantiated as Command objects whose CommandText queries support parameter-driven queries or stored procedures. Notice that the ADOc CreateParameter method is gone; it's been replaced with the generic .NET Add method used to add items to all types of collections. .NET supports several new Add method constructors for use with the Parameters collection. These new constructors make it very simple to create input parameters—the most common style. The following example illustrates one of these

---

13. Code for this section can be found in "\Examples\Chapter 03\Parameter Query" folder on the CD.

constructors. It appends an input Parameter object including the default value setting. This constructor is especially cool because it can be used for any datatype—string or number (even a floating-point value). Note that this particular constructor *requires* a value which is evaluated to set the Parameter object properties.

```
da.SelectCommand.Parameters.Add("@State",txtStateWanted.Text);
        da.Fill(ds,"PublishersIn" + txtStateWanted.Text);
        dataGrid1.DataSource =ds.Tables[0];
    }
    catch (SqlException sex) {
        Debug.WriteLine(sex.ToString());
    }
}
```

Reviewing the Parameter Object Constructors[14]

Throughout the rest of the book I illustrate use of parameter queries because they play such a pivotal role in best practice designs. In the following discussion I demonstrate how ADO.NET supports a bevy of Parameter constructors that make the process of populating the Parameters collection easy—even easier than in ADOc. This section walks through many of these constructors and shows a couple of coding tips that don't appear in the documentation, but that make the process of creating the Parameters collections consume fewer lines of code and generate fewer hair-pulling episodes.

Let's start from the list of SqlParameter constructors. Yes, these same constructors are available for the OleDb and Odbc .NET Data Providers. Each of these constructors initializes a new instance of the SqlParameter class. Here are examples of the constructors:

```
SqlParameter myParm1 = new SqlParameter();
```

Frankly, I don't use this first constructor very much, if at all. I find it easier and faster to use the Add method overloads instead of having to assign each Parameter property one-by-one.

---

14. Example code is located in the "\Examples\Chapter 03\Parameter Constructors" folder on the CD.

However, sticking with Parameter Object constructors for now, the next five constructors accept a parameter name followed by an object that describes the Parameter. In this case, the object's properties are used to set the Parameter properties. This means you can pass a string and get the Type property set to the appropriate (in this case SQL Server) datatype. No, this constructor does not try to set the length for Varchar or Char columns—it leaves this value set to 0. Pay particular attention to the constructors I use for myParm3 and myParm4—both use a Windows textbox object to initialize the Parameter; I coerce the type using Convert.ToInt32() only in the construction of myParm4.

IPHO *Because a Windows Forms control object is a class instance variable, it means that in C# you can only use this constructor inside of a method. In any case, it is a best programming practice to only use these instantiation constructors inside* try/catch *blocks inside Functions.*

An alternative is just to explicitly use a datatype enumeration—as in constructor for myParm6—which is especially useful when the Parameter can accept all of the defaults given a specific datatype.

```
// Create a parameter of SqlDbType.NVarChar (String)


SqlParameter myParm2 = new SqlParameter("@ParmName2", "Value");
SqlParameter myParm3 = new SqlParameter("@ParmName3", txtTextBox.Text);

// Create a parameter of SqlDbType.Int (Int32)

SqlParameter myParm4 =
     new SqlParameter("@ParmName4", Convert.ToInt32(txtTextBox.Text));
SqlParameter myParm5 = new SqlParameter("@ParmName5", 123);
SqlParameter myParm6 = new SqlParameter("@ParmName6", SqlDbType.Int);
```

The following constructor accepts the Parameter name, the datatype, and the argument size (used for variable-length columns or string lengths). This is especially useful when the Parameter can accept all of the defaults given a specific variable-length datatype—such as a VarChar.

```
// Create a parameter of SqlDbType.VarChar (String), size 20


SqlParameter myParm7 = new SqlParameter("@ParmName7", SqlDbType.VarChar, 20);
```

TIP *Incidentally, it does not seem to matter that the Size property of the variable-length datatypes is not set; ADO.NET does not worry about it—regardless of the setting.*

This next constructor accepts the Parameter name, the datatype, the argument size, and the *SourceColumn* value ("City"). Basically, the SourceColumn property binds a resultset column back to a Parameter. I discuss the SourceColumn property in Chapter 7 when I illustrate construction of action queries used to update a data source.

```
// Create a parameter of SqlDbType.VarChar (String), size 50 and source column
//   of "city"

SqlParameter myParm8 = new SqlParameter("@ParmName8", SqlDbType.VarChar, 50,
    "City");
```

If you want to define most of the properties in a Parameter object with a single line of code, you can use the following constructor. It accepts the same set of arguments as the previous constructor, but adds the IsNullable, Precision, Scale, and Version properties to the list. I also discuss the Version properties and why they are interesting in Chapter 7.

```
// Create a parameter of SqlDbType.Float, size 0, Parameter in, is not nullable
//   Precision 4, Scale 2 and source column of "Discount", Original Row Version

SqlParameter myParm9 = new SqlParameter("@ParmName9", SqlDbType.Float, 0,
    ParameterDirection.Input, false, 4, 2,"Discount", DataRowVersion.Original);
```

This last constructor simply adds the Value property to the previous list of arguments.

```
// Create a parameter of SqlDbType.VarChar(String), size 100, Parameter in,
// is nullable, Precision 0, scale 0, source column of "Description",
// Default Row vesion, value of "garden hose"
// Precision 4, Scale 2 and source column of "Discount", Original Row Version

SqlParameter myParm10 = new SqlParameter("@ParmName10", SqlDbType.VarChar, 100,
    ParameterDirection.Input, true, 0, 0, "Description", DataRowVersion.Default,
    "garden hose");
```

Using the Add Method to Construct Parameters[15]

As I said earlier, I found that I don't usually create Parameter objects ahead of time. Instead, I use the Add method and its own constructors to build the Parameter objects and set their properties—very much like the ADOc CreateParameter method. The following example illustrates each of the current[16] set of Add method constructors. Notice how all of these Add method constructors parallel the new Parameter constructors I just reviewed. However, there are is another nuance here: When you use the Add method, you can also tack on another Property setting as shown in some of the following examples. For example, to set the Value property when it's not included in the overloaded argument list in the constructor, you can code:

```
cmd.Parameters.Add("@ParmName", SqlDbType.Int).Value = 22;
```

This technique works for any of the Parameter properties. Cool. The following examples illustrate each of the other syntax variations.

```
try {
    SqlCommand cmd = new SqlCommand();
    cmd.Parameters.Add ("@ParmName2", "Value");
    cmd.Parameters.Add ("@ParmName3", txtTextBox.Text);
    cmd.Parameters.Add ("@ParmName4", Convert.ToInt32(txtTextBox.Text));
    cmd.Parameters.Add ("@ParmName5", 123);
    cmd.Parameters.Add ("@ParmName6", SqlDbType.Int);
    cmd.Parameters.Add ("@ParmName7", SqlDbType.VarChar, 20);
    cmd.Parameters.Add ("@ParmName8", SqlDbType.VarChar, 50,"City");
    cmd.Parameters.Add ("@ParmName9", SqlDbType.Float, 0,"Discount").Direction =

ParameterDirection.Input;

    SqlParameter myParm20 = new SqlParameter();
    cmd.Parameters.Add (myParm20);
}
catch(Exception ex) {
    Console.WriteLine(ex.ToString());
}
```

---

15. Add Method example code is located in the "\Examples\Chapter 03\Parameter Constructors" folder on the CD.
16. I expect Microsoft to add additional constructors as the product matures.

Managing Multiple-Table Queries

Keep reading if you want to execute a query that returns rows from several tables and if you want ADO.NET to manage the intertable navigation and parent/child relationships between these tables (as in Customer/Order/Item or Author/TitleAuthor/Titles). There are two approaches you can take in this scenario:

- **Construct SelectCommand objects to round trip for each (possibly related) individual rowset.** This is useful if you are extracting data from a variety of data sources—possibly on different servers or in different databases.

- **Author a single batch-SELECT statement that returns several (possibly related) rowsets from the same data source with a single round trip.** This technique leverages ADO.NET's ability to automatically parse multiple-resultset queries. Of course, it also assumes your provider can execute a batch query and return multiple resultsets—not all providers can.

Both of these techniques can be implemented in code or via the IDE drag-and-drop techniques I've already discussed. In addition, both of these techniques construct multiple DataTable objects within the DataSet object. After the data arrives (and not before), you want to tell ADO.NET how these DataTable objects are related so it can navigate from row to row.

Executing Individual SelectCommands

The following example[17] uses two DataAdapters—each containing its own SelectCommand with its own SELECT statement. The first SELECT returns selected rows from the Publishers table; the second returns related rows from the Titles table. How do I know they are related? Well, I created the database so I know they are. How does ADO.NET know they are related? It doesn't—not until you describe these relationships in code. As with the previous example, I construct a Parameter object and use the Add method to append it to the Parameters collection. My first version of this code created two separate DataAdapters, but once written, I noticed that the two DataAdapters were identical except for the query—they both connected to the same data source and used the same input parameters. After this discovery I rewrote the example to reuse the objects. The result was a tighter piece of code that simply changed the CommandText in the SelectCommand.

---

17. Located in the "\Examples\Chapter 03\Muliple DataAdapter" folder on the CD.

```
try {
    // Create a DataSet
    DataSet ds =new DataSet();

    // Create the DataAdapter providing connection and SELECT Command
    // For Publishers
    SqlDataAdapter da = new SqlDataAdapter("SELECT pubid, pubname, city, state "
        +" FROM publishers WHERE state = @State",
        "data source=.;database=biblio;uid=admin;pwd=pw");

    // Initialize the Select Command Parameters - for Publishers (and Titles !)
    da.SelectCommand.Parameters.Add("@State", SqlDbType.VarChar, 2);
    da.SelectCommand.Parameters["@State"].Value = txtStateWanted.Text;

    // Fill the dataset with the results and name the Table "Publishers"
    da.Fill(ds, "Publishers");


    // Reuse the DataAdapter resetting the SELECT Command - For Titles
    da.SelectCommand.CommandText = "SELECT title, price, pubid FROM titles "
        +" WHERE pubid in (SELECT pubid FROM publishers WHERE state = @State)";

    // Fill the DataSet with the results and name the Table "Titles"
    da.Fill(ds, "Titles");

    // Call our AddRelation() method to relate Publishers and Titles
    AddRelation(ds);

    // Bind the Publishers DataTable to the Grid
    DataGrid1.DataSource = ds.Tables["Publishers"];
}
catch (SqlException sex) {
    Console.WriteLine(sex.ToString());
}
```

After the DataSet is constructed you'll discover two DataTable objects inside. You can dump the DataSet to a grid, but the two rowsets are shown independently. If that's what you want, fine, you're done. If not, you must set the relationships between the two rowsets. Do this with the DataSet Relations collection. To inform ADO.NET of these relationships, create a DataColumn object for each column in the relationship and use these to create a new DataRelation on these columns. After this is done, the Grid control shows the selected Publisher rows with a + sign to indicate that there are related Titles rows. Early in the subroutine I check to see if this routine has already been called by checking the

Relations.Count property for 0. If the Count property is 0, the routine has not been called before—or someone stole your relations sometime in the night.[18]

```
private void AddRelation(DataSet ds) {
    try {
        // if we don't already have a relationship defined
        // then define one.
        if (ds.Relations.Count == 0)
        {

            // Create new DataColumn objects for parent and child
            DataColumn parentCol = new DataColumn();
            DataColumn childCol = new DataColumn();

            // Declare a DataRelation object
            DataRelation relPublishers;

            // Assign the parent and child columns
            parentCol = ds.Tables["Publishers"].Columns["PubID"];
            childCol = ds.Tables["Titles"].Columns["PubID"];

            // Create DataRelation.
            relPublishers = new DataRelation("PublishersTitles", parentCol, childCol);

            // Add the relation to the DataSet.
            ds.Relations.Add(relPublishers);
        }
    }
    catch( Exception ex ) {
        Console.WriteLine(ex.ToString());
    }
}
```

Executing Multiple-Resultset SelectCommand Objects[19]

The following example is very similar to the preceding code except that, instead of executing individual SelectCommand operations (with two round trips), the

---

18. I have a list of relations if any thieves are interested!
19. Located in the "\Examples\Chapter 03\Multiple Resultset" folder on the CD.

code combines the two SELECT statements into a single batch and uses the Fill method to populate the DataSet's DataTable objects in a single operation. I expect this technique to be far faster because it only requires one round trip instead of two. If your query returns more than two rowsets (parent, child, grand-child . . .), then you'll gain even more. You can also execute a stored procedure to generate the individual rowsets as described here. I demonstrate how to execute stored procedures a little later—see "Managing Stored Procedure Queries."

NOTE *Oracle users can skip on down. I'm told that Oracle does not support multiple-resultset batches as illustrated here.*

First, I declare my instance variables. Note that I do not instantiate them at declare time.

```
public class Form1 : System.Windows.Forms.Form {
    // Instance object variable Declarations
    private SqlConnection cn;
    private SqlDataAdapter da;
    private SqlCommand sc;
    private DataSet ds;
```

I then instantiate the instance variables within a `try/catch` block within the default Form constructor method:

```
public Form1() {
    try {
        InitializeComponent();
        // Create a connection object
        cn = new SqlConnection(
            "data source=.;database=biblio;uid=admin;pwd=pw");
```

The SQL used in this example was *not* generated by the .NET Query Builder; it did not know how to deal with multiple resultsets. Instead, I used Query Analyzer to author the SQL. Each query is fed with the same WHERE clause criteria as supplied to the first query in order to limit query scope to just children of the previous level. Yes, this type of query can be written in a variety of ways.

```
        // Create the Select Command
        sc = new SqlCommand("SELECT pubid, pubname, city, state FROM publishers"
            + " WHERE state = @StateWanted "
```

```
         + " SELECT pubid, isbn, title, price FROM titles WHERE pubid in "
         + " (SELECT pubid FROM publishers WHERE state = @StateWanted)",cn);

    // Add a Parameter to the Select Command
    sc.Parameters.Add("@StateWanted", SqlDbType.VarChar, 2).Value =
         txtStateWanted.Text;

    // Create a DataAdapter - initializing the Select Command
    da = new SqlDataAdapter(sc);
```

Unlike earlier examples, this example requires that I alter the automatically generated DataTable names because the Fill method uses "Table", "Table1" . . . "TableN" as the default names. The DataAdapter TableMappings collection lets me rename the default names to something more meaningful.

```
    // Set the DataAdapter Table Mappings
    da.TableMappings.Add("Table", "Publishers");
    da.TableMappings.Add("Table1", "Titles");

    // Create a DataSet Object
    ds = new DataSet();
}
```

And to round off, I include an exception handler. Folks often ask me why I prefer to write to the console output window instead of say using a MessageBox for my rudimentary exception handler. It is of course personal preference, however, if you have dumped exceptions to the console output window when the program has finished executing, they are still there to refer to when you start editing the code; whereas, if you use a MessageBox to report the exception, then once you have closed it, it is gone.

```
catch (Exception ex) {
    Debug.WriteLine(ex.ToString());
    }
}
```

The following button click-event clears the DataSet of its previous contents, passes the input parameter, opens the connection (ADO.NET does this for us via the Fill method), and uses the Fill method to run the query and return the two (in this case) resultsets. As with the previous example, the code sets up the inter-rowset (inter-DataTable) relations so that the data hierarchy can be seen and navigated using the grid control.

```
private void btnFind_Click(object sender, System.EventArgs e) {
    try {
        // Clear the DataSet
        ds.Clear();

        // Set the parameter value on the Data Adaptor Select Command
        // with the value from a TextBox control
        da.SelectCommand.Parameters["@StateWanted"].Value = txtStateWanted.Text;

        // Populate the DataSet
        da.Fill(ds);

        // Relate the DataTables in the DataSet
        AddRelation(ds);

        // Populate the DataGrid with the "Publishers" DataTable
        DataGrid1.DataSource = ds.Tables["Publishers"];
    }
    catch(Exception ex) {
        Debug.WriteLine(ex.ToString());
    }
}
```

Managing Stored Procedure Queries[20]

As with ADOc, ADO.NET is fully capable of executing stored procedures so you should not expect any surprises here. The unique characteristics of stored procedures include handling input, OUTPUT, INPUT/OUTPUT, and Return Value parameters, as well as the ability to generate multiple resultsets, print statement, RAISERROR messages, and complex COMPUTE BY resultsets. This section addresses how to capture most of these, as well as how to deal with simple rowsets. In the next section I discuss how to manage multiple resultsets—if ADO.NET has not already dealt with these for you.

To execute a stored procedure with ADO.NET, you won't have the luxury of simply executing the named stored procedure as a method of the Connection object—that's not supported like it is in ADOc. Instead, you must set up a SelectCommand similar to how you set up a Command object in ADOc. This is really pretty simple to do in ADO.NET.

---

20. Located in the "\Examples\Chapter 03\StoredProc Query" folder on the CD.

I start with the same instance object variables and create the same ConnectionString in the Form Constructor method—just as in the other examples:

```
private SqlConnection cn;
private SqlDataAdapter da;
private SqlCommand sc;
private DataSet ds;

public Form1() {
    try {
        InitializeComponent();

        // Create a connection object
        cn = new SqlConnection(
            "data source=.;database=biblio;uid=admin;pwd=pw");
```

In this example, I describe the stored procedure using a SelectCommand—setting the CommandText to the stored procedure name and the CommandType to CommandType.StoredProcedure. Do not leave off this step because doing so can really confuse ADO.NET; you'll get a syntax error when you try to execute the query. Adding the two input parameters is easy—even easier than using the CreateParameter method in ADOc. You can create the Parameter object and set its Value property at the same time by using the correct overloaded method arguments—then it is the usual creation of a DataSet and a DataAdapter.

```
        // Create a Select Command, Add (and configure) the Parameters
        sc = new SqlCommand("Au42",cn);
        sc.CommandType = CommandType.StoredProcedure;
        sc.Parameters.Add("@YearLow", SqlDbType.Int).Value = txtYearLow.Text;
        sc.Parameters.Add("@YearHigh", SqlDbType.Int).Value = txtYearHigh.Text;

        // Create a DataSet
        ds = new DataSet();

        // Create a DataAdaptor initializing the SelectCommand
        da = new SqlDataAdapter(sc);

    }
    catch (Exception ex) {
        Debug.WriteLine( ex.ToString() );
    }

}
```

Populating (and repopulating the grid) is as easy as clearing the DataSet, assigning the parameters for the SelectCommand, filling the DataSet, and then finally setting the DataGrid DataSource to the first table in the DataSet.

```
private void btnFind_Click(object sender, System.EventArgs e) {
    try {
        // Clear the DataSet
        ds.Clear();

        // Assign the Parameters for the Select Statement
        da.SelectCommand.Parameters["@YearLow"].Value  = txtYearLow.Text;
        da.SelectCommand.Parameters["@YearHigh"].Value = txtYearHigh.Text;

        // Populate the DataSet
        da.Fill(ds);

        // Populate the DataGrid
        DataGrid1.DataSource = ds.Tables[0];
    }
    catch (Exception ex) {
        Debug.WriteLine(ex.ToString());
    }
}
```

Capturing the Return Value and OUTPUT Parameters[21]

All SQL Server stored procedures return a @ReturnValue whether you ask for one or not. However, if you don't set up a Parameters collection with a parameter named "@ReturnValue", you won't see it. Stored procedures can also return OUTPUT parameters or even support bidirectional (INPUT/OUTPUT) parameters. If you want to capture or pass these, you also have to construct Parameter objects to manage them and correctly set the Direction property. But you knew all that (I hope). ADO.NET is no different from ADOc in this respect. However, constructing the Parameters collection is very different (as you've already seen). ADO.NET also throws a few curves our way, but if you keep ADOc in mind, you'll figure it out soon enough.

First, consider that while there is a CreateParameter method in ADO.NET, it does not take any arguments, so it can't be used in the same way. I experimented with a number of techniques to create parameters and ended up with the following examples. Remember that you have to deal with any rowsets returned by the

---

21. Located in the "\Examples\Chapter 03\SP With Output Parms" folder on the CD.

stored procedure before your OUTPUT parameters are returned into the Parameters collection. This is because the OUTPUT parameters are not resolved by the DBMS engine until the rowset is complete and they don't appear in the data stream until last. As with ADOc, if you check too soon (before rowset population), the individual OUTPUT, INPUT/OUTPUT, and ReturnValue parameters will be set to null. Even if your query does not return a rowset, you still need to pretend that it does—or so it seems.

Consider the following stored procedure:

```
CREATE PROCEDURE TestInOutRowset
    (
        @TitleWanted varchar(20) =  'Hi%',
        @TitlesFound int OUTPUT,
        @MaxPriceFound smallmoney OUTPUT,
        @MinPriceFound smallmoney OUTPUT,
        @AvgPriceFound smallmoney OUTPUT

    )
AS
SELECT @TitlesFound = (SELECT COUNT(*)
 FROM titles WHERE title LIKE @TitleWanted)
SELECT @MaxPriceFound = (SELECT MAX(price)
 FROM titles WHERE title LIKE @TitleWanted)
SELECT @MinPriceFound = (SELECT MIN(price)
 FROM titles WHERE title LIKE @TitleWanted)
SELECT @AvgPriceFound = (SELECT AVG(price)
 FROM titles WHERE title LIKE @TitleWanted)

SELECT @titlesfound TitlesFound,
    @maxpricefound MaxPriceFound,
    @minpricefound MinPriceFound,
    @avgpricefound AvgPriceFound     /* Rowset */

RETURN @@Rowcount
```

This stored procedure accepts a single input parameter (@TitleWanted) and returns four OUTPUT parameters along with a ReturnValue (set with @@RowCount) and a final single-row resultset. This variation of the stored procedure also returns a rowset generated with the SELECT @TitlesFound at the end of the stored procedure.

You can use the following code to execute this stored procedure, pass a string containing the desired title as an input parameter, and extract the Return Value and OUTPUT parameters. The initial phase of this code should be very familiar by now—it's the same as the last few examples, with one exception: I create a working Parameter object. It's really not necessary, but it does illustrate one technique used to create individual parameter objects. I found that there were not sufficient overloads on the Add method to create OUTPUT or Return Value parameters. Because of this, I created the Return Value parameter by brute force and used the Add method on the Parameters collection with the prefab-constructed Parm object.

```
public class Form1 : System.Windows.Forms.Form {
    private SqlConnection cn;
    private SqlDataAdapter da;
    private SqlCommand sc;
    private DataSet ds;
    private SqlParameter parm;
. . .

public Form1() {
    try {
        InitializeComponent();

        // Create a connection object
        cn = new SqlConnection(
            "data source=.;database=biblio;uid=admin;pwd=pw");

        // Create (stored procedure) SqlCommand, Add & configure the Parameters

        sc = new SqlCommand("TestInOutRowset",cn);
        sc.CommandType = CommandType.StoredProcedure;
```

This is all there is to creating and adding an @ReturnValue parameter:

```
        parm = new SqlParameter("@ReturnValue",SqlDbType.Int);
        parm.Direction = ParameterDirection.ReturnValue;
        sc.Parameters.Add(parm);
```

I used the Add method for the input parameter—it fits perfectly.

```
sc.Parameters.Add("@TitleWanted", SqlDbType.VarChar, 20);
```

However, for the OUTPUT parameters, I simply created input parameters and then changed their direction—it seemed the simplest way to do the job.

```
sc.Parameters.Add("@TitlesFound", SqlDbType.Int).Direction =
                                        ParameterDirection.Output;
sc.Parameters.Add("@MaxPriceFound", SqlDbType.SmallMoney).Direction =
                                        ParameterDirection.Output;
sc.Parameters.Add("@MinPriceFound", SqlDbType.SmallMoney).Direction =
                                        ParameterDirection.Output;
sc.Parameters.Add("@AvgPriceFound", SqlDbType.SmallMoney).Direction =
                                        ParameterDirection.Output;
sc.Parameters["@AvgPriceFound"].Precision = 2;
```

Then to complete the preparation, I instantiated a SqlAdapter using the prepare SqlCommand and a DataSet to hold the results.

```
da = new SqlDataAdapter(sc);
ds = new DataSet();
}
```

And importantly, don't forget to catch any exceptions!

```
catch(Exception ex) {
    Debug.WriteLine(ex.ToString());
}
}
```

When it comes time to execute the stored procedure, nothing really needs to be changed. I pass in the input parameter (or any INPUT/OUTPUT) parameters and execute the stored procedure using the Fill method because I expect the routine to return a rowset.

```
private void btnFind_Click(object sender, System.EventArgs e) {
    try {
        // Clear the DataSet
        ds.Clear();

        // Assign the Input Parameter to pass for the Stored Procedure
        sc.Parameters["@TitleWanted"].Value = txtTitleWanted.Text;
```

```
    // Populate the DataSet
    da.Fill(ds);

    // Populate the DataGrid
    DataGrid1.DataSource = ds.Tables[0];
```

To capture the Return Value and OUTPUT parameters, I simply reference the Parameters collection by name and extract the values. Note that you don't need null value handling—it's done for you behind the scenes. Another tip, be sure to fully qualify all references to the objects being passed to the Text property. You want a String value—not a Parameter object—passed to the Label control used to show the returned parameter. Cut back on the syntax shown here and you'll find some surprising results.

```
        lblRows.Text = sc.Parameters["@TitlesFound"].Value.ToString();
        lblMaxPrice.Text = sc.Parameters["@MaxPriceFound"].Value.ToString();
        lblMinPrice.Text = sc.Parameters["@MinPriceFound"].Value.ToString();
        lblAvgPrice.Text = sc.Parameters["@AvgPriceFound"].Value.ToString();
        lblReturnValue.Text = sc.Parameters["@ReturnValue"].Value.ToString();
    }
    catch { ... }
}
```

Using the DataReader Instead of a DataSet[22]

Because I used the Fill method to execute the previous queries, I didn't have to worry about opening (or closing) the connection or populating the DataSet. However, in the following example I use the DataReader to execute the query, so I have to worry about these details. That's all I need, more stuff to worry about. Remember, the DataReader is the low-level data I/O code that does all of the actual data reading and writing for ADO.NET. Behind the scenes, the DataReader is called by the Fill method to populate the DataSet.

In the following example I use the DataReader object's *ExecuteReader* method to execute the query stored in the DataAdapter object's SelectCommand. Whenever you use the DataReader directly, you must first use the Open method on the Connection object and close the DataSet when you're done dumping the rowset—or program the DataReader to do so. It's a fatal mistake to depend on .NET to close the Connection object for you when the Connection object falls out of scope. The documentation says that the Connection object will not be closed and its resources not released if the Connection object falls out of scope—so be

---

22. Located in the "\Examples\Chapter 03\SP With Output Parms ExecuteReader" folder on the CD.

careful. If you don't properly close the Connection object, your code might trap when the Connection object is "reactivated" with a "Syntax or Access Denied" exception. For example, if you have a subroutine that declares a Connection object, but the routine fails to close it before ending, the next time the subroutine is called, the orphaned Connection object associated with the subroutine might confuse the CLR.

Let's take a closer look at the code. Here I create a DataReader (SqlClient.SqlDataReader) to stream in the rowset. It's a lot more efficient than using the Fill method because it's doing less (far less) work. Remember the DataReader returns a RO/FO firehose data stream similar to the default ADOc Recordset. Before the code can process the OUTPUT parameters, the DataReader itself must be closed.

```
private void btnFind_Click(object sender, System.EventArgs e) {
    try {
        SqlDataReader dr;

        // Assign the Input Parameter to pass for the Stored Procedure
        sc.Parameters["@TitleWanted"].Value = txtTitleWanted.Text;

        // Explicitly Open the Connection and execute the DataReader
        cn.Open();
        dr = sc.ExecuteReader();

        { ... Do something with the DataReader ... }

        // Until the dataReader is closed we can't get at the OUTPUT parameters
        // or return value.
        dr.Close();

        // Populate the controls with output parameters (and Return Value) from
        // the Stored Procedure
        lblRows.Text = sc.Parameters["@TitlesFound"].Value.ToString();
        lblMaxPrice.Text = sc.Parameters["@MaxPriceFound"].Value.ToString();
        lblMinPrice.Text = sc.Parameters["@MinPriceFound"].Value.ToString();
        lblAvgPrice.Text = sc.Parameters["@AvgPriceFound"].Value.ToString();
        lblReturnValue.Text = sc.Parameters["@ReturnValue"].Value.ToString();
    }
    catch (Exception ex) {
        Debug.WriteLine(ex.ToString());
    }
```

You also have to close the connection because you opened it in code; I do this in a finally clause so that, even if an exception occurs in the try block, then at least the Connection object will still be closed. As a rule of thumb: If *you* open it, *you* have to close it. Your mom told you this years ago during the same lecture about looking down before you sit on the porcelain. I discuss the DataReader in more detail in the next chapter.

```
finally {
    // It is important to explicitly close the connection
    cn.Close();
}
}
```

TIP *If you're having problems with "data not available" when using the DataReader, be sure you've executed the* Read *method first . . .*

Managing Multiple-Resultset Queries[23]

In ADOc if the query returns more than one relevant resultset, you use the NextRecordset method to step from resultset to resultset. Remember, a resultset might not contain rows—as when you execute an action query. The resultset for an action query does contain the number of rows affected so you might want to capture this value to verify that things are going as planned. This section discusses how to capture the SELECT-generated rowsets in ADO.NET, as well as the rows-affected values.

For the next example, I execute the following stored procedure. It returns both selected rowsets (one of which is empty), as well as a resultset generated by an action query. It also returns a rows-affected value from the action query. Actually, it returns rows-affected values from the SELECT statements too, but ADO.NET throws these out.

```
ALTER  PROCEDURE dbo.MultipleResultsetRowsetAction
(@TitleWanted varchar(20) = 'Hi%')
AS
    SELECT Title, Year_published, price FROM titles
        WHERE title LIKE @TitleWanted
```

---

23. Code located in "\Examples\Chapter 03\MultipleResultset SP NextRecordset" folder on the CD.

```
SELECT Authors.Author, Titles.Title,
    Titles.Year_Published,
    Titles.Price
FROM Authors INNER JOIN
  Title_Author
  ON Authors.Au_ID = Title_Author.Au_ID INNER JOIN
  Titles ON Title_Author.ISBN = Titles.ISBN
WHERE (Titles.Title LIKE @TitleWanted)

SELECT  Title
FROM titles WHERE 1 = 0    /* returns empty resultset */

BEGIN TRANSACTION
  UPDATE     Titles
  SET              Price = Price * 1.1
  WHERE      (Title = @titlewanted)
  SELECT avg(price) AvgPrice FROM titles
  WHERE   Title = @TitleWanted
ROLLBACK TRANSACTION
RETURN @@Rowcount
```

The .NET code used to execute this stored procedure and parse the resultsets is pretty straightforward. I start by setting up a SelectCommand with the name of the stored procedure and CommandType of stored procedure—as I did in the earlier example. I construct a Parameters collection and wait until the user presses the **Find** button.

```
public class Form1 : System.Windows.Forms.Form {
    private SqlConnection cn;
    private SqlCommand sc;
{ ... }

public Form1() {
        try {
            InitializeComponent();

            // Create a connection object
            cn = new SqlConnection(
                "data source=.;database=biblio;uid=admin;pwd=pw");

            // Create a (stored procedure) SqlCommand, Add (and configure)
            //  the Parameters
            sc = new SqlCommand("MultipleResultsetRowsetAction",cn);
            sc.CommandType = CommandType.StoredProcedure;
```

```
            sc.Parameters.Add("@ReturnValue", SqlDbType.Int);
            sc.Parameters.Add("@TitleWanted", SqlDbType.VarChar, 20);
            sc.Parameters["@ReturnValue"].Direction =
                    ParameterDirection.ReturnValue;
        }
        catch { ... }
    }
```

In the Find button click-event I open the Connection object and use the ExecuteReader method to run the query

```
private void btnFind_Click(object sender, System.EventArgs e) {
    try {
        // Declare a DataReader
        SqlDataReader dr;

        cn.Open();
        sc.Parameters["@TitleWanted"].Value = txtTitleWanted.Text;
        dr = sc.ExecuteReader();
```

Next, the code loops through the resultsets dumping each resultset having fields (a rowset). When I'm ready to step to the next resultset, I use the NextResult() method until it returns False.

```
        while (dr.NextResult()) {
            Console.WriteLine("Records affected = " + dr.RecordsAffected);
            if (dr.FieldCount > 0) {
                ShowRows(dr);
            }
            else {
                Console.WriteLine("No rowset in this result set");
            }
        }
```

When I have finished looping (the loop—Whoopee!!), just as before, I need to close the DataReader before I can access the @ReturnValue and OUTPUT parameters.

```
        dr.Close();
        lblRows.Text = sc.Parameters["@ReturnValue"].Value.ToString();
    }
    catch { ... }
```

Hopefully, having caught any exceptions, I finally close the connection.

```
finally {
    cn.Close();
}
}
```

The ShowRows routine simply reads the data rows out of the data stream and dumps the values to the debug window.

```
private void ShowRows(SqlDataReader pDr) {
    try {
        while (pDr.Read()) {
            for( int i = 0; i < pDr.FieldCount - 1; i++) {
                Console.Write(pDr.GetName(i) + " - ");
                Console.Write(" DataTypeName=" + pDr.GetDataTypeName(i));
                Console.WriteLine(" = " + pDr.GetValue(i));
            }
        }
        Console.WriteLine("_____");
    }
    catch{ ... }
    }
}
```

Capturing the RecordsAffected Value

ADO.NET exposes both a RecordsAffected property on the DataReader object, as well as a value (integer) returned from the ExecuteNoQuery method. As with ADOc, if you use the SET NOCOUNT ON phrase in your SQL query (with SQL Server), the @@RowsAffected value is not automatically returned with your query resultset. If you examine the RecordsAffected value for SELECT queries or when the rows-affected value is disabled, ADO.NET returns -1. When working with multiple-resultset batches or stored procedures, the DataReader.RecordsAffected property returns a value with each resultset.

Exploring the Command Execute Methods

ExecuteReader is not the only Command (OleDbCommand, SqlCommand, OdbcCommand) Execute DataReader method to execute SQL with ADO.NET. There are several alternatives that can (potentially) yield better performance as shown in Table 3-2.

Table 3-2. DataReader Methods

Command Methods	Returns	Purpose
ExecuteReader	DataReader object	For rowset returning queries—at least for queries where you need to capture the rowset. Executes commands that return rows so it might not behave as expected when executing action queries such as SQL SET statements.
ExecuteNoQuery	Integer (rows affected)	For action queries such as SQL INSERT, DELETE, UPDATE, and SET statements. No rowset is generated, but it does return the number of rows affected.
ExecuteScalar	Scalar value	To execute queries that return a "scalar" value. For example, the results of an aggregate such as Max, Min, or Count. ADO.NET only captures the first column of the first row returned. There's an ExecuteScalar example later in this chapter.
ExecuteXMLReader	XMLReader object	To execute a query and return an XMLReader object. Supported only with the SqlClient provider. Requires data source to return XML as from a FOR XML query. This is discussed in Chapter 10.

By choosing the right Command method, instead of one that creates a rowset or a DataSet, you can reduce the overhead involved in executing your query. As with ADOc, I expect that any technique that eliminates the (rather expensive) process of constructing a DataSet is another best practice.

> **TIP** *If a fatal OleDbException, OdbcException, or SqlException is generated (for example, a SQL Server severity level of 20 or greater), the Connection object may be closed. However, the application can reopen the Connection object and continue.*

The ExecuteReader method also expects you to choose a CommandBehavior option that determines how the DataReader is to be constructed. In most cases this argument instructs the .NET data provider to optimize the DataReader construction in one way or another. These command behaviors are not implemented in all of the .NET data providers—at least not in the same way. Most typically, you want to use the CloseConnection behavior. These behaviors are listed in Table 3-3.

Table 3-3. ExecuteReader CommandBehavior Arguments

Command Behavior	Description
CloseConnection	After the command is executed, the associated Connection object is closed *when the associated DataReader object is closed* so you don't need to specifically close the Connection object. The problem with this option is that it now means you *must* close the DataReader instead of the Connection object!
KeyInfo	The query returns column and primary key information. The query is executed without any locking on the selected rows. When using KeyInfo, the SQL Server .NET data provider appends a FOR BROWSE clause to the statement being executed. The user should be aware of potential side effects, such as interference with the use of SET FMTONLY ON statements. See SQL Server Books Online for more information.
SchemaOnly	The query returns column information only and does not affect the database state. This permits you to find out the structure of the SELECT statement's resultset. This is handy when creating equivalent structures on the client.
SequentialAccess	The results of the query are read sequentially to the column level. This allows an application to read large binary values (BLOB)—such as pictures—using the GetChars or GetBytes methods of a .NET data provider. Execution of the query may affect the database state.

(continued)

Table 3-3. ExecuteReader CommandBehavior Arguments (continued)

Command Behavior	Description
SingleResult	The query returns a single result. Execution of the query may affect the database state.
SingleRow	The query is expected to return a single row. Execution of the query may affect the database state. Some .NET data providers may—but are not required to—use this information to optimize the performance of the command. When you specify SingleRow with the ExecuteReader method of the OleDbCommand object, the OleDb .NET Data Provider performs binding using the OLE DB IRow interface if it is available. Otherwise, it uses the IRowset interface. If your SQL statement is expected to return only a single row, specifying SingleRow can also improve application performance. This is similar to the ADOc Recordset object.

WARNING *If you use a DataReader, you* must *make sure the Connection object gets closed. This means that if you use the CloseConnection option, you must ensure that the DataReader itself is closed before you leave scope. If you don't, your connection pool will fill and you'll start getting time-out errors.*

Another best practice is to always make sure that you choose a CommandBehavior that matches the structure you expect to get back from the query. This ExecuteReader method argument lets you disable parts of ADO.NET that are not needed to process your inbound resultset. Anything you can do to reduce this overhead will help performance.

Using ExecuteScalar

It's clear that for action queries, the ExecuteNoQuery method is the best choice unless you expect to return a single value. In this case, the ExecuteScalar would be a better choice—especially when compared to the ExecuteReader method, which assumes a rowset is to be returned. Note that when you use ExecuteScalar, ADO.NET returns only the first column of the first row in the resultset.

The following example illustrates a typical use of the ExecuteScalar method. In this case I'm simply counting the number of titles whose price is greater than ten. As with each of the DataReader methods, you have to open and (more importantly) close the Connection object when you're done.

```
private void button1_Click(object sender, System.EventArgs e) {
    try {
        SqlConnection cn = new SqlConnection(
            "data source=.;database=biblio;uid=admin;pwd=pw");
        SqlCommand cmd = new SqlCommand(
            "SELECT COUNT(*) FROM titles WHERE Price >" + txtBookPrice.Text, cn);
        int intCount;
        cn.Open();
        intCount = Convert.ToInt32(cmd.ExecuteScalar());
        MessageBox.Show(
            "Books over $" + txtBookPrice.Text + " : " + intCount.ToString());
        cn.Close();
    }
    catch { ... }
}
```

When working with XML streams, the obvious choice is the SqlClient's ExecuteXMLReader. This returns an XML data stream that can be used in a variety of ways. I revisit these methods in subsequent chapters (see Chapter 10).

 NOTE *I noticed that not all of these Command methods are implemented in all of the .NET data providers. For example, the ExecuteXMLReader method is only implemented in the SqlClient provider. Each of these methods suggests a specific type of SQL query. I discuss the ExecuteXMLReader method again in Chapter 10.*

Binding to Resultset Columns

I've been getting more and more mail on ADO.NET and too many folks are having difficulty figuring out the best/fastest/easiest/correct way to address the collections or other data structures returned by ADO.NET. For example: How should one code a reference to a desired row value buried in the DataSet Tables, Rows, and Items collections?

The following chart (Figure 3-14) illustrates the difference in performance between nine different coding techniques; I show you some of the code I used to generate it in just a minute.[24] By judicious coding you can yield up to thirteen times performance boost over techniques which rely upon resolving string literals.

The code loops through several different coding techniques one million

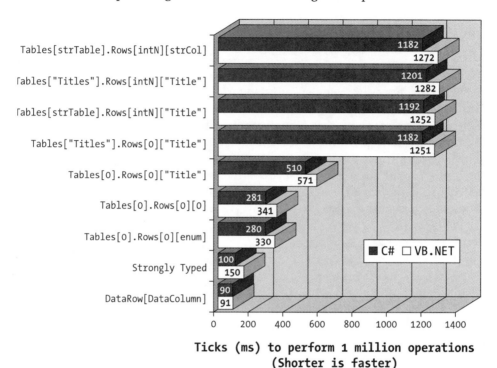

Ticks (ms) to perform 1 million operations (Shorter is faster)

Figure 3-14. Comparing .NET object reference performance

times each. This averages out the individual object reference times and provides a reasonable number to compare the benefits of each technique. Note that I used the Environment.TickCount method to capture the tick values. This is roughly equivalent to the Windows API TickCount call which simply captures the current system tick count—the number of milliseconds since the system was started. No, this is not as accurate as some other timing techniques, but it's easy to use and accurate enough for my purposes. I also expect that these tests are not particularly scientific so your mileage may vary. As with any performance claim, be sure to test the premise out on your own system with your own application and your own stopwatch.

---

24. Code is located in the "\Examples\Chapter 03\Perftest with TicCount" folder on the CD.

TIP *When testing .NET code performance always compile for "Release" and execute your project outside of the IDE. This point about outside the IDE is an important one since in my testing I found that projects—even those compiled for release—executed more than twice as slowly when launched from within the IDE.*

This first test uses the most common form of addressing—the use of literal strings such as "Titles" and "Title" to address the Tables and Items collections. Sure, this is easy for *you* to read, but it requires the CLR to add code to look up the addressed item in the collection using a serial string-comparison search. Incidentally, my test query only contained two columns, so the tests were optimized in favor of this technique. If you have more items in the collection to search, your performance gets worse—perhaps a lot worse. This particular technique took just over a second to complete (1201 milliseconds).

```
Sample1 = Environment.TickCount;
for (i = 0; i < intLoops; i++) {
    strA[i] = ds.Tables["Titles"].Rows[0]["Title"].ToString();
}
Sample2 = Environment.TickCount;
result = Sample2 - Sample1;
```

The variation on this technique where "Titles" and "Title" are passed as string variables is just a slight touch faster (1182 milliseconds).

The next technique addresses the Table object using an ordinal (number). This dramatically improves performance by directly addressing a specific item in the Tables collection. The result in this case (for a million loops) is 960 milliseconds, but I'm not done yet. *(Ahem! I hear VB .NET is just about to slip a gear.)*

```
// Test 2
Sample1 = Environment.TickCount;
for (i = 0; i < intLoops; i++) {
    strA[i] = ds.Tables[0].Rows[0]["Title"].ToString();
}
Sample2 = Environment.TickCount;
result[2] = Sample2 - Sample1;
```

The third test addresses both the Table object and the Items collection using ordinals. At this point I have eliminated both serial searches for the desired item.

This technique took 474 milliseconds—another 2X gain over the previous technique and a 4X gain over the string-literal technique in the first test (and most documentation), and 1.3X gain over the same technique in VB .NET. The problem with these last two techniques is that they don't provide very readable code—for the human developer that is. The CLR reads them just fine, it's just more difficult to figure out what's going on or how to fix it.

```
// Test 3
Sample1 = Environment.TickCount;
for (i = 0; i < intLoops; i++) {
    strA[i] = ds.Tables[0].Rows[0][0].ToString();
}
Sample2 = Environment.TickCount;
result[3] = Sample2 - Sample1;
```

The fourth test attempts to improve the readability of the second test's ordinal techniques by replacing the Items collection (column) ordinal with an enumeration. In this case I set up an enumeration to index the items in the Items collection. This enumeration corresponds to the columns returned by the SELECT statement. If this SELECT changes, you have to change the enumeration to match. The result of this change is actually poorer performance, but only by a tiny (very tiny) fraction. It also results in code that's easier to read—and far easier to code because the enumerations are available at statement completion time. The tick count for this test returned 479—five ticks longer than the all-ordinal test. Note that the Enum must be declared outside the scope of a procedure.

```
enum enuTitles { Title ,Price, PubDate }
 . . .
// Test 4
Sample1 = Environment.TickCount;
for (i = 0; i < intLoops; i++) {
    strA[i] = ds.Tables[0].Rows[0][(int) enuTitles.Title].ToString();
}
Sample2 = Environment.TickCount;
result[4] = Sample2 - Sample1;
```

Remember the best technique of all from ADOc? If you need a reminder, here's a hint: pre-binding. In this technique I declare an object ahead of time to contain the address of a chosen column. I set this address using any chosen technique, but I do so once, early in the application. After the address is set, there's no need to resolve it later when you need to retrieve data or change the value in the addressed item. Yes, you can use this technique in .NET just as you did in Visual

Basic 6.0. In this case I declared a variable `colTitle` pointing to a specific column (`Item`) of the first Table object in the DataSet. In the referencing loop I simply referred to this column object variable name. The result? Blindingly fast performance. If you can figure out how to set the object reference once (pre-bind it), and not do it each time you need to reference the object, you can eliminate virtually all performance-robbing addressing overhead. The tick count returned for this technique after one million loops was just 52 ticks. Now *that's* fast *(and VB .NET was only 1 tick behind!)*.

```
// Test 5
DataColumn colTitle = new DataColumn();
Sample1 = Environment.TickCount;
colTitle = ds.Tables[0].Columns[0];
for (i = 0; i < intLoops; i++) {
    strA[i] = colTitle.ToString();
}
Sample2 = Environment.TickCount;
result[5] = Sample2 - Sample1;
```

David Sceppa provided several hints when I was searching for a good timing technique and also suggested that creating a strongly typed DataSet would also further improve performance. The results indicated that the DataSet technique came in second—at around 220 ticks for a million operations. He thinks it's easier to code this way—I'll leave this up to you to decide after I discuss how to do this in Chapter 5. Strongly typed DataSets set up a class that contains hard-coded object references for each column in the DataSet. However, I'm not convinced that the drag-and-drop XML/XSD approach has proven itself—at least not quite yet.

Can I tear you away from your crocheting, Bill?

CHAPTER 4

ADO.NET DataReader Strategies

OK, NOW THAT YOU'VE constructed a Command and executed a SELECT query you undoubtedly want to access the data returned. As with ADOc, ADO.NET can return data in a structure that contains both schema and data and additional metadata used to help in updating the data. You can also use lighter-weight (and faster) mechanisms that simply access the low-level data stream or a single value—that's a DataReader, the subject of this chapter.

Because ADO.NET is built around XML, support for XML resultsets is also included. This chapter explores these mechanisms—examining interesting properties, methods, and events. Unlike ADOc and its relatively simple object interface, ADO.NET supports a seemingly bottomless pit of properties, methods, and constructors that can make learning how to use it a real challenge. To make things easier, I focus on just those options that form ADO.NET's core functionality and gloss over or simply bypass those more obscure operators.

With all of these choices when retrieving data, how is one to know which makes the most sense for a particular situation? Well, if your data is highly structured, the DataSet is a good match. The DataSet knows how to consume XML, provided it includes schema information. The DataSet can be populated with data providers or directly from XML as the situation demands. If you use the .NET Data Providers (such as Odbc, OleDb, or SqlClient[1]), you can leverage the OdbcCommand, SqlCommand, or OleDbCommand to do batch optimistic updates against the database.

Behind the scenes, ADO.NET uses the DataReader to execute all of its low-level I/O regardless of the data access technique you use. In the case of the SqlClient .NET Data Provider, this means submitting queries and returning resultsets at the TDS level—just like DB-Library. Why is this important? Well, it means that there are fewer (far fewer) layers between your code and the data engine, yielding better performance. If you simply need to return data rows and

---

1. I expect that by the time you read this, there will be more than three .NET Data Providers from which to choose.

don't need the overhead imposed by constructing and managing a DataSet object, the DataReader can be a good choice. If you're working with a bound control on a WebForm, you can also bind directly to a DataReader—but not on a Windows Form.

The Command object is used to tie a SELECT or action query to a Connection object—just as it does in ADOc. It also exposes the Parameters collection. It's the Command object that's used to create a DataReader—the equivalent to a firehose resultset in ADOc.

The nice thing about ADO.NET and the XML Framework is that they play well together. If you want to do XPath queries on top of the DataSet, or transform the data using XSL/T, you can map an XmlDataDocument on top of the DataSet you just populated and plug into all of the XML services. The XmlDataDocument is just a data-aware subclass of the XmlDocument. These XML details are discussed in detail in Chapter 10, "ADO.NET and XML."

Comparing ADOc with ADO.NET

It occurred to me that to help ADOc developers better understand how the ADO.NET data structures—such as the DataSet and DataReader—map to the ADOc objects, properties, and methods, there should be a Rosetta stone[2] or at least a comparison chart to highlight the differences. While Microsoft insists that ADO.NET is "just like" or "based on" COM-based ADO, I think the following table (4-1) will make it clear that this is simply not the case.

Table 4-1. ADOc Compared with ADO.NET

Operation	ADOc	DataSet	DataReader
Open Connection	Connection object or connection string	.NET Data Provider Connection object or connection string	.NET Data Provider Connection object or connection string
Set SQL for query	Source property or Open argument or Command	SelectCommand	Select Command
Run SELECT query	Open, Execute	Fill method	ExecuteReader
Run action query	Execute adExecuteNoRecords	Not recommended	ExecuteNoQuery
Run scalar query	Open, Execute	Not recommended	ExecuteScalar

(continued)

---

2. For those of you who slept through history class, the Rosetta Stone, discovered in 1799, is a black basalt slab bearing an inscription that was the key to the deciphering of Egyptian hieroglyphics and thus to the foundation of modern Egyptology (Microsoft Encarta, 2001).

Table 4-1. ADOc Compared with ADO.NET (continued)

Operation	ADOc	DataSet	DataReader
Return XML from query	Not available (except via SQL Server 2000 FOR XML)	DataSet.GetXML	ExecuteXMLReader
Specify query parameters	Command.Parameters	xxCommand.Parameters	xxCommand.Parameters
Define cursor types	FO, static, keyset, dynamic, client/ batch disconnected	Client/batch disconnected	Forward-only rowset (FO)
Define lock type	RO, optimistic, pessimistic, BatchOptimistic	Batch Optimistic	RO
Fetch first row	(Automatic)	Fill (automatic)	Read (FO)
Fetch next row	MoveNext	Not available	Read (FO)
Fetch previous row	MovePrevious	DataRow(n-1)	Not available
Fetch last row	Loop MoveNext, MoveLast	Loop read, close DataAdapter	Loop Read
Fetch n rows	GetRows, GetString, MaxRecords, SELECT TOP	SELECT TOP	Loop Read n times
Fetch row n starting at x	GetRows, GetString	Not available	Not available
Fetch multiple hierarchical rowsets	Shape provider	Fill	Read
Fetch next resultset	NextRecordset	(See Command object)	NextResult
Bind to Grid	MSHFlexGrid. Recordset DbGrid. DataSource	DataGrid.DataSource	DataGrid.DataSource (WebForm only)
# Rows returned by SELECT	RecordCount	DataView.Count	Not available

(continued)

Table 4-1. ADOc Compared with ADO.NET (continued)

Operation	ADOc	DataSet	DataReader
# Columns returned by SELECT	Fields.Count	DataTable.Items.Count	DataReader.FieldCount
Find	Find method	DataView RowFilter, DataTable Select	Not available
Sort	Sort method	DataTable Select, DataView object	Not available
Filter	Filter method	DataTable RowFilter, Select method	Not available
Seek	Seek (Jet 4.0 only)	Similar to Rows.Find	Not available
Clone	Clone	DataTable.Copy	Not available
Copy schema (only)	Not available	DataTable.Clone	Not available
Update rows	Update, UpdateBatch	DataAdapter.Update	Not available
Save, restore position	Bookmark	DataRow(n)	Use array or bind to control
Move to position	Move, AbsolutePosition, PercentPosition	DataRow(n)	Not available (only one row visible)
Create from XML	Open	DataSet.ReadXML	Not available
Persist to XML	Save adPersistXML	GetXML	Not available
Persist to binary	Save adPersistADTG	Not available	Not available
Persist to Response	Save Response	GetXML	Not available
Persist to file	Save	WriteXML	Not available

Understanding the DataReader

As you've seen from the examples in the previous chapter, the DataReader is implemented by ADO.NET's data providers as the OdbcDataReader, SqlDataReader, and OleDbDataReader. All .NET Data Providers implement a DataReader class—they have to, it's required to perform low-level data I/O operations. In addition, as a reminder, the DataReader exposes data returned from the SelectCommand property as an RO/FO, single-row stream—sort of like the ADOc firehose Recordset. However, there is little similarity between the DataReader and the Recordset. ADOc simply does not expose the low-level data I/O as we have seen in DB-Library, PL/SQL,[3] or even the ODBC API. In ADOc, if you want rowset data, you have to construct an (expensive) Recordset. That's one reason why the DataReader is so cool. If I think of another reason, you'll be the first to know.

 IMHO *One problem with the DataReader is that there is no way to bind it in Windows Forms applications (it is bindable in WebForms), and no way to extract the data in bulk. I would love to see a routine to extract to an array . . . but then one could always us the DataSet instead, which uses the DataReader behind the scenes. I just think the DataSet is like using a bulldozer to load a little red wagon.*

One important difference between the DataSet and the DataReader is how ADO.NET manages the connection used to execute the query. When you use a DataSet, ADO.NET can open and close the connection for you. However, this feature is *not* available when you use the DataReader. You *must* open the connection with the Connection object's Open method before you use one of the Execute methods. Yes, you can ask ADO.NET to close the connection for you by using the CloseConnection CommandBehavior—but the connection is only closed *if you remember to close the DataReader*! Because there is the chance that a connection might get left open, this can be a potential nightmare. Remember, if the connection is not closed before the Connection object loses scope, you're pooched;[4] it won't be long before you run out of connections and your application freezes up waiting for a free connection to continue.

As you saw in Chapter 3 in the "Exploring the Command Execute Methods" section, there are several Execute methods used to instantiate a DataReader (and execute the query). You must call one of these Execute methods—for example, the Command.ExecuteReader method of the SqlCommand object—rather than declaring and using a constructor method to instantiate the DataReader. Choosing the right Execute method (as I describe later) can have a significant impact on the performance of your query. The Command object's SelectCommand contains the

---

3. PL/SQL: the low-level protocol used by Oracle.
4. Fred wants me to define "pooched." It's like being SOL, in deep kimchi, up the creek without a paddle, or . . . well, you get the idea.

query used to populate the DataReader—assuming you want a rowset. However, you can (should) also use the DataReader to execute action queries—such as INSERT, UPDATE, DELETE, or maintenance queries. ADO.NET has a number of tuned Execute methods designed just for this purpose, which further improves performance by circumventing the row-retrieval mechanism. This approach is the same one you used with the adExecuteNoRecords option in ADOc.

After the DataReader is opened, the associated Connection object is blocked and cannot be used for other operations until the DataReader.Close method is executed; remember this also closes the connection if (and only if) you used the CloseConnection CommandBehavior. This is no different from what went on behind the scenes in ADOc. If you tried to execute another query in ADOc but the connection was tied up populating a Recordset, ADOc often created and opened another Connection object to execute the query behind the black curtains.

When working with any of the DataReader objects, you *must* use the Read method first to read the first row—and each subsequent row. That's because when the DataReader is initialized, its current row pointer is positioned *before* the first row for some reason. So, if you don't use Read before trying to "get" DataReader data, you get an exception: "Invalid attempt to read when no data is present." While the name and datatype of the columns returned are available, the data is not—not until you execute the first Read.

When Read returns False, there is no (further) data. When working with ADOc, you had to remember to use the MoveNext method to position the current row pointer to the next available row in the rowset. In ADO.NET, you have to remember to use the Read method *before* you attempt to access the row. I'm sure no one will be confused by this change. At least not until it has bit them about a thousand times. The following diagram (Figure 4-1) illustrates the difference.

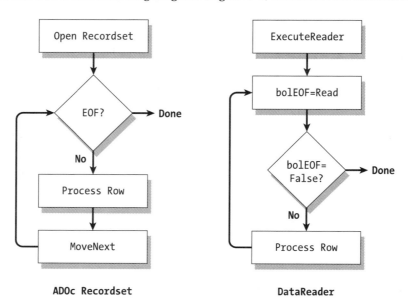

Figure 4-1. ADOc Recordset versus the ADO.NET DataReader processing loop

The DataReader FieldCount property can be used to return the number of columns in the current row. The RecordsAffected property returns the number of rows affected by the last action query (not the current SELECT). RecordsAffected returns -1 except for action queries. This choice of names is a little strange since most references to ADO.NET data refers to "Rows" and "Columns," not "Fields" and "Records" as in ADOc. I guess someone didn't get the memo about this change.

After the DataReader is closed, you can reference (just) the RecordsAffected property and the IsClosed property. The DataReader properties are listed in the following table (4-2). No, there is no RecordCount property to see how many rows were returned by the query—not when working with a DataReader. However, if you remember, the ADOc Recordset didn't have a RecordCount either; it always returned -1 on its default firehose cursor. You had to activate a full-blown cursor—static, keyset, or (heaven forbid) dynamic—to get a valid RecordCount.

Instead of forcing developers to use the DataSet for everything, ADO.NET consciously implemented a separate mechanism for the DataReader. Although it has very few features, its simplicity and proximity to the low-level I/O protocols makes it a very efficient way to extract data from your data source. My tests show it to be very fast—even when it had to retrieve individual rows and do column-by-column data extractions.

Tables 4-2 lists the properties of a (typical[5]) DataReader.

Table 4-2. DataReader Properties

Property	Purpose
Depth	Gets a value indicating the depth of nesting for the current row. This is important for hierarchical resultsets.
FieldCount	Gets the number of columns in the current row.
IsClosed	Gets a value indicating whether or not the DataReader is closed.
Item	Gets the value of a column in its native format. In C#, this property is the indexer for the DataReader.
RecordsAffected	Gets the number of rows changed, inserted, or deleted by execution of the action query. Always -1 for SELECT queries.

The DataReader "operational" methods are used to Read the data rows, close them, position to the next resultset of a multiple-resultset query, and otherwise manage the DataReader class. Table 4-3 lists these methods.

---

5. Each .NET Data Provider can implement the DataReader as it sees fit. Some properties might not appear in all providers' DataReader objects or they might work differently.

Table 4-3. DataReader Operational Methods

Method	Purpose
Close	Closes the DataReader object. If you set Command object's Execute method CommandBehavior to CloseConnection; this also closes the associated Connection object.
GetName	Gets the name of the specified column given its number.
GetOrdinal	Gets the column number (ordinal) given the name of the column.
GetSchemaTable	Returns a DataTable that describes the column metadata of the DataReader.
IsDBNull	Gets a value indicating whether or not the column contains non-existent or missing values. Be sure to use this method when columns might contain NULL before using other data Get methods. I show an example of this later in this chapter.
NextResult	Advances the data reader to the next result, when reading the results of batch SQL statements.
Read	Advances the DataReader to the next row in the resultset. Returns False if there are no (more) rows.

The following methods (Table 4-4) are those inherited from the DataReader object's parent object.

Table 4-4. DataReader Common Methods Inherited from Parent Object

Method	Purpose
Equals (inherited from Object)	Overloaded. Determines whether two Object instances are equal.
GetType (inherited from Object)	Gets the Type of the current instance.
GetHashCode (inherited from Object)	Serves as a hash function for a particular type, suitable for use in hashing algorithms and data structures like a hash table.
GetLifetimeService (inherited from MarshalByRefObject)	Retrieves a lifetime service object that controls the lifetime policy for this instance. For the default Lifetime service this will be an object of type ILease.

(continued)

Table 4-4. DataReader Common Methods Inherited from Parent Object (continued)

Method	Purpose
InitializeLifetimeService (inherited from MarshalByRefObject)	Objects can provide their own lease and so control their own lifetime. They do this by overriding the InitializeLifetimeService method provided on MarshalByRefObject.
ToString (inherited from Object)	Returns a String that represents the current Object.

Once positioned to a row of data in the DataReader, you'll discover there is no collection of Field objects (as you used in ADOc) to access the data. Instead, you're faced with a long list of "Get" methods—one for each datatype supported and another (GetValue) that tries to figure out the datatype. You can index the Get methods using either the ordinal (column number) or the column name, but I recommend use of the ordinal or an enumeration that maps the inbound columns to their ordinal.

Table 4-5 lists the Get data-retrieval methods. Each .NET Data Provider's DataReader implementation supports these basic datatypes.

Table 4-5. DataReader Get methods Common to All Providers

Method	Purpose
GetBoolean	Gets the value of the specified column as a Boolean.
GetByte	Gets the value of the specified column as a Byte.
GetBytes	Reads a stream of bytes from the specified column offset into the buffer as an array starting at the given buffer offset.
GetChar	Gets the value of the specified column as a single character.
GetChars	Reads a stream of characters from the specified column offset into the buffer as an array starting at the given buffer offset.
GetData	(Not currently supported.)
GetDataTypeName	Gets the name of the source datatype.
GetDateTime	Gets the value of the specified column as a DateTime object.
GetDecimal	Gets the value of the specified column as a Decimal object.
GetDouble	Gets the value of the specified column as a double-precision floating point number.
GetFieldType	Gets the Type that is the datatype of the object.

(continued)

Table 4-5. DataReader Get methods Common to All Providers (continued)

Method	Purpose
GetFloat	Gets the value of the specified column as a single-precision floating point number.
GetGuid	Gets the value of the specified column as a globally-unique identifier (GUID).
GetInt16	Gets the value of the specified column as a 16-bit signed integer.
GetInt32	Gets the value of the specified column as a 32-bit signed integer.
GetInt64	Gets the value of the specified column as a 64-bit signed integer.
GetString	Gets the value of the specified column as a string.
GetValue	Gets the value of the specified column in its native format.
GetValues	Gets all attribute columns in the collection for the current row.

The following methods are unique to the SqlClient .NET Data Provider and are used to access native datatypes returned from SQL Server.

Table 4-6. DataReader Get Methods Unique to SqlClient Provider

Method	Purpose
GetSqlBinary	Gets the value of the specified column as a SqlBinary.
GetSqlBoolean	Gets the value of the specified column as a SqlBoolean.
GetSqlByte	Gets the value of the specified column as a SqlByte.
GetSqlDateTime	Gets the value of the specified column as a SqlDateTime.
GetSqlDecimal	Gets the value of the specified column as a SqlDecimal.
GetSqlDouble	Gets the value of the specified column as a SqlDouble.
GetSqlGuid	Gets the value of the specified column as a SqlGuid.
GetSqlInt16	Gets the value of the specified column as a SqlInt16.

(continued)

Table 4-6. DataReader Get Methods Unique to SqlClient Provider (continued)

Method	Purpose
GetSqlInt32	Gets the value of the specified column as a SqlInt32.
GetSqlInt64	Gets the value of the specified column as a SqlInt64.
GetSqlMoney	Gets the value of the specified column as a SqlMoney.
GetSqlSingle	Gets the value of the specified column as a SqlSingle.
GetSqlString	Gets the value of the specified column as a SqlString.
GetSqlValue	Gets an Object that is a representation of the underlying SqlDbType Variant. In other words, you choose the datatype to fetch as an input parameter.
GetSqlValues	Gets all the attribute columns in the current row.

TIP *For optimal performance, DataReader avoids creating unnecessary objects or making unnecessary copies of data. As a result, multiple calls to methods such as* GetValue(System.Int32) *return a reference to the same object. Use caution if you are modifying the underlying value of the objects returned by methods such as* GetValue(System.Int32).

Using the DataReader Get Methods to Retrieve Data

I thought you might like an example[6] showing how to extract data from a DataReader using one or more of these myriad methods. The following code illustrates a couple of techniques that might prove helpful. As much as I hate to do it, the only way to access DataReader resultset data is via a row loop—unless you resort to constructing a DataSet from the DataReader.

---

6. Located in the "\Examples\Chapter 04\DataReader GetValues" folder on the CD.

WARNING   *One of the issues you'll have to deal with as you work with the Get methods is figuring out which Get method to use for each datatype returned by the query. For example, in a demo I wrote for VBits, I returned the Discount column from the Customers table. Its datatype was defined as a float (8). When I executed the GetDataTypeName method, ADO.NET returned "float". Cool. But the GetFloat method did not work. Only after repeated experimentation did I discover that the DataReader expected me to use GetSqlDouble to fetch this value. You'll want to use the correct Get method though and not fall back on the GetValue method as it costs more time and resources to execute.*

The following example illustrates using an OleDb .NET Data Provider to open a connection, run a simple query, and use an OleDbDataReader to return the values from the rowset returned. In this example, I used as many constructors as I could to illustrate how they can simplify the code. After you get used to them, constructors are pretty intuitive and should not pose a real problem for you. The first few lines construct the Connection object, the Command, and the DataReader. Note that you can't use a constructor when creating the DataReader—it's initialized (and constructed) by the ExecuteReader method.

```
private void btnFind_Click(object sender, System.EventArgs e)
{
    try
    {
        OleDbConnection cn = new OleDbConnection("Provider=SQLOLEDB.1; "
            +"Integrated Security=SSPI;Initial Catalog=biblio;Data Source=.");
        OleDbCommand sc = new OleDbCommand(
          "SELECT TOP 10 Title, Price FROM Titles WHERE title LIKE '"
            + txtTitleWanted.Text + "'", cn);
        OleDbDataReader dr;
```

Now you're ready to open the connection. Because you're not filling a DataSet (with the Fill() method), ADO.NET won't open the connection for you. This also means that you need to make sure it gets closed when you're done. You can accomplish this by using the CommandBehavior.CloseConnection option when you use the Command ExecuteReader() method and by remembering to close the DataReader before it falls out of scope. The ShowRows routine dumps the data to a ListBox control.

```
        cn.Open();


        dr = sc.ExecuteReader(CommandBehavior.CloseConnection);

        if (dr.FieldCount > 0)
        {
            ShowRows(dr);
        }
        else
        {
            Console.WriteLine("No rowset in this result set");
        }
        dr.Close();
    }
    catch { ... }
}
```

The ShowRows routine dumps the data rows from the DataReader column-by-column and row-by-row. Make sure to test for DBNull values or you'll end up with trappable exceptions. The CLR is not very forgiving when it gets a data exception. I guess those coming from Visual Basic were just spoiled for too many years.

```
private void ShowRows(OleDbDataReader pDr )
{
    try
    {
        int intRow = 0;
        string strData;
        string strPrice;
        ListBox1.Items.Clear();
        while (pDr.Read())
        {

            if (pDr.IsDBNull(1))
            {
                strPrice = "UK";
            }
            else
            {
                strPrice = pDr.GetDecimal(1).ToString();
            }
```

```
                    strData = strPrice + "\t" + pDr.GetString(0);
                    intRow = ListBox1.Items.Add(strData);
            }
            if (ListBox1.Items.Count == 0)
            {
                    ListBox1.Items.Add("No data found!");
            }
        }
    }
    catch { ... }
}
```

I'd like to mention a couple more points before I move on. First, if you don't use a specific Get method that matches the datatype being returned in your rowset, you'll get a trappable exception. However, you can try to use the GetValue method because it seems to work for a variety of data sources. For example, the Price column returned from the titles table is defined in the SQL Server database as Smallmoney (used to store values too insignificant to give a congressman). When I tried GetFloat and GetDouble, I tripped an exception; however, GetValue worked—seemingly as well as GetDecimal. Because this code was written using the OleDb .NET Data Provider, the GetSqlMoney method was not available. However, I recoded and retested using the SqlClient .NET Data Provider and found that GetSqlMoney worked fine—but there was no Get method for Smallmoney.

Next, the preceding code does not illustrate the (mandatory) try/catch exception handler needed to prevent data exceptions (situations where the data does not match the expected datatype) from crashing your application. I discuss exception handling in Chapter 9, "ADO.NET Exception Management Strategies."

I'm not thrilled with designs that loop through resultsets column-by-column and row-by-row as illustrated here. I show you how to use the GetValues() method next—it eliminates the inner loop. Perhaps they perform fast enough to overcome my concerns. I do know that ADO.NET and the CLR are doing some fancy footwork to manage the pointers used in this technique to make things work as quickly as possible, but I expect your mileage will vary from provider to provider.

Using GetValues to Fetch a Row

If you want to get an entire row at a time, you can use the GetValues() method to extract the data into an array of type object[]. In this case, you simply declare an array that has enough elements to hold all of the data columns you want to extract. If the array is too small (but instantiated), ADO.NET stops processing columns after the array row is filled. (You can pass a larger than necessary array without any difficulties.) I set the array to fit the number of columns returned. A single call to GetValues() loads the array. In my testing I found that this method was (usually) very slightly faster than using the various Get methods of the last section and certainly more convenient to use.

```csharp
private void ShowRowsGet(OleDbDataReader pDr )
{
    object[] strData = new object [pDr.FieldCount];
    string strValues;
    int intCr;
    ListBox1.Items.Clear();
    try
    {
        while (pDr.Read())
        {
            intCr = pDr.GetValues(strData);
            strValues = "";
            for(int intCol = 0; intCol <= intCr - 1; intCol++)
            {
                if (Convert.IsDBNull(strData[intCol]))
                {
                    strValues += " < null > ";
                }
                else
                {
                    strValues += strData[intCol].ToString() + "\t";
                }

            }
            ListBox1.Items.Add(strValues);
        }
    }
    catch { ... }
}
```

Cleaning Up After Your DataReader

As a best practice you should *always* close your ADO.NET Connection and DataReader objects—especially because ADO.NET is not opening and closing the Connection object for you (as it does when you use the Fill() method against a closed Connection). Unlike Visual Basic 6.0, where you could set an object to Nothing to release its resources, .NET has no guarantee regarding when objects may be cleaned up. This is because the .NET CLR is a garbage-collected environment. Since the DataReader, the Connection object and the pooled server connection hold valuable system and server resources, they must be closed as soon as they are no longer needed in order to free their resources. Even more significant, there may be issues with some providers that require that their resources be freed by the same thread that created them.

One easy technique is to automate this process as illustrated in the previous example. That's where I used the `CommandBehavior.CloseConnection` that closes the Connection object for me after the DataReader is closed. If you leave this option out of the ExecuteReader method call, you have to close the Connection object yourself—or suffer the consequences (eventually). You still need to remember to close the DataReader when you're done with it.

CHAPTER 5

Using the DataTable and DataSet

WE'VE COME A LONG WAY TOWARD learning about ADO.NET, but so far I've glossed over most of the details you need to understand ADO.NET's newest concept: the DataSet. Well, it's all new for ADOc developers. The ADO.NET DataSet is basically a collection of DataTable objects with a mechanism to tie the tables together relationally and manage those tables as related sets of data. It also serves as a data source for bound controls. This means you won't need a separate data source control—such as an ADO Data Control—to bind resultsets to data-aware controls.

As I've said before, the DataSet is different in a number of ways. First, it's designed to handle one or many resultsets by managing one or many DataTable objects. If you add code to interrelate these DataTable objects, you can bind to complex hierarchical controls—such as the ADO.NET DataGrid control—or navigate in code from parent to child to grandchild (and beyond). For the ADOc developer, the DataSet can be somewhat daunting at first, but this chapter should clear up the mysteries.

The DataTable object is an *in memory* data store and is about as close to an ADOc Recordset as you're going to get in ADO.NET. However, the Recordset is about as similar to the DataTable as a 1975 Ford pickup is to a fancy SUV. When was the last time you loaded a half-ton of loose zoo-doo into the back of your new Acura MDX? But, at the same time, if your goal is to impress your new boss, driving up in an old pickup full of manure will probably not help your ascent up the job ladder.

The ADOc Recordset and DataTable end up doing many of the same things with your data, but each has its own particular benefits and shortcomings. Both have their own unique set of properties, methods, events, and most importantly, unique behaviors. Consider that the Recordset traces its lineage back to ISAM data sources that required bookmarks, percent-position, and other row-oriented navigation techniques used by the dBase and Jet data access architectures. In contrast, ADO.NET DataTable objects don't support any type of "scrolling"—you simply fill a DataTable and position to any row desired by number. The DataTable does not support any of the Move methods—it does not need to.

This chapter will help you understand the differences and similarities between the ADOc Recordset and the new ADO.NET DataTable and DataSet (at least that's the goal). The next chapter focuses on sorting, filtering, and finding data after you've populated your DataSet and DataTable objects. I first introduced the DataSet in previous chapters, so I won't revisit the rationale and code behind its construction. At this point, it's time to discuss how to *use* the DataSet and its collection of DataTable objects.

I think you'll find the DataTable and DataSet are pretty flexible—despite being very different from the ADOc Recordset. Both the DataTable and DataSet support lots of ways to manage the rows returned—many (but not nearly all) of the features exposed by the Recordset are supported by the DataSet or DataTable, but usually in different ways. Then again, the ADO.NET paradigm has some "new and improved" features that the Recordset will never have[1]— but I suspect there is a feature or six exposed by the ADOc Recordset that you might also miss.

NOTE *No, the Data**Table** object does not necessarily "map" to a specific table in the database. It might, but generally, that would be a poor design choice. Think of the DataTable as an in-memory cache of data and Data Description Language (DDL) reflecting a single-rowset product of a query.*

Data passed to the DataTable can come from virtually anywhere—one or more databases, XML, your own code, mail, or anywhere else (okay, not parts of rural Sandpoint, Idaho, but *almost* anywhere else). In addition, data can be drawn from more than one source at a time—each rowset managed in a separate DataTable object. However, any primary-key/foreign-key relationships between these rowsets (stored in the DataTable objects) are up to you to define; don't worry, I'll show you how. The .NET IDE provides a way to use drag-and-drop to define these relationships and construct an XSL schema to manage them.

An important and often glossed-over feature of the DataTable is its ability to have additional data appended to it or merged with it. That is, when you open an ADOc Recordset, you're stuck with the rowset population. Sure, you can use the AddNew method to add more rows, but you can't run another query and append the rows to the end of a Recordset or, better yet, merge rows from another Recordset into an existing Recordset. Both of these features are built into a DataTable. This means that if you have an existing DataTable and you use the DataAdapter Fill method to run a query, the DataTable will have both the original set of rows *and* the new set. As Arte Johnson used to say, "Interesting. Very interesting—but weird."

After the DataTable is filled with data, you can find or position to a specific DataRow in the Rows collection. If there is more than one DataTable in a DataSet

---

1.   I wouldn't be shocked if there was another revision of the MDAC stack that did anything but provide additional compatibility with ADO.NET.

and you define the intertable relationships, you can locate and navigate to related children. For example, if you have Customer and Addresses DataTable objects and define the columns that define the relationship, you can choose a specific customer and then navigate to each related address. Even the basic DataSet supports use of a (fairly limited) SELECT query to get a subset of the rows meeting a criterion, filter out a subset of the rows, sort the rows, and much more. By the time you finish this chapter, you'll know how to do all of this (I hope).

Understanding the DataSet and DataTable Structure

Before I start wading into the specifics of the DataTable and DataSet methods and properties, you need a better understanding of what these objects look like under the hood. As I said, these ADO.NET objects don't really resemble the Recordset, so I'll have to start from scratch. Let's revisit the chart you saw in Chapter 1; it's the same chart, but now it's named Figure 5-1.

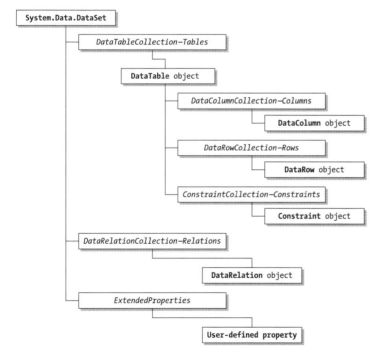

Figure 5-1. ADO.NET DataSet object hierarchy.

NOTE *This chart was originally drawn based on the namespace definitions exposed by the .NET object browser. I had a bit of trouble using this chart when coding until I realized that it is not really helpful. Sure, it reflects the System.Data.DataSet namespace, but it does not reflect how one codes to the namespace. Sigh. For example, once I construct a DataSet, the DataTables that make up this DataSet are referenced as items in the* Tables *collection—not the DataTableCollection. Unlike Visual Basic 6.0's object browser that shows all of the objects we code to (by the names we use in code), the Visual Studio .NET IDE's object browser does not. Nowhere does it show the Tables, Rows, or Columns collections. Double sigh. I guess their C++ obfuscation bit was set when they designed this part of the IDE. Isn't that* special?

The code used to reference these collections is, fortunately, brutally simple and very intuitive once you discover the right object collection names. The Table objects returned from a query into a DataSet can be referenced as follows. I show you how to build a DataSet in a minute.

```
private DataTable dt = new DataTable();
dt = ds.Tables[0];
```

In a similar fashion, the DataColumn and DataRow objects in the DataTable object are referenced through the Columns and Rows collections respectively.

```
DataColumn dcFirst;
DataRow drowFirst;
drowFirst = dt.Rows[0];
dcFirst = dt.Columns[0];
```

Are you having fun yet? Fortunately, all of these collections are highly intuitive—better yet, they match the terms I've been using in relational databases for decades. I corrected the chart (Figure 5-1) to add the "correct" collection object names.

Consider that a query can result in the creation of one or several DataTable objects—as when executing a multiple-resultset stored procedure or simply a query containing several SELECT statements. If you construct a DataSet to administer the DataTable object(s) and their interrelationships, the DataSet manages the DataTables and the DataRelation objects in three separate collections (Table 5-1):

Table 5-1. DataSet Collections

DATASET COLLECTIONS	PURPOSE
DataTableCollection (Tables)	0 to *n* DataTable objects used to hold schema and data.
DataRelationCollection (Relations)	0 to *n* DataRelation objects used to hold inter-DataTable relationships.
ExtendedProperties	0 to *n* DataSet properties

TIP *I spend most of the time discussing the first of these three collections—the DataTableCollection and the knobs and switches in the DataTable objects it contains. Remember that you need to refer to the DataTableCollection as* Tables *in code.*

Typed Versus Untyped DataSets

ADO.NET introduces the concept of "typed" and "untyped" DataSets. A typed DataSet—sometimes referred to as a "strongly typed DataSet"—exposes the DataTable name and each column name as objects visible at design time. To implement a typed DataSet, you can spend a couple of hours writing code and laying out an XSD file to describe each and every object or you can get the Visual Studio IDE to do it for you.

IMHO *I'm not convinced (at this point) that strongly typed DataSets are the best way to go; but they are a fast techique. Setting them up and keeping the extra code straight might be enough to send some poor developer over the edge; but using this technique results in faster object addressing. See the end of Chapter 3 for details.*

After you create a strongly typed DataSet, ADO.NET promotes the tables and column references to "first-class" objects by name. This permits you to reference tables and columns using named object-style dot notation as if the columns were individually named objects in the namespace (because they are). That is, you can reference the DataSet DataTable(s) by name along with the columns returned by the query as shown here:

```
string strCustName = Ds.Customers[intRow].CustName;
```

In this case, the typed DataSet exposes the CustName column in a specified (intRow) row of the Customers table.

Unless you specifically create a strongly typed DataSet, ADO.NET exposes your DataSet as untyped. In the case of an untyped DataSet, the DataSet has no schema associated with it at design time because the DataSet's structure is exposed only as collections—as I have discussed up to this point. So, to expose the same data using an untyped DataSet, you might code:

```
string strCustName = ds.Tables["Customers"].Rows[intRow]["CustName"].ToString();
```

In this case, there are at least three run-time bindings that must be resolved to fetch a single string value. There are more opportunities for error and (as I have shown) considerably slower performance.

Typed DataSets are certainly easier for humans to read, assuming you recognize what you're seeing. They are also supported by Visual Studio IntelliSense™ so the object names appear in the statement drop-down list as shown in the following figure (Figure 5-2). In this example, the individual columns City, CustID, CustName, and Discount are exposed in the IntelliSense drop-down list.

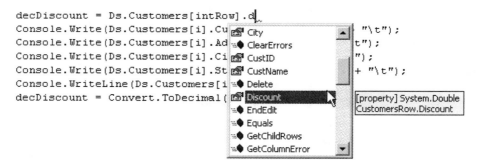

Figure 5-2. IntelliSense exposing DataSet members.

Another benefit of typed DataSets is their built-in type checking. That is, you don't (always) have to take special steps to ensure that assignments to and from typed DataSets are correct—the compiler does this for you before run time.

Generally, you'll find that Visual Studio .NET uses XSD schemas and typed DataSets quite widely. While you can use either type of DataSet in your applications, Visual Studio has more tool support for typed DataSets, and they make programming with the DataSet easier and less error-prone.

Addressing Data in DataSet Objects

As I illustrated in the discussion at the end of Chapter 3, there are several basic choices for addressing data in DataSet objects that don't require you to provide a string to address a specific DataTable in the Tables collection or a specific column in the Columns collection. While most of the examples in this book don't use these techniques, use of ordinal, strongly typed DataSets or prebinding is a better choice. That is, instead of coding:

```
DataTable dt = myDataSet.Tables["Titles"];
```

you would code:

```
DataTable dt = myDataSet.Tables[0];
```

This also applies to all situations where you use a string to refer to a member of a collection—in ADO.NET or anywhere else. So, if you're interested in performance, don't get hooked on using string-referenced collection members.

Typed DataSets have a lot to offer—as you saw at the end of Chapter 3. They provide one of the fastest techniques for addressing data in DataSets, but they do come attached with a maintenance price tag. So, when the structure of the underlying data changes on say a remote data source (for example, fields are deleted, renamed, added, etc.), then you may very well find that you need to reengineer (and redistribute) the typed DataSet.

Constructing Strongly Typed DataSets

In order to construct a strongly typed DataSet, you or the Visual Studio IDE have to construct XSD schema and named DataSet.cs[2] files to instantiate your DataSet *based on the XSD,* instead of on the base DataSet object in the System.Data namespace. This simple fact is difficult to harvest from the MSDN documentation on typed DataSets. While it seems more-or-less obvious now that I understand how it's done, I hope this section makes the revelation easier for you. I show lots of examples of constructing strongly typed DataSets in this section, using both Visual Studio and more "manual" techniques.

---

2.   Or DataSet.vb file.

TIP *At run time you can also construct and save an existing DataSet's schema by using the WriteXmlSchema method. This file can be used subsequently to construct a typed DataSet.*

To make this process easy, the Visual Studio IDE exposes drag-and-drop techniques used to generate the XSD and C# (or VB) files for typed DataSets. I discussed these techniques in Chapter 2 when I walked you through creating DataSet's using the IDE. I won't go through this again, but this is an easy way to generate both the XSD and language-specific files.

Another (more difficult) way to construct the language-specific file from an existing XSD file is to use the .NET Framework SDK executable XSD.exe. This utility generates the new XSD-specific DataSet class to be included into your project. The XSD.exe-generated C# file for a relatively simple DataSet is about 15K in size and contains a considerable amount of code used to implement the typed DataSet based on the XSD.

For those into command-line development, the syntax for generating a DataSet using the XSD.exe command-line tool is as follows:

```
xsd.exe /d /l:CS XSDSchemaFileName.xsd /n:XSDSchema.Namespace
```

In this syntax, the /d directive tells the tool to generate a DataSet (the source code for the XSD-based DataSet). The /l: tells the tool what language to use—for example, C# (CS) or Visual Basic .NET (VB). The optional /n: directive tells the tool to generate a namespace for the DataSet—in this case called XSDSchema.Namespace. The output of the command is—based on the /l:CS argument—XSDSchemaFileName.cs, which can be compiled and used in an ADO.NET application. The generated code can be compiled as a library or a module.

For example, with a typed DataSet, the CustName column of the first row of the Customers DataSet is addressed as follows:

```
strCustName = dsCustOrders1.Customers[0].CustName;
```

In contrast, if you are working with an untyped DataSet, the equivalent code is:

```
dsCustOrders1.Tables["Customers"].Rows[0]["CustName"].ToString();
```

Access to tables and columns in a typed DataSet is also faster at run time because when a newly typed DataSet is instantiated, all its component-exposed table and column objects are bound to tables and columns in the DataSet—actually using literal addressing techniques. But, this is a one-time binding cost since, thereafter, access is through these bound objects rather than through the resolution of any string literals or ordinals.

NOTE *Consider that this language-specific file is based on an XSD file that was, in turn, created ahead of time based on a known database resultset schema. This means that if the database or query schema changes, even subtly, the approach breaks down. I also expect that the considerable code required to implement the XSD-derived DataSet class will be expensive to execute—at least initially—so this approach might warrant close evaluation for performance when compared with untyped DataSets.*

Manually Assembling a Strongly Typed DataSet

I'm not a whole-hearted fan of the drag-and-drop approaches exposed by Visual Studio. For the most part, this is because of the voluminous code that Visual Studio crams into my application behind the scenes—code that's sometimes unneeded and often difficult for "ordinary" developers to fathom, debug, or remove when things go wrong. Because of this, I figured out how to create a strongly typed DataSet of my own using Visual Studio's drag-and-drop IDE-generated XSD DataSets, the automatically generated DataSet.cs files, and a few other lines of code. The example of this implementation is on the book's CD[3] and the highlights are described here. To accomplish this, follow these steps:

1. Create a new project.

2. Use the drag-and-drop techniques to drag **DataAdapter** to the form.

3. Complete the dialogs to establish a connection to a selected data source.

4. Specify how the DataSet is to be constructed—either with an SQL query or a stored procedure—with or without parameters.

5. Use the **Generate DataSet** dialog to create a DataSet.

---

3. Located in the "\Examples\Chapter 05\Typed DataSet Construction" folder.

6. Save the generated XSD and C# files in the **Solution Explorer** window.

7. Drill down into the **Windows Form Designer Generated Code** and locate the Visual Studio-generated line of code that includes the TableMappings block. Copy that line into the working clipboard. Without setting the TableMappings, the DataSet will seem like it's set up correctly, but ADO.NET will not populate the DataSet properly. This mapping block will look something like this:

```
this.da.TableMappings.AddRange(new System.Data.Common.DataTableMapping[]
{
    new System.Data.Common.DataTableMapping
    ("Table", "Customers",
      new System.Data.Common.DataColumnMapping[]
      {
          new System.Data.Common.DataColumnMapping("CustName", "CustName"),
          new System.Data.Common.DataColumnMapping("Discount", "Discount"),
          new System.Data.Common.DataColumnMapping("Addr1", "Addr1"),
          new System.Data.Common.DataColumnMapping("Addr2", "Addr2"),
          new System.Data.Common.DataColumnMapping("City", "City"),
          new System.Data.Common.DataColumnMapping("StateCode", "StateCode"),
          new System.Data.Common.DataColumnMapping("Zip", "Zip"),
          new System.Data.Common.DataColumnMapping("AddrID", "AddrID"),
          new System.Data.Common.DataColumnMapping("CustID", "CustID")
      }
    )
});
```

8. Return to the target project (or create a new one).

9. Add the XSD and C# files created earlier to the new project by right-clicking and choosing **Add Existing Item** in the Solutions Explorer window. These two files should now appear in your Solution Explorer.

10. Paste the **TableMappings** code into your form's or class's constructor method.

11. Declare your Connection, DataAdapter, DataTable, and Command objects as usual.

12. Declare the typed DataSet using a reference to the XSD-generated C# DataSet added to your project. See the following example.

13. After this, you can reference the table and its columns as named references in the code.

The following code declares an instance of the strongly typed DataSet dsTitles (as constructed with the DataSet generation dialog). It then declares a variable, tRow, to address a new DataRow as returned by the dsStrong.Titles.NewTitlesRow() method. Next, I populate tRow with new data, and then add this to the Titles table in the strongly ty   ped DataSet by calling the AddTitlesRow() method. I can now address the row. Of course, I could have populated the DataSet by calling a Fill() method on an appropriate DataAdapter. Simple? Perhaps, for an OO purist.

```
dsTitles dsStrong = new dsTitles();
dsTitles.TitlesRow tRow = dsStrong.Titles.NewTitlesRow();
tRow.Title = "ADO and ADO.NET Examples and Best Practices, Second Edition";
tRow.ISBN = "1893115682";
tRow.BookNo = 1;
{ . . . populate the rest of the required Fields . . . }
dsStrong.Titles.AddTitlesRow(tRow);
string strA = dsStrong.Titles[0].Title;
```

Using Untyped DataSets

Without this XSD schema information, your application must provide the column mapping on its own—ideally by ordinal (column number) or by name (not so ideal). Unfortunately, if you use by-name referencing, this slows down the run-time code considerably[4] because of late binding; so, typed DataSets are preferred whenever possible. You may find it beneficial to instantiate and bind DataRow and/or DataColumn objects for use in referencing with untyped DataSets; in some circumstances this can provide roughly a ten percent increase in performance over using strongly typed DataSets alone.

You might find it impossible or impractical to create a strongly typed DataSet—as when you simply don't know how the DataSet will be structured ahead of time, or when the structure is subject to change. Creating XSD files against multiple-resultset stored procedures can also be problematic. In any case, strongly typed DataSets are probably not a good idea in the early stages of database development when the schema is not firmly nailed down and is still subject to change.

---

4. A double-string reference (ds["Titles"].Rows[0]["ISBN"]) vs. an all-ordinal reference (ds[0].Rows[0][0]) is over 3 times slower (1726 vs. 528 ticks per million operations).

More generally, there are many times when you might create a DataSet dynamically without having a schema available. In this case, the DataSet is simply a convenient structure in which you can keep information, as long as the data can be represented in a relational way. At the same time, you can take advantage of the DataSet's capabilities, such as the ability to serialize the information to pass to another process or to write out an XML file.

Importing ADOc Recordsets

One of the first things people migrating from ADOc will want to do is import an ADOc Recordset returned from a middle-tier component into an ADO.NET data structure of some kind, for example a DataTable in a DataSet. Most likely, your ADOc COM component has been in place for some time, but you want to be able to leverage that work and the data it returns in a .NET application. Well, good news: ADO.NET can import that ADOc Recordset with a simple single call to a DataAdapter's Fill() method. However, the bad news is that the only DataAdapter that supports this is OleDbDataAdapter. The further bad news is that there is not (yet) an automated mechanism for extracting a Recordset from a DataTable. This means that you will have to be responsible for marshaling any changes occurring on the DataTable back into your recordset if you need the changes updated to that recordset.

 IMHO *This is a serious oversight on Microsoft's part and I think this should be resolved soon. That does not mean it will be, but I still think it's too big a problem for Microsoft to ignore for long.*

The following example illustrates use of the OleDbDataAdapter Fill method to import an ADOc Recordset. The full example is provided on the CD.[5]

```
private void btnImportRS_Click(object sender, System.EventArgs e) {
OleDbDataAdapter da = new OleDbDataAdapter();
DataSet ds = new DataSet();
da.Fill(ds, ADOcRs, "AuthorsByYearBorn");
DataGrid1.DataSource = ds.Tables[0];
}
```

---

5.   Located in the "\Examples\Chapter 05\Import ADOc Recordset (OleDB)" folder.

After the Recordset is imported you're free to bind it to controls, update it, and execute whatever code you choose (against the DataSet) to update it. No, there is no direct mechanism to export the Recordset. You might try saving the data to XML and reconstructing an ADOc Recordset from this XML; but that would be a waste of time. The XML format persisted and understood by ADOc is, shall I say, "different" from that used by ADO.NET; ADOc uses XDR (XML-Data Reduced[6]) and ADO.NET uses XSD schema format. I hear that Microsoft is working on an XSL transform to permit you to export your ADO.NET data back to ADOc. This is a pretty squeaky wheel so I expect this converter will be done before long.

TIP *The* `Fill()` *method, once it has "imported" a Recordset to a* `DataSet` `DataTable`, *tries to be helpful and always closes any Recordset it is passed. This might not be what you want; so, if you need to keep the Recordset around after* `Fill()`, *then pass a clone of the Recordset to the* `Fill()` *method instead. For example:*

```
da.Fill(ds, ADOcRs.Clone(LockTypeEnum.adLockUnspecified),
"AuthorsByYearBorn");
```

Also don't forget that you will probably want to disconnect the recordset from the connection with a `Recordset.ActiveConnection = null` *so that the data in it can persist after the Connection object has been closed.*

Comparing ADOc Recordsets and DataTable Objects

After your ADOc Recordset is imported via the DataAdapter `Fill()` method, you'll discover one or more ADO.NET DataTable objects holding your data. Let's compare the ADOc Recordset and the ADO.NET DataTable once more. In ADOc, you use the Fields collection to manage or create the schema used to correctly store and format the data, as shown in Figure 5-3. The Field object holds the data state (Value, OriginalValue, and UnderlyingValue) as well as properties for datatype (Type), variable-length column size (DefinedSize and ActualSize),

---

6. XDR was one of the first attempts at Recordset persistence (after ADTG) and one of Microsoft's first XML implementations. It fell short for a number of philosophical (and technical) reasons so it was replaced by the now "standard" XSD format.

decimal precision and scale (Precision and NumericScale), and update status (Status). Can you find any match to the Recordset with its Fields, Errors, and Properties collections in ADO.NET's DataSet or DataTable object? I can't either; however, the DataSet does bear some resemblance to Data Access Objects (DAO) with its hierarchy of collections. I guess those folks were itching to create another hierarchical object model.

NOTE *The DataSet is not defined or implemented by the .NET Data Providers—it's built into the CLR System.Data namespace. This means the properties, methods, and events are not subject to change based on which provider you happen to use—at least not much.*

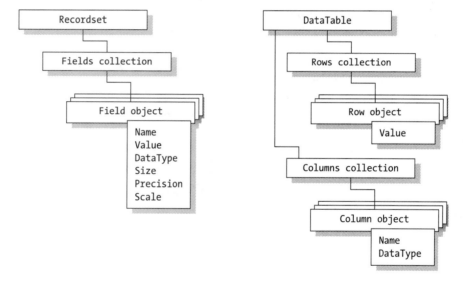

Figure 5-3. ADOc Recordset vs. ADO.NET DataTable structure.

The primary difference between the ADOc Recordset and the ADO.NET DataTable object is that ADO.NET separates DDL schema and data into *separate* collections in the DataTable object. In ADO.NET, schema is stored in the DataTable DataColumnCollection (Columns) in DataColumn objects. The data itself is stored in the DataRowCollection (Rows) in DataRow objects. Let's take a closer look at these objects and their collections.

Table 5-2 shows how the ADOc Fields collection properties and methods map to the new ADO.NET data structures—wherever they reside. One thing you'll notice about this table is that ADO.NET (and .NET in general) is not designed around "pure" properties with which you (and I) are used to working. All too often, we find that object references are implemented as overloaded methods with (many) additional enumerated options.

Table 5-2. ADOc Fields Collection Compared with ADO.NET DataColumnCollection

ADOC FIELDS COLLECTION	DATACOLUMNCOLLECTION EQUIVALENT
Rs.Fields	DataSet.Tables[n].Columns
.Count	.Count
[n] (indexes Field objects)	["FieldName"] [n] (indexes Column objects) ["ColumnName"]
.Append (add another Field) (underlying Recordset must be closed)	.Add (add another Column) (DataTable can be populated)
.Delete (remove a Field) (underlying Recordset must be closed)	.Clear(removes all columns) .Remove("ColumnName") .Remove(DataColumn) .RemoveAt(intcolumnindex) (DataTable can be populated)

Table 5-3 shows how the ADOc Field object properties and methods map to the new ADO.NET data structures. Notice that the DataTable object is missing a number of properties and methods. In some cases, these are no longer needed by the ADO.NET technology, but in other cases, this functionality was reported AWOL at morning roll call.

Table 5-3. ADOc Field Object Compared with DataSet

ADOC FIELD OBJECT	DATASET, DATATABLE, OR DATACOLUMN OBJECT EQUIVALENT
.ActualSize	Use Len method against Row item
.Attributes	Only a few of these are supported via DataColumn object properties
.DataFormat	Not supported
.DefinedSize	DataColumn.MaxLength
.Name	DataColumn.ColumnName
.NumericScale	Accessible via datatype mapping
.OriginalValue	DataRow[i, DataRowVersion.Original] DataRow["ColName", DataRowVersion.Original]
.Precision	Accessible via datatype mapping
.Properties	ExtendedProperties collection
.Status	RowState supports a few of these Status enumerations
.Type	DataColumn.DataType
.Value	DataRow(i) DataColumn.DefaultValue
.UnderlyingValue	DataRow[i, DataRowVersion.Current] DataRow["ColName", DataRowVersion.Current]
.AppendChunk	Not required
.GetChunk	Not required

Building DataTables

You don't have to create a DataSet to work with DataTable objects—but it's the easiest and most common way. While it's not yet clear what it will cost in time,

CPU, RAM, and patience to do so, I can see several situations where creating a DataSet to manage a single DataTable might be overkill. This section discusses how to get ADO.NET to construct a DataTable using a variety of techniques including use of the DataAdapter Fill method, accessing XML data sources, and others.

Building DataTables with the Constructor

The easiest way to create an empty DataTable is to use its constructor:

```
DataTable dt = new DataTable("MyDataTable");
```

After the DataTable is constructed, it's up to you to populate the DataColumnCollection (Columns) with DataColumn objects using constructor arguments passed to the Add method of the Tables collection.[7] You can also define a primary key column for the table, and create and add Constraint objects to the Constraints collection of the table. After you have defined the schema for a DataTable, you can add rows of data to the table by adding DataRow objects to the Rows collection of the table.

Microsoft seems to think that developers will want to create their own DataTable objects from scratch and fill in the Columns collection programmatically. Frankly, I can't see many applications for this approach but I can see lots of problems trying to keep an application-defined table in sync with a parallel table in the database—if there are any. So, if you want to roll your own DataTables, see the DataColumn object in MSDN documentation. I prefer to discuss techniques that are less likely to cause problems later.

Building DataTables Using the DataAdapter Fill Method

The DataAdapter object exposes the Fill() method that essentially executes the SelectCommand query and constructs a shell DataTable object for each resultset in the query containing only the column names—no other DDL is filled in. However, if the MissingSchemaAction property is set to AddWithKey, appropriate primary keys and constraints are also created.

---

7.   I won't illustrate that here. The online Help topics do a fine job documenting this (rather obscure) technique.

An important point that I can't emphasize enough: The `Fill()` method does *not replace* the current contents of the DataTable.[8] That is, if the DataTable already contains a rowset, use of the `Fill()` method *adds* the rows returned by the query to the DataTable. The process of adding the new data is also pretty smart. For example, consider the following example.[9] In this code, I use the Fill method three times—each time with a different SQL SELECT query. In the first two cases, the SELECT statement returns a row from the Titles table, but the query orders the columns differently. In the third SELECT, I return data from another table.

```
private SqlConnection cn;
private SqlCommand cmd, cmd2, cmd3;
private DataSet ds;
private SqlDataAdapter da;
private DataTable dt;

public Form1() {
    try {
        InitializeComponent();
        cn = new SqlConnection("data source=.;database=biblio;uid=admin;pwd=pw");
        cmd = new SqlCommand(
            "SELECT TOP 1 Title, Price, ISBN FROM Titles WHERE price > 10", cn);
        cmd2 = new SqlCommand(
            "SELECT TOP 1 Price, Title, ISBN FROM Titles WHERE price < 10", cn);
        cmd3 = new SqlCommand("SELECT TOP 1 Author FROM Authors", cn);

        ds = new DataSet("Composite");
        da = new SqlDataAdapter(cmd);
        dt = new DataTable();

        da.Fill(ds);
        da.SelectCommand = cmd2;
        da.Fill(ds);
        da.SelectCommand = cmd3;
        da.Fill(ds);
```

---

8. That is unless you are passing a Recordset to `Fill()`. When you pass a recordset to `Fill()` then the DataTable is replaced with the content of the Recordset and the previous contents of the DataTable disappear.

9. Located in the "\Examples \Chapter 05 Multiple Fills" and "\Examples\Chapter 05\CreateDataTable" folder on the CD.

```
        DataGrid1.DataSource = ds.Tables[0];
    }
    catch (Exception ex) { ... }
}
```

When ADO.NET starts to fill an existing DataSet, it compares the inbound resultset (generated by the SELECT) against the DataTable (in this case the first and only DataTable in the DataSet ds) and tries to match the inbound resultset columns with existing columns by name. If the column names match, a new row is added using the existing column order. Cool. However, if an inbound resultset has columns that don't match the existing DataTable Columns collection, ADO.NET adds a new column to the existing DataTable and inserts a new row with the new column. This means all of the previous rows end up with a new column set to null. Very cool. The following screen shot (Figure 5-4) illustrates the DataGrid control bound to the DataTable created by the preceding example.

This means you can create a composite of several queries in a single DataTable. This also means that if you reexecute the Fill method repeatedly, the

	Title	Price	ISBN	Author
▶	dBASE III : A Practical Guide	22.5	0-0038307-6-4	(null)
	Oracle Triggers and Stored Procedure Programming	0	0-0134436-3-1	(null)
	(null)	(null)	(null)	Jacobs, Russ
✱				

Figure 5-4. Results of several Fill methods with different SELECT statements.

existing data in the DataSet DataTable(s) is not replaced as you might expect—that's what happens with an ADOc Recordset.

I think this is an important new feature that can be very useful—especially in this disconnected architecture. If this is not the desired effect, you must use the DataSet or DataTable Clear method to clear the contents of the target DataTable before you reexecute the Fill method.

If the query contains more than one resultset, you might (just might) get more than one DataTable object constructed and appended to the Tables collection—one for each rowset returned. Each of these DataTables can be filled independently, or as we have seen earlier, managed by a DataSet object, in which case the DataSet is constructed to contain 1 to *n* DataTable objects. The Fill methods require you to pass an instantiated DataTable or DataSet (if you expect more than one DataTable).

Here's another simple example[10] of the Fill method technique to construct and populate a couple of DataTable objects. Notice how the DataTable constructor can be used to name the newly constructed DataTable. Without this setting, the new DataTable has no name using this syntax. However, the Fill method can be used to name the table, but only if the Fill method is used to create a DataSet.

```
public Form1() {
    try {
        InitializeComponent();
        cn = new SqlConnection("server=.;database=biblio;uid=admin;pwd=pw");
        cmd = new SqlCommand("SELECT State, StateCode FROM ValidStates", cn);
        da = new SqlDataAdapter(cmd);
        dt = new DataTable("ValidStatesData");
        dt2 = new DataTable();

        da.Fill(dt);
        da.Fill(dt2);
        DataGrid1.DataSource = dt;

        // Returns "ValidStatesData"
        Console.WriteLine(dt.TableName.ToString());

        // Returns ""
        Console.WriteLine(dt2.TableName.ToString());
    }
    catch (Exception ex) { ... }
}
```

If the query returns more than one resultset and you're filling a DataTable (as opposed to a DataSet), only the first resultset is placed in the DataTable. Any other resultsets are discarded whether they result from action queries or subsequent SELECT statements. This also means that if there are resultsets with no rowsets before the desired rowset-returning query, ADO.NET will step over these without complaint. On the other hand, if your Fill method references a DataSet instead of a DataTable, each resultset returned is used to populate individual DataTable objects within the DataSet. I discuss this in the next section.

Note that the Fill method can be executed multiple times (as in the previous example). ADO.NET figures out what to do—depending on whether or not you're working with a DataTable or a set of DataTables managed by a DataSet. This

---

10. Located in the "\Examples\Chapter 05\Naming Tables with Fill" folder on the CD.

technique can be used to replace a DataTable or simply add another DataTable to an existing set of DataTables in a DataSet. You can use the Fill method multiple times on the same DataTable. If a primary key exists, incoming rows are merged with matching rows that already exist; if no primary key exists, incoming rows are appended to the DataTable.

> **NOTE** *When handling batch SQL statements that return multiple results, the implementation of FillSchema for the OleDb .NET Data Provider retrieves schema information for only the first result. To retrieve schema information for multiple results, use Fill with the MissingSchemaAction property set to* AddWithKey.

You can also fill a DataTable object from a properly-formatted XML query. No, you can't use the ADOc Save() method formatted XML document as a source. However, a SQL Server 2000 FOR XML query does return correctly formatted XML. As I said earlier, you can also use the Fill() method against an ADOc Recordset object to construct a DataTable.

If the DataAdapter encounters duplicate columns while populating a DataTable with the Fill method, it generates artificial names for the subsequent columns, using the pattern columnname1, columnname2, columnname3, and so on. If the incoming data contains unnamed columns, they are placed in the DataSet according to the pattern Column1, Column2, and so on.

Building DataTable Objects Within a DataSet

When the query contains one or more resultsets and you pass a DataSet to the Fill() or FillSchema() methods, each resultset is added to the DataSet one at a time—each adding a separate DataTable to the DataSet Tables collection. Well, the DataTable objects are not actually "added" to the DataSet. In reality the slight of hand behind the smoke and mirrors is achieved by the manipulation of pointers both in the DataSet, which has a list of pointers to DataTable objects (Tables—tablecollection), and in the DataTable, which has a pointer back to the DataSet. These pointers are implemented in such a way that a DataTable cannot be appended to more than one DataSet at a time.

> **NOTE** *You can move DataTable objects from one DataSet to another: First, remove it from one DataSet and then add it to another. Why might you want to do this? Well, for one, you might want to serialize a DataSet and its contents to an XML file (see how to do this later in Chapter 10) or you might set up a DataSet containing only those tables that you want to serialize.*

The following diagram (Figure 5-5) illustrates how the individual SELECT commands of a query are used to generate individual DataTable objects.

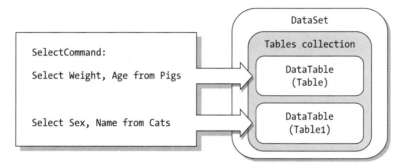

Figure 5-5. Creating DataTables from multiple resultsets.

When your query returns more than one resultset—as shown in the diagram—the first DataTable object created and appended to the Tables collection is named `Table`. Additional resultsets are named by appending integral values to the specified table name (for example, `Table`, `Table1`, `Table2`, and so on). Another advantage to this approach is the fact that only one round trip is made to populate both DataTables.

The following example[11] shows how the `Fill()` method can be used to populate a DataSet with several DataTables at once.

```
public Form1() {
    try {
        InitializeComponent();
        cn      = new SqlConnection("server=.;database=biblio;uid=admin;pwd=pw");
```

---

11. Located in the "\Examples\Chapter 05\DataTable Fill Multiple Tables" folder on the CD.

```
    strSQL = "SELECT State, StateCode FROM ValidStates "
        + SELECT ZipCode FROM ZipCodes";


    cmd = new SqlCommand(strSQL, cn);
    da  = new SqlDataAdapter(cmd);
    dt  = new DataTable("ValidStatesData");
    ds  = new DataSet("DataSetName");


    da.Fill(dt);


    // Returns "ValidStatesData"
    Console.WriteLine(dt.TableName.ToString());
    DataGrid1.DataSource = dt;
    da.Fill(ds, "srcTable");


    foreach  (DataTable dtTemp in ds.Tables) {
        Console.WriteLine(dtTemp.TableName.ToString());
    }
  }
  catch(Exception ex) { ... }
}
```

In this case, ADO.NET creates three DataTable objects. The first (dt) is named ValidStatesData because that's how the object was constructed. The remaining two are automatically named Table and Table1. I show you how to "map" these to better, more readable, more meaningful names in a minute. However, you can easily change the "base" table name by passing in a string to the Fill method, as shown here:

```
 da.Fill(ds, "MyData");
```

This causes ADO to generate one DataTable named MyData. Any subsequent DataTables generated by query resultsets are named based on the base name— MyData1, MyData2 . . . MyDataN.

 WARNING *Make sure that name collisions don't occur when defining your table and column names.*

Using FillSchema to Retrieve DDL

The DataAdapter also exposes the FillSchema() method that runs the DataAdapter SelectCommand query, constructs one or more DataTable objects, and appends them to the DataTables collection—just like the Fill() method. However, in this case, the FillSchema() method simply populates the Columns collection and does not attempt to extract any data rows from the resultset(s). The FillSchema method can be very handy to construct empty DataTable objects that you intend to fill with data by some other means.

 NOTE *Remember that the* Fill() *and* FillSchema() *methods open and close the connection associated with the DataAdapter as needed—assuming the connection isn't already open.*

Both the Fill and FillSchema methods add columns to the DataColumnCollection (Columns) of the DataTable. These methods also configure the following DataColumn properties if they exist at the data source: AllowDBNull and AutoIncrement. You must set AutoIncrementStep and AutoIncrementSeed separately. The MaxLength, ReadOnly, and Unique properties are also set.

FillSchema also configures the PrimaryKey and Constraints properties according to the following rules:

- If one or more primary key columns are returned by the SelectCommand, they are used as the primary key columns for the DataTable.

- If no primary key columns are returned, but unique columns are, the unique columns are used as the primary key if, and only if, all of the unique columns are nonnullable. If any of the columns are nullable, a UniqueConstraint is added to the ConstraintCollection, but the PrimaryKey property is not set.

- If both primary key columns and unique columns are returned, the primary key columns are used as the primary key columns for the DataTable.

NOTE   *Primary keys and unique constraints are added to the ConstraintCollection according to the preceding rules, but other constraint types are not added. I talk about adding other constraints later in this chapter.*

If ADO.NET encounters duplicate columns while populating a DataTable, it generates artificial names for the subsequent columns using the same technique I just discussed for the Fill method. That is, it generates names based on the pattern columnname1, columnname2, columnname3, and so on. If the incoming data contains unnamed columns, they are placed in the DataSet according to the pattern Column1, Column2, and so on.

When handling queries that return multiple results, FillSchema for the OleDb provider retrieves schema information for only the first resultset. To retrieve schema information for multiple resultsets, use Fill with the MissingSchemaAction property set to AddWithKey.

WARNING   *When using FillSchema with the OLE DB provider for Oracle (MSDAORA), extra columns not present in the SELECT statement may be added to the DataSet. If the SELECT statement does not include primary key or indexed columns, FillSchema retrieves the extra columns and adds them to the DataColumnCollection. Subsequent calls to Fill do not add data to the extra columns. If any of these columns do not allow NULL values, an error occurs. To avoid this situation, include primary key or indexed columns in the SELECT statement.*

Accessing DataTable Data

Up to this point, I've been talking about the structure of the DataTable, but not about the gold-bearing ore it contains—the data. The next sections address retrieving data from the Rows collection and the DDL from the Columns collection. I also examine some of the more interesting properties, try some of the useful methods, and experiment with some of the events.

Accessing the DataColumnCollection (Columns)

The Columns collection contains one or more DataColumn objects that expose a (relatively limited) set of properties to describe the column's DDL. No, the data returned by a query is not stored here—that's stored in the Rows collection in a Row object that I discuss next. As was shown in Table 5-3, the properties you used when accessing the Recordset Field object are not exposed in the same way, if at all, in ADO.NET. However, there are a number of new ADO.NET properties to which you never had access in ADOc. Consider that most of the bit flags exposed by the ADOc Field Attributes property are *not* supported; the few attributes that *are* supported are indicated in Table 5-4, which lists and briefly describes the DataColumn properties. Remember, each provider exposes a core set of properties but then adds additional properties that extend its functionality to match its features. This means that not all provider properties are exposed in all other providers.

Table 5-4. DataColumn Object Public Properties

ADO.NET PROPERTY	ADOC PROPERTY	DESCRIPTION
AllowDBNull	Similar to ADOc Field Attribute adFldIsNullable.	Does the column permit NULL values?
AutoIncrement	Similar to ADOc Field Attribute adFldRowID.	Does the column automatically increment for new rows added to the table?
AutoIncrementSeed	Not exposed in ADOc	The starting value for an AutoIncrement column.
AutoIncrementStep	Not exposed in ADOc	The increment used by an AutoIncrement column.
Caption	Not exposed in ADOc	Column caption. This is the human-readable column name.
ColumnMapping	Not exposed in ADOc	The column MappingType that determines how a column's values will be written when the DataSet WriteXml method is called.
ColumnName	Same as Field Name property in ADOc.	The column name as stored in the database.
DataType	Similar to ADOc Field Type property.	Gets or sets the type of data stored in the column. (See Table 5-5).
DefaultValue	Similar to ADOc Field Value property.	Gets or sets the default value for the column when creating new rows.
Expression	Not exposed in ADOc	Used to filter rows, calculate the values in a column, or create an aggregate column.

(continued)

Table 5-4. DataColumn Object Public Properties (continued)

ADO.NET PROPERTY	ADOC PROPERTY	DESCRIPTION
ExtendedProperties	Not exposed in ADOc	Defines custom user information.
MaxLength	Similar to ADOc Field Size property.	Maximum permitted length of a text String or Char column.
Namespace	Not exposed in ADOc	Used when reading and writing an XML document into a DataTable using the various DataSet XML methods.
Ordinal	Not exposed in ADOc	Gets the position of the column in the DataColumnCollection collection. This was implemented in RDO, but not ADOc.
Prefix	Not exposed in ADOc	Gets or sets an XML prefix that aliases the namespace of the DataTable.
ReadOnly	Similar to ADOc Field Attribute adFldUpdatable.	Indicates whether the column allows changes once a row has been added to the table.
Table	SourceTable property	DataTable to which the column belongs.
Unique	Not exposed in ADOc	Indicates whether the column values in each row must be unique.

Supported DataType Settings

When you define your DataColumn object or after it's retrieved from the data source, the DataType property returns one of the valid datatypes (System.Type), as shown in Table 5-5. Note that UInt16, UInt32, and UInt64 (unsigned integer) types are not compliant with the Common Language Specification (CLS). Note that the DataColumn object (and ADO.NET) does not support Precision or NumericScale properties. That's because when you're working with values with decimal points, you simply choose one of the floating-point datatypes (Decimal, Double, Single);the precision and numeric scale are set automatically.

 WARNING   *It's also not a good idea to use UInt64 on Intel 32-bit platforms because they are not thread safe; they do not load the registers atomically so unpredictable results are possible.*

Table 5-5. Supported Datatypes

DATATYPE	CLS COMPLIANT	C# TYPE	RANGE
System.Boolean	✔	bool	True or False
System.Byte	✔	byte	0 to 255 (hex 0x00 to 0xFF)
System.Char	✔	char	Unicode values from hex 0x0000 to 0xFFFF
System.DateTime	✔	DateTime	12:00:00 AM, 1/1/0001 CE (Common Era) to 11:59:59 PM, 12/31/9999 CE
System.Decimal	✔	decimal	-79,228,162,514,264,337,593,543,950,335 to +79,228,162,514,264,337,593,543,950,335
System.Double	✔	double	(64 bit float) -1.79769313486232e308 to +1.79769313486232e308, as well as positive or negative zero, PositiveInfinity, NegativeInfinity, and Not-a-Number (NaN).
System.Int16	✔	short	32768 through positive 32767
System.Int32	✔	int	2,147,483,648 through positive 2,147,483,647
System.Int64	✔	long	-9,223,372,036,854,775,808 through +9,223,372,036,854,775,807
System.SByte	✔	sbyte	-128 to +127
System.Single	✔	float	(32-bit float) -3.402823e38 to +3.402823e38, positive or negative zero, PositiveInfinity, NegativeInfinity, and Not-a-Number (NaN).
System.String	✔	string	An "immutable" string of characters (of any length).
System.TimeSpan	✔	TimeSpan	Represents a period of time expressed in "ticks"—the smallest unit of time (100 nanoseconds)—either positive or negative.
System.UInt16		ushort	0 to 65535
System.UInt32		uint	0 to 4,294,967,295
System.UInt64		ulong	0 to 184,467,440,737,095,551,615

When working with the SqlClient provider, you can also reference the SQL Server-specific datatypes. See "System.Data.SqlTypes" in online Help. This topic maps the SQL Server datatypes to their ADO.NET equivalents.

> **WARNING** *The DataSet stores data using the set of .NET Framework types as shown in Table 5-5. This is generally the most convenient representation for the user, but may cause problems when the back-end type is a SQL Server decimal datatype. The .NET Framework decimal type allows a maximum of 28 significant digits, while the SQL Server decimal data type allows 38 significant digits. If an application attempts to fill a .NET Framework decimal datatype with a SQL Server decimal datatype, an exception is thrown and the Fill operation terminates because data cached in the DataSet would lose the extra precision.*

To reference the DataType property in your code, you must specify the selected datatype in a somewhat convoluted fashion. For example,[12] when creating a DataTable with a single string-type column you code:

```
// Create a DataTable.
DataTable NameTable = new DataTable("Names");
// Create a DataColumn and set various properties.
DataColumn FirstNameCol = new DataColumn();
FirstNameCol.DataType = System.Type.GetType("System.String");
FirstNameCol.AllowDBNull = true;
FirstNameCol.Caption = "Author's First Name";
FirstNameCol.ColumnName = "FirstName";
FirstNameCol.DefaultValue = "Fred";
FirstNameCol.MaxLength = 20;
// Add the column to the table.
NameTable.Columns.Add(FirstNameCol);
```

Note that in this example, there is no enumeration (as there is in ADOc) to refer to the datatypes—you have to use the GetType method of the System.Type object and pass a string containing the name of the desired property.

---

12. Located in the "\Examples\Chapter 05\DataTypesTest" folder on the CD.

As expected, an exception is generated when changing the DataType property after the column has begun storing data. If AutoIncrement is set to True before setting the DataType property, any attempt to set the type to anything except an integer type generates an exception.

Accessing the Columns collection is not difficult. Remember, it's only necessary to touch the DataColumn object when describing a new column from scratch or when inspecting one of the properties to manage the data (from the Rows collection) or when setting up a variable object for fast prebinding techniques.

DataSet Case Sensitivity

By default, DataSet table and column names are case-insensitive—that is, a table in a DataSet called DogFights can also be referred to as dogfights or DogFIGHTS. This case-insensitivity might match the naming conventions in your database—including SQL Server—where the names of data elements cannot be distinguished by case alone—unless the DB is created in Case-Sensitive mode.

 WARNING *Unlike DataSet objects, XML documents are case-sensitive, so the names of data elements defined in schemas are case-sensitive. For example, schema protocol allows the schema to define a table called Customers and a different table called* customers. *This can result in name collisions when a schema is used to generate a DataSet class.*

Case sensitivity can be a factor in how data is interpreted within the DataSet. For example, if you filter data in a DataSet DataTable, the search criteria might return different results depending on whether or not the comparison is case-sensitive.

You can control the case sensitivity of filtering, searching, and sorting by setting the DataSet object's CaseSensitive property. All the DataTables in the DataSet inherit the value of this property by default. (You can override this property for each individual DataTable.)

Creating Your Own Columns Collection

The previous example illustrates how to create an individual DataColumn object and use the Add method to append it to the Columns collection of a DataTable object. I expect this approach will be useful if you want to build a stand-alone (in memory) data structure. If you expect to write this DataTable to a database, you must take care to match the DDL described with the DDL in the database.

Understanding the DataRow Object

Before I wade hip-deep into the code used to access the data returned from your query, let's take a closer look at the DataRow object itself. There aren't many properties here—the two most important are the DataRow class indexer (Item property to Visual Basic .NET folks) and ItemArray, which expose the data values in much the same way that the `Field.Value` property does in ADOc. Table 5-6 lists and describes these properties.

Table 5-6. DataRow Properties

PROPERTY	DESCRIPTION
HasErrors	Indicates if there is an error string associated with the row (RowError) or one or more columns.
[Indexer]	Gets or sets data stored in a specified column. Equivalent to the ADOc Field object's Value property.
ItemArray	Gets or sets all of the values for this row through an array. See an example of this "property" later in this chapter.
RowError	Gets or sets the custom error description for a row.
RowState	Gets the current state of the row. See "Filtering on RowState" in Chapter 6.
Table	Gets the DataTable associated with this DataRow.

I expand on each of these properties (even the ones that look like methods) as I work through the rest of this chapter.

Accessing the DataRowCollection (Rows)

I think I'm finally ready to access the data returned from a query or simply set a data value in a self-defined DataTable. This is where the DataRow object comes into play. As I said earlier, ADO.NET stores its data separately from its column DDL so you'll find that the DataRow object only contains the data values and little else. I suspect this is because ADO.NET is built around XML and the schema (DDL) is managed in a different part of the XML structure (or in an entirely separate structure) from the data.

The Item Property

The DataRow object is used to fetch and manipulate the data in a DataTable—
regardless of how it got there in the first place. The DataRow class's Indexer and
ItemArray properties are used to access the data values in the DataRow object. To
access a specific row value, select the row using an index and a specific column of
the rowset using another index as shown in the following example.[13]

```
DataRow dr;
int i, j;

da.Fill(ds, "Authors1947");
dt = ds.Tables[0];

for(i = 0; i < dt.Rows.Count; i++) {
    dr = dt.Rows[i];
    for( j = 0; j < dt.Columns.Count; j++) {
        Console.WriteLine(dr.ItemArray[j].ToString());
    }
    Console.WriteLine(" ");
}
Console.WriteLine("For each loop");
foreach( DataRow dr1 in dt.Rows) {
    for (j = 0; j <dt.Columns.Count; j++) {
        Console.Write(dr1[j].ToString() + "\t");
    }
    Console.WriteLine(" ");
}
```

TIP   *In the MSDN examples and elsewhere, the Index is
invariably referenced by name—using a "late binding"
technique that I don't recommend in ADOc. But this is not
a COM-based environment, so many of the old rules no
longer apply. I asked the folks at Microsoft about this and
they suggested using ordinals to refer to Indexed objects.
I agree. My tests clearly show that this approach is (far) faster
than leaving the CLR to resolve string-literal index values.
Okay, so why do my examples still show late binding?
Because it's easier to read.*

---

13.   Located in the "\Examples\Chapter 05\DataRows" folder on the CD[0].

This approach is very (very) different from the techniques we used to reference rows in a rowset in ADOc. Consider that the DataTable is in memory—all of the rows are visible at once so they can be accessed using their row ordinal index starting with row 0. The Row Item property is another collection of values—one for each data column.

NOTE *No, there is no "Bookmark" property in ADO.NET to position to a saved location. I discuss how to position your current row pointer in ADO.NET DataTable objects later in this chapter and again in Chapter 6.*

To provide a bit of contrast from the documentation, let's look at a more typical example of creating a DataTable and its associated Rows collection—I execute a SELECT query and use the DataAdapter Fill() method to create the table. Once created, accessing the returned DataColumn and DataRow objects can be accomplished in the same fashion.

```
SqlConnection cn = new
   SqlConnection("data source=.;uid=admin;pwd=pw;initial catalog=biblio");
DataTable dt =  new DataTable("AuthorsIn1947");
SqlCommand cmd = new
   SqlCommand("SELECT Author, year_born FROM authors WHERE year_born = 1947",cn);
SqlDataAdapter da = new SqlDataAdapter(cmd);
DataSet ds = new DataSet();

DataRow dr;
int i, j;

da.Fill(ds, "Authors1947");
```

After the DataTable is created, it's a simple matter to loop through the Columns collection dumping each DataColumn object's ColumnName property (as headings) and through the Rows collection dumping each DataRow object's Item property (as referenced by its index).

```
dt = ds.Tables[0];

foreach (DataColumn dc in dt.Columns) {
    Console.Write(dc.ColumnName + "\t");
}
Console.WriteLine(" ");
```

```
for(i = 0; i < dt.Rows.Count; i++) {
    dr = dt.Rows[i];
    for( j = 0; j < dt.Columns.Count; j++) {
        Console.WriteLine(dr[j].ToString() + "\t");
    }
    Console.WriteLine(" ");
}
Console.WriteLine("For each loop");
foreach( DataRow dr1 in dt.Rows) {
    for (j = 0; j <dt.Columns.Count; j++) {
        Console.Write(dr1[j].ToString() + "\t");
    }
    Console.WriteLine(" ");
}
```

Using the ItemArray Method

Another approach to fetching data from a DataTable Row object is to use the ItemArray method. In this case, ADO.NET retrieves all of the data items in a single operation. This is handy in cases where you can more easily work with an array. The following code[14] illustrates this technique. To access the array of items, you need an array of type Object. This is the datatype used instead of Variants. The problem with this approach is performance. Because you force ADO.NET to construct generic Object references instead of strongly typed variable references, you'll discover this approach is slower than referencing individual columns—one at a time.

```
private SqlConnection cn;
private string sql;
private SqlDataAdapter da;
private DataTable dt;
private object[] ia;

public Form1() {
    try {
        InitializeComponent();
        cn= new SqlConnection("server=.;database=biblio;uid=admin;pwd=pw");
        sql= "SELECT Addr1, Addr2, City, StateCode FROM Addresses" +
            " WHERE CustID = 106558";
```

---

14. Found in the "\Examples\Chapter 05\ItemArray" folder on the CD.

```
        da = new SqlDataAdapter(sql, cn);
        dt = new DataTable();
        da.Fill(dt);
        ia = dt.Rows[0].ItemArray;          // Fill DataRow array with row data

        for(int i = 0; i <= ia.GetUpperBound(0); i++) {
            Console.WriteLine(ia[i]);
        }
    }
    catch (Exception ex) { ... }
}
```

Yes, you can also use the ItemArray property to assign the data values to a row in a single operation. This technique is similar to syntax to pass arrays of ADOc Field names and values to the Update or AddNew methods in ADOc.

The following example illustrates filling in an array:

```
private void CreateRowsWithItemArray(DataTable dt) {
    try {
        DataRow dr;
        // Declare the array variable.
        object[] rowArray = new object[2];
        // Create 10 new rows and add to Rows collection.
        for(int i=0; i <= 9; i++) {
            rowArray[0] = "TS" + i.ToString();
            rowArray[1] = "Test State " + i.ToString();
            dr = dt.NewRow();
            dr.ItemArray = rowArray;
            dt.Rows.Add(dr);
        }
    }
    catch(Exception ex) { ... }
}
```

Testing for Results

Did your query return any rows? When you execute a SELECT to return the names of ducks that have a college degree in the Animals table, you *should* get an empty resultset (but now-a-days you never know—especially in parts of Oregon). If you execute a multiple-resultset query (or stored procedure that returns more than one resultset), you might encounter an action query embedded in the resultsets that has no rowset at all. You need to be prepared to test for either contingency or any of a number of potential exceptions that could crop up.

When trying to see if any rows resulted from your query, one approach is to test the Count property of the Rows collection. This determines how many rows resulted from the query.

```
int rowcount = dt.Rows.Count;
```

To determine how many *columns* are in your query, you can inspect the SELECT statement (in other words you should already know because you didn't use SELECT *), or you can check the DataTable.Columns.Count property. If you use the ItemArray technique, the Ubound() or GetUpperBound() methods can return the number of columns fetched.

Working with NULL Values

Okay, suppose your data column contains a NULL value. As with ADOc, you need to test for this contingency before assigning or referencing the data willy-nilly. The following example illustrates use of the IsNull() method, which is used to test if the DataRow Item contains a NULL. You'll discover that IsNull() can be applied to either the DataRow or DataColumn objects.

 TIP　*No, you can't use the empty string concatenation technique like in ADOc—it simply does not work in ADO.NET.*

The MSDN documentation illustrates a couple ways to assign NULL to a DataRow Item. I've seen both:

```
dr.[0] = System.Type.GetType("DBNull");
```

and

```
dr.[0] = DBNull.Value;
```

I expect you'll discover a few more before long. The following code[15] adds a few lines to the previous example (which created the in-memory table). Notice how I assign a NULL value to the last row of the DataTable and test for NULL using IsNull:

15.　Located in the "\Examples\Chapter 05\DataColumn DataRow" folder on the CD.

```
myRow = NameTable.NewRow();
myRow["FirstName"] = System.Type.GetType("DBNull");
// or in a simpler form . . .
// myRow["FirstName"] = DBNull.Value;
NameTable.Rows.Add(myRow);
for (i = 0; i <= 10; i++) {
    if (NameTable.Rows[i].IsNull("FirstName")) {
        Console.WriteLine("Row " + i.ToString() + " – Null value");
    }
    else {
        Console.WriteLine("Row " + i.ToString() + " – " +
            NameTable.Rows[i]["FirstName"]);
    }
}
```

Indicating DataRow Errors

ADO.NET permits you to manage errors in a variety of ways. New to ADOc developers is the concept of row-based and column-by-column error strings. These can be set in code and persisted along with the other data. I suspect that these can be warning messages or other informational (non-fatal) tidbits of information that can be used to inform you (or the educated user) about conditions set on the DataColumn.

To set an error string that applies to an entire row, use the DataRow RowError method shown here.

```
NameTable.Rows[0].RowError = "ERROR somewhere in this row ";
```

You can also persist error strings with each data column. To see whether your Columns collection contains any persisted error strings or whether there is an error string set on the row, you can use the DataRow HasErrors method. This method is applied to the DataRow, not the DataColumn. There's an illustration of this method in one of the following examples.

When you want to save an error string and associate it with a specific column, you can use the DataRow SetColumnError method. This method accepts a pointer (either index or string) to indicate the column to mark and a string to indicate the nature of the error. You can set this error string to anything that makes sense to you and your application as shown here:[16]

---

16.   See the DataRow.GetColumnError method in online Help.

```
private void SetColError(DataRow myRow, int ColIndex){
    string errorString;
    errorString = " Something is amiss here . . . too old.";
    // Set the error for the specified column of the row.
    myRow.SetColumnError("Age", errorString);
}
```

Use the GetColumnError method to return errors from a chosen column. Again, this method is overloaded so it can accept a variety of indexing syntaxes.

```
private void PrintColError(DataRow myRow, int ColIndex){
    // Print the error of a specified column.
    Console.WriteLine(myRow.GetColumnError(ColIndex));
}
```

The GetColumnsInError method can be used to return an array of all DataColumn objects that contain errors. As with the previous techniques, this method is overloaded so it also accepts a variety of indexing syntaxes.

```
private void GetAllErrs(DataRow myRow){
    // Declare an array variable for DataColumn objects.
    DataColumn[] colArr;
    // If the Row has errors, check use GetColumnsInError.
    if(myRow.HasErrors){
        // Get the array of columns in error.
        colArr = myRow.GetColumnsInError();
        for(int i = 0; i < colArr.Length; i++){
            // Insert code to fix errors on each column.
            Console.WriteLine(colArr[i].ColumnName);
        }
    // Clear errors after reconciling.
    myRow.ClearErrors();
    }
}
```

The ClearErrors method clears all errors for the row. There does not seem to be a way to clear errors for specific columns.

Accessing DataSet Data

Okay, now that you understand the DataTable object I'm ready to briefly revisit the DataSet object used to manage one or more (probably related) DataTables.

After the DataSet is filled from your data source, your data can be accessed through the DataTable objects it contains.

As I've said repeatedly, the DataSet is implemented with XML at its foundation. This permits seamless—albeit bulky—interprocess communication and persistence of either the DataSet data or schema as XML. The WriteXML extrudes both schema and data while the WriteXmlSchema method extrudes just the schema. Use the ReadXml method to construct a DataSet from an XML document that contains both schema and data. I discuss many of the XML aspects of the DataSet in Chapter 10.

In Chapter 7, I discuss how to use the GetChanges method to create a new DataSet containing a subset of DataSet rows—just those which have changed—and the Merge method to manage update operations. I also discuss the remaining aspects of updating and persisting DataSets.

Positioning the Current Row Pointer

At this point, I would like to contrast how data is accessed in ADO.NET with how it is accessed in ADOc. First, consider that the approach taken by DAO, RDO, and ADOc to position the current row pointer (CRP) was based on a flat, sequential model as exposed initially by ISAM databases and later by relational interfaces such as DB-Library and ODBC. Legacy architecture notwithstanding, ADO.NET's hierarchical model really calls for a new approach.

The Rows collection can be directly accessed only by ordinal (row number) starting at 0. When working with a DataReader I've shown that there's no need to "move" the CRP to another row—there is only one active row. This row pointer advances each time you use the Read method. When working with a DataTable, there is no need to move the CRP to populate the Rows collection, as it's either fully populated or in the process of being populated in a background thread.

What's the impact on your ADOc experience here? Well, you won't find any of the Move methods (Move N, MoveNext, MovePrevious, MoveLast, and MoveFirst) or any of the Bookmark methods (Bookmark, AbsolutePosition, and PercentPosition) implemented in ADO.NET. To move the CRP to a specific row in the ADO.NET resultset, simply set the index of the Rows collection to an integer value. To save this location for later, simply save this integer value in a variable. To return to this location, simply set the Rows collection index to this saved value. Folks, things have gotten a lot simpler.

```
MyDataTable.Rows[i][enuFields.FirstName];
```

Binding to DataSets

Microsoft has done considerable work on its binding technology and this work did not stop in their design of the .NET Framework. Consider, however, that the Framework was designed primarily as a new approach for browser-driven Visual Basic Script ASP applications and not so much as a replacement for Windows applications—at least in my opinion. Both the Windows Forms and WebForm .NET architectures support binding, but in very different ways. I am going to leave the WebForm-based architectures to other authors and focus (even if briefly) on the traditional Windows Forms applications.

When you "bind" to a data source, you basically connect to a number of ADO.NET "black box" code blocks to perform operations such as displaying the results, capturing changes from the user, and posting changes to memory. However, ADO.NET stops there. ADO.NET bound controls don't expect a data source control—such as a Data control or the ADO Data Control—to automatically connect and query (before Form_load). In addition, its bound controls do not try to update the database on their own. They assume you're working in a disconnected environment and leave to you the task of posting changes to the database. I discuss how this works in Chapter 7.

Some binding operations are brutally simple to implement but perhaps tedious to code. Other operations are more complex and thus prone to error. The ADO.NET binding technology must make a number of assumptions about the nature, structure, volume, and composition of the data, as well as how that data is fetched, its updatability, and volatility. In some (okay, many) cases, these assumptions are not correct—at least not completely. This means that data binding often works in many simple situations, but gets progressively worse as the complexity and volume of the data increases.

The ADO.NET data binding implementation is as flexible as data binding goes, but this also means it's tougher to code. Yes, you can set up data binding with Visual Studio and its drag-and-drop tools, but these wizards and other techniques often introduce code in your application that's difficult to learn, understand, and change as the data schema later changes.

Even with all of these caveats, I've found it far simpler and safer to bind to data-aware controls in Visual Studio .NET than it ever was in Visual Basic 6.0 or Visual C++ 6.0. The binding mechanism is far less intrusive and less complex. I like the fact that I have full control over the connection and the query and its parameters. The DataGrid control is intuitive and easy to use (once you get used to it). I think Microsoft has moved in the right direction. In this case, less is more.

CHAPTER 6

Filtering, Sorting, and Finding

As you saw in earlier chapters, ADO.NET supports a bevy of ways to manage the memory-resident data returned in a DataSet. In this section you'll see that ADO.NET exposes additional functionality to the ways you can address, sort, filter, and find data—and for the first time, "select" data (well, in a way).

Because of the very nature of the disconnected DataSet architecture used in ADO.NET, it's often impractical or impossible to requery a remote data source to reorder or further filter data. Of course, this assumes that you're not implementing a traditional client/server application, which can execute further server-side sorting, filtering, and detailed row selections as the need arises. But keep in mind that it's still expensive to execute a full round-trip query to further filter or sort a resultset—especially since ADO.NET already has the code to make these refinements loaded into memory and ready to be used.

As I've said before, if you go to the expense of creating a DataTable or DataSet, you might as well take advantage of the best practice features they expose—in this case, sorting, filtering, and finding.

The ADOc client-side cursor engine provided sort, filter, find, and seek functionality, but ADO.NET's approach is different in many ways. I discuss two fundamental approaches for performing these operations in this section:

- **Using the DataTable Select method**: This method is overloaded to accept arguments to filter and sort data rows returning an array of DataRow objects.

- **Using DataView object sort, filter, and find methods**: This object uses the same filter arguments supported by the Select method, but the DataView extrudes structures that can be bound to data-aware controls.

IMHO *To sort or not to sort. As you well know, the initial query that constructs your DataSet can include an ORDER BY clause to set the initial rowset order. If the server-side Query Optimizer (QO) references an index, your rowset(s) might simply return the chosen rowset based on that index. However, if there aren't indexes or ORDER BY clauses to affect the data order, the server must stop what it's doing and sort the rows on its own. Because the order-by operation can take place* before *the WHERE clause restrictions are applied, quite a few rows might be sorted and stored temporarily on the server—only to be discarded when the WHERE clause restriction is applied to the ordered rowset.*

So, in some cases, you might find that it is actually faster to sort the data after *it arrives at the client—especially when large unindexed (or improperly indexed) data structures are being queried. That's because the data engine might have to perform a complex sort against one or more large tables before returning a rowset to the client. Creating appropriate database indexes can reduce or eliminate the need for these time- and resource-consuming sorts. Not sure what's happening? Use the Query Analyzer to view the query plan to make sure and to suggest improvements in your indexes.*

As I said in the previous chapter, case sensitivity can be a factor in how data is interpreted within the DataSet. For example, if you filter data in a DataSet table, the search criteria might return different results depending on whether or not the comparison is case-sensitive. You can control the case sensitivity of filtering, searching, and sorting by setting the DataSet object's CaseSensitive property. All the DataTable objects in the DataSet inherit the value of this property by default. (You can override this property for each individual table.)

Filtering and Sorting with the Select Method

The DataTable Select method accepts a filter argument to return an array of DataRow objects that conform to the criteria in a FilterExpression passed as a Select method argument. This method is vaguely similar to the ADOc Filter method so don't confuse it with a SQL SELECT statement. The FilterExpression argument is evaluated as a Boolean and bears some resemblance to a SQL

WHERE clause. That is, if the expression returns True, the row is included. For example, a FilterExpression might look like this:

```
Title like 'Hitch%' and Price < 10.50
```

The FilterExpression can reference column values by name (as in the preceding example), property values, or literal values. See "DataColumn.Expression Property" in online Help for detailed information. Before you run off and dig up that (rather long) Help topic, consider that if your FilterExpression is trying to reference a comparand that contains a single quote, you have to apply the "O'Malley" rule to the string. For example, to find a title "Hitchhiker's Guide," you would code:

```
"Titled LIKE 'Hitchhiker''s Guide%' "
```

Note how the apostrophe (single quote) in the title name is doubled. Without this extra single quote, ADO.NET throws an exception.

As with ADOc, the DataTable Select method does not affect the original DataTable Rows collection order or content. Unlike ADOc, the Select method returns an array of DataRow objects based on the FilterExpression, sort string, and other criteria. If any rows qualify based on the Select method's FilterExpression, the GetUpperBound method (applied to the returned array of DataRow objects) returns a value greater than or equal to 0. If no rows qualify, GetUpperBound returns -1.

TIP *Another nuance crops up when ADO.NET returns an array—as with the Select method. The GetUpperBound property returns the highest elements array index. Because of this, if there is a single row in the array, GetUpperBound returns 0, not 1. If there are no rows in the array, GetUpperBound returns -1. This is because the array is 0-based, not 1-based.*

Sorting with the Select Method

The DataTable Select method also supports the ability to sort a DataTable's rowset returned as an array of DataRow objects. The sort criteria arguments passed to the Select method seem to be similar if not identical to those passed to the ADOc Sort property. A typical sort expression is simply the name of the column to sort by followed by an optional direction (ASC or DESC) argument—just as you used in ADOc. For example, to sort by the DataTable's Title column, you specify the sort expression "Title" for an ascending sort (lowest values first) or "Title DESC" for a descending sort (highest first). However, you can also sort by the value of any expression, including calculated values. As you'll see in the next section, if you are using a DataView, you specify the sort expression to the DataView object's Sort property.

 IMHO *The fundamental problem with the Select method for some ADOc developers (like me) is that it does* not *return a filtered Table object as expected—it returns an array of DataRow objects. This means you can't directly bind this array to a DataGrid or other bound controls. Later on I show you how to use a DataView to accomplish this a little easier— see "Filtering and Sorting with the DataView Object."*

The following example illustrates how to filter and sort using the DataTable Select method. It begins by setting up a Command object used to execute a parameter-based stored procedure. The Form constructor sets up the query and calls the RunQuery routine. This code is provided—as are all of the other examples, indexed by chapter—on the book's companion CD.[1]

```
public Form1() {
    try {
        InitializeComponent();
        cn = new SqlConnection("server=.;database=biblio;uid=admin;pwd=pw");
        cmd = new SqlCommand("GetTitlesByYear", cn);
        cmd.CommandType = CommandType.StoredProcedure;
        cmd.Parameters.Add("@TitleWanted", SqlDbType.VarChar, 20);
        cmd.Parameters.Add("@YearLow", SqlDbType.Int);
        cmd.Parameters.Add("@YearHigh", SqlDbType.Int);
        da = new SqlDataAdapter(cmd);
        ds = new DataSet();
        RunQuery();
        txtFilter.Text = txtQTitle.Text;
    }
    catch (Exception ex) { ... }
}
```

---

1.   Located in the "\Examples\Chapter 06\Filter" folder on the CD.

The following subroutine runs the query based on the current parameter settings. It also displays the rowset in a DataGrid and passes a DataRow array (containing the entire rowset) generated by the Select method to the ShowTable routine (as described later).

```
private void RunQuery() {
    try {
        // Run query based on current parameter settings
        da.Fill(ds, "Titles");
        DataGrid1.DataSource = ds.Tables[0];
        ShowTable(ds.Tables[0].Select());
        FillSortCriteria();
    }
    catch (Exception ex) { ... }
}
```

The Filter button filters the contents of the first DataTable based on the FilterExpression, again using the Select method. Note that the GetUpperBound method returns -1 if no rows qualify based on the Filter.

```
private void btnFilter_Click(object sender, System.EventArgs e) {
    try {
        DataRow[] FilteredRowArray;
        txtShowRows.Text = "";
        FilteredRowArray = ds.Tables[0].Select("Title LIKE '"
            + txtFilter.Text + "'");
        Debug.WriteLine(FilteredRowArray.GetUpperBound(0));
        if( FilteredRowArray.GetUpperBound(0) >= 0) {
            ShowTable(FilteredRowArray);
        }
        else {
            MessageBox.Show("No titles meet criteria (filtering).");
        }
    }
    catch ( Exception ex ) { ... }
}
```

The Sort button executes the Select method passing both the Filter and Sort arguments. The routine concatenates either " ASC" (the default) or " DESC" to indicate either ascending or descending sort direction. Don't forget the leading space in front of this sort direction argument.

```
private void btnSort_Click(object sender, System.EventArgs e) {
    try {
        DataRow[] SortedRowArray;
        string strSortType;
        string strSort;
        string strFilter;
        if (rbAsc.Checked) {
            strSort = cmbSortArg.Text + " ASC";
        }
        else {
            strSort = cmbSortArg.Text + " DESC";
        }
        if (txtFilter.Text == "") {
            strFilter = "";
        }
        else {
            strFilter = "Title LIKE'" + txtFilter.Text + "'";
        }
        txtShowRows.Text = "";
        SortedRowArray = ds.Tables[0].Select(strFilter, strSort);
        Debug.WriteLine(SortedRowArray.GetUpperBound(0));
        if( SortedRowArray.GetUpperBound(0) >= 0 ) {
            ShowTable(SortedRowArray);
        }
        else {
            MessageBox.Show("No titles meet criteria (sorting).");
        }
    }
    catch (Exception ex) { ... }
}
```

After you have an array of DataRow objects, you're ready to dump the array to a multiline TextBox control. This array could have been dumped to a DataGrid, but you would have had to do so row-by-row.

```
private void ShowTable(DataRow[] RowArray ) {
    try {
        string strS=null;

        for (int i =0 ; i<= RowArray.GetUpperBound(0);i++) {
            for ( int intCol = 0; intCol <=
                RowArray[i].ItemArray.GetUpperBound(0); intCol++) {
                strS = strS + RowArray[i][intCol].ToString() + "\t";
```

```
        }
        strS = strS + "\r\n";
        txtShowRows.Text = strS;
    }
}
catch(Exception ex) {
    Debug.WriteLine(ex.ToString());
    MessageBox.Show(ex.ToString());
}
}
```

To illustrate different ways to bind to a Parameter, note that the first two references use ordinals (correctly/faster) and the last reference a string (easier to read/slower).

```
private void btnQuery_Click(object sender, System.EventArgs e) {
    try{
        ds.Clear();
        cmd.Parameters[0].Value = txtQTitle.Text;
        cmd.Parameters[1].Value = txtQYearLow.Text;
        cmd.Parameters["@YearHigh"].Value = txtQYearHigh.Text;
        txtFilter.Text = cmd.Parameters[0].Value.ToString();
        RunQuery();
    }
    catch (Exception ex) { ... }
}
private void FillSortCriteria() {
    try {
        if (cmbSortArg.Items.Count > 0) {
            return;
        }
        foreach (DataColumn dc in ds.Tables[0].Columns) {
            cmbSortArg.Items.Add(dc.Caption);
        }
    }
    catch (Exception ex) { ... }
}
```

If the example application needs to rerun the query, the btnQuery_Click routine (shown in the previous code) captures current parameters, clears the current contents of the target DataTable (in the DataSet), and reexecutes the query.

as a collection of DataTable objects. If you choose to use a DataView object, you can add one to a form or component in much the same way you do other data elements—namely, by dragging it onto a designer and setting its properties. You can also bind to the DataView. The DataViewManager is located on the Tools menu in the Data tab. However, once you create a DataTable, the DataView is already exposed through the DefaultView property, so it's only visible at run time.

If you create a custom DataView—either manually or in code—in addition to the DataView exposed by the DefaultView property, you can also create multiple views on a single set of data and assign names to your DataView objects. I suspect that the DataView is simply constructing a set of pointers akin to ADOc Bookmarks that are used to reference the original DataTable Rows collection.

Both the DataView and Select method techniques provide roughly the same filtering and sorting capabilities. The primary difference is that you can call a DataTable's Select method only in code at run time. In contrast, the DataView provides these additional advantages:

- **You can create and configure the DataView at design time, with the option to set its properties at run time as well.** No, the DataView does not have a separate design-time component.

- **You can use the DataView in data binding.** This means you can display rows managed by a DataView using a bound control such as the DataGrid. As I mentioned before, the array of DataRow objects extruded by the Select method is not bindable.

- **You can create multiple DataView objects to see the data in a resultset in different ways.** For example, one DataView might display data in an Orders table in date order and another DataView might show it in customer order.

 TIP *Be sure to set the DefaultView.RowFilter property to an empty string if you plan to requery. If you don't, the new resultset will be filtered based on the FilterExpression.*

You'll also find that the way you approach problems with the DataView is different on a number of planes. For instance, remember that you're working with the DataTable itself when referencing a DataView, not an extruded array of DataRow objects. This means you can potentially change/affect the behavior of any operation that touches the DataTable—sometimes in subtle, but sometimes in not so subtle, ways.

Filtering on RowState and Version

As with ADOc Recordset objects, the DataTable object is designed to maintain not only the current columns' values as fetched from the database, but the changed values as well—and all at the same time. As I discuss in the next chapter, ADO.NET saves the original, proposed, and current, as well as the default version of your data. If your code or a bound control changes the DataRow Value property, ADO.NET saves the original value for later retrieval if necessary (as when you wish to "undo" changes). Rows are flagged according to their status: new, unchanged, deleted, or modified.

You can use filters to access subsets of the DataTable Rows collection based on these distinct versions of the data. That is, you can filter for just the rows that have been changed, just those deleted, or those not changed at all. If you loop through all of the rows in a DataTable, you'll step through new, changed, deleted, along with unchanged records unless you set a filter beforehand to see only a subset of the rows.

If you are calling the DataTable Select method and passing a filter expression, you can also add a parameter indicating what row state or version you want to use as a filter criterion. If you are using a DataView object (discussed next), you can set the RowStateFilter to indicate what version or state of a row you want. I fully discuss the RowState values in Chapter 7, "ADO.NET Update Strategies," when I discuss update operations.

Filtering and Sorting with the DataView Object

ADO.NET also exposes an entirely new[2] DataView object that supports a number of methods that work something like a data engine's SQL VIEW, with a number of enhancements. If you look closely, the DataView is similar to the ADOc Filter property in many ways; it even inherits some of its "issues."

Basically, the DataView is an object designed to provide an additional data-management layer on top of DataTable data. A DataView provides ways to filter, sort, navigate, as well as help edit a defined set of DataRow objects in an associated DataTable. As with a SQL View, the DataView is not a copy of the data, but simply another "view" on the same data. The DataRows stored in the DataView can be sorted, filtered, and otherwise manipulated in a variety of ways using the DataView properties and methods discussed in this section. For the most part, I expect you'll find the DataView easier to use than the Select method just discussed—even though it also has a few issues you should watch out for.

ADO.NET also exposes the DataViewManager object, which acts as a collection of DataView objects—not unlike the way that the DataSet acts

---

2.   New at least to ADOc developers.

Setting DataView Filter Properties

While the DataTable object exposes the Select method with a number of arguments to filter the DataTable rows, the DataView object exposes the RowFilter property to perform (roughly) the same filtering operation. The RowFilter property documentation suggests that the only valid filter expression is a column name expression such as:

"City = 'Seattle'"

> **WARNING** *The filter expression uses single quotes to frame the comparand ('*Seattle*'). I suspected that this string would have the same "O'Malley" issue as other strings with imbedded single quotes. I was right: This property does* not *support imbedded single quotes in the comparand.*

However, I've found that other, more complex expressions are also supported. For example, to return only those columns set to null values, use the following expression:

"Isnull(Col1,'Null Column') = 'Null Column'"

The DataView also supports the RowStateFilter property to filter rows with specific RowState values—as I discussed earlier in this chapter.

After you set the RowFilter property, ADO.NET hides (but does not eliminate) all rows in the associated DataTable object's Rows collection that don't match the filter expression. The DataView.Count property returns the number of rows remaining unhidden in the view. If you've managed to hide all of the rows, DataView.Count returns 0.

To sort a DataView, construct a sort expression string as you did for the ADOc Recordset object's Sort property and for the Select method's sort argument. Note that the Sort property can accept any number of (well, at least several) columns on which to sort the Rows collection. For example, to sort on Year_Published and Title, use the following sort expression string:

"Year_Published, Title ASC"

Either sort argument can use either ASC or DESC as a postfix. For example, to sort by a descending price (highest first) and title, use the following sort expression string:

"Price DESC, Title"

Set the RowFilter to an empty string ("") to reset the RowFilter or Sort properties and to show all of the rows in the DataTable object's Rows collection in the original order.

The following example[3] is similar to the previous Select method example in some respects, but it's more refined and illustrates use of the DefaultView. No drag-and-drop DataView was added to the project; I simply used the existing DataTable object's DefaultView RowFilter and Sort properties to filter and sort the DataTable object's Rows collection.

This version of the solution uses the same setup routine as the previous example. I also use a DataGrid control bound to the first DataTable in the DataSet (initially) and later to the DataTable[0].DefaultView.

```csharp
public Form1() {
    try {
        InitializeComponent();
        cn = new SqlConnection("server=.;database=biblio;uid=admin;pwd=pw");
        cmd = new SqlCommand("GetTitlesByYear",cn);
        cmd.CommandType = CommandType.StoredProcedure;
        cmd.Parameters.Add("@TitleWanted", SqlDbType.VarChar, 20);
        cmd.Parameters.Add("@YearLow", SqlDbType.Int);
        cmd.Parameters.Add("@YearHigh", SqlDbType.Int);

        da = new SqlDataAdapter(cmd);
        ds = new DataSet();

        RunQuery();
        txtFilter.Text = txtQTitle.Text;
    }
    catch (Exception ex) { ... }
}
```

This routine fills a couple of drop-down column pick lists.

```csharp
private void FillSortCriteria() {
    try {
        if (cmbSortArg.Items.Count > 0) {
            return;
        }
        foreach( DataColumn dc in ds.Tables[0].Columns) {
            cmbSortArg.Items.Add(dc.Caption);
            cmbFields.Items.Add(dc.Caption);
```

---

3.   Located in the "\Examples\Chapter 06\DataView" folder on the CD.

```
            }
        }
        catch (Exception ex) { ... }
    }
```

This routine opens the connection, executes the query (both operations executed by the Fill method), and binds the initial resultset to the DataGrid.

```
private void RunQuery() {
    try{
        da.Fill(ds, "Titles");
        objDb = DataGrid1.DataSource;
        DataGrid1.DataSource = ds.Tables[0];
        FillSortCriteria();
    }
    catch (Exception ex) { ... }
}
```

The following three routines capture user input from a form and call the SetFilter subroutine to set the DataView filter.

```
private void btnFilterTitle_Click(object sender, System.EventArgs e) {
    try {
        SetFilter("Title LIKE '" + txtFilter.Text + "'");
    }
    catch (Exception ex) { ... }
}

private void btnFilteronColumn_Click(object sender, System.EventArgs e) {
    try {
        SetFilter(cmbFields.Text + " " + txtFilterColumn.Text);
    }
    catch (Exception ex) { ... }
}

private void btnGeneralFilter_Click(object sender, System.EventArgs e) {
    try {
        SetFilter(txtGeneralFilter.Text);
    }
    catch (Exception ex) { ... }
}
```

The `SetFilter` routine accepts a string passed from the click-events. This string is passed to the DefaultView RowFilter property thus activating the filtering mechanism. If no rows remain after the filter is set, a dialog box is displayed. This routine also supports an error handler to trap syntax errors caused by incorrect filter arguments.

```
private void SetFilter(string strFilterExpression) {
    try {
        DataGrid1.DataSource = objDb;
        ds.Tables[0].DefaultView.RowFilter = strFilterExpression;
        if ( ds.Tables[0].DefaultView.Count > 0 ) {
            DataGrid1.DataSource = ds.Tables[0].DefaultView;
        }
        else {
            MessageBox.Show("No titles meet criteria.");
        }
    }
    catch (Exception ex) { ... }
}
```

The Sort button activates a routine to capture and cobble together a sort criteria string to be passed to the DataView Sort property. Once constructed, the string is applied to the DataView object's Sort property.

```
private void btnSort_Click(object sender, System.EventArgs e) {
    try {
        string strSort;

        if (rbAsc.Checked) {
            strSort = cmbSortArg.Text + " ASC";        // Note space after "
        }
        else {
            strSort = cmbSortArg.Text + " DESC";       // Note space after "
        }
        ds.Tables[0].DefaultView.Sort = strSort;
        DataGrid1.DataSource = ds.Tables[0].DefaultView;
    }
    catch (Exception ex) { ... }
}
```

The Query button sets the Command object parameters and reexecutes the command set up earlier. Note that I clear the DataSet to prevent resultsets from accumulating from query to query.

```
private void btnQuery_Click(object sender, System.EventArgs e) {
    try {
        ds.Clear();        // Remove any existing rowset from a previous query
        cmd.Parameters[0].Value = txtQTitle.Text;
        cmd.Parameters[1].Value = txtQYearLow.Text;
        cmd.Parameters["@YearHigh"].Value = txtQYearHigh.Text;
        txtFilter.Text = cmd.Parameters[0].Value.ToString();

        ds.Tables[0].DefaultView.RowFilter = "";
        RunQuery();
    }
    catch (Exception ex) { ... }
}
```

Creating DataView Objects with Visual Studio

As you've probably guessed by now, I'm not sold on many of the drag-and-drop approaches, but the impact of dragging a DataView to your project is minimal. Yes, Visual Studio supports the ability to drag a DataView object from the **Tools | Data** menu to your form. If you do so, Visual Studio adds a single line of code to instantiate a DataView so that you can manipulate the DataView programmatically or connect it to other design-time-generated DataTable references. As with the DataView object exposed by the DataTable object's DefaultView property, you can bind this new DataView to bound controls.

Updating a DataView

Remember that a DataView is simply an alternate pathway to the DataTable object and the Rows collection—a view in every sense. You can also UPDATE, INSERT, and DELETE rows from the DataTable using views, assuming that ADO.NET can isolate individual rows. But that's always been a restriction with ADOc or any of the data access interfaces. If there's a primary key or one or more other columns that can be used to uniquely identify a row, ADO.NET should (okay, might) be able to update the row. You also need to make sure that the DataView object "allow" properties are set to True: AllowEdit, AllowNew, and AllowDelete. I discuss ADO.NET update strategies and techniques in the next chapter.

Working with the DataViewManager

If your DataSet contains multiple tables, an alternative is to create a DataViewManager object, which works something like a DataSet global DataView. This new object provides a single object that manages a collection of DataView objects, each of which is associated with a specific DataTable in the selected DataSet object. You can define individual DataView objects that sort or filter the data in each DataTable in your DataSet; as a matter of fact, ADO.NET creates one for you as it creates each DataTable—all of which can be managed by the DataViewManager. Remember, each DataTable object supports a DefaultView property and you can create additional DataView objects as needed to provide different "views" on your rowsets.

The DataViewManager object is especially useful when working with related tables and when you want to sort or filter child records from a master table. For example, suppose you create a DataSet containing multiple DataTable objects which contain rows from the Orders and Items tables, as well as a DataRelation object that links the two tables. In this scenario, you can use individual DataView objects to sort the Orders table by CustomerID and the Items table by ItemNumber.

To use a DataViewManager object, you must create and configure it in code; there is no design-time object that you can add to a form or component. This is no disappointment for me. This also means that if you want to bind controls to the DataView Manager, you must also do so in code because there is no design-time component to which to bind them.

 NOTE *The DataRow object does not implement the interfaces needed for DataBinding, but the DataRowView does; this means that you can bind to a DataRowView but not to a DataRow. However, if you are using a strongly typed DataSet, you can bind to the strongly typed DataRow because it has properties (provided by the XSD schema) that map to the fields in the underlying DataRow.*

It's not difficult to create a new DataView Manager—just follow these steps (I expect your code has already done most of these already):

1. Create and populate a DataSet. You ought to know how to do this by now.

2. Create an instance of the DataViewManager class as shown here:

```
DataViewManager dvm = new DataViewManager();
```

3. Set the DataViewManager object's DataSet property to the DataSet you created in Step 1.

4. Set sort and filter expressions by accessing individual tables through the DataViewSettings collection.

Not too tough. As soon as you access a DataTable object through the DataViewSettings collection, ADO.NET constructs a new DataView for the table. You can't add or remove a DataViewSetting from the collection, but you can change the properties of the DataViewSetting corresponding to a particular DataTable. Adding or removing a DataTable from the DataSet adds or removes the corresponding DataViewSetting from the collection.

If you want to bind controls to the DataViewManager, set the bound control's data-binding properties after configuring the DataViewManager object. For example, in a Windows Form, you can set a control's DataSource property to the DataViewManager and its DataMember property to the name of the DataTable (and thus, DataView) to which to bind.

 NOTE *When you use individual DataView objects to sort the DataRows in the associated DataTable object, the Relation object's GetChildRecords method does not returned sorted rows. However, if you use a DataViewManager, the method will return sorted rows.*

The DefaultViewManager Property

The DataViewManager returned by the DataSet object's DefaultViewManager property allows you to create custom settings for each DataTable in the DataSet. When you add DataTable objects to the DataTableCollection, each table is automatically configured to display rows according to the specified property settings of the DataView—including sort order, filtering, and DataViewRowState.

Using the Find Methods

If you remember the ADOc Seek method, you'll recognize the ADO.NET Rows collection Find and the DataView Find methods. These "Find" methods permit a direct lookup of a row based on the primary key if (and only if) you set them up correctly. There's also a new method—the Contains method—that returns a Boolean if the Rows collection contains a match based on the PrimaryKey. This section tells you how to use each of these methods. Before I get started, consider that, unlike ADOc, these Find methods, regardless of the technique, do *not* execute any queries and require no round trips to the server to locate rows. These searches—as with all of the Sort, Filter, and Find techniques discussed so far—are executed by ADO.NET against the in-memory data store.

 IMHO *No, I don't know why the Microsoft folks didn't call this the* Seek *method. I guess they wanted to avoid further confusion with ADOc.*

ADO.NET implements three basic forms of Find—like what you've seen with the Filter method:

- **The Find method as applied to the Rows collection.** This form returns a DataRow object based on a primary key match.

- **The Find method as applied to the DataView object.** This form points to the matching row by returning an integer row number—assuming you have set the Sort property to the column to search.

- **The Contains method as applied to the Rows collection.** This method returns True if a row matching the primary key exists in the DataTable object's Rows collection.

The Rows Collection Find Method

Similar to the DataTable Select method, the Rows collection Find method returns a DataRow object—in this case a single row instead of an array. This method requires that you set the PrimaryKey property before using it. If you don't, you'll trip a trappable exception.

Setting the PrimaryKey Property

When you execute a query that executes a stored procedure, ADO.NET is not likely to discover and set the PrimaryKey for you. Even if you execute an ad hoc query, I have yet to see evidence that the PrimaryKey property is ever set automatically. This means you'll probably have to set it manually—at least most of the time. Setting the PrimaryKey property is not that tough, but it needs a few words of discussion. Basically, the PrimaryKey property holds an array of DataColumn objects—one for each column that constitutes the unique identifier for the row. For example, the Titles table has a single-column PrimaryKey—the ISBN—so you have to create an array containing a single DataColumn item. On the other hand, the Orders table has a two-column PrimaryKey—CustID and OrderID—so in this case the array would hold two DataColumn items.

To set the PrimaryKey property, you have to:

1. Create an array of DataColumn objects large enough to hold the unique identifier columns. However, to create a single-element "array" simply code:

```
<datatype>[] objPkArgs = new <datatype> [1];
```

2. Fill the array with DataColumn objects describing each element of the PrimaryKey.

The following example illustrates setting the PrimaryKey property when there are two columns in the PrimaryKey:

```
DataColumn[] colPk = new DataColumn[2];
colPk[0] = dsOrderItem.Tables[0].Columns["CustID"];
colPk[1] = dsOrderItem.Tables[0].Columns["OrderID"];
dsOrderItem.Tables[0].PrimaryKey = colPk;
```

At least one of the Microsoft folks suggested I use the FillSchema method to populate the PrimaryKey property. I tried it, but it did not work.

```
daOrderItem.FillSchema(dsOrderItem.Tables[0], SchemaType.Source);
```

Executing the Rows.Find Method

After the PrimaryKey is set, using the Rows collection Find method is fairly straightforward. The real question is: What do I do with the resulting row? You must use one of the methods described earlier to display or pass the resulting row to another layer.

The following example,[4] part of a large sample application on the CD, sets up and executes the Find method against a Rows collection. Find returns a DataRow

---

4. Located in the "\Examples\Chapter 06\Find Method SqlClient" folder on the CD.

object based on the PrimaryKey passed as an argument. Note that I simply reference the "columns" returned by the Find method.

```
private void btnFindRow_Click(object sender, System.EventArgs e) {
    try {
        DataRow drFound;
        DataColumn[] colPk = new DataColumn[1];
        colPk[0] = ds.Tables[0].Columns["Title_ID"];
        ds.Tables[0].PrimaryKey = colPk;
        drFound = ds.Tables[0].Rows.Find(txtFindArg.Text);
        if (drFound ==null ) {
            MessageBox.Show("No PK matches " + txtFindArg.Text);
        }
        else {
            txtFoundRow.Text = drFound[0].ToString() + " : " +
                    drFound["Title"].ToString();
        }
    }
    catch(Exception ex) { ... }
}
```

If the Rows collection's Find method does not locate a match, the returned DataColumn (drFound in this case) is set to null.

This next example[5] illustrates use of multiple keys. In this case the DataSet was created against the Orders table with its rows uniquely identified by Customer ID and Order ID (CustID and OrderID). In this case, I create an object array of the desired CustID and OrderID values and pass the text values to search for. As with the earlier example, if one or both of these values is not located, the Find method returns null.

```
private void btnFind_Click(object sender, System.EventArgs e) {
    try {
        DataRow drFound;
        DataColumn[] colPk = new DataColumn[2];
        colPk[0] = dsOrderItem.Tables[0].Columns["CustID"];
        colPk[1] = dsOrderItem.Tables[0].Columns["OrderID"];
        dsOrderItem.Tables[0].PrimaryKey = colPk;

        object[] objFind = new object[2];
```

---

5.   Located in the "\Examples\Chapter 06\DataView Find Array" folder on the CD.

```
        objFind[0] = cmbCustList.Text;
        objFind[1] = txtOrderID.Text;
        drFound = dsOrderItem.Tables[0].Rows.Find(objFind);
        if (drFound == null) {
            MessageBox.Show("No PK matches search arguments");
        }
        else {
            string strData="";
            for (int i = 0; i<= drFound.ItemArray.GetUpperBound(0); i++) {
                strData = strData + drFound[i].ToString() + " ";
            }
            txtFoundRow.Text = strData;
        }
    }
    catch(Exception ex) { . . . }
}
```

The DataView Object's Find Method

For some reason, the folks at Microsoft working in the DataView team thought they also needed a Find method. It's relatively under documented, so these tips should help get this working for you.

First, the DataView object's Find method could care less about the PrimaryKey—regardless of what the documentation says. It *does* care about the DataView object's Sort property—which the documentation fails to mention (but it does show up in the MSDN example). Once you understand this, it's really easy to code the Find method. It also has a couple of overloads—one to accept a string to match against the Sort property column and another to accept an array of strings to match.

 WARNING *If you don't set the DataView object's Sort property prior to executing the Find method, Find returns a pseudo random number—well, it seems that way. Instead of failing, Find returns an integer that seems to have no bearing on anything. Just be careful before assuming that this method is working!*

Passing Arguments to Find

The code shown next[6] illustrates two DataView object Find method techniques. The first simply passes a text argument to the Find method while the second passes an object array containing the Find method arguments. I illustrate passing multiple arguments in the example provided in the following section. In both of these implementations of the Find method, if ADO.NET fails to locate a matching row, Find returns a -1 as the row number. The trick here is to make sure the object array (objPkArgs) is declared to be the right width. When there is only one element in the PrimaryKey, the "array" is only one member wide. In this case, declare the array with 0 width.

```
private void btnFind_Click(object sender, System.EventArgs e) {
    try{
        int intRow;
        ds.Tables[0].DefaultView.Sort = "Title_ID";
        intRow = ds.Tables[0].DefaultView.Find(txtFindArg.Text);
        if (intRow == -1) {
            MessageBox.Show("Could not find " + txtFindArg.Text);
        }
        else {
            DataGrid1.CurrentRowIndex = intRow;
        }
    }
    catch (Exception ex) { ... }
}


private void btnFindArray_Click(object sender, System.EventArgs e) {
    try {
        int intRow;
        object[] objPkArgs = new object[1];
        ds.Tables[0].DefaultView.Sort = "Title_ID";
        objPkArgs[0] = txtFindArg.Text;     // contains valid PK
        intRow = ds.Tables[0].DefaultView.Find(objPkArgs);
        if (intRow == -1) {
            MessageBox.Show("Could not find " + txtFindArg.Text);
        }
        else {
            DataGrid1.CurrentRowIndex = intRow;
```

---

6. Located in the "\Examples\Chapter 06\Simple Find" folder on the CD.

```
        }
    }
    catch (Exception ex) { ... }
}
```

Passing Multiple Arguments to Find

The following example[7] illustrates using *multiple* primary key columns passed as
an object array to the Find method—just as I did for the Rows collection Find
method shown previously. Multiple arguments are necessary in situations where
the PrimaryKey or unique identifier requires more than one column to resolve
a row. Note that the DataView I'm using is referenced by the DataTable object's
DefaultView property. As with the previous example, you have to set the
DataView Sort property, but in this case you have to set it to *both* columns referenced by the Find arguments. If you don't, you'll get bogus results.

```
private void btnFind_Click(object sender, System.EventArgs e) {
    try {
        DataRow drFound;
        DataColumn[] colPk = new DataColumn[2];
        colPk[0] = dsOrderItem.Tables[0].Columns["CustID"];
        colPk[1] = dsOrderItem.Tables[0].Columns["OrderID"];
        dsOrderItem.Tables[0].PrimaryKey = colPk;

        object[] objFind = new object[2];
        objFind[0] = cmbCustList.Text;
        objFind[1] = txtOrderID.Text;
        drFound = dsOrderItem.Tables[0].Rows.Find(objFind);
        if (drFound == null) {
            MessageBox.Show("No PK matches search arguments");
        }
        else {
            string strData="";
            for (int i = 0; i<= drFound.ItemArray.GetUpperBound(0); i++) {
                strData = strData + drFound[i].ToString() + " ";
            }
            txtFoundRow.Text = strData;
        }
    }
    catch(Exception ex) { ... }
}
```

---

7. Located in the "\Examples\Chapter 06\DataView Find Array" folder on the CD.

The Rows Collection Contains Method

Another way to locate a row based on your DataTable object's PrimaryKey property is to use the Rows collection Contains method. This method works very much like the Find method in that it expects you to set the PrimaryKey property (one way or another) with an array of PrimaryKey column objects. However, instead of returning a DataRow, the Contains method simply returns a Boolean— True, if the row is found, and False, if not. After the PrimaryKey property is set, you can use the Contains method by passing it a string to match against the PrimaryKey.

The following example[8] uses a combination of the Find methods and the Contains method to remove a selected row from a DataSet. I discuss the Remove method in Chapter 7 coming up next.

```
private void btnSearch_Click(object sender, System.EventArgs e) {
    try {
        DataTable tb = ds.Tables[0];
        int intRow;
        DataColumn[] dcolPk = new DataColumn[1];
        dcolPk[0] = tb.Columns["ISBN"];
        tb.PrimaryKey = dcolPk;
        tb.DefaultView.Sort = "ISBN";
        if (tb.Rows.Contains(txtSearchFor.Text)) {
            // at least one row matches primary key
            rowFound = tb.Rows.Find(txtSearchFor.Text);
            intRow = ds.Tables[0].DefaultView.Find(txtSearchFor.Text);
            if ((rowFound == null) | (intRow == -1)) {
                MessageBox.Show("Could not find row ");
            }
            else {
                DataGrid1.CurrentRowIndex = intRow;
            }
        }
        else {
            MessageBox.Show("No row found that matches " + txtSearchFor.Text);
        }
    }
    catch(Exception ex) { ... }
}
```

---

8.   Located in the "\Examples\Chapter 06\Remove and Insert via Method" folder on the CD.

CHAPTER 7

ADO.NET Update Strategies

Up to this point I've written a lot about extracting and massaging data from your data sources, but hardly a word about saving changes to the database or simply transporting the resultset data to some other tier. I expect that most of you work with applications where you need to change the data from time to time. This chapter focuses on the mechanics of persisting your changes to a data source or transporting your in-memory DataTable or DataRow data. Remember that ADO.NET is basically an "in-memory" data manager so "updating" might be as simple as changing the Value property in a DataRow; deleting a row could be implemented by using the RemoveAt method against the Rows collection. Updating might also be as complex as calling a series of conditional SQL queries that update a related set of tables applying complex business rules and triggers under a strict permissions regimen with convoluted referential integrity constraints.

In some architectures you might have another tier write to a database or simply process the information you send back; that's why I talk about transport mechanisms in this chapter. Using this approach you have to maintain the DDL metadata to ensure that the receiving code can figure out which row to update or delete. ADO.NET can assist with this process in a number of ways—as I explain in this chapter.

If you read the Visual Basic version of this book you know I'm of the opinion that ADO.NET does not *directly* support pessimistic locking or any type of server-side cursor management—at least none that a typical ADOc developer would use. Of course, you can always bypass ADO.NET and execute a block of SQL that creates a server-side cursor to perform some operation or even lock an individual row—assuming your back end supports it. However, if you're creating a client/server application, I don't recommend any form of client-side transaction management. For middle-tier code, I prefer use of stored procedures that handle locking/concurrency issues.

On the other hand, if you're running SQL Server or other back ends that support UPDATE row isolation, you can get ADO.NET to manage a pessimistic locking update for you:

1. Open a connection (and leave it open).

2. Begin an ADO.NET transaction specifying "RepeatableRead" isolation level.

3. Execute an UPDATE statement that addresses the individual row to be changed and returns a row's affected or operation status as a parameter.

4. Commit or rollback the transaction based on the returned status.

In this scenario, if another operation attempts to access the row being updated, an exception is thrown. Be sure to keep the user out of these operations. That is, don't let the user decide to finalize or validate the UPDATE—doing so cripples scalability and can leave rows locked for indeterminate lengths of time.

Because of the current ADO.NET architecture, the number of update strategies available to you is more limited—at least when compared with ADOc. I only wish that Microsoft had chosen to give us a hint as to what they plan to do to address these issues.

Yes, even with these and the other limitations discussed earlier you can still save your data; however, the ADO.NET architecture suggests that you design your systems from the outset to support optimistic locking strategies whenever possible—but that's true for ADOc applications as well.

If you've read any of my previous books, you'll know that I've been encouraging optimistic locking designs for some time. Yes, there are some (quite a few) situations where locking is an integral part of a data access strategy; if you're sure your design falls into this category, ADO.NET might not the best solution for you—it's not your only alternative. In these cases, you can consider use of ADOc from your .NET application—it still supports pessimistic locking just as it always has—but I'm hesitant to encourage anyone to build new ADOc applications at this point in time. I just hate to see you waste your time with ADOc development when there are new versions of ADO.NET Data Providers and new server-side architectures being developed that should provide all of this missing ADOc functionality—someday.

Changing Data—The Fundamentals

I was well into this chapter when I realized that I had left off one little, but very important, detail: how to change the data in a DataTable. That is, how to take a value from a variable (perhaps provided by the user) and save it into a DataRow Value property. I've already discussed the data structures involved—the DataTable, DataRow, and Rows collection—so you have probably already guessed how to write to the DataRow object's Value property. Addressing the Value property is a little different when compared with ADOc—so let's revisit it.

If the DataSet is strongly typed (see Chapter 4), you can refer to the Value property with far less code (because you provided additional code earlier to expose the DataSet as an object). But let's start with an untyped DataSet.

 NOTE *One important difference between ADOc and ADO.NET is the concept of the "current row." When you address rows in ADO.NET you must refer to a **specific** DataRow object or a **specific** member of the Rows collection by number; there is no current row pointer as there is in ADOc. That said, I think it would be interesting to have ADO.NET support bulk change operations against an entire (filtered) set of rows—perhaps in a future version.*

Addressing the Value Property with Untyped Datasets

After you have a new row, or if you're dealing with existing rows, you can simply reference the Value property using a variety of syntaxes. Note that the Value property is assumed in the following examples. I understand that default properties are legal when the property is parameterized.

```
myRow[0] = "Fred";
myRow[1] = "Soccer Coach";
```

Yes, you can also use a string to reference the DataRow column to be changed; however, this approach is far slower than using ordinals as in the previous example.[1] As with ADOc, you can set up enumerations to refer to the columns in the DataRow for the same reasons I discussed before—they're faster and easier to read.

---

1. See the performance comparisons at the end of Chapter 3.

```
myRow["FirstName"] = "Fred";        // Avoid this syntax
myRow["Job"] = "Soccer Coach";      // Ditto
```

This row (myRow in the examples) just sits in memory, not associated with any collection of DataRow objects; it won't be until you add it to the Rows collection using the Add method.

```
MyTable.Rows.Add(myRow);
```

Addressing the Value Property with Typed Datasets

Because a strongly typed DataSet and its members are exposed to the development environment as objects, the DataTable and its columns can be referenced by name. This makes the coding easier when it comes time to perform updates—despite the fact that it took longer to build the typed DataSet in the first place. The performance here *is* faster than using an ordinal.

The following example shows how to add new records using typed DataSet objects:

```
dsAuthors Ds = new dsAuthors();
dsAuthors.AuthorsRow myRow = Ds.Authors.NewAuthorsRow();
myRow.Author = "Fred";
ExistingTable.Rows.Add(myRow);
```

Creating New DataRows

ADO.NET's approach to adding rows to a DataTable requires another step or two when compared with how it's done in ADOc. The following steps walk you through this process.

To add rows to an *existing* DataTable you need to:

1. **Declare a variable to address the DataRow and use the DataTable object's NewRow method to construct the new DataRow.** This new row is not initially associated with the DataTable object's Rows collection, so the RowState is initially set to Detached.

   ```
   DataTable myTable = MakeTable();
   DataRow myRow;
   myRow = myTable.NewRow();
   ```

2. **Append the new DataRow object to the DataTable Rows collection.**
At this point the RowState changes to Added.

```
myTable.Rows.Add(myRow);
```

3. **Modify the row as desired.** Note that this does *not* affect the RowState—
it won't until the AcceptChanges method is called.

```
myRow["FirstName"] = "Fred";
```

4. **Accept the changes (add and modify).**

```
myTable.AcceptChanges();
```

5. **Modify the row again.** Now the RowState shows Modified. If you read in a
row, the RowState starts out as Unchanged and is set to Modified after you
change a value.

```
myRow["FirstName"] = "Scott";
```

6. **Mark the row for deletion.** This leaves the row in the Rows collection until
you execute AcceptChanges again. At this point the RowState changes to
Deleted.

```
myRow.Delete();
```

7. **Undo the delete operation using the RejectChanges method.** This
restores the previous RowState.

```
myRow.RejectChanges();
```

As shown in the previous examples, when it comes time to create a new
DataRow, you need to use the NewRow method of the DataTable object. This is
something like the DAO Edit method in that it creates a new empty row that you
can edit at will. As in ADOc, you don't need to do anything special to begin
changing the DataRow Item property (equivalent to the ADOc Field.Value
property).

As in DAO, you have to use the ADO.NET DataRow.BeginEdit method to
enable changes to an existing row (one already in the DataTable). To commit those
changes to the database you have to use the Update method, and if that's
successful, the AcceptChanges method. No, don't use the AcceptChanges method
before you successfully execute the Update method. This approach is very
different from what you're probably used to working with in ADOc where there's
no need to "activate" a row for editing and where virtually any action commits the
rows to the database.

Deleting DataSet Rows

You can remove rows from a DataTable object's Rows collection using a logical or a physical approach (or both). That is, you can use the RemoveAt method to *physically* remove a specific row from the Rows collection as shown here:

```
DataRowCollection rc = ds.Tables[0].Rows;
// No rows to delete?
if (rc.Count == 0) {
    return;
}
// intRowToDelete = row number
rc.RemoveAt(intRowToDelete);
```

There's also a Rows.Remove method to physically remove a specific Row object from the Rows collection. The trick is to get a DataRow somehow. Suppose you have a routine that finds a row to delete and then returns that row as a DataRow object. With this scenario it is easy to remove the row from the Rows collection:

```
myDataSet.Tables[0].Rows.Remove(myRowToDelete);
```

 NOTE *I wrote a full-blown example to illustrate the Remove method (and the Contains method). See "Chapter 07\Remove and Insert via method" on the CD.*

The downside of these Remove approaches is that ADO.NET won't construct appropriate DELETE SQL calls to remove the data row in the database. You also can't "undo" the delete operation; the data is gonzo and can only be recovered from the loose chad strewn all over the floor. These Remove methods should be used to manage the local DataTable rows in situations where you don't care about keeping the remote database in sync.

 You can also use the Delete method to get ADO.NET to *logically* mark a selected row for deletion. Basically, the Delete method simply changes the RowState property to Deleted, but it does not remove the row from the Rows collection and still does not post this change in status to the database—not until you use the Update method. Remember, if you use the Delete method, the

Rows.Count property is unchanged because it includes *all* rows in the Rows collection; any deleted rows are still included. To determine how many "live" undeleted rows are still in a DataTable object's Rows collection, you can maintain the count on your own (risky), loop through the Rows collection looking for rows that don't have the RowState set to Deleted (slow), or better yet and as a best practice, examine the DataTable's DataView Count property (via DefaultView property filtered on RowState).

NOTE   *No, as I said, there is no concept of a "current row" in ADO.NET so the Delete method must be used against a specific row—addressed by ordinal in the Rows collection.*

The following example deletes a specific row (intRowToDrop) from the DataSet:

```
DsItems.Tables[0].Rows[intRowToDrop].Delete();
```

"Undoing" a Delete Operation

Oops, you decide that you want to roll back a change you just made to a DataSet, DataTable, or DataRow. Well, there are several options for doing this. First, if you make this decision *before* you execute the Update method, you can use the RejectChanges method. The DataRow, DataTable, and DataSet objects all support the RejectChanges method. Depending on which object you choose, changes in the specific row referenced (DataRow), changes in the specific DataTable, or all changes in all DataTables in a DataSet are rolled back; the RowState is reset to Original and the original values are applied to the Value property. No, you can't use RejectChanges after you've executed AcceptChanges—but didn't your mom tell you, you're not supposed to use AcceptChanges until after using the Update method.

You can also undo changes made to your DataRow or DataRowView objects by using the CancelEdit method. However, in order for CancelEdit to work, you must use BeginEdit prior to making changes. I discuss the CancelEdit method in the next section.

Of course, you also can use transactions to manage changes as well. I mentioned transactions earlier—in Chapter 2.

Postponing Constraint Enforcement

I discuss ADO.NET constraints in Chapter 8, but I do need to mention a few points now while I'm on the topic of making changes to your data. Remember that the ADO.NET architecture manages data constraints *in memory*—assuming you coded them. That is, if there are primary key/foreign key relationships, or unique key constraints defined for the table(s) in the DataSet, you can easily get into a situation where ADO.NET detects exceptions as rows are being changed *before* you're finished changing the data. For example, suppose you have a look-up table with valid part numbers and an order comes in that references a new part. Ordinarily, you would define a PK/FK relationship between the PartID column in the Items table and a PartID in the ValidParts table. If you add the new item before adding the new part, ADO.NET will throw an exception.

To avoid this problem, you can tell ADO.NET to delay checking the PK/FK or other constraints until further notice by setting the EnforceConstraints property to False. Toggling the EnforceConstraints property back to True tells ADO.NET to recheck any constraints established for the DataSet. It is at this time that constraint exceptions will be thrown—assuming there are still constraint problems.

Using BeginEdit

Another approach to temporarily suspend data-validation events associated with data modifications is to use the DataRow object's BeginEdit method. As with the DAO Edit method (no, ADOc does not require use of the Edit method), BeginEdit signals ADO.NET that you're performing data-manipulation operations on several rows. Before you edit each row participating in a multirow edit, use the DataRow.BeginEdit method.

If you don't explicitly call BeginEdit when working with a bound control (such as the DataGrid), BeginEdit is automatically called when the user changes a value in the control (such as a grid cell). EndEdit is automatically called when you execute the AcceptChanges method. This means AcceptChanges can trigger one or more data validation events and exceptions.

Because the data is not posted to the DataTable until EndEdit is called, you can retrieve the new values using the Item property passing `DataRowVersion.Proposed` as the Version argument. As I discussed earlier, you can also undo any edits within the BeginEdit scope by using the CancelEdit method. The next section, which discusses managing the persisted data version data, includes further discussion of the BeginEdit method.

Data Validation

Okay, some of your data sources are not that reliable. In many cases the source of your data might be ordinary people with limited typing skills and poor eyesight. Remember that the world population is aging and not everyone sees as well as a 22-year-old computer wiz. In any case you're going to have to validate your data somewhere, and while .NET has a few controls, methods, properties, and events to help, it won't add these validation rules on its own.

To start with, you can build data validation into the DataSet itself in the following ways:

- **Establish keys and unique constraints as part of the DataSet schema.**
  I discuss this in Chapter 8.

- **Set properties on the DataColumn object.** For example, you can set MaxLength, AllowDBNull and Unique properties. As data is entered, ADO.NET throws exceptions if the data does not comply with these constraints.

- **Add code behind an event that fires when column or row currency is changed.** You can implement this by adding your own events to the DataTable or by using one or more of the events exposed by the .NET Data Provider.

Coding Event Handlers

ADO.NET and the .NET Data Providers all expose a number of events that can be used to validate your data as it is entered. The following code assigns a handler to the DataTable to fire when the data in the row changes.

```
// add a RowChanged event handler for the table.
this.dt.RowChanged += new
    System.Data.DataRowChangeEventHandler(this.DataTableRow_Changed);
```

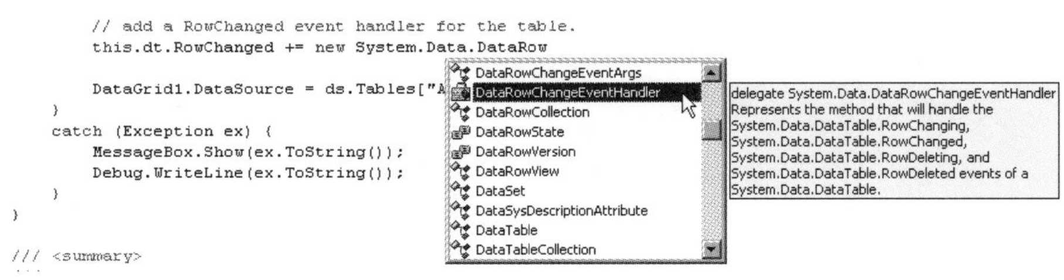

Figure 7-1. Assigning an event handler method.

Each event handler is passed a number of arguments depending on the event. For example, the RowChanged event handler is passed two arguments: an Object (Sender) and the DataRowChangeEventArgs (e). This second argument contains pointers to the data row being altered and why the event was fired.

```
private void DataTableRow_Changed(object Sender,
    System.Data.DataRowChangeEventArgs e)
```

The following example[2] illustrates coding a DataTableRow_Changed event handler that simply dumps the incoming events to the debug window so you can see when they fire and what arguments are passed. Notice that there is no "cancel" argument[3] passed in this case, so it's up to you to rollback the change if needed. To illustrate this, I do a simple (really pretty dumb) validity check on the Year_Born column and use the DataRow.RejectChanges method if something is amiss. Note that this operation also fires the event handler so watch out for recursive functions.

```
private void DataTableRow_Changed(object Sender,
  System.Data.DataRowChangeEventArgs e) {
    try {
        // The DataRow has changed. Validate the contents
        string strA="";
        switch ( e.Action) {
            case DataRowAction.Add:
                strA = "Add";
                ValidateRow(e.Row);
                break;
            case DataRowAction.Change:
                strA = "Change";
                ValidateRow(e.Row);
                break;
            case DataRowAction.Commit:
                strA = "Commit";
                break;
```

---

2. Located in the "\Examples\Chapter 07\Update" folder on the CD.

3. Some event handlers—such as the RowUpdated event—do support return arguments to indicate whether or not to throw an exception to the invoking code.

```
        case DataRowAction.Delete:
            strA = "Delete";
            if (MessageBox.Show("Are you sure you want to delete this row?",
                "Question", MessageBoxButtons.OKCancel ,
                MessageBoxIcon.Question,
                MessageBoxDefaultButton.Button1)
                == DialogResult.Cancel ) {
                e.Row.RejectChanges();  // Cancel proposed changes
            }
            break;

        case  DataRowAction.Nothing:
            strA = "Nothing";
            break;
        case DataRowAction.Rollback:
            strA = "Rollback";
            break;
    }
    Debug.WriteLine("Row_Changed Event: AU_ID=" + e.Row["Au_ID"].ToString()
        + " -- " + strA);
}
catch (Exception ex){...}
}
```

This is the (lame) row-validation routine. No, I'm not a fan of putting this type of logic in an application because it has a tendency to change frequently. Sure, you can code a better one that won't require updating as often, but these business rules really belong on the server in database rules—not here.

IPHO   *For applications that are disconnected from a server for much of their time (replicating/updating only when connected to a server), it's a good idea to perform business rule type validation on the client. Identifying a data validation problem as close as possible to the user entering the data helps to ensure that data integrity is maintained by getting that user to address the data entry problem right at the time it is most fresh in their minds. Bill is right, however, in that this does lead to a maintenance problem when you need to update the business rules on 10,000 PDAs running the Compact Framework—all because the vice president's spouse has just pointed out that it's not a good idea to allow the cosmetics sales force to book orders on their PDAs giving a 110 percent discount.*

```
private void ValidateRow(DataRow dr) {
    try {
        int intYb;
        if (dr["Year_born"].Equals(DBNull.Value)) {
            return;
        }
        intYb = Convert.ToInt32(dr["Year_Born"]);
        if ((intYb < 1)  | (intYb > 2100)) {
            MessageBox.Show("Year born value is invalid");
            dr.RejectChanges();  // Cancel proposed changes
        }
    }
    catch (Exception ex){
        Debug.WriteLine(ex.ToString());
        MessageBox.Show(ex.ToString());
    }
}
```

TIP *Notice how the preceding routine checks for a* null *value.*

There are other interesting row-change events as well. For example, the SqlDataAdapter exposes RowUpdated and RowUpdating.

When you execute the Update method, two events fire as each data row is changed as follows:

1. The values in the DataRow are moved to the parameter values.

2. The RowUpdating event is raised.

3. The command executes.

4. If the command is set to FirstReturnedRecord, then the first returned result is placed in the DataRow.

5. If there are OUTPUT parameters, they are placed in the DataRow.

6. The RowUpdated event is raised.

7. AcceptChanges is called.

Other event handlers exposed by ADO.NET include the DataTable ColumnChanging, ColumnChanged, RowChanging, and RowChanged events.

Remember that the BeginEdit method disables the RowChanging and RowChanged events after individual column changes. When the EndEdit method is executed, these events are raised once—just once—even if several columns have changed. Choosing a highly granular event—such as ColumnChanging—can make coding easier in some respects because your code can be structured to catch exceptions while the attention of the user is on that column; however, it also means more processing behind the scenes which might degrade performance.

Checking RowState

The RowState property indicates the "state" of the row (no, not "Louisiana"). This is similar to the Recordset.*Status* property in ADOc, but very few of the equivalent ADOc Status values are implemented in ADO.NET. Table 7-1 lists the various RowState values and what they indicate. Note that several methods alter the RowState—most if not all are discussed in this chapter.

Table 7-1. DataRow RowState Values

RowState	Description
Added	The row has been added to a DataRowCollection; AcceptChanges has not been called.
Deleted	The row was deleted using the Delete method of the DataRow.
Detached	The row has been created but is not part of any DataRowCollection. A DataRow is in this state immediately after it has been created and before it is added to a collection, or if it has been removed from a collection.
Modified	The row has been modified and AcceptChanges has not been called.
Unchanged	The row has not changed since AcceptChanges was last called.

Determining the Data Version

As you update the data in a DataRow Item, ADO.NET maintains the previous value behind the scenes. To be more precise, ADO.NET stores the Default, Original, Current, and Proposed values—referred to as data "versions." These values are stored along with the Item value for a total of up to five data values. You have to use the HasVersion property[4] to determine whether one of the alternate data versions is available. No, don't try to reference a version that doesn't exist—you'll trip an exception. ADOc also supported this functionality, but only the Value, OriginalValue, and Underlying values were maintained.

The following example[5] uses the HasVersion property to determine whether one or more of the data version values are present. If so, the code dumps that version to the debug (output) pane. If the version has not been set, you can't just reference it in code—that trips an exception.

Because I defined the DefaultValue as "Fred", this code returns "Fred" in the Output window. Note that I'm using the DataRowVersion.Default class to return this value. For purposes of this example, I start by "manually" creating a DataTable instead of creating one from a query.

```
// Create a DataTable.
DataTable NameTable = new DataTable("Names");

// Create a DataColumn and set various properties.
DataColumn FirstNameCol = new DataColumn();
FirstNameCol.DataType = System.Type.GetType("System.String");
FirstNameCol.AllowDBNull = true;
FirstNameCol.Caption = "Author's First Name";
FirstNameCol.ColumnName = "FirstName";
FirstNameCol.DefaultValue = "Fred";
FirstNameCol.MaxLength = 20;

// Add the column to the table.
NameTable.Columns.Add(FirstNameCol);

DataRow myRow;
string NameIn;
```

---

4. The distinction between "properties" and "methods" has become pretty clouded here. Both IsNull and HasVersion look like methods to me, but the documentation calls them properties.

5. Located in the "\Examples\Chapter 07\DataColumn DataRow" folder on the CD.

The first few lines of code dump the current default value.

```
for (int i = 0; i <= 9; i++) {
    myRow = NameTable.NewRow();
    if (myRow.HasVersion(DataRowVersion.Default)) {
        Debug.WriteLine("Pre-set value default:" + myRow[0,
            DataRowVersion.Default].ToString());
    }
```

The next block of code sets a new value into the row. After this, the default value is now the same as the Item value. If you don't supply an Item value before updating, the DefaultValue property is used.

```
    switch (i) {
    case 0:
        myRow["FirstName"] =   "Fred";
        break;
    case 1:
        myRow["FirstName"] =   "Betty";
        break;
    case 2:
        myRow["FirstName"] =   "Sam";
        break;
    case 3:
        myRow["FirstName"] =   "Victoria";
        break;
    case 4:
        myRow["FirstName"] =   "Bill";
        break;
    case 5:
        myRow["FirstName"] =   "Marilyn";
        break;
    case 6:
        myRow["FirstName"] =   "Jim";
        break;
    case 7:
        myRow["FirstName"] =   "Mary";
        break;
    case 8:
        myRow["FirstName"] =   "Alice";
        break;
    default:
        myRow["FirstName"] = null;
        break;
```

```
    }
        // Be sure to add the new row to the DataRowCollection.
        NameTable.Rows.Add(myRow);
        if( NameTable.Rows[i].HasVersion(DataRowVersion.Default)) {
            Debug.WriteLine("Pre-edit default:" + NameTable.Rows[i][0,
              DataRowVersion.Default].ToString());
        }
    }
```

The next few lines of code visit each of the version values—if they are available—and dump them to the output window.

```
        NameTable.Rows[0].BeginEdit();
        NameTable.Rows[0][0] = "New Name";
        if (NameTable.Rows[0].HasVersion(DataRowVersion.Proposed)) {

            Debug.WriteLine("Proposed:" + NameTable.Rows[0][0,
                DataRowVersion.Proposed].ToString());
        }
        if (NameTable.Rows[0].HasVersion(DataRowVersion.Original)) {
            Debug.WriteLine("Original:" + NameTable.Rows[0][0,
                DataRowVersion.Original].ToString());
        }
        if (NameTable.Rows[0].HasVersion(DataRowVersion.Current)) {
            Debug.WriteLine("Current:" + NameTable.Rows[0][0,
                DataRowVersion.Current].ToString());
        }
        if (NameTable.Rows[0].HasVersion(DataRowVersion.Default)) {
            Debug.WriteLine("Default:" + NameTable.Rows[0][0,
                DataRowVersion.Default].ToString());
        }
        NameTable.Rows[0].AcceptChanges();
    }
    catch (Exception ex) {...}
}
```

As you fetch and modify your data, ADO.NET saves, deletes, and refreshes the various versions. The DataRowVersion is your window on these versions and changes based on the following conditions (as shown in Table 7-2):

Table 7-2. How Editing Data Impacts DataRowVersion

Method	Effect on DataRowVersion
DataRow.BeginEdit	If the Value changes, the Current and Proposed values are activated.
DataRow.CancelEdit	Proposed value is cleared.
DataRow.EndEdit	Proposed value becomes the Current value.
DataRow.AcceptChanges	Proposed value becomes the Current value—the Original value persists.
DataRow.RejectChanges	Proposed value is cleared and the version is set to Current.
DataTable.AcceptChanges	Original value is set to CurrentValue.
DataTable.Update	Original value is set to CurrentValue and the Proposed is cleared.

When you set up your Parameters collection, you might want to map the Parameters being passed to and from your update queries to a specific version of the data. In some cases you'll want to pass DataRowVersion. Figure 7-2 illustrates how the DataRow versions are affected by changes in the data.

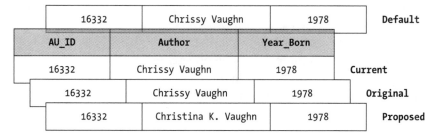

AU_ID	Author	Year_Born	
16332	Chrissy Vaughn	1978	**Default**
16332	Chrissy Vaughn	1978	**Current**
16332	Chrissy Vaughn	1978	**Original**
16332	Christina K. Vaughn	1978	**Proposed**

ADO.NET maintains multiple versions of your data

Figure 7-2. DataRowVersion management.

Setting the Correct Version for Parameters

The stored procedures you (or ADO.NET) construct to update the database are driven with parameters that get their Value property set automatically by the Update method. You must, however, program the Update method to extract these values from the correct DataRow column and version. Remember, there are three sets of data in each column—one for each version: Original, Proposed, and Current.

There are two Parameter object properties used to tell the Update statement which column contains the value and which version of the data to use:

- **The SourceColumn property**: Maps one of your DataRow columns to one (or more) Parameter objects. No, ADO.NET won't be happy if you set this to a non-existent column.

- **The SourceVersion property**: Tells the Update method which version of the data should be referenced.

If you set these properties correctly, ADO.NET can map the correct values into your stored procedure calls. If you don't set them at all, the values passed to the stored procedure will probably be the Current value.

The following lines of code were generated by Visual Studio using the DataAdapter configuration wizard, which I discussed in Chapter 3 (see "Using the DataAdapter Configuration Wizard") and will also discuss again later in this chapter. Notice how the SourceColumn (Au_ID) and version (System.Data.DataRowVersion.Original) are specified.

```
this.SqlUpdateCommand1.Parameters.Add(new
System.Data.SqlClient.SqlParameter("@Original_Au_ID", System.Data.SqlDbType.Int,
4, System.Data.ParameterDirection.Input, false, ((System.Byte)(0)),
((System.Byte)(0)), "Au_ID", System.Data.DataRowVersion.Original, null));
```

I discuss how to construct these Parameter objects and how to (try to) get Visual Studio or ADO to do it for you later in this chapter; see the "Constructing the Parameters Collection Using DeriveParameters" section.

Update Strategies

As with ADOc, you have several choices when updating data. A few of the interesting ones (there are others) are:

- **Create an updatable DataSet.** With this approach you specify additional DataAdapter Command objects to perform each modification task—inserting, updating, and deleting a row. ADO.NET helps you manage collisions and determine which rows were changed and which failed to change.

- **Execute ad hoc queries to perform the updates on your own.** In this case you create your own SQL procedures or simply reference stored procedures to perform changes. You have to handle collisions on your own with this strategy.

- **Simply create a DataTable and make changes to the in-memory Rows collection.** This data structure can be persisted or transported elsewhere to be processed.

The following sections discuss each of these approaches in some detail. Which is best for you really depends on the complexity of your resultsets and other factors. In many cases you'll find that ADO.NET is incapable of constructing the needed SQL statements to change complex resultsets, so you might be on your own anyway. However, if your `SelectCommand` SQL is fairly simple or accesses a table directly, there's a good chance ADO.NET can construct the needed INSERT, UPDATE, and DELETE queries for you and help manage collisions.

Creating Updatable DataSets

ADO.NET approaches the update task from a somewhat familiar tack for ADOc developers. Do you remember the Visual Basic 6.0 Data Object wizard, and how it asked you to point to four procedures to fetch, INSERT, UPDATE, and DELETE rows? Well, ADO.NET uses a similar approach to perform its queries and updates; Visual Studio .NET also provides a wizard to fill in these Command objects for you.

When you set up a .NET Data Provider DataAdapter—such as SqlDataAdapter, OleDbDataAdapter, or OdbcDataAdapter—you'll find that each supports four Command objects—one for each of the following basic operations as listed in Table 7-3:

Table 7-3. DataAdapter Properties Used to Manage Operational Queries

DataAdapter Property	Description
SelectCommand	Returns rowset(s) based on SELECT query.
DeleteCommand	Removes specific row using DELETE query.
UpdateCommand	Changes specific row using UPDATE query.
InsertCommand	Adds new row using INSERT query.

To create an updatable DataSet, you have to set up the DataAdapter associated with the DataSet to contain pointers to each of the Command objects you expect to use. That is, if you don't want to modify the rowset returned by the SelectCommand, you don't have to fill in any of the other Command properties.

You have several options when it comes time to generate the data-modification Command objects and the SQL action queries they contain. If your SelectCommand query is fairly simple, Visual Studio can generate these for you. The ADO.NET CommandBuilder class can (try to) do it for you. However, in many cases you'll find it easier to simply code the INSERT, UPDATE, and DELETE SQL statements yourself; Visual Studio can help code the SQL statements in this case as well if you use its Query Builder.

Incidentally, there's nothing to stop you from using stored procedures for any or all of these operations. As a matter of fact, I would suggest this approach for better scalability, stability, and performance; in fact, it's another best practice.

Using the CommandBuilder Class

When your SelectCommand query is not fixed at design time you can (try to) get ADO.NET to automatically generate the three data-modification queries—assuming your SELECT query is a simple single-table SELECT. The CommandBuilder object can't generate the action queries for joined tables or stored procedures that contain JOIN operators in the SQL query nor for tables that are part of a relationship. In addition, I found the Command Builder somewhat challenged when I tried to use it in one of my applications. For example, when I wrote an update query (with or without a stored procedure), I returned the new row identity value to make sure I had added addressability to the new row. The CommandBuilder did not place anything in the query to return the row ID and there was no way to add it. Here are a few more rules and restrictions:

- **Your** SelectCommand **needs to retrieve at least one PrimaryKey or unique column as part of the query.** Having a TimeStamp column without a PrimaryKey of some kind won't work.

- **The** SelectCommand **query cannot refer to SQL queries, stored procedures, or views that include JOIN operators.**

- **As with the Refresh method, the CommandBuilder makes its own round trip to the server to fetch metadata**—and you know how I feel about the Refresh method (just say "no").

- **The CommandBuilder makes no attempt to add code to retrieve output arguments from the action query.**

- **If the CommandText, Connection, CommandTimeout, or Transaction properties of the** SelectCommand **change, you have to notify the CommandBuilder by executing the RefreshSchema method.** This causes another round trip to the server to refresh the schema.

- **The UpdateCommand and DeleteCommand will not change any row that has been changed (modified or deleted).** If you need to force through an update, you can't use the CommandBuilder.

- **The CommandBuilder is designed to be used with unrelated tables.** That is, you can't expect to update tables with primary key/foreign key relationships. You have to create these update statements yourself.

- **You can't change the** SelectCommand **after the CommandBuilder has constructed the data-modification commands.** If you do, the results are not predictable unless you use the RefreshSchema to reconstruct the commands.

- **If the column names contain special characters such as spaces, periods, quotes, or non-alphanumeric characters, you can't use the CommandBuilder**—even if you use the QuotePrefix/QuoteSuffix properties.

Basically, the CommandBuilder takes the query you supply in the SelectCommand and generates the DataAdapter InsertCommand, UpdateCommand, and DeleteCommand queries. Figure 7-3 illustrates how the Update method manages the four Command objects generated by the CommandBuilder to query and update the data.

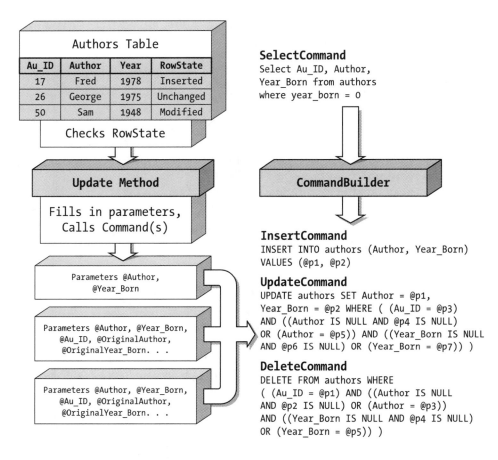

Figure 7-3. ADO.NET CommandBuilder.

As I just said, to be able to generate the data-modification code, a run-time round-trip query is executed by ADO.NET each time the CommandBuilder class is instantiated. An example of the DDL query executed to determine the schema of the SelectCommand is shown here:

```
EXEC sp_executesql N'
SET FMTONLY OFF;
SET NO_BROWSETABLE ON;
SET FMTONLY ON;
SELECT Au_ID, Author, Year_Born FROM authors
WHERE year_born = 0'
```

If your SelectCommand invokes a stored procedure, this procedure had better return the same schema each time the query is executed, or the action query commands won't match the SELECT—this could be bad. This might not be the case if the logic of the stored procedure branches to alternate sections based on date/time variations, input parameters, or other variables.

If you define one or more of the three DataAdapter Command classes before using the CommandBuilder, these are not disturbed—just those Command classes set to null are filled in.

Initiating the CommandBuilder Class

Each of the SQL action queries generated by the CommandBuilder is constructed using the guidelines—see the following code for an example. Setting up a CommandBuilder class is as simple as instantiating it. In this example I've created a CommandBuilder class (cb) using the SqlClient SqlCommandBuilder class passing the SqlDataAdapter (da) as an argument.

```
cn = new SqlConnection ("data source=.;uid=admin;pwd=pw;initial
        catalog=biblio");

cmd= new SqlCommand("SELECT Au_ID, Author, Year_Born FROM authors" +
        "WHERE year_born < 100",cn);
da = new SqlDataAdapter(cmd);
ds= new DataSet();
da.Fill(ds, "Authors");

DataGrid1.DataSource = ds.Tables[0];

SqlCommandBuilder cb = new SqlCommandBuilder(da);
```

No, don't try to examine the CommandBuilder.CommandText property directly—you can't. You have to use one of the GetXXCommand methods—as shown in the following example—to fetch these strings.

```
Debug.WriteLine("InsertCommand:" + cb.GetInsertCommand().CommandText);
Debug.WriteLine("UpdateCommand:" + cb.GetUpdateCommand().CommandText);
Debug.WriteLine("DeleteCommand:" + cb.GetDeleteCommand().CommandText);
```

Generating the InsertCommand

The CommandBuilder constructs an SQL INSERT statement matching the syntax of the provider. For example, if you use the SqlClient provider, the CommandBuilder uses Transact SQL syntax to construct the INSERT.

An example of a typical TSQL INSERT follows. Note the use of parameters that are filled in by ADO.NET when the command is executed.

```
InsertCommand:INSERT INTO authors( Author , Year_Born )
 VALUES ( @p1 , @p2 )
```

The INSERT statement SQL generated by the CommandBuilder is saved in the InsertCommand property and referenced when the Update method is executed.

Each updatable column is included in the statement as illustrated in the following generated code. This means columns generated by expressions or system-generated values—such as row identity or time stamp values—are *not* included in the INSERT.

SQL Server (captured with the Profiler) executes the following SQL statement when the Update method is executed. In this example, I added several rows to a DataGrid control bound to the DataTable associated with the SqlDataAdapter. Note that this INSERT statement is only one of several executed. As I said, each action query uses a round trip to the server. This particular operation is managed by the sp_executesql stored procedure, which is used to improve query performance.

```
exec sp_executesql N'INSERT INTO authors( Author , Year_Born )
 VALUES ( @p1 , @p2 )', N'@p1 varchar(5),@p2 smallint',
 @p1 = 'test2', @p2 = 2
```

Generating the UpdateCommand

The CommandBuilder generates an SQL UPDATE statement and saves it to the UpdateCommand property based on the SelectCommand using an algorithm similar to that used to generate the InsertCommand. As with the InsertCommand, only updatable columns are included in the generated SQL. Note that the UPDATE query is fairly complex—it has to account for NULL values being passed as parameters, as well as compare the original values with those currently in the database. I expect most of us can write more efficient SQL UPDATE queries, but consider that this method has to implement a generic (OSFA) query that's designed to work in a variety of situations and data sources.

```
UpdateCommand:UPDATE authors
SET Author = @p1 , Year_Born = @p2
WHERE ( (Au_ID = @p3) AND ((Author IS NULL AND @p4 IS NULL)
OR (Author = @p5)) AND ((Year_Born IS NULL AND @p6 IS NULL)
OR (Year_Born = @p7)) )
```

After I changed several rows in the DataGrid, and executed the Update method, ADO.NET executed the following action query to update the database. Again, this is only one of several UPDATE statements executed by the Update method; each required its own round trip.

```
exec sp_executesql N'UPDATE authors SET Author = @p1 ,
Year_Born = @p2 WHERE ( (Au_ID = @p3)
AND ((Author IS NULL AND @p4 IS NULL) OR (Author = @p5))
AND ((Year_Born IS NULL AND @p6 IS NULL)
OR (Year_Born = @p7)) )', N'@p1 varchar(5),
@p2 smallint,@p3 int,@p4 varchar(8000),
@p5 varchar(8000),@p6 smallint,@p7 smallint',
@p1 = 'Test1', @p2 = 1, @p3 = 16103, @p4 = NULL,
@p5 = NULL, @p6 = 0, @p7 = 0
```

Generating the DeleteCommand

As with the other CommandBuilder commands, the DeleteCommand is generated by parsing the SelectCommand with the metadata retrieved when polling the database—as discussed earlier. The DELETE query removes a specific row based on the primary key column value where the current row values match the original values fetched from the database. A typical DeleteCommand follows:

```
DeleteCommand:DELETE FROM  authors WHERE ( (Au_ID = @p1)
AND ((Author IS NULL AND @p2 IS NULL) OR (Author = @p3))
AND ((Year_Born IS NULL AND @p4 IS NULL)
OR (Year_Born = @p5)) )
```

After having deleted several rows from the test table, I execute the Update method and SQL Server's Profiler reports that the following statement was executed. As with the other examples, a query like this is executed for each row deleted—each requiring a round trip.

```
exec sp_executesql N'DELETE FROM  authors
WHERE ( (Au_ID = @p1) AND ((Author IS NULL AND @p2 IS NULL)
OR (Author = @p3)) AND ((Year_Born IS NULL AND @p4 IS NULL)
OR (Year_Born = @p5)) )', N'@p1 int,@p2 varchar(5),
@p3 varchar(5),@p4 smallint,@p5 smallint', @p1 = 16103,
@p2 = 'Test1', @p3 = 'Test1', @p4 = 1, @p5 = 1
```

Trying to Understand the Update Plan

The `UpdateCommand` generated by ADO.NET seems complex, but if you understand what it's trying to do, it (almost) makes sense: The SQL is attempting to create a "safe" update.

If you start from the base query:

```
SELECT au_id, author, Year_born FROM authors
```

a simple Update statement would reference the specific row by PrimaryKey and set the new values passed in as parameters:

```
UPDATE authors
SET author = @p1, Year_born = @p2
WHERE au_id = @p3
```

However, if someone else had changed the row since it was last visited, this Update would simply overlay the existing data. This is precisely how some DBMS systems are set up: The last change is kept. But what if the user selected a row at 1:00 P.M. and sat on the row for four hours and didn't change it until just before going home at 5:00 P.M., while others with access to the database continued to make changes? All of the changes made to the data row since the initial fetch (at 1:00 P.M.) would be lost. Without row locking or some mechanism (even artificial) to ensure that there is no chance that two or more clients change the same row(s), this scenario has potentially severe problems. I discussed how to implement pessimistic locking a little earlier—but make sure there aren't other alternatives before you wade into that swamp.

To address this issue, ADO.NET has chosen to add a number of WHERE clause statements to ensure that the originally fetched rows are the same at the instant the UPDATE executes as they were when the row was initially fetched with the SELECT. With the CommandBuilder syntax generated for the `UpdateCommand` and `DeleteCommand` queries, each column fetched is compared to the existing data. If it's not the same, the UPDATE fails. Thus you end up with an UPDATE statement that looks something like this:

```
UPDATE authors
SET author = @p1, Year_born = @p2
WHERE au_id = @p3
AND (Author = @p4)
AND (Year_Born = @p5)
```

For example, the current row value Author is tested against the input parameter @p4, which ADO.NET saved from the original SELECT query. If it doesn't match, the RowsAffected value for this UPDATE returns 0 and ADO.NET knows something went wrong. No, there's no indication what column changed and no way to tell ADO.NET that you don't really care about that column.

But there are still issues with this statement. These "equality" expressions do not work with null values. This means some accommodation has to be made for each column to ensure that if the table-resident column is null and the input parameter is null, the query expression (Author = @P4) does not fail.[6] Thus, our UPDATE statement has evolved to the monster we saw earlier.

IMHO *My fundamental problem with the CommandBuilder is that it's the only run-time-automated Update code generator available in ADO.NET. This means developers are missing several important features ADOc developers have had for years. For example, ADO.NET lacks the ability to set the Update Criteria that tells ADOc how to construct the Update statements. This property gives developers the option of having Update statements reference a TimeStamp column to determine whether the data has changed since it was last visited. One could also specify if all columns or just "touched" columns were part of the generated Update Set list to reduce needless trigger and rule executions. I think these features will be sorely missed until Microsoft has the time to get them back in place in .NET.*

Dealing with Imbedded SQL Punctuation

Some data sources support imbedded spaces or punctuation in their object names. For example, both SQL Server and Access support imbedded spaces, commas, and semicolons in Table, Column, and other object names. ADO.NET permits you to frame these object names in the CommandBuilder-generated SQL by setting the QuotePrefix and QuoteSuffix properties. I suggest that you set these to left and right bracket ([and]) respectively to frame the object names in a bracketed expression. You must set these properties before the CommandBuilder generates the commands or after the Update has been executed. However, another limitation listed earlier indicates that these properties won't help with imbedded "invalid" characters.

---

6. In SQL when you compare any value using "=" against a null, the expression always returns false.

IMHO *Remember how ADOc could generate* UPDATE *queries and let you choose how those were created with the Update Criteria property? Remember how ADOc would let you specify the database, owner, and table of joined tables in complex queries using the Unique properties? Remember how ADOc would batch together the UPDATE, INSERT, and DELETE SQL statements into one or more batches to reduce round-trip overhead? Well, all of these features are still in COM-based ADO, but they weren't carried forward to ADO.NET. Too bad.*

Constructing the Parameters Collection Using DeriveParameters

You can use the CommandBuilder DeriveParameters method to construct a Parameters collection for queries or stored procedures referenced in the SelectCommand. Actually, as it turns out, the DeriveParameters method is simply another implementation of the ADOc Refresh method. To use it, the Connection associated with the DataAdapter must be open and, when executed, ADO.NET executes the following query (passing the name of the TestInOutNoRowset stored procedure).

```
exec sp_procedure_params_rowset
  @procedure_name = N'TestInOutNoRowset'
```

In my example,[7] this query took 1285 milliseconds to execute (that's 1.2 seconds). That's a long, long time as far as queries go. Like the ADOc Refresh method, you still have to go back into the Parameters collection and fix up the Direction property—as in the following code—because they still haven't figured out how to differentiate between INPUT/OUTPUT and OUTPUT parameters or how to set the Precision or NumericScale correctly.

```
public Form1() {
    try { ...
        cn = new SqlConnection("data
            source=.;database=biblio;uid=admin;pwd=pw");
            sc = new SqlCommand("TestInOutNoRowset",cn);

    sc.CommandType = CommandType.StoredProcedure;
        da = new SqlDataAdapter(sc);
        da.SelectCommand = sc;
```

---

7. See the "\Examples\Chapter 07\DeriveParameters on the CD" folder on the CD.

After the DataAdapter is set up, open the connection (sigh) and use the CommandBuilder to construct the Parameters collection. You still have to loop through all but the first of the Parameters to reset the Direction property; this stored procedure uses OUTPUT parameters, not INPUT/OUTPUT.

```
        cn.Open();

        // Populate the DataAdaptor's SelectCommand Parameters.
        SqlCommandBuilder.DeriveParameters(da.SelectCommand);

        // Close the Connection...
        cn.Close();
    }
    catch (Exception ex) {...}
}
```

How the CommandBuilder Deals with Concurrency Issues

As I've said previously, ADO.NET's default locking scheme assumes the rows fetched from the server are not locked. As illustrated earlier, you'll be able to implement a form of pessimistic locking assuming your back end supports it. I do, however, expect a richer implementation of pessimistic locking to appear in a version somewhere down the road; whether that road is as long and fraught with peril and evil witches as the yellow-brick road to Oz, I'm not sure. This means that (by default) when you ask ADO.NET to populate the Rows collection, the data sent to your application is simply a snapshot of the data as it exists at that instant in time. Other users can access the same data and can make changes to it—assuming they have rights to do so.

Just because your ADO.NET application does not implement pessimistic row (or page/table) locking does not mean that other applications or even other data interfaces in your application do not. In other words, other applications or even your own application can use an ADO.NET pessimistic lock (using transactions with an appropriate isolation level[8]), ADOc, DAO, or any other data interface to request the server to lock specific rows, blocks of rows, or entire pages or tables of data. Your ADO.NET application must be prepared to deal with this situation. Generally, when your application is denied access to a locked row, the server will wait for a specified (CommandTimeout) length of time with the expectation that the row will be freed in time to complete your query. If the query time-out period expires (the lock(s) were not released quickly enough), your application trips an exception.

---

8. See the discussion of pessimistic locking ("Update Strategies") earlier in this chapter.

The commands generated for the UpdateCommand and DeleteCommand contain WHERE clauses that make sure that the targeted row (based on PrimaryKey) exists and is the same (column for column) as when it was originally read. If the row is not the same, ADO.NET triggers a DBConcurrencyException. If you want to force your changes through regardless of any other changes to the database, you have to construct your own UpdateCommand and DeleteCommand.

What Happens When Update Is Executed?

Regardless of how the DataAdapter data-modification commands are generated or coded, when the Update method is executed against the DataSet,[9] ADO.NET walks the DataRows collection of each referenced DataTable (there might be several) and checks the RowState property. If the row is new (DataRowState.Added), ADO.NET executes the InsertCommand; if it has been changed (DataRowState.Modified), it executes the UpdateCommand; and if it has been dropped (DataRowState.Deleted) it executes the DeleteCommand. This process is repeated for each row in the Rows collection—each query requiring a round trip to the server. In each case, ADO.NET expects to get back a RowsAffected value of 1—one row added, one row updated, one row deleted. Any other value indicates that the change failed to complete correctly, in which case ADO.NET throws an exception.

But what if something goes wrong in the update? What if a row is not there to update (someone deleted it) or the row has been changed since you last fetched it? What if a row is locked because some application (even yours) is using pessimistic locking? What if a server-side rule prevents the update from completing? What if a trigger fires and returns an error (RAISERROR in SQL Server)? Stay tuned, I discuss each of these contingencies later in this chapter.

 TIP *ADO.NET might be confused if the* UpdateCommand *does not return the RowsAffected value. This might be due to the query or stored procedure used to execute the UPDATE statement. To attempt to resolve this issue,* **add** SET NOCOUNT OFF, *or* **remove** SET NOCOUNT ON *in the stored procedure to ensure that the rows-affected value* **is** *returned.*

---

9.   I discuss the Update method and its use later in this chapter, see "Understanding the UpdateMethods."

Using Visual Studio to Generate Action Queries

The CommandBuilder is not the only way to generate the action queries needed to SELECT, UPDATE, INSERT, and DELETE rows in your database. Visual Studio .NET also includes wizards that can do the job—and do it better. No, they still don't come up to the standard set by ADOc, but they do provide a workable starting point. This section discusses how to use these wizards to generate the ad hoc queries and, if desired, the stored procedures to modify your database table. Yes, I'm afraid this technique is constrained by the same restrictions as the Command-Builder—it can't deal with joined tables. So, if you need to work with a single table under the same restrictions as before, but want to generate the code at design time, these Visual Studio wizards are the ticket.

Reviewing the Generated Stored Procedures

Return for a moment to Chapter 3 and review the use of the DataAdapter configuration wizard (DACW) to construct queries. In this chapter, I would like to drill into these queries and the stored procedures ADO.NET generates to see how they are better than the queries generated by the CommandBuilder. For this section, I used the DACW to generate new stored procedures for a simple SELECT and for each of the action queries. I used the Query Builder (launched by the DACW) to generate the SELECT query, as well as each of the other queries that follow here:

```
SELECT Au_ID, Author, Year_Born FROM Authors
WHERE (Year_Born < 1800)
```

The DACW also generated the following stored procedures based on the SELECT statement:

- The SELECT stored procedure:

    ```
    CREATE PROCEDURE dbo.AuthorsInvalidDate
    AS
      SET NOCOUNT ON;
      SELECT Au_ID, Author, Year_Born
      FROM Authors WHERE (Year_Born < 1800)
    ```

- The INSERT stored procedure:

```
CREATE PROCEDURE dbo.AuthorInsert
 (@Author varchar(50),
  @Year_Born smallint)
AS
  SET NOCOUNT OFF;
  INSERT INTO Authors(Author, Year_Born)
   VALUES (@Author, @Year_Born);
  SELECT Au_ID, Author, Year_Born FROM Authors
   WHERE (Au_ID = @@IDENTITY)
```

I changed the last SELECT in this stored procedure to better deal with the identity issues by substituting @@IDENTITY with SCOPE_IDENTITY(), which my SQL Server 2000 system supports. This addresses some race conditions caused by secondary table triggers firing when a new row is inserted.

```
SELECT Au_ID, Author, Year_Born FROM Authors
  WHERE (Au_ID = SCOPE_IDENTITY())
```

- The UPDATE stored procedure:

```
CREATE PROCEDURE dbo.AuthorUpdate
(    @Author varchar(50),
     @Year_Born smallint,
     @Original_Au_ID int,
     @Original_Author varchar(50),
     @Original_Year_Born smallint,
     @Au_ID int )
AS
     SET NOCOUNT OFF;
UPDATE Authors SET Author = @Author, Year_Born = @Year_Born
WHERE (Au_ID = @Original_Au_ID)
AND (Author = @Original_Author
  OR @Original_Author IS NULL AND Author IS NULL)
AND (Year_Born = @Original_Year_Born
  OR @Original_Year_Born IS NULL AND Year_Born IS NULL);
SELECT Au_ID, Author, Year_Born
FROM Authors
WHERE (Au_ID = @Au_ID)
```

- The DELETE stored procedure:

```
CREATE PROCEDURE dbo.AuthorDelete
(    @Original_Au_ID int,
     @Original_Author varchar(50),
     @Original_Year_Born smallint )
AS
  SET NOCOUNT OFF;
DELETE FROM Authors WHERE (Au_ID = @Original_Au_ID)
 AND (Author = @Original_Author
  OR @Original_Author IS NULL AND Author IS NULL)
 AND (Year_Born = @Original_Year_Born
  OR @Original_Year_Born IS NULL AND Year_Born IS NULL)
```

It's immediately clear that Visual Studio's CommandBuilder is smarter than the one built into the ADO.NET .NET Data Providers. While the "safe" queries are similar, there are other factors here that make the code easier to work with and more functional. First, the parameters generated are spelled out. For example, the original values are passed in the UPDATE and DELETE queries and the parameters are marked as such.

```
 OR @Original_Year_Born IS NULL AND Year_Born IS NULL)
```

Another very important difference is the inclusion of the second resultset generated for the UPDATE stored procedure. This returns the newly generated columns including the new Identity value.

```
SELECT Au_ID, Author, Year_Born FROM Authors
WHERE (Au_ID = @Au_ID)
```

Because this value is generated by the query, you can map it back into your bound controls and manage this value more easily. I illustrate this technique later in this chapter.

Another, more serious issue I have with this generated SQL Server code is that it uses @@Identity. This is a global variable that returns the last-generated Identity value. That's cool if you have a simple system without triggers firing when rows are inserted. If, however, you upgrade your system later and fire a trigger or two when a row is inserted, things can go wrong when using @@Identity. I discuss this issue later in this chapter (see "Retrieving Autonumber, Identity, or GUIDs"), so suffice it to say you should be using the new SCOPE_IDENTITY() function—assuming you're running SQL Server 2000.

David Sceppa (fellow author and ADO guru) informed me of yet another issue that can turn the use of the DACW or the CommandBuilder into an exercise in frustration. It seems that this was not an issue in pre-beta 2 versions of .NET because object names were delimited with brackets ([My Table]), but in the released version of ADO.NET these brackets disappeared. Yes, we both tell developers to avoid imbedding spaces in database, table, column, view, or stored procedure names, but even the sample NorthWind database contains lots of object names with imbedded spaces. It's one of the (litany of) reasons I don't recommend use of NorthWind. Okay, what does this mean to you? Well, all is not lost; you can (must) set the QuotePrefix and QuoteSuffix properties to [and] respectively in the **Tool | Options | DataBase Tools | Query/ViewDesigner** dialog or in code.

Reviewing the Generated Code

Another job of the DACW is to construct code to build and populate the Connection, Command, and DataAdapter objects. When you specify stored procedures to manage the action query tasks, the DACW adds a considerable amount of code to your project. I'm not going to dump the entire project into these pages[10] but I will highlight some of the more interesting parts that you might want to strip out and use in your own projects.

The Generated SelectCommand

Let's start with the SelectCommand. It's pretty straightforward, but notice how the @Return_Value Parameter object is constructed. Also note that the DACW makes no attempt to use With syntax (which improves readability and (probably) performance).

```
// SqlSelectCommand1
//
this.SqlSelectCommand1.CommandText = "[AuthorsInvalidDate]";
this.SqlSelectCommand1.CommandType = System.Data.CommandType.StoredProcedure;
this.SqlSelectCommand1.Connection = this.SqlConnection1;
this.SqlSelectCommand1.Parameters.Add(new
    System.Data.SqlClient.SqlParameter("@RETURN_VALUE",
    System.Data.SqlDbType.Int, 4, System.Data.ParameterDirection.ReturnValue,
    false, ((System.Byte)(0)), ((System.Byte)(0)), "",
    System.Data.DataRowVersion.Current, null));
```

---

10. I did, however, dump the whole project on the CD. See the "\Examples\Chapter 07\Create Author Update SPs" folder.

In this case, the DACW-generated code that initializes a new instance of the SqlParameter class with the constructor arguments is shown in Table 7-4:

Table 7-4. Arguments Passed to the SqlParameter Constructor

Argument	DataType	Setting
Name	String	@RETURN_VALUE
Type	SqlDbType	SqlDbType.Int
Size	Integer	4
Direction	ParameterDirection	ParameterDirection.ReturnValue
IsNullable	Boolean	False
Precision	Byte	(System.Byte)(0)
Scale	Byte	(System.Byte)(0)
Source Column	String	"" (not referenced)
DataRowVersion	DataRowVersion	DataRowVersion.Current
Value	Object	null

By this time, all of these properties should make sense—I've discussed them all at least once. Notice that the Source Column argument is not filled in so the code won't try to return this value into the target DataTable. Remember that the SourceColumn property tells ADO.NET to insert the returned value into a specified column of the DataTable (at least when you set the Direction to ReturnValue, InputOutput, or Output). What's a little strange here is that the DACW chose to use the constructor that references the Precision and Scale Parameter object properties and not the simpler constructor used to build integer-only Parameters. There aren't many (okay, any) Return_Value arguments that have a decimal component—they're all integers.

The Generated InsertCommand

The INSERT query generated for the SqlInsertCommand is, by contrast, mapped back to the DataTable, so after the Command executes, the new data values are inserted into the DataTable object in memory to keep it in sync. This is programmed by setting the SourceColumn property using the SourceColumn argument in the SqlParameter constructor.

```
// SqlInsertCommand1
//
this.SqlInsertCommand1.CommandText = "[AuthorInsert]";
this.SqlInsertCommand1.CommandType = System.Data.CommandType.StoredProcedure;
this.SqlInsertCommand1.Connection = this.SqlConnection1;
this.SqlInsertCommand1.Parameters.Add(new
    System.Data.SqlClient.SqlParameter("@RETURN_VALUE",
    System.Data.SqlDbType.Int, 4, System.Data.ParameterDirection.ReturnValue,
    false, ((System.Byte)(0)), ((System.Byte)(0)), "",
    System.Data.DataRowVersion.Current, null));
this.SqlInsertCommand1.Parameters.Add(new
    System.Data.SqlClient.SqlParameter("@Author", System.Data.SqlDbType.VarChar,
    50, "Author"));
this.SqlInsertCommand1.Parameters.Add(new
    System.Data.SqlClient.SqlParameter("@Year_Born",
    System.Data.SqlDbType.SmallInt, 2, "Year_Born"));
```

Note that the `@Author` and `@Year_Born` columns are "mapped" to correspond to the second SELECT statement's return columns in the AuthorInsert procedure as shown again here:

```
SELECT Au_ID, Author, Year_Born FROM Authors
  WHERE (Au_ID = @IDENTITY)
```

The Generated UpdateCommand

The DACW-generated `UpdateCommand` is very different from the Command object generated by the CommandBuilder. Note that it constructs parameters for the original values because these are (still) used in the stored procedure to determine whether the row has changed. I wondered if the SELECT query would affect this approach. That is, suppose the database table has a TimeStamp instead of or in addition to an Identity value as the PrimaryKey? If I were going to write an UPDATE query, I would certainly try to use the TimeStamp value to see if changes were made since the row was last visited. Well, I tried it—there was no change. Apparently, this is as good as it gets—the brute-force update technique. Sigh. Perhaps next time.

```
// SqlUpdateCommand1
//
this.SqlUpdateCommand1.CommandText = "[AuthorUpdate]";
this.SqlUpdateCommand1.CommandType = System.Data.CommandType.StoredProcedure;
this.SqlUpdateCommand1.Connection = this.SqlConnection1;
this.SqlUpdateCommand1.Parameters.Add(new
    System.Data.SqlClient.SqlParameter("@RETURN_VALUE",
    System.Data.SqlDbType.Int, 4, System.Data.ParameterDirection.ReturnValue,
    false, ((System.Byte)(0)), ((System.Byte)(0)), "",
    System.Data.DataRowVersion.Current, null));
this.SqlUpdateCommand1.Parameters.Add(new
    System.Data.SqlClient.SqlParameter("@Author", System.Data.SqlDbType.VarChar,
    50, "Author"));
this.SqlUpdateCommand1.Parameters.Add(new
    System.Data.SqlClient.SqlParameter("@Year_Born",
    System.Data.SqlDbType.SmallInt, 2, "Year_Born"));
this.SqlUpdateCommand1.Parameters.Add(new
    System.Data.SqlClient.SqlParameter("@Original_Au_ID",
    System.Data.SqlDbType.Int, 4, System.Data.ParameterDirection.Input, false,
    ((System.Byte)(0)), ((System.Byte)(0)), "Au_ID",
    System.Data.DataRowVersion.Original, null));
this.SqlUpdateCommand1.Parameters.Add(new
    System.Data.SqlClient.SqlParameter("@Original_Author",
    System.Data.SqlDbType.VarChar, 50, System.Data.ParameterDirection.Input,
    false, ((System.Byte)(0)), ((System.Byte)(0)), "Author",
    System.Data.DataRowVersion.Original, null));
this.SqlUpdateCommand1.Parameters.Add(new
    System.Data.SqlClient.SqlParameter("@Original_Year_Born",
    System.Data.SqlDbType.SmallInt, 2, System.Data.ParameterDirection.Input,
    false, ((System.Byte)(0)), ((System.Byte)(0)), "Year_Born",
    System.Data.DataRowVersion.Original, null));
this.SqlUpdateCommand1.Parameters.Add(new
    System.Data.SqlClient.SqlParameter("@Au_ID", System.Data.SqlDbType.Int, 4,
    "Au_ID"));
```

The Generated DeleteCommand

The DeleteCommand generated by the DACW is faced with the same challenges faced by the UpdateCommand. ADO.NET has generated a parameter query to ensure that the target row (to be deleted) has not changed since it was last read. It uses the same approach as the UpdateCommand.

```
// SqlDeleteCommand1
//
this.SqlDeleteCommand1.CommandText = "[AuthorDelete]";
this.SqlDeleteCommand1.CommandType = System.Data.CommandType.StoredProcedure;
this.SqlDeleteCommand1.Connection = this.SqlConnection1;
this.SqlDeleteCommand1.Parameters.Add(new
    System.Data.SqlClient.SqlParameter("@RETURN_VALUE",
    System.Data.SqlDbType.Int, 4, System.Data.ParameterDirection.ReturnValue,
    false, ((System.Byte)(0)), ((System.Byte)(0)), "",
    System.Data.DataRowVersion.Current, null));
this.SqlDeleteCommand1.Parameters.Add(new
    System.Data.SqlClient.SqlParameter("@Original_Au_ID",
    System.Data.SqlDbType.Int, 4, System.Data.ParameterDirection.Input, false,
    ((System.Byte)(0)), ((System.Byte)(0)), "Au_ID",
    System.Data.DataRowVersion.Original, null));
this.SqlDeleteCommand1.Parameters.Add(new
    System.Data.SqlClient.SqlParameter("@Original_Author",
    System.Data.SqlDbType.VarChar, 50, System.Data.ParameterDirection.Input,
    false, ((System.Byte)(0)), ((System.Byte)(0)), "Author",
    System.Data.DataRowVersion.Original, null));
this.SqlDeleteCommand1.Parameters.Add(new
    System.Data.SqlClient.SqlParameter("@Original_Year_Born",
    System.Data.SqlDbType.SmallInt, 2, System.Data.ParameterDirection.Input,
    false, ((System.Byte)(0)), ((System.Byte)(0)), "Year_Born",
    System.Data.DataRowVersion.Original, null));
```

Retrieving Autonumber, Identity, or GUIDs

Many of our tables use an "identity" column or other automatically incrementing primary key to make sure that each row is identified with a unique value. Even if you dozed off during the early chapters of this book, you'll probably know there are a number of issues with this strategy:

- After you add a new row, how can you determine the new unique value?

- Suppose the database is being replicated. How do remote sites add rows and retrieve unique values for their new rows and still guarantee that these row identifiers are not duplicated at other sites?

- When the identity value is created, the server can return this value as a variable. What if some other process generates its own identity value for another row in another table? Which is returned?

ADO.NET architecture makes this issue even more complex because it assumes that the memory-resident copy of the resultset supports auto incrementing without fear of collisions with other clients adding rows to the same base table(s). Well, to resolve this issue, ADO.NET assumes that it's the server's responsibility to create new identity values. This means that when you execute an INSERT statement or add a row to the Rows collection, you don't attempt to set the auto-increment value yourself—you leave it up to the server to resolve. But this is not a new strategy; we've always done it this way. ADO.NET also can deal with identity values created independently of the database engine. When I get to the last section in this chapter where I discuss merging DataTables, you'll see how ADO.NET resolves these values.

The next challenge is to retrieve the newly generated identity values. This can still be accomplished using techniques we've all been using for some time. One approach with which most of us are comfortable is to use an OUTPUT parameter from a stored procedure to return the newly created identity value. This value can be mapped back to a specific column in the DataSet quite easily—as I illustrate in a minute. Of course, not all data sources support stored procedures, and others don't support OUTPUT parameters. If this is the case, you'll need to find another approach. It has been suggested that you add code to the RowUpdated event to requery the data source and retrieve the new identity value.[11] My suggestion would be to find a more serious server if this is a critical issue for you.

The following example illustrates several interesting points—all of which are new to ADOc developers:

- Constructing an `InsertCommand` to call a stored procedure whose input arguments are "bound" to a DataRow column.

- Using the Update method to pass the input arguments from a new data row to the stored procedure.

- Using an OUTPUT parameter in the stored procedure to fill in the new row identity.

Let's start with the stored procedure. In this case, it's a simple INSERT statement that accepts a couple of input arguments followed by a Set statement that returns the new identity value. Note that I use the new SQL Server 2000 `SCOPE_IDENTITY()` function. This function is not confused by any triggers that fire as a result of adding a new row to the target table. It's far safer to use than the old `@@IDENTITY` global variable.

---

11. There is an example of using the RowUpdated event in MSDN Help.

```
CREATE PROCEDURE ReturnIdentityFromInsert
(  @NameIn Varchar(50),
    @StateIn Varchar(50),
    @NewID Integer OUTPUT  )
AS

INSERT INTO TestInsert ([Name], State) VALUES (@NameIn, @StateIn)

SET @NewID = SCOPE_IDENTITY()
```

The setup code sets up two commands—the SelectCommand and the InsertCommand. The SelectCommand returns three columns from the TestInsert table; it's small, so the fact that there is no WHERE clause is not important here. I also set up the InsertCommand to execute a stored procedure—as in the preceding ReturnIdentityFromInsert.

The magic here is in how the InsertCommand Parameters collection is created. Notice that the SourceColumn argument is provided for each of the input and OUTPUT parameters. This string is used to tie the parameter back to the DataRow by column name. After these columns are mapped, ADO.NET can fill in the input parameters before the InsertCommand is executed and then retrieve the OUTPUT parameter into the correct DataRow column after the query is executed. Cool? I think so.

```
private SqlConnection cn;
private SqlDataAdapter da;
private SqlCommand scSelect;
private SqlCommand scInsert;
private DataSet ds;
public Form1() {
    try{...
        cn = new SqlConnection("data
            source=.;database=biblio;uid=admin;pwd=pw");
        da = new SqlDataAdapter();
        scSelect = new SqlCommand("SELECT ID,Name,State FROM TestInsert", cn);
        scInsert = new SqlCommand("ReturnIdentityFromInsert",cn);
        scInsert.CommandType = CommandType.StoredProcedure;

        scInsert.Parameters.Add("@Return_Status", SqlDbType.Int);
        scInsert.Parameters.Add("@NameIn", SqlDbType.VarChar, 50, "Name");
        scInsert.Parameters.Add("@StateIn", SqlDbType.VarChar, 50, "State");
        scInsert.Parameters.Add("@NewID", SqlDbType.Int, 1, "ID");
        scInsert.Parameters["@Return_Status"].Direction =
            ParameterDirection.ReturnValue;
        scInsert.Parameters["@NewID"].Direction = ParameterDirection.Output;
```

```
            ds = new DataSet();

            da.SelectCommand = scSelect;
            da.InsertCommand = scInsert;
            da.Fill(ds, "TestInsert");
            DataGrid1.DataSource = ds.Tables[0];


        }
        catch (Exception ex) {...}
}
```

The last part of the example will look like magic if you don't understand that
ADO.NET has already been told what to do earlier. This example[12] captures the
two input parameters from TextBox controls and inserts these into a new
DataRow which is added to the Rows collection. The Update method executes the
InsertCommand—passing in the mapped DataRow values as input arguments to
the stored procedure and returning the new Identity (ID) value into the new row.
It does not get much easier.

```
private void btnInsert_Click(object sender, System.EventArgs e) {
    DataRow Newdr;
    try{
        Newdr = ds.Tables["TestInsert"].NewRow();
        Newdr["Name"] = txtName.Text;
        Newdr["State"] = txtState.Text;
        ds.Tables[0].Rows.Add(Newdr);
        da.Update(ds, "TestInsert");
        txtNewId.Text = scInsert.Parameters["@NewID"].Value.ToString();
    }
    catch (Exception ex) {...}
}
```

Using Visual Studio to Create Commands

Another approach (that I'm not going to revisit) is to use Visual Studio
drag-and-drop to create the Command objects. Frankly, while the SQL
commands constructed here are better (Visual Studio apparently does not use
the CommandBuilder), they are only useful for fairly simple applications or as a
starting point for writing (or learning to write) your own queries.

---

12.   Located in the "\Examples\Chapter 07\Identity Value Via OUTPUT Parm" folder on the CD.

To get Visual Studio to create your Command objects, use the technique described in Chapter 2 to run the DACW. This process builds the `SelectCommand` and one or all of the Update, Delete, and Insert commands for you.

Note that you don't have to let Visual Studio drop a bunch of complex code into your application to take advantage of Visual Studio's ability to generate SQL. It's easy to get Visual Studio to open a Query Builder window; just follow these steps:

1. Open the **Server Explorer** and create or open a connection.

2. Choose your target table—even if you intend to select from more than one table—and open it.

3. Click the **Show Diagram**, **Show Grid**, and **Show SQL** pane buttons near the top of the screen. These expose the functionality of the Query Builder. You'll find it easier to use than its Visual Studio 6.0 DaVinci Tools parent.

4. When you're ready, copy the code from the SQL pane into your application and clean up the line breaks.

Another really useful/long-awaited/stolen-from-Visual InterDev feature is Visual Studio's ability to insert SQL directly into the stored procedures you're building. Simply open a new or existing stored procedure and right-click to **Insert SQL**. The Query Builder opens and permits you to interactively construct and test SQL statements that are subsequently (and automatically) inserted into your stored procedure.

Understanding the Update Methods

One of the challenges that "classic" Visual Basic developers will have to face is that there is not a single set of arguments for many of the methods on which we rely. Not only are there more objects, properties, and methods, but many of these objects have a number of implementations—"overloaded" extensions. Ah the joys of true inheritance and object-oriented programming. The Update method is a typical example. Remember that the Update method in each case simply calls the respective Update, Delete, and Insert Command objects (if any) for each updated, deleted, or inserted row in the specified DataTable or array of DataRow objects. The difference is that you can invoke the Update method against the DataRow, DataSet, or DataTable. Table 7-5 lists the DataAdapter Update methods—at least for one of the .NET Data Providers (SqlClient):

Table 7-5. DataAdapter Update Method Overload List

Update Overload	Description
Update(DataRow( ))	Executes data modification commands against the selected DataRow (and just that row).
Update(DataSet)	Walks the DataSet Tables collection and executes data-modification commands against each row in each Table object's Rows collection.
Update(DataTable)	Executes data modification commands against each DataRow in the specified DataTable object.
Update(DataRow( ), DataTableMapping)	Walks the array of DataRows executing the data modification commands for each DataRow objects and in the array.
Update(DataSet, String)	Walks the DataSet Tables collection and executes data modification commands against each row in the Table object indicated by the string argument.

What the documentation does not say is that the Update method, like the Fill method, opens the connection associated with the Update Command objects and closes it (actually releases it to the pool) when the update operations are complete. Of course, if the connection is already open, it's simply used to perform the update operations and remains open after they are complete.

The Update method (regardless of the overload) returns an integer value (RowsAffected) that indicates the number of rows affected by the operation(s). This means if you add fifteen rows, change twenty rows, and drop fifty rows, the Update method returns eighty-five rows after eighty-five round trips to the server.

The following diagram (Figure 7-4) illustrates how the data versions maintained by ADO.NET are used to feed the UpdateCommand and DeleteCommand parameters.

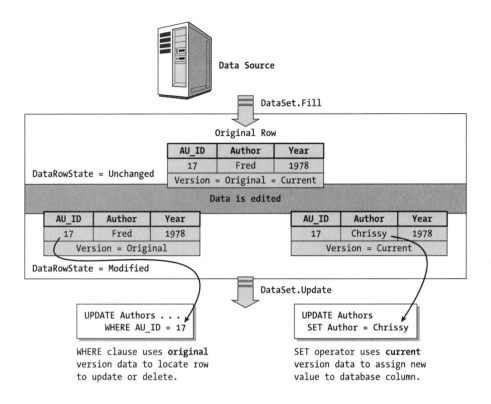

Figure 7-4. How ADO.NET passes data versions to update parameters.

Update Performance

Your update strategy and the chances of it succeeding really depend on a number of factors—many of which are determined by the way you construct your initial SELECT query. For example, if your query returns a single indexed row, you'll have an easier time updating it when contrasted to attempting to update a subset of a thousand rows. In any case, if you want ADO.NET to execute the UpdateCommand for you, it will attempt to do so one row at a time. In most (okay, all) cases this is very inefficient because it requires a round trip for each row.

A more efficient approach, especially when there are many rows to update, is to use a bulk INSERT statement *on the server*. That is, write a WHERE clause for the UPDATE statement that changes all of the targeted rows in a single operation. Like this:

```
UPDATE Employees SET Salary = Salary * 1.10
WHERE YearsInService > 15
```

As I discussed earlier in the ADOc section, you might find it far faster to construct blocks of INSERT statements to insert many rows at once or more complex queries that bind several update operations into a single transaction. More typically, complex update operations are handled by stored procedures.

A few more points you might want to consider:

- **Consider that when you fetch a row from a table without a TimeStamp, you can't always tell if another user changes the row.** For example, if you fetch a row with a column HairColor set to "red" and change the color to "black," you won't be able to tell that someone else has already changed the color to "black" because your update will succeed as long as none of the other columns are changed as well.

- **When you change a row, be sure to avoid changing the primary key.** When you do so, you're really executing a DELETE followed by an INSERT.

Another Approach to Bulk Inserts: Use XML

In a recent e-mail[13] dialog on one of the list servers,[14] I heard about a new idea that leverages both stored procedure and XML at the same time to perform bulk INSERTs. The challenge was to use a stored procedure to execute a set of INSERT queries, but to avoid repetitive and expensive round trips. The solution only works with SQL Server 2000,[15] but it's an elegant way to resolve this nagging problem. Basically, you construct a stored procedure that uses OPENXML to feed an INSERT statement—like in the following example. First, the stored procedure accepts a Varchar string (up to 8000 bytes in length) parameter containing a set of INSERT queries expressed as an XML document. This string is converted to an in-memory XML document with the sp_xml_preparedocument stored procedure which returns a pointer to the XML document as an OUTPUT parameter. This document is fed to the INSERT statement via a SELECT * FROM OPENXML statement that points to the in-memory XML document.

---

13. Thanks to Pratick Mukherjee (http://www.rdacustomsoftware.com) of Atlanta, GA for this tip. He's a consultant at RDA Corp who's into peanuts and cricket.

14. VBDATA-L@Peach.Ease.Lsoft.com

15. This technique is described in SQL Server 2000 books online under OpenXML.

```
CREATE PROCEDURE [dbo].[sp_candidate_SaveSurveyResults]
@surveyResult varchar(8000),
AS
DECLARE @hDoc int
EXEC sp_xml_preparedocument @hDoc OUTPUT, @surveyResult
INSERT INTO MyTargetTable
SELECT * FROM OPENXML(@hDoc, '/Root/Results',1)
WITH MyTargetTable
EXEC sp_xml_removedocument @hDoc
```

The XML structure is also pretty simple with just a Root node and Results nodes for the records. Each Results node represents a record to be inserted and the table fields are the attributes of each Results node. The only thing to watch out for is case-sensitivity in comparing the node attributes and the table fields. You can also have nested nodes to represent a one-to-many or a many-to-many relationship. Just change the XML pattern-matching expression in case you must deal with nested nodes—and wash your hands afterwards.

Updating the Authors Table—An Example

The following example[16] walks you through a simple scenario that uses a stored procedure to fetch a set of rows from and posts an update to the Authors table. These rows are bound to a WinForm DataGrid control, which is used to add, change, and delete selected rows. The code contains an exception handler that deals with a few of the typical collision-handling issues, but not nearly all of the potential exceptions that could occur. The example executes four stored procedures to query and change the rows. The action queries were all auto-generated by Visual Studio as discussed earlier in this chapter, and then tuned to make them more...well, suitable. These changes were, for the most part, minor. I used a different SELECT query to return the rows; it accepts Year_Born as an input parameter to limit the number of rows returned.

This example is a little more complete than others. While simple,[17] it performs several basic steps and illustrates many of the points you need to understand before being comfortable updating with ADO.NET.

Figure 7-5 is a screen-shot of the completed example. It queries the Authors table based on a given Year_Born value and permits the user to edit the values in a DataGrid control. After a change is made and the **Show Versions** button is clicked, the application posts the various versions found to the TextBox controls in the

---

16. Located in the "\Examples\Chapter 07\Update".

17. Despite being "simple," this application is fairly large as examples go. It has over 800 lines of code—but I wrote only about 200 of those—Visual Studio .NET IDE added the rest.

IMHO *The technique illustrated in this example has a number of benefits over Visual Basic 6.0 data binding. Because ADO.NET does not attempt to execute any queries until told to do so, you have a lot more control over the connection and your database. This is a big step in the right direction.*

center of the form. When the **Update** button is clicked, the application calls the Update method to post any changes to the table. The new data values continue to appear in the DataGrid control—even if the change disqualifies the row based on the initial query. If any rows fail to update and the **Stop on First Error** option button is checked, a dialog appears that prompts the user for instructions. However, if the **Continue After Error** option button is checked, then the Update method skips over any exceptions and simply marks the DataRow so it can be filtered out later.

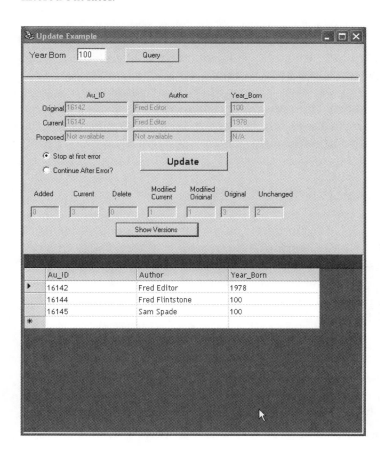

Figure 7-5. The completed Update example.

NOTE *While the names of the previously mentioned "authors" might appear to be valid real-world authors, this is only test data. Any similarity to real authors is mostly coincidental.*

Working with an Updatable DataGrid Control

When you set the DataGrid control's DataSource property to the DataTable generated by your query it displays and becomes a direct path to the Rows collection. The DataGrid automatically populates itself with the DataRows and fills in its headings from the Columns collection. It does not, however, automatically set the column widths,[18] so you still have to do that yourself. When you select a row in the DataGrid, you're essentially selecting a specific DataRow in the Rows collection. Any changes you make to the DataGrid are made to the DataRow, just as any changes made to the DataTable through other code paths are reflected in the DataGrid. For example, if you create a DataView on the DataTable and set the DataView.RowStateFilter property to `DataViewRowState.Added`, all rows in the DataGrid disappear except the newly added rows. Of course, the other rows are still there, but only the filtered rows are shown. Setting the DataView object's RowStateFilter property can also change the DataGrid.CurrentRowIndex property, so the DataGrid row on which you think you're working might change.

Showing the Available Data Versions

The example application is programmed to display the contents of each data version stored by ADO.NET on demand. This can help you understand what these various versions are set to and when they change in the course of updating a rowset. When you click the **Show Versions** button on the form, two routines are called. The first dumps each of the versions and the second dumps each of the row counts based on the RowStateFilter enumerations.

---

18. The beta 2 version of Visual Basic .NET did support an "auto-resize" mode that used the data values from the first ten rows to set the column widths. This was removed because it was too slow (or the Microsoft developers were too … let's not go there). Setting column widths in ADO.NET is an order of magnitude harder than it was in the MSHFlexGrid or any grid control in Visual Basic 6.0.

Let's take a look at the first routine. It simply fetches each of the version types, but not until the HasVersion method returns True to indicate that the particular version is available. If you ask for a version type that's not available, you trip an exception. Notice that this method applies to the entire row, not to a particular column. If the version information is not present, the routine sets the TextBox control to "Not available" or "N/A".

```
private void ShowVersions(int dgRowNumber) {
    try {
        DataRow dr = ds.Tables[0].Rows[dgRowNumber];
        string strNa = "Not available";

        if (dr.HasVersion(DataRowVersion.Current)) {
            txtAuIDCurrent.Text = dr["Au_ID",
                DataRowVersion.Current].ToString();
            txtAuthorCurrent.Text = dr["Author",
                DataRowVersion.Current].ToString();
            txtYear_BornCurrent.Text = dr["Year_Born",
                DataRowVersion.Current].ToString();
        }
        else {
            txtAuIDCurrent.Text = strNa;
            txtAuthorCurrent.Text = strNa;
            txtYear_BornCurrent.Text = "N/A";
        }
        if( dr.HasVersion(DataRowVersion.Proposed)) {
            txtAuIDProposed.Text = dr["Au_ID",
            DataRowVersion.Proposed].ToString();
            txtAuthorProposed.Text = dr["Author",
            DataRowVersion.Proposed].ToString();
            txtYear_BornProposed.Text = dr["Year_Born",
            DataRowVersion.Proposed].ToString();
        }
        else {
            txtAuIDProposed.Text = strNa;
            txtAuthorProposed.Text = strNa;
            txtYear_BornProposed.Text = "N/A";

        }
        if (dr.HasVersion(DataRowVersion.Original)) {
            txtAuIDOriginal.Text = dr["Au_ID",
                DataRowVersion.Original].ToString();
            txtAuthorOriginal.Text = dr["Author",
```

```
            DataRowVersion.Original].ToString();
        txtYear_BornOriginal.Text = dr["Year_Born",
            DataRowVersion.Original].ToString();
    }
    else{
        txtAuIDOriginal.Text = strNa;
        txtAuthorOriginal.Text = strNa;
        txtYear_BornOriginal.Text = "N/A";
    }
    ComputeRowCounts();
}
catch (Exception ex){...}
}
```

When the ShowVersions subroutine runs, the TextBox controls look something like Figure 7-6.

	Au_ID	Author	Year_Born
Original	16142	Fred Editor	100
Current	16142	Fred Editor	1978
Proposed	Not available	Not available	N/A

Figure 7-6. DataRowVersion displayed in the Update example.

Showing the Row Counts

In order to compute how many rows are going to be modified, I capture the number of rows added, deleted, or modified. I then compare that value to the RowsAffected argument returned from the Update method. To this end, I created the ComputeRowCounts subroutine to capture those values and display them on the form; the code for that routine follows. It creates a DataView object and sets each of the RowStateFilter enumerations, capturing the Count each time. Notice that I save the DataGrid control's CurrentRowIndex so I can reset it at the end of the routine. This is because the CurrentRowIndex—that points to the working or current row in the grid—is changed if the number of rows shown in the grid changes. Many of the RowStateFilter settings affect the number of rows displayed, as discussed earlier.

```
private void ComputeRowCounts() {
    try {
        // Save the grid index--changing the RowStateFilter can change it
        int intDataGridIndex = DataGrid1.CurrentRowIndex;
        dv = ds.Tables["Authors"].DefaultView;

        Debug.WriteLine("---- " + DateTime.Now.ToLongDateString() + "------");
        dv.RowStateFilter = DataViewRowState.Added;
        Debug.WriteLine("Added:" + dv.Count);
        intAdded = dv.Count;
        txtAdded.Text = intAdded.ToString();

        dv.RowStateFilter = DataViewRowState.CurrentRows;
        Debug.WriteLine("Current Rows:" + dv.Count);
        intCurrent = dv.Count;
        txtCurrent.Text = intCurrent.ToString();

        dv.RowStateFilter = DataViewRowState.Deleted;
        Debug.WriteLine("Deleted:" + dv.Count);
        intDeleted = dv.Count;
        txtDelete.Text = intDeleted.ToString();

        dv.RowStateFilter = DataViewRowState.ModifiedCurrent;
        Debug.WriteLine("Modified Current:" + dv.Count);
        intModifiedCurrent = dv.Count;
        txtModifiedCurrent.Text = intModifiedCurrent.ToString();

        dv.RowStateFilter = DataViewRowState.ModifiedOriginal;
        Debug.WriteLine("Modified Original:" + dv.Count);
        intModifiedOriginal = dv.Count;
        txtModifiedOriginal.Text = intModifiedOriginal.ToString();

        dv.RowStateFilter = DataViewRowState.OriginalRows;
        Debug.WriteLine("Original Rows:" + dv.Count);
        intOriginal = dv.Count;
        txtOriginal.Text = intOriginal.ToString();

        dv.RowStateFilter = DataViewRowState.Unchanged;
        Debug.WriteLine("Unchanged:" + dv.Count);
        intUnchanged = dv.Count;
        txtUnchanged.Text = intUnchanged.ToString();

        dv.RowStateFilter = DataViewRowState.CurrentRows;
        DataGrid1.CurrentRowIndex = intDataGridIndex;
    }
    catch( Exception ex) {...}
}
```

When this routine ends, the TextBox controls on the form look something like Figure 7-7.

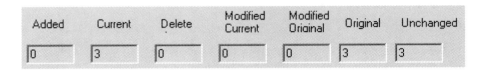

Added	Current	Delete	Modified Current	Modified Original	Original	Unchanged
0	3	0	0	0	3	3

Figure 7-7. DataView using RowStateFilter.

Using GetChanges to Manage Modified Rows

The GetChanges method is an alternative to getting each of the DataViewRowState counts to determine how many total data-modification operations are expected. GetChanges simply returns a new DataTable or DataSet containing just the changes. This method is especially interesting to those application architectures that don't do the updates on their own, but that pass a data structure to another tier for posting or processing.

The GetChanges method can be applied to the entire set of DataTables in a DataSet or to a single DataTable. Each returns a duplicate data structure containing just the altered rows. You can also choose to filter the rows passed to the new data structure by setting an argument in the GetChanges method. This way you can pass the added rows to one routine, the deleted rows to another, and the modified rows to yet another.

The following code is drawn from the Update button click-event in the example. The final version of the example includes code to make sure the Update button click-event does not fire until the data has changed. This avoids an exception that can be tripped if you try to extract the changes when nothing has changed. This event handler creates a new DataTable drawn from the altered DataTable that contains all of the changed rows. I then check the Rows collection Count property to see how many changes were made. This value is compared to the previously computed count of modified rows to verify that both arrive at the same value.

```
DataTable dtChanges = new DataTable();
int IntChanges;
dtChanges = ds.Tables["Authors"].GetChanges();
IntChanges = dtChanges.Rows.Count;
if (IntChanges != intModified) {
    MessageBox.Show("GetChanges count (" + IntChanges + ") does not match
        computed count (" + intModified + ").");
}
```

Update Exception Handling Strategies

When you execute the Update method and several rows are going to be changed, remember that, by default, ADO.NET *stops* at the first sign of trouble, abandons the operation, and trips a trappable exception (DBConcurrencyException). This means that if there are twenty rows to be changed ahead of the row that caused the exception, these twenty rows will be changed, but the rows following the exception will not. That is, those rows will not be changed unless you set the (all-important) DataAdapter ContinueUpdateOnError property or use transactions. Frankly, I would have expected the Update method to automatically continue by default if there was an exception. Fortunately, the ContinueUpdateOnError property makes the Update statement work more reasonably. However, if the Update fails, you won't get a trappable exception—that's the bad news. The good news is that you can still filter out the rows that had problems and revisit them to see what went wrong and try to figure out what can be done to fix them. The problem with this approach is that it might take several (many, many) attempts to work down through the collisions because the first collision causes the Update method to throw an exception.

The application example shown throughout this chapter illustrates use of the ContinueUpdateOnError technique. You'll also notice that the DataGrid in the example automatically marks rows that have update problems with a big red exclamation mark (!) as shown in Figure 7-8.

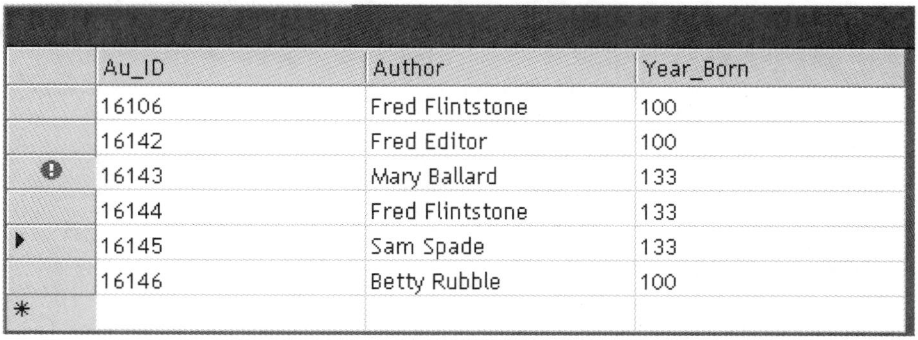

	Au_ID	Author	Year_Born
	16106	Fred Flintstone	100
	16142	Fred Editor	100
●	16143	Mary Ballard	133
	16144	Fred Flintstone	133
▶	16145	Sam Spade	133
	16146	Betty Rubble	100
∗			

Figure 7-8. DataGrid shows which row(s) failed to update.

The ability for the DataGrid to show which row(s) failed to update can save you lots of time and code. It's a very cool feature.

Using the ContinueAfterError Property

The DBConcurrencyException exception won't fire if you have set the DataAdapter object's ContinueAfterError property to True. In this case, you must add a test after each Update statement to see if the action query (or queries) actually completed successfully. The example illustrates a technique that approaches the problem by using the DataView with the RowStateFilter property set to return a count of added, deleted, and other available values. These integer counters were summed to compute the number of rows to be updated. Why I had to go to this amount of trouble escapes me—all of the information was there, I just had to compute it by hand. Why doesn't ADO.NET add a RowsModified RowStateFilter enumeration? BHOM. The next few lines of code (okay, there are about a dozen) capture the first few of these values from the DataTable's DefaultView property. I applied the DataViewRowState enumerations to the RowStateFilter one-by-one to extract the integer values.

```
dv = ds.Tables["Authors"].DefaultView;

Debug.WriteLine("---- " + DateTime.Now.ToLongDateString() + "------");
dv.RowStateFilter = DataViewRowState.Added;
Debug.WriteLine("Added:" + dv.Count);
intAdded = dv.Count;
txtAdded.Text = intAdded.ToString();

dv.RowStateFilter = DataViewRowState.CurrentRows;
Debug.WriteLine("Current Rows:" + dv.Count);
intCurrent = dv.Count;
txtCurrent.Text = intCurrent.ToString();

dv.RowStateFilter = DataViewRowState.Deleted;
Debug.WriteLine("Deleted:" + dv.Count);
intDeleted = dv.Count;
txtDelete.Text = intDeleted.ToString();
...
```

After the values have been captured, I sum them to compute the number of rows to be updated. This should match the RowsAffected value returned by the Update statement—if all goes as planned.

```
intModified = intAdded + intDeleted + intModifiedOriginal;
```

Next, the Update method (framed in a try/catch block) executes to post the changes to the database. When the ContinueAfterError property is set to `true`, the Update method does not branch to the catch—it falls through. I throw up a message box to alert the user, but this is probably not a good idea—especially on a Web page or middle-tier component.

```
try{ ...
        RowsAffected = da.Update(ds.Tables["Authors"]);
        ds.Tables["Authors"].AcceptChanges();
        if (intModified != RowsAffected) {
            MessageBox.Show("Something went wrong with the update. \r\n"
              +"We expected to update " + intModified + " rows, but actually"
              +" affected " + RowsAffected + " rows.","Update Example"
              ,MessageBoxButtons.OK, MessageBoxIcon.Stop);
        }
...
```

Another approach you might take is to use the HasErrors property of the DataSet object to determine whether the DataSet has any rows that have errors. If HasErrors returns `true`, you can walk the DataTable and use the GetErrors method to extract the error string for any (or all) columns—as in the following code:

```
if( ds.HasErrors) {
    string errStr = "";
    foreach ( DataRow dr in ds.Tables["Authors"].GetErrors()) {
        errStr = errStr + "Au_ID = " + dr["Au_ID"].ToString() +
            " Author:" + dr["Author"].ToString() +
            " Born:" + dr["Year_Born"].ToString() + " Error = " +
            dr.RowError + "\n\r"; }
    MessageBox.Show(errStr,"DataTable Error",MessageBoxButtons.OK,
    MessageBoxIcon.Information);
}
```

 WARNING *A serious issue with this approach is that ADO.NET also bypasses exceptions generated by the .NET Data Provider—SqlClient in this case. This means you can't tell if the exception was caused by a rule, a trigger, or a blown referential integrity rule. All you know is that the RowsAffected does not match the expected count of changed rows. In some cases (as least with the current builds), HasErrors does not return True when there are Delete errors. I'm sure this is a bug and will be corrected soon.*

What to Do When an Update Fails

Okay, the Update method threw an exception. Now what? This isn't as fatal as blowing out a poorly manufactured tire on an overpass, but the result can be the same if you're not ready. If an Update method exception is thrown, you probably have a DataSet that has one or more rows that failed to get updated, added, or deleted. At this point, you are going to have to jump through a few hoops to get the database to reflect what you want it to be. Part of the problem here might be your basic update strategy. One issue is trying to determine if rows have changed based on column data comparisons. I think update concurrency tests based on TimeStamp values are a far better approach—they're faster and far easier to code. No, ADO.NET does not (yet) provide the flexibility that ADOc Update Criteria provided. I hear that the next version should support better control over action command generation.

You have several choices when you find that some or all of the action commands did not go through. For example, you can force through the UPDATE by removing all of the column value tests. However, this technique requires another Command object that leaves out the check to see if anyone else has changed the row. If this is the strategy you expect to use in the event of a data collision, you probably should have used it in the first place. The UPDATE statement is really easy to write in this case:

```
UPDATE Authors SET Author = @p1, Year_Born = @p2
WHERE Au_ID = @p3
```

But this strategy won't work for an INSERT. If the row is already there, you have to read back the current values and decide what to do and (perhaps) execute an UPDATE query. This is another reason why I don't like to execute INSERT statements in the blind—hoping that they will work. If your data strategy ensures that your insert operations will always succeed (perhaps because you have constructed the unique identifier yourself) this is not an issue. But if you depend on computer-generated identifiers, you might want to consider creating these in bulk ahead of time and mark the rows as "inactive" until you post the actual data using an UPDATE which also sets the rows as "active."

Of course, you usually have another choice—you can take the passive approach and leave the data as is if there is a collision. This means you ignore the collision and a requery on the target row to report back the current data state to the user.

Handling Update Method Exceptions

When you set up your application's Update exception handler, there is a litany of things that you must be prepared to trap. These include the same list of "exceptions"[19] that occur in ADOc. As a short refresher, be prepared for:

- **Connection is no longer available.** The server might be down or simply out of available connections, or it might have been replaced with a Linux box by a cost-conscious accountant who watches too much TV.

- **The changes you're making violate a primary key/foreign key relationship.** For example, you can't delete an author or publishers that have related titles in the Titles table.

- **The new row you're adding violates a unique constraint.** If you're not using an Identity key or a GUID, this is fairly likely.

- **The data added or updated violates a server-side rule.** Perhaps a data column has a range limit. It's still an integer, but a valid value for a person's age might be 0 to 120 (or so).

- **Some other application, component, or ASP has the data locked and your query timed out waiting for the lock to be released.** Unfortunately, the data is locked by your boss's workstation and he went skydiving last week and hasn't returned.

- **A trigger fired and you've broken one or more business rules.** Perhaps the customer with whom you're working has exceeded his credit limit.

This list is by no stretch of the imagination complete or comprehensive. As I said before (many times), you must be prepared for a boat-load of issues, business rules, and office politics when working with relational databases—regardless of the interface, server, platform, or DBMS.

---

19. As I have said earlier, these "exceptions" are a normal part of any program that handles data in a relational database.

All of the previously listed exceptions (and many more) are trapped by the .NET Data Provider's exceptions handler—assuming you've created an appropriate Catch statement. For example, this means that with the SqlClient provider, you need to add a Catch statement for `SqlClient.SqlException`. There are a bevy of things that can go wrong with an Update, but ADO.NET exposes only the three exceptions listed in Table 7-6:

Table 7-6. Update Exceptions

Exception Type	Condition
ArgumentNullException	The DataSet is invalid.
InvalidOperationException	The source table is invalid.
DBConcurrencyException	An attempt to execute an INSERT, UPDATE, or DELETE statement resulted in zero records affected (see following notes).

Some typical[20] exceptions you are likely to encounter include:

- **Could not locate the specified row (based on PrimaryKey) to change.** This could be due to someone deleting the row since it was last read.

- **Found the row, but discovered that someone else had already changed it**. The values originally fetched did not match the current row values.

- **More than one row qualified based on the PrimaryKey.** In other words the PrimaryKey did not turn out to be unique after all.

- **The target row no longer exists.** It was deleted or the row identifier was changed (which basically deletes the row). Just exactly who did the deleting is anyone's guess.

- **The inserted row did not get added to the database for some reason.** Perhaps it's already there. Perhaps the database is full or just sick of all of your constant requests to change stuff.

- **The target row is there but the columns have changed.** If you use the "compare all the database columns with the originals" technique to determine if the rows have changed, any change to any column will prevent the update or delete operation from returning 1 as the number of rows affected.

---

20. Again, this list does not include all possible contingencies—there's not enough paper to print them all in a list.

WARNING *ADO.NET won't trip an exception if someone changed a row to the same values your UPDATE is changing them to. If this is a concern, use a TimeStamp column to manage concurrency.*

The DBConcurrencyException does not give you much to work with besides the Message and a pointer to the DataRow that failed. However, the DataRow has quite a bit of information, including the exception message, as illustrated in the example I discussed earlier in this chapter. This is usually enough to determine what went wrong.

As the Update method scans the Rows collection searching for RowState values that indicate something has changed, it executes the operations in no particular order—but usually top-to-bottom starting at the top (ordinal 0) of the Rows collection. If you wish to control the sequence in which the data-modification queries are fired, you can execute the GetChanges method and selectively build a DataSet that contains just Updated, Deleted, or Inserted rows using the matching DataRowState enumerations. Once selected, the Update method can be executed against each subset. For example, to capture just those rows that have been modified into another DataSet you can execute:

```
xDataSet = myDataSet.GetChanges(DataRowState.Modified);
```

Coding the Update DBConcurrencyException Trap

If you don't set the ContinueUpdateOnError property to True (discussed earlier in this chapter), you can expect to trip an exception in your Catch handler. Yes, you had better have traps for exceptions generated by the .NET Data Provider, as well as for the more common DBConcurrencyException exception. The DBConcurrencyException Catch handler in the example calls the ConcurrencyErrorMessage subroutine, which constructs a string that contains information about the exception message and row being changed; it then prompts the user for advice.

TIP *Again, I'm not in favor of prompting the user for this type of advice. They rarely know how to resolve the issue and all too often delay while trying to figure it out. This, in turn, leads to more issues than before. Generally, you should plan to resolve these issues on your own.*

```
catch (SqlException sex) {
    MessageBox.Show(sex.Message);
}
catch (DBConcurrencyException dbconex){
    if (dbconex.Row.HasErrors ) {
        ConcurrencyErrorMessage(dbconex);
        dbconex.Row.ClearErrors();
    }
    else {
        MessageBox.Show("Exception with no errors on the row passed");
    }
    ShowVersions(DataGrid1.CurrentCell.RowNumber);
}
```

Executing Ad Hoc Queries to Perform Updates

Another approach, in contrast to having ADO.NET (or Visual Studio) construct the INSERT, UPDATE and DELETE queries for you, is to develop these action queries yourself. I expect that most shops will tend to choose this option because they already have a suite of stored procedures designed to maintain their data stores. Consider that ADO.NET can still do much of the front-end management of updates for you even if you use roll-your-own stored procedures to do the heavy-lifting when it comes time to update the data.

I've already discussed the techniques of creating stored procedures to perform updates and how to execute them, so I don't think I need to discuss this again. As a matter of fact, the example discussed earlier in this chapter was driven with stored procedures.

The advantage to using stored procedure or ad hoc action queries is that you can code far more sophisticated and technologically aware procedures. These types of procedures can take advantage of TimeStamp columns and situations where you want to SET only those data columns that have changed. This avoids unnecessary server-side overhead caused by extra rules and trigger code firing.

 IMHO *However, that said, consider that Microsoft is undoubtedly already enhancing ADO.NET to incorporate more sophisticated routines that implement the same (and better) update strategies to which we've become accustomed in ADOc. Remember the Update Criteria property? I expect that same flexibility to be incorporated into later versions of ADO.NET.*

Merging and Transporting Data

Unlike ADOc, ADO.NET excels at the ability to modify the schema of existing DataTable objects and cleverly merge two (or more) DataTables or DataSets as easily as shuffling cards—even if they are different shapes—well, within reason.

The DataSet Merge method can easily amalgamate two DataSet objects that have roughly the same schema. This method is usually used to incorporate changes made to a DataSet by another application or another part of the same application. Think of this process as being like the process of merging changes made to a document as several writers contribute to the content. Typically, the Merge method is the final operation executed after the data is validated, any exceptions are resolved, the data is posted to the database, and the local DataSet is refreshed.

For example, a client application can gather data from the user and validate it before sending it to a middle-tier component. To implement this scenario, GetChanges is used to capture just the changed rows into another DataTable or DataSet. This reduces the memory and data transmission loads because only the "delta" (the changes) are transmitted between tiers. Next, the data is transmitted by argument to the middle tier.

Note that the DataSet is always transmitted as XML between tiers. The middle-tier component can process the data as needed, either by updating the database based on the structures passed or by simply crunching the data in any way necessary. The middle tier can respond to the client by returning a Boolean indicating that the operation was successful or, more typically, it can rerun the original query to return the latest data from the data source. For example, when rows are added and the unique primary keys are generated on the server, the middle-tier query can retrieve these new values and insert them into the middle tier's copy of the DataSet. After the modified DataSet is returned to the client it can be merged (using the Merge method) with the memory-resident copy to reconcile the differences.

When discussing the Merge method you need to understand the gazintas and gazoutas—or what goes into what from where. In easier terms, ADO.NET refers to the current DataSet as the "target" and the second DataSet as the "source." Remember that the Merge method does not affect the source DataSet in any way; it's the target that gets changed.

In some cases, the schema of the two DataSet objects might not be the same. It's possible for an application or middle-tier component to add columns to a DataSet to deal with a special data situation. I've done this to add extra exception or informational data to a data structure so the client application can more easily deal with special conditions. You can get ADO.NET to add these new columns to the target DataSet by setting the missingSchemaAction argument to `MissingSchemaAction.Add`.

If you started this process by using the GetChanges method, the original DataSet sent to the middle tier did not have all of the rows. In this case, if you use the GetChanges method, ADO.NET assigns each row a unique identifier that's used later when it comes time to use Merge. No, you can't get at it—it's hidden behind the curtains. This means that the copy (clone) of the source DataSet has the same unique ID values as the original rows in the target. These internally generated ID values are used to match the source and target rows. After a match is found, the original values are overlaid with the values from the source DataSet; the changed values remain untouched.

In cases where Merge is executed but you did *not* use GetChanges to generate the DataSet to transmit to the middle tier, ADO.NET searches the target for a matching row (using the primary key) if the source row's DataRowState is set to Unchanged, Modified, or Deleted. If the DataRowState is set to New, the same search is done but with the new primary key value.

While Merge is executing, the data constraints are disabled. After Merge is completed, any constraints that cannot be enabled cause a ConstraintException to be generated. At this point the EnforceConstraints property is set to false; the merged data is retained as long as the constraints remain disabled. All rows that fail to pass the constraints are marked with an exception. All of these exceptions must be cleared (and resolved) before attempting to reenable the constraints by setting the EnforceConstraints property to true.

ADO.NET
Constraint Strategies

I JUST FINISHED ANOTHER LONG E-MAIL exchange with David Sceppa about some of the finer details of ADO.NET. I told him that I didn't agree with some of the approaches Microsoft has taken toward handling data constraints, referential integrity, and data validation. He reminded me that developers don't have to use them. That's very true. IMHO, these features will be handy for a subset of the developers using ADO.NET—but not nearly all. This chapter discusses how ADO.NET has implemented referential and data constraints and also how to specify the relationships between tables in your database. I know, you've already done that and you're wondering why ADO.NET doesn't figure this out by itself. That's a question I'm not prepared to answer.

Understanding .NET Constraints

When a relational database is designed it usually (almost always) includes a number of mechanisms used to help the database engine maintain and enforce the data and referential integrity of the data it stores, manages, and protects. Generally, we refer to these mechanisms as "constraints." In ADO.NET, a constraint is an automatic rule applied to a column or related columns that determines the course of action when the value of a row is changed. All serious (and some not so serious) database management systems use constraints, at least to some extent, to manage data and to help their Query Optimizer construct a high-efficiency plan to retrieve the data. Remember that ADO.NET constructs an in-memory database that also must (should) enforce these constraints. Because of this, it's often necessary to create parallel constraints in your ADO.NET data structures that replicate the constraints in the server-side data source database.

Let's walk into the new building Microsoft has constructed to manage referential integrity in .NET. You don't have to come if you're worried your SA will get mad. First, consider that data and referential integrity is (or should be) defined in the database and enforced by the DBMS engine. Most of the professional DBAs with whom I've discussed this agree with me on at least this point. That is, you normally use the referential integrity tools that ship with your DBMS to ensure that when you add an item to an invoice, the part number is in the ValidParts table. Moreover, when you add the new invoice to the Invoices table, the constraints ensure that the Invoice ID does not already exist in that table. This is done using primary key/foreign key relationships and unique constraints.

In SQL Server, these constraints can be created using TSQL code scripts or in SQL Enterprise Manager or Visual Studio by making changes to your database diagram.[1] The point is, these referential integrity constraints are stored as an integral part of the database—not generally as part of your application, middle-tier component, or ASP page. Regardless of the tool, language, application, component, or data access interface you use, these constraints are enforced; the part number must be included in the ValidParts lookup table and the new invoice number must be unique—or the update operation that violates the constraint is rolled back and no changes are made.

ADO.NET's approach suggests that developers replicate/emulate these constraints (at least the ones that make sense) by building a parallel ConstraintCollection each time the DataSet is constructed. This way ADO.NET can perform needed checks to ensure continued referential integrity, permitting the DataSet to be managed in a totally isolated environment without benefit of a DBMS connection. This means you have to add code to your application to clone the database-side constraints and somehow ensure that they stay in sync as the business rules and other factors that morph the constraints change.

Data validation rules apply to individual columns or to logically related sets of columns. For example, a valid postal code or phone number should conform to a specific mask—a known and understood pattern of numbers, punctuation, and letters. However, in different parts of the world, postal codes and phone number formats change quite a bit. For example, in parts of Texas, you simply tell Mabel to get Sam on the line and your "postal code" is "Fourth place on the Austin road past the crick." Other rules might specify how large a number might be. For example, within the state of Washington, valid postal (Zip) codes must be between 98000 and 99499. While this type of rule is generally fixed (until a Republican administration takes over), businesses (and governments) often have to deal with rules that can change at any time. As we all well know, airline ticketing and healthcare pricing systems are clogged with these ever-changing rules. If you're writing an application that has to work despite these rules, you might want to consider a system that permits your application or component to morph itself based on server-side (DBMS-defined) rules. While this was tough in the past, some of the more sophisticated DBMSs (including SQL Server 2000) support extended properties that can be used to store and retrieve these business rules as often as they are needed.

---

1.   See a diagram of the Biblio database in Figure 8-2 in the "Creating DataRelation Objects" section.

ADO.NET does not implement any equivalent functionality beyond low-level datatype checking and string-length checks—and even those are far less stringent than those implemented in ADOc. In other words, ADO.NET can throw an exception if you provide an invalid number or a string `null` when it is not permitted, and it does not have a built-in mechanism to make sure the data conforms to a given mask or range. However, there are .NET controls that can provide this functionality.

How ADO.NET Implements Constraints

There are several different types of constraints and ADO.NET implements many of them—one way or another:

- **Null constraints**: The ability to indicate if the column can permit `null` values. The ADO.NET DataColumn class exposes the Boolean AllowDBNull property that, when set to True, permits the value in the column to be set to `null`. See the discussion of how `null` values are handled in code in the "Working with Null Values" section in Chapter 5.

- **Check constraints**: Used to enforce data integrity by limiting the values that can be assigned to a column. These are implemented in SQL Server using Rules or `CONSTRAINT` operators when a data table is created. There is no direct equivalent in ADO.NET, nevertheless, you can set the DataColumn class's MaxLength property to limit the number of characters in a variable-length (text) datatype and include additional code to validate data on your own. If your database has check constraints installed, you had better be prepared for additional exceptions caused by `UPDATE` or `INSERT` queries that violate these constraints.

- **Primary key constraints**: Identify the column(s) whose values uniquely identify a row in a table. Primary key columns cannot be defined as permitting `null` values. This is implemented in ADO.NET by the DataTable that exposes the PrimaryKey property, which holds an array of DataColumn objects that make up the primary key columns. I illustrated how to set the PrimaryKey property array in the "Setting the PrimaryKey Property" section in Chapter 6.

- **Unique constraints**: Used to ensure that each row in a data table is unique. After a unique constraint is created (or enabled), the engine verifies that each row has a unique value in the specified column(s) specified by the constraint. This means that no two rows are completely identical. This permits fetch and maintenance operations to focus on individual rows. ADO.NET implements the unique constraint by exposing the UniqueConstraint object that can be assigned to a single or array of columns in a DataTable. See the discussion of the UniqueConstraint object later in this chapter in the "Implementing Unique Constraints" section.

- **Foreign key constraints**: Define the relationships between two related tables. For example, in the Biblio database, there is a primary key/foreign key relationship between the Titles table and the Publishers table. This constraint makes sure that before you add a new row to the Titles table that the PUB_ID column contains a valid entry pointing to a valid PUB_ID value in the Publishers table. This foreign key constraint also prevents you from deleting a row from the Publishers table that has related rows in the Titles table. ADO.NET implements foreign key constraints through use of the ForeignKeyConstraint object discussed later in this chapter in the "Implementing Foreign Key Constraints" section.

Managing the Constraints Collection

Constraint objects are maintained in the ConstraintCollection collection and associated with specific DataTable objects through the Constraints property. These constraints are not enforced if the EnforceConstraints property is set to false—as I discussed in Chapter 7.

Basically, the DataTable.Constraint is used to:

- **Ensure that when a value is changed in a "constrained" column that the in-memory Table maintains data integrity.** If the Table object's ConstraintCollection contains a ForeignKeyConstraint, the constraint properties can specify if the values in the foreign table are deleted, the changed column's properties are set to `null`, or if a specified default value or an exception is thrown.

- **If a column has a UniqueConstraint in the ConstraintCollection, ADO.NET simply makes sure that the row identifier does not exist in the table when new rows are added.** It has no bearing on collisions with rows not fetched or those that might have been added to the database since the data was initially fetched.

 NOTE *These constraints must be added using code and are not persisted anywhere outside the application or classes where the constraints are defined. If the constraints, or business rules associated with them, change, you have to change them in code as well. There are no wizards (yet) to help you maintain these "parallel" constraints.*

Implementing Unique Constraints

Setting up a unique constraint in ADO.NET is not hard. The unique constraint can consist of one or several columns in your DataTable. It can be constructed using a number of techniques:

- **Set the PrimaryKey property.** This automatically sets up the ConstraintCollection and sets the Unique property on indicated DataColumn objects.

- **Establish a DataRelation between two tables.** This automatically creates UniqueConstraint and ForeignKeyConstraint constraints.

- **Set the Unique property of a single DataColumn object to True to create a single-column unique constraint.** Note that the Unique property is only set if a *single* column constitutes the UniqueConstraint. If the column is married or even has a steady girlfriend, it won't work.

- **Choose the one or more columns in the Columns collection that make the data row unique.** Assign these to elements of the UniqueConstraint array.

- **Use the UniqueConstraint constructor to help build a ConstraintCollection.**

- **Use the Add method to append UniqueConstraint objects to the ConstraintCollection.**

The following examples[2] illustrate several of these techniques. One approach to creating constraints is to create a UniqueConstraint object and populate it using the new constructor. There are several overloads available. The technique used in this example accepts one (or more) DataColumn objects. In this case I extracted these DataColumn objects from an existing table created with the Fill method. I used this approach because the documentation usually illustrates this concept by creating a table in memory. Note that you have to actually create the DataTable objects before trying to access the Columns collection. The first Debug statement indicates that the ISBN DataColumn object's Unique property is False before creating the UniqueConstraint and True afterwards.

---

2.   Located in the "\Examples\Chapter 08\Create UniqueConstraints" folder on the CD.

```
da.Fill(ds, "Titles");
dt = ds.Tables["Titles"];

// false
Debug.WriteLine("TitleID Unique? " + dt.Columns["ISBN"].Unique.ToString());
UniqueConstraint uc = new UniqueConstraint("CustConstraint", dt.Columns["ISBN"],
    true);

dt.Constraints.Add(uc);

// Now true
Debug.WriteLine("TitleID Unique? " + dt.Columns["ISBN"].Unique.ToString());
```

Another approach[3] to adding constraints to a DataTable is to get ADO.NET to do it for you. While ADO.NET won't fill them all in for you, the DataAdapter FillSchema method can do the trick. Unfortunately, this method requires another round trip to the server—something that I usually try to avoid. First, this method requires an available Connection to the data source, which might not be the case if the code is running on a remote client. Next, the extra round trip must be repeated each time the object is created.

```
da.Fill(ds, "Titles");
dt = ds.Tables["Titles"];

Debug.WriteLine("TitleID Unique? " + dt.Columns["ISBN"].Unique); // False

// Generates round trip FMTONLY query
da.FillSchema(ds.Tables["Titles"], SchemaType.Source);

Debug.WriteLine("TitleID Unique? " + dt.Columns["ISBN"].Unique); // Now true
```

What about situations where there are several columns included in the PrimaryKey? The Title_Author table in the Biblio database is a typical example. In this case the PrimaryKey includes both the ISBN (which points to a valid title in the Titles table) and the AU_ID (which points to a valid author in the Authors table). To set up a UniqueConstraint for this table, you could use the UniqueConstraint new constructor to build a UniqueConstraint with multiple columns.

---

3. Located in the "\Examples\Chapter 08\FillSchema to build Constraints" folder on the CD.

```
da.Fill(ds, "TitleAuthor");
dt = ds.Tables["TitleAuthor"];

Debug.WriteLine("Constraints.count: " + dt.Constraints.Count); // 0
Debug.WriteLine("Enforce Contstraints? " + ds.EnforceConstraints);    // True

DataColumn[] myColumns = new DataColumn[2];
myColumns[0] = dt.Columns["ISBN"];
myColumns[1] = dt.Columns["AU_ID"];

UniqueConstraint myUC = new UniqueConstraint("CustConstraint",  myColumns);

dt.Constraints.Add(myUC);
Debug.WriteLine("Constraints.count: " + dt.Constraints.Count);
Debug.WriteLine("Enforce Contstraints? " + ds.EnforceConstraints);    // True
```

This example[4] also illustrates the Count property of the Constraints collection and the Boolean EnforceConstraints property which returns true—even before the UniqueConstraint property is set.

Implementing Foreign Key Constraints

Generally, the ForeignKeyConstraint is established between one or more DataColumn objects designated as the DataTable object's primary key. This type of constraint implements the traditional relational database PK/FK relationship. This constraint prevents changes to a PK value in one table (a parent) that's linked by a relationship to a PK value (called a "foreign key") in another table (a child). This means that, depending on the actions you program when you create the ForeignKeyConstraint, you won't be able to delete a parent row with related child rows or even change its PK value (which essentially deletes the row anyway). However, as I said earlier, the UniqueConstraint and the ForeignKeyConstraint are not enabled and their rules are not enforced if the EnforceConstraints property is set to False. This means if there are situations where you need to violate referential integrity (that ForeignKeyConstraint objects protect), you can do so by turning off the constraints.

---

4.   Located in the "\Examples\Chapter 08\UniqueIndex With Multiple Columns" folder on the CD.

WARNING *Consider that your database probably already has foreign key constraints installed. No, ADO.NET won't use these to set up your ForeignKeyConstraint objects for you—even with a round trip to the server. You must do this yourself. You must also modify your code whenever the server-side foreign key constraints are changed or you risk creating invalid constraints for your in-memory "database."*

Creating a ForeignKeyConstraint object is done automatically if you create a relationship between two or more tables; I discuss this in the next section. The process of creating ForeignKeyConstraint objects in code is not that different from creating UniqueConstraint objects, but there are a number of additional options that determine what actions ADO.NET performs when a row is updated or deleted. These actions also determine what actions are taken if changes are made to related tables. You set what actions are to be taken by setting the rule properties of the ForeignKeyConstraint. These rule properties are:

- **AcceptRejectRule**: Determines what ADO.NET does when AcceptChanges or RejectChanges is invoked. Default is None.

- **DeleteRule**: Determines what ADO.NET does when a row is deleted. Default is Cascade.

- **UpdateRule**: Determines what ADO.NET does when a row is updated. Default is Cascade.

Valid action settings for the rules are outlined in Table 8-1.

Table 8-1. ForeignKeyConstraint DeleteRule Actions

ACTION	APPLIES TO	DESCRIPTION
Cascade	AcceptRejectRule, DeleteRule, UpdateRule	Deletes or updates related rows (see later). Default for DeleteRule and UpdateRule.
SetNull	DeleteRule, UpdateRule	Sets the Value property of the child row's related key to DBNULL. However, this assumes that the column is programmed to accept null values—it probably isn't.

(continued)

Table 8-1. ForeignKeyConstraint DeleteRule Actions (continued)

ACTION	APPLIES TO	DESCRIPTION
SetDefault	DeleteRule, UpdateRule	Sets values in related rows to the default value.
None	AcceptRejectRule, DeleteRule, UpdateRule	Specifies that no action be taken on related rows. This can also be bad because it could wreck referential integrity. (See later.)

Understanding the Cascade Action

The default action for the UpdateRule and DeleteRule is Cascade and the AcceptRejectRule can also be set to Cascade (but its default action is None). By setting a rule to Cascade, ADO.NET ensures that *all* child rows in a PK/FK relationship are automatically deleted when the related parent row is deleted. It sounds kinda brutal, but remember folks, it's only data.

WARNING *Cascading operations can be a very powerful tool in the hands of a skilled developer or disastrous in the hands of someone who's ADO-challenged. For example, if you set the DeleteRule to Cascade on a lookup table (such as ValidStates) that's part of a ForeignKeyConstraint and you delete one of the ValidStates rows such as Texas, you have also (and quite quickly, I might add) deleted all of the related children in the relationship—and possibly all of their children as well—but only for the state of Texas.*

When you perform deletes on relational data, the action queries you execute must ensure and maintain the referential integrity of your database. As you know, every child row in a relationship must refer to a valid parent row. This means parent rows should not (must not) be deleted as long as the parent has viable children. Sure, it's okay to delete the children along with the parents such as when you delete an order and all of the items associated with that order. But deleting an order and leaving the items in the database is not good. In most cases, ADO.NET trips an exception if you attempt to perform an `Update` or `Delete` method that violates the ForeignKeyConstraint rules. Remember that you can disable constraints when using the Update method. See Chapter 7 for details.

Understanding Parent/Child Primary Key/ Foreign Key Relationships

There are many types of relationships when working with relational databases; the one-to-many relationship is the most common type. In a one-to-many (sometimes shown as 1- ∞) relationship, a row in Table A can have many matching rows in Table B, but a row in Table B can have only one matching row in Table A. For example, there can only be one ValidStates..StateCode for the Addresses..State-Code. Many tables in the Biblio database have one-to-many relationships. The Customers and Titles tables also have a one-to-many relationship; each customer can have many Addresses, but an Address only applies to one customer—at least in the Biblio database. As seen in Figure 8-1, Customers is the one side (the parent) and the Addresses table is the many side (the child).

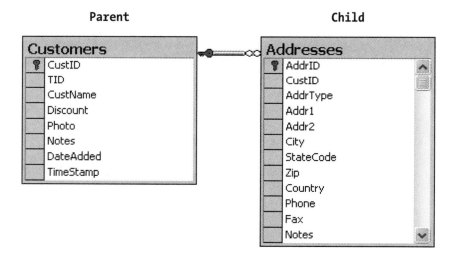

Figure 8-1. Database diagram showing one-to-many relationship.

When you set up a ForeignKeyConstraint, the one side of the one-to-many relationship is the parent and the many side is the child. This means that the ValidStates table would be the parent and the Addresses table would be the child.

The one-to-many relationship can only be created if one (and only one) of the related columns is a primary key or has a unique constraint. In the case of the ValidStates to Addresses example, the StateCode in the ValidStates table is the primary key and is unique.

TIP   *When you view or manage the database relationships using Visual Studio, the primary-key side (the parent) of a one-to-many relationship is denoted by a key symbol 🔑). The foreign-key side (the child) of a relationship is denoted by an infinity symbol (∞). Remember that a mom (a parent) can have many children, but a child can have only one biological mom. No, Aunt Mary does not count—at least not in this case.*

Creating ForeignKeyConstraint Objects

If you want to add a ForeignKeyConstraint object for your in-memory DataSet, you can use the ForeignKeyConstraint constructor that supports enough overloads to deal with all of the options. However, the most challenging part might be figuring out which table is the parent and which is the child. I know a number of families where this is an issue—especially when it comes to deciding whether the parent or the child gets control over the TV remote on a Thursday night. It's not much easier with relational databases.

The following example[5] illustrates setting up a ForeignKeyConstraint between the ValidStates table and the Addresses table. Remember that the Add method on the DataTable Constraints collection is also flexible enough to help build these constraints.

```
try { ...
    SqlConnection cn = new SqlConnection(
        "database=biblio;Data Source=.;integrated security=sspi");
    SqlCommand scStates = new SqlCommand(
        "SELECT StateCode, State FROM ValidStates ", cn);
    SqlCommand scAddr = new SqlCommand(
        "SELECT AddrID, CustID, StateCode, City FROM Addresses WHERE StateCode " +
        " IN (SELECT StateCode FROM ValidStates)", cn);
    SqlDataAdapter da = new SqlDataAdapter(scStates);
    DataTable dt = new DataTable();
    DataSet ds = new DataSet("CustomerAddress");
```

---

5.   Located in the "\Examples\Chapter 08\ForeignKeyConstraint" folder on the CD.

```
        da.Fill(ds, "States");
        da.SelectCommand = scAddr;
        da.Fill(ds, 1, 50, "Addresses");      // Get the first 50 rows.

        DataColumn parentCols;
        DataColumn childCols;
        ForeignKeyConstraint FKC;

        // Set parent and child column variables.
        childCols = ds.Tables["Addresses"].Columns["StateCode"];
        parentCols = ds.Tables["States"].Columns["StateCode"];
        FKC = new ForeignKeyConstraint(parentCols, childCols);

        // Set constraint Rule properties.
        FKC.DeleteRule = Rule.SetDefault;
        FKC.UpdateRule = Rule.Cascade;
        FKC.AcceptRejectRule = AcceptRejectRule.Cascade;

        // Add the constraint, and set EnforceConstraints to true.
        ds.Tables["Addresses"].Constraints.Add(FKC);
        ds.EnforceConstraints = true;
    }
    catch( Exception ex ) { ... }
```

In cases where there are multiple columns involved in the primary key/foreign key relationship (they must be matching pairs in this case), simply create arrays of DataColumn objects and pass these arrays to the ForeignKeyConstraint constructor. You can also pass the rule settings to the constructor as arguments.

Using the FillSchema Method

The DataAdapter Fill method fetches the data rows from the DataSource, but does not fetch the schema. You can use the FillSchema method to fill in the primary key constraints to populate the DataSet with the current database schema information. Foreign key constraint information is not included and will need to be explicitly created as the previous examples illustrate. As I said before, the FillSchema method causes ADO.NET to perform another round trip to the server for this information.

WARNING *If one of the columns in your data set is identified as auto-incrementing (such as an identity column), the FillSchema or Fill methods set the AutoIncrement property to True but do not set the AutoIncrementStep or AutoIncrementSeed properties—you have to do that yourself.*

Make sure the schema information is filled in *before* you fill your DataSet with data. This ensures that when additional calls to the Fill method are made, primary key information from the inbound rows can be used to update the current DataSet data. If you just append to the DataSet you get duplicate rows. Not good.

NOTE *If the FillSchema method is called for a command that returns multiple resultsets, only the schema information from the first resultset is returned. When returning schema information for multiple resultsets, Microsoft recommends that you specify a MissingSchemaAction of AddWithKey and obtain the schema information when calling the Fill method.*

Creating DataRelation Objects

The DataRelation object is the new ADO.NET mechanism used to specify relationships between related DataTable objects within a DataSet. There are no "constraints" or "data relations" objects in ADOc,[6] which is why this might seem new to you. The first questions you should be asking are: Why do I need to define these relationships? Aren't they already defined in the database? These are good questions. The answer: You don't need to define these relationships unless you want ADO.NET to handle navigation and referential integrity issues for you. These relationships are already defined in the database, but ADO.NET has no way to retrieve them.

The DataSet manages the inter-DataTable (interrowset) relationships in the DataRelationCollection (`Relations`), which holds one or more DataRelation objects. You can also access DataRelation objects through the Relations property of the DataSet and through the ChildRelations and ParentRelations properties of the DataTable.

As a reminder, the following diagram (Figure 8-2) shows the sample Biblio database and its intertable relationships.

---

6.   ADOMD and the Shape provider do implement similar functionality.

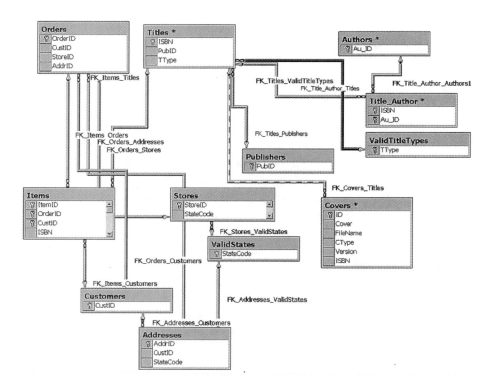

Figure 8-2. The Biblio database and its intertable relationships.

Each DataRelation object links two tables together based on specific matching columns. For example, in the Biblio database, the Pub_ID column in the Titles table is matched with the Pub_ID column in the Publishers table—as illustrated in Figure 8-2 (FK_Titles_Publishers). When I defined this relationship in the Biblio database, I did so to ensure that no Title could be created without a valid publisher on file. This is called a "primary key/foreign key relationship."

When you write code to establish relationships between the DataTable objects you fetch (or create), the DataColumn objects specified must have identical datatypes and lengths (if the DataColumn objects use Varchar or Char DataTypes). The DataRelation objects created for your table can determine the actions that ADO.NET will take when rows are added, updated, or deleted between related tables in your in-memory DataSet "database." Also, the rules you define when using the Constraint objects determine how ADO.NET reacts when there is a violation.

You can't create a DataRelation that has a Constraint or a relationship that has already been violated. For example, if a row already in the Titles table has an invalid Pub_ID before creating a DataRelation between two DataTable objects, ADO.NET throws an exception and it prevents you from creating a DataRelation between the DataTable objects using the Pub_ID column.

WARNING *You must create these relationships (populate the Relations collection) **each** time you build and populate the DataSet object if you want to activate the ADO.NET features that depend on them. Ideally, these relationships should match relationships already established in the database. I can see it would be very easy to get these out of sync. Good luck keeping them straight.*

After a relationship is established, ADO.NET throws an exception if any change to the data would result in a violation in that relationship. This is the same action that would prevent rows from being added to the database when primary key/foreign key relationships are established on the server. You can also enforce unique key identifiers on the table to ensure that new rows are not already in the DataTable based on the primary key(s) you define.

The following example[7] is subroutine from a larger example program (Customer Access 1) that fetches data from the Customers table based on a pre-selected CustID (Customer ID). The following code is used to fetch and display the Order and Item data for the selected customer. The code also shows how to set the intertable relations between the Orders and Items tables. Unlike examples in the documentation, this example illustrates how to set more than one column in the DataRelation. That is, to identify a specific order or item, the query uses two columns: CustID and OrderID.

NOTE *This example follows the .NET convention of establishing the ADO.NET objects each time they are used. It's not clear that this is any more or less efficient than using global objects.*

The first part of the function initializes required variables. Note the use of the `Declaration` constructor to preset the Row and Col values to DataGrid control row and column values.

```
private void ShowOrderItemData( DataGrid dg,  SqlConnection cn) {
    try {
        int lRow = dgCustomers.CurrentCell.RowNumber;
        int lCol = dgCustomers.CurrentCell.ColumnNumber;
        int lCurRow = dgCustomers.CurrentRowIndex;
        int lCustID = Convert.ToInt32(dgCustomers[lRow, 0]);
```

---

7.   Located in the "\Examples\Chapter 08\Customer Access1" folder on the CD.

The following code builds new DataAdapter, Command, and DataSet objects, as well as two arrays of DataColumn objects used to set the Relations later.

```
SqlDataAdapter da = new SqlDataAdapter();
SqlCommand sc = new SqlCommand();
DataSet ds = new DataSet();
DataColumn[] ParentCols = new DataColumn[2];
DataColumn[] ChildCols = new DataColumn[2];
DataRelation relPublishers;
```

Next, I set up the Command object to call the stored procedure used to retrieve the orders and items for the selected customer. I expect that you could set this up ahead of time, but in a Web environment, this might not save you any time or other resources.

```
sc.CommandText = "GetOrdersItemsByCustomer";
sc.CommandType = CommandType.StoredProcedure;
sc.Parameters.Add("@CustIDWanted", SqlDbType.Int).Value = lCustID;
sc.Connection = cn;
da.SelectCommand = sc;
```

When I create a DataSet (to contain the fetched DataTable data) the default DataTable names are "Table" and "Table1". The following code "remaps" those tables so that I can refer to them by more intuitive names: "Orders" and "Items".

```
da.TableMappings.Add("Table", "Orders");
da.TableMappings.Add("Table1", "Items");
```

The following code runs the stored procedure and fills the specified DataSet. This process constructs two DataTable objects and appends them to the Tables collection. Note that the table mapping is done before the Fill.

```
da.Fill(ds);
```

I'm finally ready to set the intertable relationships. I accomplish this by building an array (of DataColumn objects) containing each column in the parent table (orders) that relates to each corresponding column in the child table (Items). Once I've filled the array, it's a simple matter to build a new Relation object with the array of columns and then add the new Relation object to the Relations collection. This process can be repeated as needed for other intertable relations.

```
ParentCols[0] = ds.Tables["Orders"].Columns["CustID"];
    ParentCols[1] = ds.Tables["Orders"].Columns["OrderID"];

    ChildCols[0] = ds.Tables["Items"].Columns["CustID"];
    ChildCols[1] = ds.Tables["Items"].Columns["OrderID"];
    // Create DataRelation.
    bool bConstraints = true;
    relPublishers = new DataRelation("OrderItem", ParentCols, ChildCols,
        bConstraints);

    // Add the relation to the DataSet.
    ds.Relations.Add(relPublishers);
```

After the relations are established, I can bind the first (Parent) table to the DataGrid DataSource property. From there, the user can navigate through the orders and see individual items by clicking on the grid. (See Figure 8-3.)

```
    dg.DataSource = null;
    dg.DataSource = ds.Tables[0];
}
catch( Exception ex){...
}
}
```

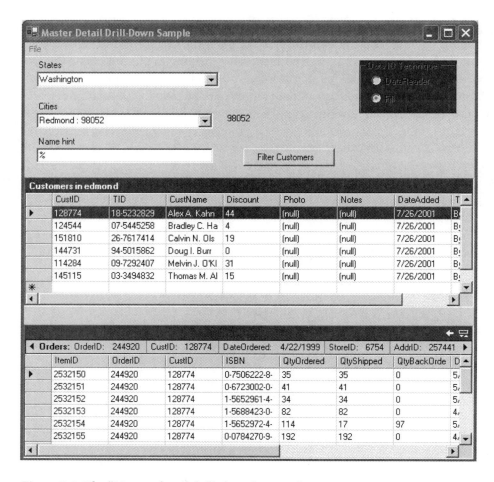

Figure 8-3. The "Master-detail drill-down" example.

ADO.NET Exception Management Strategies

ONE OF THE FUNDAMENTAL CONCEPTS you'll encounter with the .NET Framework (regardless of the language you use) is how exceptions are exposed and managed. While the Visual Basic developer can still use the `On Error GoTo` syntax, it might not make much sense in light of how .NET exposes exceptions. Frankly, as long as On Error management evolves in Visual Basic .NET it remains moving target. Many fundamental On Error features were not implemented in the beta versions, which created quite a disturbance in the developer community. As a result (or so it seems), On Error handling has been almost completely restored. However, this chapter focuses on use of the try/catch exception handler. I also outline the various types of Exception classes you're bound to trip as you work with ADO.NET.

NOTE *Yes, many of these points are beyond the scope of this book. .NET exception handling is not specific to ADO.NET. It is part of the CLR, but I thought that this issue was important enough and new enough if coming from Visual Basic 6.0 to justify including it in the book. I know that it was confusing for me when I first got started with .NET, but if you already know how all of this works, skip to the next chapter on XML.*

The .NET Framework supports two types of exception handling:

- **Unstructured**: For the Visual Basic developer, this is activated when you code an On Error statement at the beginning of a block of code. This type of error handling has no effect on variable scope. The On Error handlers that you used in Visual Basic should work in Visual Basic .NET, but because there are so many other subtle behaviors involved, I don't really recommend their use.

- **Structured**: This approach uses try/catch constructs. In overview: A try block is always followed by one or more catch blocks. If an exception occurs or is explicitly "thrown" (with a call to throw) while executing statements in the try block, then the exception is trapped and control is first passed to the most appropriately matching catch block. Don't fret if that was a little confusing; I spend most of the chapter explaining how this mechanism works.

Structured Exception Handling

IPHO   *The SEH (Structured Exception Handling) learning curve is steepest for those coming from Visual Basic; after all, in my experience "Structured anything" and "Visual Basic code" are almost industry oxymorons. Okay, I'll accept that **your** code wasn't, but the vast majority of Visual Basic code just happened like lava spewing from a volcano, and the venerable defacto exception handler OnError Goto is definitely unstructured. Those coming from C++ will have an easier time here.*

The documentation refers to this new type of exception handling as "structured" because it folds into the seams of object-oriented programming. It's really quite different from the "unstructured" error handling you used in older versions of Visual Basic. Because of this difference, you'll probably have to make fundamental design changes in your functions and subroutines to deal with the realities of this new approach.

This chapter addresses the following points in relation to structured exception handling:

- The C# trap mechanism for Exception handling is the try/catch syntax.

- The try/catch blocks also determine variable scope.

- The try/catch blocks must be defined around executable lines of code so errors might be encountered outside of their control.

- Exception catch statements should be coded with the most specific handlers first, followed by more generic handlers.

- The try/catch blocks can be nested, but not overlapped.

Understanding try/catch

The recommended way to handle errors is *try/catch*—whether you're using C#, Visual Basic .NET, or any of the CLR object-oriented languages. The following discussion should help clear up the mysteries of try/catch to make your transition to this new error-management paradigm.

try/catch Syntax

The try/catch syntax is not that tough to code. Basically, just open a try/catch block with the same try statement you've seen coded many times in the examples in this book.

The catch statement expects you to provide a variable name (I usually use ex) to address the incoming Exception or specialized exception object such as SqlException. No, don't expect to use e as the variable name because this is usually already in use by a parent event handler. If there is more than one catch statement (there usually are), be sure to provide *different* variable names for each one. If you don't, Visual Studio statement completion won't work correctly (but the code will still work).

```
try{
    // your code to "try" goes here
}
catch(SqlException sex) {
    // SqlException or other specific exception handler goes here…
}
catch (SystemException ex) {
    // General-case exception handler goes here…
}
```

Standard Exceptions

As you probably guessed, the specific exception handlers are tripped by specific error conditions. Table 9-1 contains a useful list of "standard" exceptions condensed from online Help that can help you decide which exception handlers you need to code.

Table 9-1. Standard Exceptions

Exception Type	Base Type	Description
Exception	Object	Base class for all exceptions.
SystemException	Exception	Base class for all run-time-generated errors.
IndexOutOfRangeException	SystemException	Thrown by the run time only when an array is indexed improperly. Indexing an array outside of its valid range.
NullReferenceException	SystemException	Thrown by the run time only when a null object is referenced.
InvalidOperationException	SystemException	Thrown by methods when in an invalid state.
ArgumentException	SystemException	Base class for all argument exceptions.
ArgumentNullException	ArgumentException	Thrown by methods that do not allow an argument to be null.
ArgumentOutOfRangeException	ArgumentException	Thrown by methods that verify that arguments are in a given range.
InteropException	SystemException	Base class for exceptions that occur or are targeted at environments outside of the run time.
ComException	InteropException	Exception encapsulating COM Hresult information. Used in COM interop.
SEHException	InteropException	Exception encapsulating Win32 Structured Exception Handling information. Used in unmanaged code Interop.

Variable Scope in try/catch Blocks

When you declare a variable within a try or catch block, the variable is instantiated upon entrance to the block and marked for tear-down as the logic exits the block. This means any variables declared within a try block will only be visible in the try block and not outside of it—like in the catch block.

Exceptions That Fire Outside of try/catch Scope

You can only put a try/catch handler in your application inside of functions—this means that instance objects cannot be instantiated at a global level within a try/catch block. The question you might be asking is: Why does that matter? Well, so long as you instantiate nonstatic instance variables inside try/catch blocks in class constructor functions, then you don't need to fret about unrecognized arguments tripping exceptions.

Nesting Exception Handlers

Yes, it's possible to nest try/catch handlers within other try/catch handlers, however, these definitions cannot overlap. For example, the following try/catch handler is valid:

```
try{
    'Your code goes here….
    try{
        // More specific code goes here
    }
    catch (Exception ex){
        // Error handler goes here
    }
}
    // More code that's monitored by outside Try/Catch handler
catch(SqlException sex) {
    // SqlException or other specific exception handler goes here…
}
catch (SystemException ex) {
    // General-case exception handler goes here…
}
finally{
    // This code is executed when the outer try/catch block ends
}
```

Note that if you get an error inside of a catch block, the error is bubbled up to the parent. If the parent has no Exception handler, your code goes down with an untrapped exception.

Trapping Specific vs. General Exceptions

When setting up your exception handlers, you might be surprised where the errors come from. For example, if your row fails to update due to a collision (see Chapter 7), you'll trip a DBConcurrencyException—not a SqlException. If, on the other hand, your update fails because of a Rule violation or a concurrency error on the server, you *will* trip a SqlException (or OleDbException or OdbcException). Clear? I didn't think so. Just be aware that if ADO.NET generates the error, it exposes one of its specific exceptions as shown in Table 9-2. However, if the SqlClient or one of the other .NET Data Providers traps the error, it throws one of its own Exception classes. The provider-specific exceptions are listed later in this chapter.

The System.Data Exceptions

The following data-related exceptions are thrown by ADO.NET as it encounters various conditions (as shown in the Description column below). No, these exceptions are not all rooted in the System.Data namespace—most root in System.Exception.SystemException.DataException. EvaluateException and SyntaxErrorException are derived from InvalidExpressionException. Yes, a serious application might well have many of these exceptions handled.

Table 9-2. System.Data Exceptions

Exception	Description—Thrown When…
ConstraintException	Attempting an action that violates a constraint. See Chapter 8.
DataException	Errors are generated using ADO.NET components.
DBConcurrencyException	During the update operation if the number of rows affected equals zero. See Chapter 7.
DeletedRowInaccessibleException	An action is attempted on a DataRow that has been deleted.

(continued)

Table 9-2. System.Data Exceptions (continued)

Exception	Description—Thrown When…
DuplicateNameException	A duplicate database object name is encountered during an add operation in a DataSet-related object.
EvaluateException	The Expression property of a DataColumn cannot be evaluated.
InRowChangingEventException	Calling the EndEdit method within the RowChanging event.
InvalidExpressionException	Attempting to add a DataColumn containing an invalid Expression to the Columns collection.
MissingPrimaryKeyException	Attempting to access a row in a table that has no primary key.
NoNullAllowedException	Attempting to insert a null value into a column where AllowDBNull is set to False.
ReadOnlyException	Attempting to change the value of a read-only column.
RowNotInTableException	Trying to perform an operation on a DataRow that is not in a DataTable.
StrongTypingException	The exception that is thrown by a strongly typed DataSet when the user accesses DBNull value.
SyntaxErrorException	The Expression property of a DataColumn contains a syntax error.
TypedDataSetGeneratorException	A name conflict occurs while generating a strongly typed DataSet.
VersionNotFoundException	Attempting to return a version of a DataRow that has been deleted.

Each of these specialized Exception classes exposes a standard set of properties inherited from the base Exception class. Table 9-3 lists these properties. Notably missing is a "message number" to which many of us have become accustomed.

Table 9-3. Exception Class Properties

Public Properties	Description
HelpLink	Gets or sets a link to the help file associated with this exception.
InnerException	Gets the Exception instance that caused the current exception.
Message	Gets a message that describes the current exception.
Source	Gets or sets the name of the application or the object that causes the error.
StackTrace	Gets a string representation of the frames on the call stack at the time the current exception was thrown.
TargetSite	Gets the method that threw the current exception.

I expect you'll be referencing the Message property for these Exception classes. There's not a lot of other detail to go on. Consider, however, that these messages are localized for different language implementations of the .NET Framework (French, German, Japanese, Texan...), so I don't recommend using hard-code string compares against these messages without consideration for the localized versions.

The SqlException Class

Each of the .NET Data Providers is responsible for implementing its own Exception class. This gives the .NET Data Provider the flexibility to return far more detailed information as Exception properties, as well as any number or type of Exception classes as they see fit. The SqlClient provider throws SqlException classes to your try/catch error handler. In addition, the SqlClient class also returns errors to the SqlError class. Table 9-4 lists properties exposed in the SqlException namespace (note properties inherited from the base Exception class):

Table 9-4. SqlException Properties

SqlException Public Properties	OleDbException?	Description
Class	No (ErrorCode— Hresult)	Gets the severity level of the error returned from the SQL Server .NET Data Provider.

(continued)

Table 9-4. SqlException Properties (continued)

SqlException Public Properties	OleDbException?	Description
Errors	Yes	Gets a collection of one or more SqlError objects that give detailed information about exceptions generated by the SQL Server .NET Data Provider.
HelpLink (inherited from Exception)	Yes	Gets or sets a link to the Help file associated with this exception.
InnerException (inherited from Exception)	Yes	Gets the exception instance that caused the current exception.
LineNumber	No	Gets the line number within the Transact-SQL command batch or stored procedure that generated the error. No, this is not the line number in your application—sorry.
Message (Overridden)	Yes	Gets the text describing the error.
Number	No	Gets a number that identifies the type of error.
Procedure	No	Gets the name of the stored procedure or remote procedure call (RPC) that generated the error.
Server	No	Gets the name of the computer running an instance of SQL Server that generated the error.
Source (Overridden)	Yes	Gets the name of the provider that generated the error.
StackTrace (inherited from Exception)	Yes	Gets a string representation of the frames on the call stack at the time the current exception was thrown.
State	No	Gets the error code for the error.
TargetSite (inherited from Exception)	Yes	Gets the method that threw the current exception.

The SqlError Class

In addition to the SqlException exposed by the SQL Server-specific SqlClient Exception class, the SqlClient .NET Data Provider also exposes a SqlErrorCollection class that's accessible through the SqlException.Errors property which points to one or more SqlError objects. The SqlError objects inherit (expose) the same properties as the SqlException class.

The "error" messages returned from SQL Server have varying severity levels. In the normal course of processing connections and running queries, SQL Server usually returns "informational" messages. The error severity is returned in the "Class" property (No, I don't know why it's not "severity"—oh well). Anyway, Table 9-5 outlines the various severity, oops, I mean Class values, and why they are set.

Table 9-5. SqlError Severity Levels and Their Causes

Class/Severity	Reason
0–10	Informational. Might not be "errors" at all. Returned by SQL Server when it switches default databases or languages. Can be raised by stored procedures to indicate anything of an informational (non-fatal) nature.
11–16	Generated by a stored procedure, but considered more "serious" than 0–10 errors. These "conditions" can be corrected by the user and aren't considered errors.
17–19	Software or hardware errors. These are serious errors, but you can continue working (at your own risk). The connection remains open with all errors less than 20.
20–-25	Fatal software or hardware errors. These are errors too serious to permit the operation to continue. The connection is usually closed but it can be reopened and the application should be able to continue—depending on what went wrong.

The OleDbException Class

The OleDbException class is not nearly as complete as the SqlException class. While it exposes an OleDbErrorCollection collection through its Errors property, it does not expose many of the other properties exposed by the SqlException class. See Table 9-4 and System.Data.OleDB.OleDBException for details.

Displaying the Error Message

I like to display more than just the Message property returned from the Exception object. Throughout my examples you will see that I typically use the ToString() method on the Exception object to coerce the CLR to dump everything it knows about the exception to a string—not just the message. This is quite helpful for Debug builds if the target of the string is the Debug object, but it would scare the britches off of your novice users at runtime—so think a little about what you send to MessageBoxes your users get to see.

There is a nifty way to mark methods that you would like compiled into the project for a debug build but not included in a release build. So, if like me, you like to have MessageBoxes pop their trivia to the screen during test execution—but not to do so in release builds—you might find this technique helpful. Start by ensuring that you are using the System.Diagnostics namespace:

```
using System.Diagnostics;
```

Create your conditionally compiled method and mark it as such with the conditional attribute:

```
[Conditional("DEBUG")]
private void DebugMessageBox(string strMessage) {
    MessageBox.Show(strMessage);
}
```

You are now able to call DebugMessageBox() and a MessageBox will only pop up in debug builds:

```
catch(Exception ex){
    DebugMessageBox(ex.ToString());
}
```

CHAPTER 10

ADO.NET and XML

EXTENSIBLE MARKUP LANGUAGE (XML) is the new[1] universal format for data. XML allows developers to easily describe and deliver rich, structured data from any application in a standard, consistent way. XML does not replace HTML; rather, it is a complementary format. Microsoft is heavily investing in XML—you'll see XML in versions of SQL Server 2000 and in many of Microsoft's new applications. But, it's clear that XML has not stopped its evolutionary process. The "original" form of XML used in ADOc is no longer used in ADO.NET and I expect further changes as the international standards committees tune and refine XML and its ancillary extensions, such as XSD and XSLT.

This chapter focuses on the XML foundations of ADO.NET and how to use the XML features to process, transmogrify,[2] and transport your data. I show how to extract XML from an existing DataSet and how to process an inbound XML data stream. SQL Server 2000 (using a FOR XML query), Web Services, and multitier components are all capable of passing data streams as XML. XML is not only used for data and schema transmission, but also to expose .NET Web Service classes and their properties, methods, and events. One of the last things this chapter illustrates is how to create a Web Service to return a DataSet (in the form of XML) back to your application.

 IMHO *I've always believed that ADO.NET should have been named "XDO" or "XDO.NET." I've said this from the beginning—even before .NET appeared in public. This is because ADO.NET is based on XML—and not on COM-based ADO. In the early days of ADO.NET's existence, the newly emerging XML-based data access interface* **was** *called XDO by the development team. I've interviewed a number of Microsoft product managers and found that the name "ADO.NET" was begrudgingly agreed upon after many contentious meetings. Regardless of what they call this new interface, we're stuck with it—at least with the name.*

---

1. The latest. I've seen several "universal" standards come and go over the last thirty years.
2. **transmogrify** *v* (-fied, -fying) to change or transform, esp. in a magical or surprising manner. **transmogrification** *n* in some cases transmogrification requires a cardboard box and a stuffed tiger.

I've been working with ADO.NET for almost a year at this point and I've never once had to manually parse XML. I have used the XML methods described in this chapter, but for the most part, I let ADO.NET manage the behind-the-scenes processing on its own. This chapter aims to provide a high-level glimpse of the XML underpinnings of ADO.NET without giving you angina.

Late in this book's development cycle, Microsoft announced and released a new XML interface for Microsoft SQL Server 2000. According to Microsoft, XML for SQL Server—also known as SQLXML—enables developers to bridge the gap between XML and relational data stored in SQL Server (version 2000 or later). You can create XML views of your existing relational data and work with it as if it were an XML document. SQLXML is a potential solution if you need to:

- Query relational data with Xpath.

- Query relational data with TSQL and return XML results.

- Update relational data as if it were XML.

- Load very large XML files into an existing SQL Server 2000 database, converting them to relational data.

- Query your SQL Server data by using URLs from your Web browser or Web application.

- Access SQL Server XML functionality with OLE DB, ADOc, or .NET Managed classes.

No, it's too late in the cycle to go any deeper into this subject. I expect to be writing a number of whitepapers over the next year and I'll certainly include this topic in one of the first. If you're yearning for more information on SQLXML and can't wait for my whitepaper, see
`http://www.microsoft.com/sql/techinfo/xml/default.asp`.

XML Support in ADO.NET

It's clear that Microsoft has wanted to incorporate XML into its data access architectures for some time now. ADOc has supported XML persistence and other XML-aware features since version 2.6; you can use the Save method to extrude an XML representation of your binary Recordset data to a Stream object, data file, or to the Response object. I discussed this feature earlier along with techniques that use the Recordset Open method to populate data and schema from a persisted (or passed) XML document. In ADO.NET, XML is used to facilitate storing, manipulating, reorganizing, and sharing your data. Whenever requested, ADO.NET converts your data to or from XML on demand.

Regardless of the source, ADO.NET DataSet objects can be accessed through two pathways: the DataSet properties, methods, and events; and the XML Document Object Model (DOM). Both of these techniques have parallel access methods that permit you to follow sequential or hierarchical paths through your data. XML data can be rendered (displayed, formatted, used in reports) using newly emerged XML standard formatting XSL/T. If desired, you can extract just the schema from the XML DOM by using the ReadXmlSchema method. This DDL schema contains a description of the data tables, as well as any relations and constraints defined for the DataSet.

NOTE   *This book cannot serve as an XML primer. Fortunately, there are many other titles that cater to beginners. This book can help you understand what's going on behind the scenes so you can manipulate your data as needed with XML or with the more "traditional" ways through the DataSet methods, properties, and events.*

Standardizing on XML Formats

As you know by now, the ADOc Recordset object can extrude an XML document if you use the Save method with the adPersistXML option or if you read a properly (ADOc) formatted XML document and rehydrate it as an ADOc Recordset. In contrast, the XML document returned by the ADO.NET DataSet does *not* contain column data as attributes of row elements—which ADOc expects. This means you can't open an ADO.NET-generated XML stream as a Recordset in ADOc. Yes, I've already shown you that ADO.NET can directly import a binary ADOc Recordset, but passing the data back to ADOc is problematic. ADO.NET can't import an ADOc Recordset-generated XML stream. This makes it tough to interoperate with ADOc COM components.

The reasons behind the decision to change the "standard" XML format in ADO.NET are fairly complex, but basically, they had to do with increasing the flexibility of the XML structure. The ADO.NET XML structure is more flexible in that it permits developers to add substructure with elements if and when needed. The ADOc structure is more rigid and compact, thus faster to transmit over the wire. This benefit in ADOc was not seen as a key factor; XML transmissions are already much bulkier than their binary Recordset counterparts. In the future we'll see tokenized (compressed) XML formats in ADO.NET that should reduce the intertier transmission loads.

 TIP *Because of the preceding issues, whenever you transmit XML from tier to tier, you should take whatever steps possible to reduce the volume of data to move across the wire. This is easily accomplished by setting filters that remove all unchanged data from updated DataSet objects before they are passed between layers.*

The XML format used by SQL Server and its `FOR XML AUTO` queries is compatible with the "new" format used by ADO.NET. This means passing XML data to and from SQL Server should be easier. Given that SQLXML is designed specifically to interoperate with ADO.NET, it's clear that the XML structure is stabilizing and working its way into every crease of SQL Server 2000 and its future versions.

Understanding XML and DataSet Objects

As I have said before, ADO.NET supports the ability to construct DataSet objects from either XML streams or documents. These XML sources can include data or schema, or both. The schema is expressed as Extensible Schema Definition language (XSD)—another form of XML. As I discussed earlier, when you import data into a DataSet, the existing data remains so you can combine data generated by "traditional" data sources with XML data sources. You can also export data from a DataSet to an XML document—with or without the schema. This is handy when you have to send data through a firewall; in most situations, a firewall won't permit you to pass binary data.

Importing DataSet Data from an XML Document

The DataSet object's ReadXML method is used to read XML data from a data file (formatted as XML), a data stream, or from an XmlReader object—as long as it is in the correct XML format. I discussed the XmlReader object along with the DataReader object earlier in the book (see Chapter 4). This section explains how the ReadXml method can be programmed to deal with the different types of XML and whether or not to extract the schema.

The ReadXML method supports a number of overloads that accept the data source and an optional XmlReadMode argument. It's this XmlReadMode argument that governs how the ReadXML method processes the XML data source.

Because these data sources, and your need for the data or schema, can vary, appropriate use of this parameter can help (or hurt) performance and resource demands. Table 10-1 summarizes the ReadXml method's XmlReadMode options.

Table 10-1. ReadXML XmlReadMode Arguments

XmlReadMode	Description
Auto	(Default) Examines the XML and chooses the most appropriate option.
ReadSchema	Reads any inline schema and loads the data and schema.
IgnoreSchema	Ignores any inline schema and loads the data into the existing DataSet schema.
InferSchema	Ignores any inline schema and infers the schema per the structure of the XML data, then loads the data.[3]
DiffGram	Reads a DiffGram and posts the data to the current schema.
Fragment	Continues reading multiple XML fragments until the end of the stream is reached.

Auto

By default, the ReadXML method's XmlReadMode Auto argument tells ADO.NET to examine the XML and choose an appropriate XmlReadMode setting. For best performance, always hard code the XmlReadMode instead of leaving it to default to Auto. This ensures that the appropriate action will be taken each time the code runs—not to mention reducing CPU overhead churning the XML document. To determine which option to use, the ReadXML method chooses what to do in the following order:

- If the XML is a DiffGram,[4] DiffGram is used.

- If the DataSet contains a schema or the XML contains an inline schema, ReadSchema is used.

- If the DataSet does not contain a schema and the XML does not contain an inline schema, InferSchema is used.

---

3. See the "InferSchema" section later in this chapter.
4. DiffGram: XML that contains changes to the data. I discuss this in the next section.

ReadSchema

If you set the XmlReadMode ReadSchema option, the ReadXML method adds new tables to the DataSet based on the XML schema. This also occurs if the Auto option is used, and if the XML source contains schema. However, if these tables are already in the DataSet, an exception is thrown. No, you can't modify existing DataTable schema using the ReadSchema option. If you choose the ReadSchema option, and there is no schema in the XML document, nothing happens.

IgnoreSchema

When you choose the XmlReadMode IgnoreSchema option, any data that does not match the existing schema is discarded. If no schema exists in the DataSet, no data is loaded. If the data is a DiffGram, IgnoreSchema has the same functionality as DiffGram.

InferSchema

Choosing the XmlReadMode InferSchema option means that if the DataSet already contains a schema, the current schema is extended by adding new tables (assuming there is not a table that matches the schema), or by adding columns to existing tables. An exception is thrown if an inferred table already exists with a different namespace, or if any inferred columns conflict with existing columns. This option is handy if you want to merge new columns and data into an existing DataTable.

DiffGram

The XmlReadMode DiffGram option merges new rows with existing rows where the unique identifier values match. I discussed merging data earlier—this is the XML approach to the problem. I discuss DiffGrams in more detail in the next section.

Fragments

If you choose the XmlReadMode Fragments option, the ReadXML method appends the XML data where the data matches the DataSet schema. Fragments that do not match the DataSet schema are discarded. I've seen references to using this option with the FOR XML queries extruded by SQL Server 2000 that contain incomplete XML documents.

What Are DiffGrams?

A DiffGram is a type of XML that's a subset of the SQL Server 2000 UpdateGram; you've probably seen this before, when I discussed FOR XML queries or in the SQL Server 2000 Books Online documentation. The DiffGram encapsulates the data and any additions, changes, or deletes made to the base data. The DiffGram also contains the original version of changed data columns.

When you make changes to a DataSet, ADO.NET uses the DiffGram XML format to load and persist the data. As I illustrate later in this chapter, when you send or receive data to and from an XML Web Server, ADO.NET also uses the DiffGram to pass the DataSet over the wire. In order to get ADO.NET to format the XML as a DiffGram, you must explicitly ask for it using the ReadXML method DiffGram option as just discussed.

Several dumps of a DiffGram follow that show how the data is broken into several distinct sections (and no, there won't be a test on this). I'm only showing you this because you might have to debug a program that sends you XML in this format or maybe you just want to impress your friends.

Let's start with the header—see Figure 10-1. It lets the target system know that you're sending XML formatted as a DiffGram.

```
<?xml version="1.0" standalone="yes" ?>
- <diffgr:diffgram xmlns:msdata="urn:schemas-microsoft-com:xml-msdata"
    xmlns:diffgr="urn:schemas-microsoft-com:xml-diffgram-v1">
```

Figure 10-1. XML DiffGram header.

Next, the individual data rows appear in the XML in one or more blocks delineated by a tag generated from the name of the DataSet. In this case, the <InfoRequest> and </InfoRequest> tags delineate this block.

If there are changes being applied to the row, the hasChanges tag indicates modified, inserted, or descent. (See Table 10-2 for more details on these settings.) No, if you're working with the Argentinean version, it does not tag the changes as <Tienen Cambios>—lo siento. See Figure 10-2.

```
 - <InfoRequest>
  - <InfoRequest diffgr:id="InfoRequest3" msdata:rowOrder="2"
      diffgr:hasChanges="modified">
      <ID>16</ID>
      <CustID>146786</CustID>
      <ISBN>0-3875840-2-1</ISBN>
      <DateRequested>2001-10-18T13:25:00.0000000-07:00</DateRequested>
      <DateShipped>2001-10-19T00:00:00.0000000-07:00</DateShipped>
      <TimeStamp>AAAAAAA6u6U=</TimeStamp>
    </InfoRequest>
  - <InfoRequest diffgr:id="InfoRequest4" msdata:rowOrder="3"
      diffgr:hasChanges="modified">
```

Figure 10-2. DiffGram InfoRequest block.

The next section of the DiffGram is the `<diffgr:before>` block—as seen in Figure 10-3. It contains deleted rows and the original row versions for changed rows.

```
 - <diffgr:before>
  - <InfoRequest diffgr:id="InfoRequest1" msdata:rowOrder="0">
      <ID>10</ID>
      <CustID>146786</CustID>
      <ISBN>0-4444292-0-4</ISBN>
      <DateRequested>2001-10-23T00:00:00.0000000-07:00</DateRequested>
      <DateShipped>2001-10-24T00:00:00.0000000-07:00</DateShipped>
      <TimeStamp>AAAAAAA6u54=</TimeStamp>
    </InfoRequest>
  - <InfoRequest diffgr:id="InfoRequest2" msdata:rowOrder="1">
      <ID>12</ID>
```

Figure 10-3. DiffGram "before" block.

Each row in the DiffGram is assigned a unique identifier—generated by ADO.NET as shown in Figure 10-2. I discussed this identifier in Chapter 7 when I talked about merging DataSet data. It's used to help identify unique rows in disjoint DataSet objects so the rows can be matched up after a remote process has posted changes to a database.

```
<InfoRequest diffgr:id="InfoRequest3 "...
```

If there are changes being applied to a row, the `hasChanges` annotation indicates that the row has changed:

```
< ...diffgr:hasChanges="modified ">
```

Valid settings for the hasChanges tag are listed in Table 10-2.

Table 10-2. Diffgram Tags

hasChanges Tag	Valid Settings
Inserted	Identifies an Added row.
Modified	Identifies a Modified row that contains an Original row version in the <diffgr:before> block. Note that Deleted rows will have an Original row version in the <diffgr:before> block.
Descent	Identifies an element where one or more children from a parent/child relationship have been modified.

NOTE *While the DiffGram format is primarily used by the .NET Framework as a serialization format for the contents of a DataSet, you can also use DiffGrams to modify data in tables in a Microsoft SQL Server 2000 database. For more information, see the SQLXML for SQL Server 2000 located at* http://www.microsoft.com/sql/techinfo/xml/default.asp.

Merging XML Data with Your DataSet

Suppose your DataSet already contains data and you use the ReadXML method. In this case, data from the XML stream is simply appended to the existing data. However, the ReadXML method does not attempt to overwrite existing data based on matching keys—that's the job of the DataSet Merge method as I've already discussed. On the other hand, loading a DiffGram using ReadXML with an XmlReadMode of DiffGram will merge rows that have the same unique identifier.

Fetching and Saving DataSet Objects as XML

Okay, you already know you can save DataSet objects to XML and you know the format is different from the one used by ADOc. What I have not told you is how to use ADO.NET to make the transformation from DataSet to XML—that's the topic of this section. Table 10-3 lists the methods for this process.

Table 10-3. DataSet XML Methods

DataSet XML Method	Description
GetXml	Extracts data stored in the DataSet in XML format. If the DataSet has changes, this method is identical to WriteXml with XmlWriteMode set to IgnoreSchema.
GetXmlSchema	Extracts data schema stored in the DataSet in XSD format. Identical to calling WriteXmlSchema, except that only the primary schema is written.
InferXmlSchema	Infers the XML schema from the specified TextReader or file into the DataSet.
ReadXml	Reads XML schema and data into the DataSet.
ReadXmlSchema	Reads XML schema into the DataSet.
WriteXml	Writes XML schema and data from the DataSet.
WriteXmlSchema	Writes XML schema from the DataSet.

No, you don't need to create a schema before you save your DataSet. Sure, if there is schema, ADO.NET can save it along with the data, but it's transformed from the internal binary data/schema arrays to the XSD format. The relation and constraints defined for the DataSet are saved along with the DataTable schema definitions. Typically you're going to want to save the "current" version of the XML data, but as I already discussed, you can read or save in DiffGram format using either the ReadXML or WriteXML methods, which save both the original and current versions of your data.

Depending on the option you choose, ADO.NET can persist the data to a file, a stream, an XmlWriter, or a string. For example, to write the DataSet to a string, use the DataSet object's GetXML method:

```
string xmlString = InfoRequest.GetXml();
```

If the DataSet has changes, calling the GetXml method is identical to calling WriteXml with XmlWriteMode set to IgnoreSchema because the XML returned contains *just* the data—not the schema. If you simply want to extract the XML (XSD) schema, use the GetXMLSchema method.

TIP *The GetXml method returns XML as a string, which generates more memory and CPU resources than using WriteXml to write XML to a file.*

The WriteXML method is used to persist a DataSet in XML format to a file, stream, or XmlWriter. As with the ReadXml method, you pass a string containing the filename path, a System.IO.TextWriter, or XmlWriter object, along with an option argument that tells ADO.NET how the XML is to be exported.

The following code snippet is part of the larger application discussed later in this chapter. It's really here just to illustrate use of the WriteXML method. It serves no other purpose than to help debug the application. I used it to determine what changes were being posted to the DataSet through a bound DataGrid control. In this case, I constructed a new DataSet containing just the changes from the working DataSet (dsInfoRequest) and dumped this to a local file using the WriteXML method as a DiffGram. You saw the contents of this file in Figures 10-1, 10-2, and 10-3.

```
DataSet dsChanges = new DataSet();
dsChanges = dsInfoRequest.GetChanges();
dsChanges.WriteXml("c:\\changes.xml", XmlWriteMode.DiffGram);
```

Table 10-4 lists the valid options for XmlWriteMode, which control how the current contents of the DataSet are processed.

Table 10-4. XmlWriteMode Option Arguments

XmlWriteMode	Description
IgnoreSchema	Write data, but no schema.
WriteSchema	(Default) Write XML data with the relational structure as inline XML Schema.
DiffGram	Writes the entire DataSet as a DiffGram.

When working with hierarchical (parent/child) DataSet objects, be sure to set the DataRelation object's Nested property to True. This constructs XML that contains child rows nested within their parent elements. Sounds cozy, doesn't it?

Loading Schema from XML

If you have the time and temperament (and your boss lets you get away with it), you can hard code DataSet schema. You can also use the Fill or FillSchema methods, as I've already discussed, to fill in (at least some) of this schema. Another alternative is to suck the schema out of an XML document using the DataSet ReadXmlSchema or InferXmlSchema methods—as the following sections describe.

ReadXmlSchema

This DataSet method extracts schema information from an XML document that contains XSD-formatted schema or inline XML schema. ReadXmlSchema is handy when you want to extract just the schema from an XML document into a DataSet. For example, if you want to create a new DataSet whose schema matches that of the inbound XML document, ReadXmlSchema is your best choice. If you want the data *and* schema, use the ReadXml method instead.

When using the ReadXmlSchema method and the target XML document does not contain an inline or XSD schema, the schema is inferred from the elements in the document. In other words, the ReadXmlSchema falls back to the InferXmlSchema technique of determining the schema to pass to the DataSet. If the target DataSet contains a schema, it's extended to include the new columns read or inferred from the XML document. If new tables are found, these are appended to the DataSet. If, however, a column definition in the source schema does not have a compatible datatype in the target schema, an exception is thrown.

InferXmlSchema

The InferXmlSchema DataSet method infers (figures out/extrapolates/conjures) the schema from the XML document while giving you the option to ignore certain named portions of the XML document. It duplicates functionality of the ReadXml method (with the InferSchema option) and the ReadXmlSchema method when there is no schema to read. To bypass named portions of the XML document, the InferXmlSchema method expects a second argument containing a string array of XML namespaces to be ignored by the operation.

The process of inferring the schema from an XML document is not really a black art—although it may appear as such to some of us. The following text is extracted and (hopefully clarified) from online Help:

First, the inference engine has to read the XML document and figure out which elements refer to tables. Next, it tries to find columns for each of these tables. If it finds nested tables, the inference engine generates nested DataRelation and ForeignKeyConstraint objects that interrelate the tables.

Here is a brief summary of inference rules:

- Elements that have attributes or child elements are inferred as tables.

- Elements that repeat are inferred as a single table.

- If the document or root element has no attributes and no child elements that would be inferred as columns, it is inferred as a DataSet. Otherwise, the document element is inferred as a table.

- Attributes are inferred as columns.

- Attributes and elements that have no attributes or child elements are inferred as columns—unless they repeat, in which case they are considered to be tables.

- A nested DataRelation is created between two tables' elements that are inferred as tables nested within other elements.

- A new, primary-key column named "TableName_Id" is added to both tables and used by the DataRelation. A ForeignKeyConstraint is created between the two tables using the "TableName_Id" column.

- A new column named "TableName_Text" is created for the text of each of the elements that are inferred as tables and contain text but have no child elements. If an element is inferred as a table and has text, but also has child elements, the text is ignored.

Clear? I hope so, because that's as far as I'm going.

Persisting XML Schema

You can use the WriteXmlSchema method to export a DataSet object's schema—the table and column definitions along with the relations and constraints—as XSD. The WriteXmlSchema method accepts one argument: the destination. As with the other XML methods, the target for the WriteXmlSchema method can be a file, a stream, an XmlWriter, or a string. If you use the DataColumn object's ColumnMapping property you can specify how a column is represented in the XSD.

Creating a Web Service as an XML Data Source

One of the primary means of leveraging the power of the disconnected DataSet that forms the core of ADO.NET's data access architecture is the ability to pass DiffGrams between tiers—even through firewalls. This section discusses one of the relatively new executable component types: the Web Service. I show how it can be used as a source of XML data, as well as an engine that can process DiffGrams passed to it.

The Web Service is a new paradigm exposed for the first time in the .NET Framework—at least for the most part. We saw the first signs of this architecture when Visual Basic 6.0 introduced "Web Classes" using the "IIS Application" template. A Web Service is an instantiated class that runs on an IIS server, not unlike ASP code or a Visual Basic 6.0 Web Class.

Frankly, a Web Service is more like a middle-tier DCOM component than anything else—except for the fact that it does not use DCOM. Unlike an ASP page, the Web Service is not "interpreted" code. It uses the same JIT or persisted-compilation technology as WinForm or other .NET Framework applications or executable components.

Unlike a COM or .NET executable, a Web Service is exposed to the invoking application through an XML "discovery" file that permits Visual Studio .NET to discover the classes, properties, methods, and events that the Web Service implements—just as a registered COM component exposes its innards through the COM iUnknown QueryInterface method. This discovery file is automatically created by Visual Studio .NET when the project is built.

To deploy a Web Service, the .vsdisco file (and you thought disco was dead), the compiled (code) .asmx, and other files are simply copied to an appropriate directory on the Web (IIS) server. No, you don't have to register them. If your development system is your IIS server, you don't have to do anything to deploy the Web Service—it's already done for you. Figure 10-4 is a screen-shot of the .disco XML discovery file from when I created the example "BiblioService1" Web Service:

```
<?xml version="1.0" encoding="utf-8" ?>
- <discovery xmlns:xsi="http://www.w3.org/2001/XMLSchema-
    instance" xmlns:xsd="http://www.w3.org/2001/XMLSchema"
    xmlns="http://schemas.xmlsoap.org/disco/">
    <contractRef
      ref="http://localhost/BiblioServices/BiblioService1.asmx?
      wsdl"
      docRef="http://localhost/BiblioServices/BiblioService1.asmx"
        xmlns="http://schemas.xmlsoap.org/disco/scl/" />
  </discovery>
```

Figure 10-4. A typical VSDisco discovery file.

Notice how the .disco file points to the executable .asmx file on the IIS server. But I'm getting ahead of myself. Let's step through the process of creating a Web Service.

TIP   *I first started this process using the Help topic walkthrough, but it seemed to be out of date. It included a number of steps that made no sense and weren't necessary. I expect this to be fixed before long, but the following steps should make the process pretty clear.*

Remember that Web Service architecture depends on the same discipline and regimen you used for COM components—at least to some extent. If you change the argument count or datatypes passed, you'll still run into problems if you don't keep the calling application aware of these changes. Frankly, this aspect caused me the most problems when working with this technology for the first time.

The Web Service that I created for the first example has two methods and exposes its own Exception class. I show you how to create that too—it's not hard. First, start a new C# .NET project, but choose **ASP.NET Web Service**, as seen in Figure 10-5. This exposes a dialog prompting for the name for your service. I named the Web Service "BiblioServices".

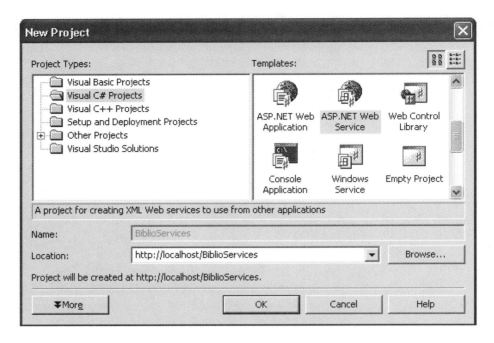

Figure 10-5. The Visual Studio .NET new project dialog.

When you click **OK**, Visual Studio .NET creates a new IIS virtual directory to manage the files for your Web Service. The next exposed window has a message that begins with "To add components to your class…" and ends with "… Click here to switch to the code pane." Switch to the code pane.

The code you write here is no different from any of the code you've written up to this point—with only a few exceptions. Consider that in this case you're creating a UI-less code component. This means that it's not a good idea (not possible) to create MessageBox dialogs—there's no user here to see them.

To permit the Web Service to return a custom exception, I created a BiblioServiceException class as follows:[5]

```
public class BiblioServiceException : System.Exception {
    public BiblioServiceException(string sMessage):base(sMessage) {
    }
}
```

---

5. This example is located in the "\Examples\Chapter 10\BiblioServices" folder on the CD.

Next, I added the following code to change the Web Service namespace (as suggested by the test harness). The default Web Service namespace is `http://tempuri.org`, which won't do for a production application.

```
[WebService(Namespace="http://betav.com/webservices/")]
public class BiblioServiceClass : System.Web.Services.WebService {
    private BiblioServiceException bseNoRows = new BiblioServiceException(
        "No Rows resulted from query");
```

After this, I created a couple of public functions used to expose the AuthorByISBN and TitlesByAuthor methods. No, there's nothing here you haven't seen before except that the public Function statement is preceded with the `[WebMethod()]` tag to indicate that this function is to be visible to the outside via the .vsdisco file. No, not all functions in this class need to be made visible. The functions create and open connections using the same ConnectionString so they should be able to reuse the same connection. They both set up SelectCommand objects to execute rowset-returning parameter-driven stored procedures. If the query does not return any rows, the code uses the `throw` operator to throw the custom BiblioServiceException error. Other errors are exposed by throwing the base exception.

```
[WebMethod]
public DataSet AuthorByISBN(string sISBN) {
    DataSet ds;
    try{
        ds = new DataSet();
        SqlConnection cn = new SqlConnection("data
            source=.;database=biblio;uid=admin;pwd=pw");
        SqlCommand cmd = new SqlCommand("AuthorsByISBN",cn);
        SqlDataAdapter da = new SqlDataAdapter(cmd);
        if (sISBN == "" | sISBN ==null) {
            sISBN = "1-5561590-6-4";
        }
        cmd.CommandType = CommandType.StoredProcedure;
        cmd.Parameters.Add("@ISBNWanted", SqlDbType.VarChar);
        cmd.Parameters["@ISBNWanted"].Value =  sISBN;
        da.Fill(ds);

        if (ds.Tables[0].Rows.Count == 0) {
            throw bseNoRows;
        }
        return ds;
    }
```

```
        catch(Exception exg) {

            Debug.WriteLine(exg.ToString());
            throw exg;
        }
    }
[WebMethod]
public DataSet TitlesByAuthor(string sAuthorWanted) {
    DataSet ds;
    try {
        ds = new DataSet();

        SqlConnection cn = new SqlConnection("data
            source=.;database=biblio;uid=admin;pwd=pw");
        SqlCommand cmd = new SqlCommand("TitlesByAuthor", cn);
        SqlDataAdapter da = new SqlDataAdapter(cmd);
        cmd.CommandType = CommandType.StoredProcedure;
        cmd.Parameters.Add("@AuthorWanted", SqlDbType.VarChar);
        cmd.Parameters["@AuthorWanted"].Value = sAuthorWanted;
        da.Fill(ds);
        if (ds.Tables[0].Rows.Count == 0) {
            throw bseNoRows;
            }
        return ds;
    }
    catch (Exception exg) {
        Debug.WriteLine(exg.Message);
        throw exg;
    }
}
```

 WARNING   *When I first created these Web Service functions, I tried to pass back a DataTable. .NET would not permit this—complaining that I was trying to pass an "Interface." No, I don't understand this, but when I switched to pass back a DataSet, the problem(s) went away.*

The Visual Studio .NET IDE makes testing the Web Service as easy as testing any Windows Forms application you've created so far. Unlike Visual InterDev, you don't have to create a custom HTML page to invoke the Web Service to test; this is done for you automatically. Now you know why it takes two hours to install Visual Studio .NET. The documentation says you should mark the .asmx file as the "Startup File," but the IDE seems to do that on its own. Just press F5 to start the test/debug test harness. Sure, you can stop execution using breakpoints just as you have before.

When you start the Visual Studio .NET test harness, a test HTML page is automatically constructed to evaluate, test, and launch your Web Service. This test harness page is launched in a separate browser window. You'll see the following (Figure 10-6) dialog (assuming you changed the namespace).

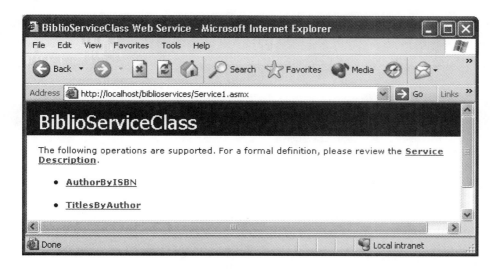

Figure 10-6. Test harness HTML page.

The test harness HTML page prompts you to choose between the public functions installed in your Web Service class. Clicking on either of the bulleted items chooses the specified function. If the function (method) in the selected Web Service expects to be passed input arguments, a dialog is exposed to capture them from you. For example, when you click on **AuthorByISBN**, the dialog in Figure 10-7 appears.

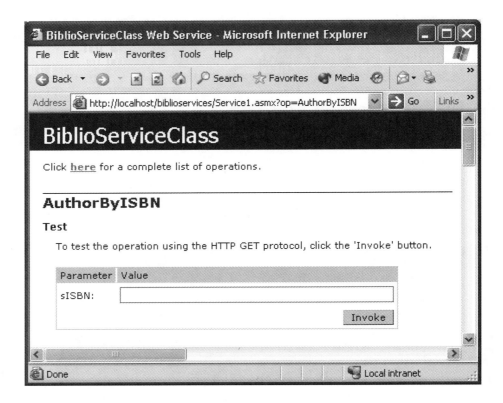

Figure 10-7. AuthorByISBN parameter prompt.

After you fill in the TextBox control prompting for ISBN and click the **Invoke** button, the value is passed as a parameter to the AuthorByISBN function.

When the function executes, a DataSet is generated and displayed in the browser window as formatted XML—as shown in Figure 10-8.

This DataSet is passed back to whatever application invokes the Web Service. To illustrate how to invoke the Web Service from a C# Windows Forms Application, I created another project to call each of the functions in the BiblioService Web Service. The application uses two TextBox controls and two buttons to capture the input parameters, call the Web Service methods, and display the DataSet in a bound DataGrid control.

Folks, it does not get much easier than this. The only "magic" is how the Web Service was added to the project and how it was instantiated. For this project I simply clicked **Project | Add Web Reference**. This exposed a rather unusual dialog that prompted me with three alternatives—as shown in Figure 10-9.

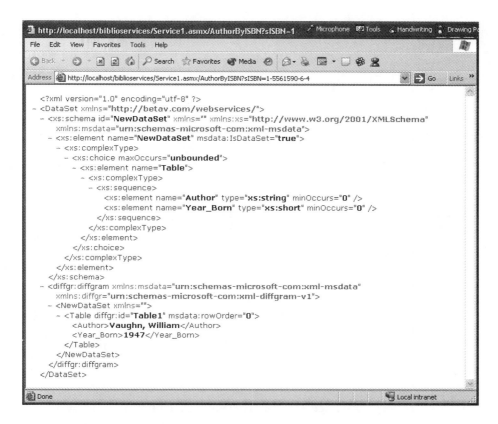

Figure 10-8. Browser rendered XML DataSet.

This dialog exposes two Microsoft-sponsored sources that contain prebuilt Web Services that you can add to your project (subject to fees in some cases). In the beta releases of Visual Studio .NET it also used to expose "Web References on Local Web Server," which listed all the Web Services on the local development machine. That feature was removed in the release version of Visual Studio .NET for security reasons—but if you look at Peter's Web site (http://www.boost.net), there's a tip there to show you how you can put that feature back in. However, doing so might compromise your site's (and your software's) security.

When you select the Web Reference you've just created (http://localhost/BiblioServices/BiblioServices.vsdisco) under **Linked reference groups**, you're confronted with yet another dialog that exposes the .vsdisco file contents and an **Add Reference** button—click that and your Web Service is referenced and added to the Web References list in your Project Explorer.

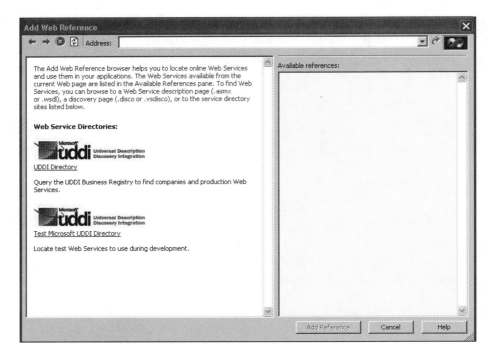

Figure 10-9. Add Web Reference dialog.

If you alter the Web Service, it's always a good idea to update this Project Explorer reference to make sure the .vsdisco file is still correct. To update a Web Reference, you can try to drill down into the Web References and right-click on **localhost** and choose **Update Web Reference**—as shown in Figure 10-10. However, in my experience, this does not work if you change the arguments passed to or from the Web Service. While there's probably a cool way to tell your calling project that the Web Service class has changed and it needs to reload it, the only way I found to get this to sync up again is to remove the Web Service from the project and add it in again. At least this is easier than accessing a DCOM component.

The code to instantiate the Web Service in your calling Windows Form (or wherever) is also pretty easy. In this case, a drop-down dialog exposed by the Visual Studio IDE's statement completion routine shows the registered classes in the Localhost namespace: BiblioServiceClass. After this, you can reference the properties, methods, and events exposed by the Web class (oops, I mean Service). Oh, well, you get the idea.

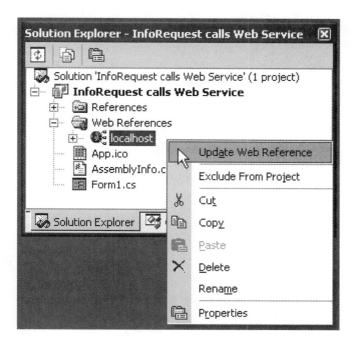

Figure 10-10. Update Web Reference drop-down in Solution Explorer.

```csharp
private DataSet ds;
private localhost.BiblioServiceClass BiblioService;

public Form1() {
    try{...
        BiblioService = new localhost.BiblioServiceClass();
        ds = new DataSet();
    }
    catch (Exception ex) { ... }
}

private void btnAuthorsByISBN_Click(object sender, System.EventArgs e) {
    try{
        ds.Clear();
        ds = BiblioService.AuthorByISBN(txtISBNWanted.Text);
        DataGrid1.DataSource = ds;
        DataGrid1.DataMember = ds.Tables[0].TableName;
    }
```

```
    catch( Exception ex) {
        MessageBox.Show(ex.ToString());
        Debug.WriteLine(ex.ToString());
    }
}

private void btnTitlesByAuthor_Click(object sender, System.EventArgs e) {
    try{
        ds.Clear();
        ds = BiblioService.TitlesByAuthor(txtAuthorWanted.Text);
        DataGrid1.DataSource = ds;
        DataGrid1.DataMember = ds.Tables[0].TableName;
    }
    catch( Exception ex) {
        MessageBox.Show(ex.ToString());
        Debug.WriteLine(ex.ToString());
    }
}
```

When you're ready to debug the Web Service, simply press F8 and step through your Windows Form code. When you reach the point where the Web Service method is invoked, the debugger loads the symbol information from the Reference.cs—the proxy class that's created when you reference the Web Service—and steps right into the Web Service code. Cool.

Passing an Updated DataSet Back to a Web Service

To illustrate the common practice of sending a disconnected DataSet to a Web Service, updating it, and sending it back for inspection, I modified one of my earlier sample applications. This little application is used to test the data-generation routines because it navigates many of the data hierarchies. The example[6] I created to illustrate the complex Web Services retrieves customer information given a selected state and city, and lets you drill down to view the customers' orders and the items for a selected order. I also added yet another layer to this hierarchy: information requests. That is, if the customer wants information on a particular title, the operator can double-click an item and a row is added to a bound grid at the bottom of the form—as shown in Figure 10-11.

---

6. Located in the "\Examples\Chapter 10\InfoRequest calls Web Service" folder on the CD.

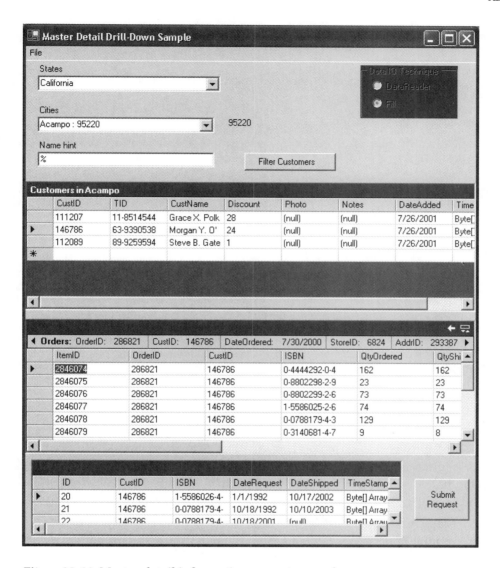

Figure 10-11. Master-detail information request example.

When the **Submit Request** button is clicked, the DataSet is passed to the Web Service. The code to do this is pretty clear. First, declare a new object based on the LocalHost1.UpdateInfoRequestClass class. If you determine that the DataSet has changes pending, proceed to call the UpdateInfoRequest method of the UpdateInfoRequestClass. If you watch the Visual Studio .NET IDE Output window you'll see a lot (a whole lot) of activity as the Web Service is located and invoked. I've seen this take ten seconds or so to get started. After the first invocation, the process seems to start faster.

```
private void btnUpdate_Click(object sender, System.EventArgs e) {
    localhost.UpdateInfoRequestClass UpdateInfoRequest;
    try{
        UpdateInfoRequest = new localhost.UpdateInfoRequestClass();
        if( dsInfoRequest.HasChanges()) {
            dsInfoRequest = UpdateInfoRequest.UpdateInfoRequest(dsInfoRequest);
            if (dsInfoRequest.HasErrors) {
                MessageBox.Show("Update failed...");
                dgInfoRequest.Refresh();
            }
        }
    }
    catch ( Exception exg2 ) {...}
}
```

TIP   *You can use the F8 key to get the debugger to step into your Web Service, however, if you linger there too long the operation might time out, which triggers an exception.*

The Web Service code to post changes to the database follows. The strategy here is to accept an inbound DataSet. The code knows that there are changes to be made, but not necessarily which kind (adds, changes, or deletes). To reduce overhead caused by the creation of DataAdapter Command objects that won't be needed, I added a few lines of code to construct only necessary Commands.

The example starts by creating a new UpdateInfoRequestClass. This class supports a single-function UpdateInfoRequest exposed as a method of the class.

The method accepts a single argument—a DataSet—and returns the updated DataSet.

```
using System.Web.Services;
using System.Data.SqlClient;
[WebService(Namespace="http://boost.net/webservices/")]
public class UpdateInfoRequestClass : System.Web.Services.WebService
```

Next, I create new Connection and DataAdapter objects, along with up to three Command objects—depending on whether or not the DataSet passed has new rows, changed rows, or deleted rows.

```
[WebMethod]
public DataSet UpdateInfoRequest(DataSet dsChanges) {

    try {
        dsChanges.WriteXml("c:\\passedxml.xml");
        SqlConnection cn = new SqlConnection(
           "data source=.;database=biblio;uid=admin;pwd=pw");
        SqlDataAdapter da = new SqlDataAdapter();
        SqlCommand UpdateCmd = new SqlCommand("InfoRequestUpdate", cn);
        byte byS = 0;
        byte byP = 0;
        DataView dv = new DataView(dsChanges.Tables[0]);
        dv.RowStateFilter = DataViewRowState.Added;
        Debug.WriteLine("Inserts:" + dv.Count);
        if (dv.Count > 0) {
            SqlCommand InsertCmd = new SqlCommand("InfoRequestInsert", cn);
            InsertCmd.CommandType = CommandType.StoredProcedure;

            InsertCmd.Parameters.Add(new SqlParameter("@CustID", SqlDbType.Int,
               2, ParameterDirection.Input, false, byS, byP, "CustID",
               DataRowVersion.Current, null));
            InsertCmd.Parameters.Add(new SqlParameter("@ISBN",
               SqlDbType.VarChar, 20, ParameterDirection.Input, false, byS, byP,
               "ISBN", DataRowVersion.Current, null));
            InsertCmd.Parameters.Add(new SqlParameter("@DateRequested",
               SqlDbType.SmallDateTime, 20, ParameterDirection.Input, false, byS,
               byP, "DateRequested", DataRowVersion.Current, null));
            InsertCmd.Parameters.Add(new SqlParameter("@DateShipped",
               SqlDbType.SmallDateTime, 20, ParameterDirection.Input, false, byS,
               byP, "DateShipped", DataRowVersion.Current, null));
```

```
                    da.InsertCommand = InsertCmd;
                    Debug.WriteLine("Insert command:" + da.InsertCommand.CommandText);
                }
            dv.RowStateFilter = DataViewRowState.ModifiedOriginal;
            Debug.WriteLine("Updates:" + dv.Count);
            if (dv.Count > 0) {
                UpdateCmd.CommandType = CommandType.StoredProcedure;

                UpdateCmd.Parameters.Add(new SqlParameter("@PreviousID",
                 SqlDbType.Int, 2, ParameterDirection.Input, false, byS, byP, "ID",
                 DataRowVersion.Original, 0));
                UpdateCmd.Parameters.Add(new SqlParameter("@CustID", SqlDbType.Int,
                  2, ParameterDirection.Input, false, byS, byP, "CustID",
                  DataRowVersion.Current, null));
                UpdateCmd.Parameters.Add(new SqlParameter("@ISBN",
                  SqlDbType.VarChar, 20, ParameterDirection.Input, false, byS, byP,
                  "ISBN", DataRowVersion.Current, null));
                UpdateCmd.Parameters.Add(new SqlParameter("@DateRequested",
                  SqlDbType.SmallDateTime, 20, ParameterDirection.Input, false, byS,
                  byP, "DateRequested", DataRowVersion.Current, null));
                UpdateCmd.Parameters.Add(new SqlParameter("@DateShipped",
                  SqlDbType.SmallDateTime, 20, ParameterDirection.Input, false, byS,
                  byP, "DateShipped", DataRowVersion.Current, null));
                UpdateCmd.Parameters.Add(new SqlParameter("@PreviousTimeStamp",
                  SqlDbType.Timestamp, 8, ParameterDirection.Input, false, byS, byP,
                  "TimeStamp", DataRowVersion.Original, null));

                da.UpdateCommand = UpdateCmd;
            }
            dv.RowStateFilter = DataViewRowState.Deleted;
            Debug.WriteLine("Deletes:" + dv.Count);
            if( dv.Count > 0) {
                SqlCommand DeleteCmd = new SqlCommand("InfoRequestDelete", cn);
                DeleteCmd.CommandType = CommandType.StoredProcedure;

                DeleteCmd.Parameters.Add(new SqlParameter("@PreviousID",
                    SqlDbType.Int, 2, ParameterDirection.Input, false, byS, byP,
                    "ID", DataRowVersion.Original, 0));
                DeleteCmd.Parameters.Add(new SqlParameter("@PreviousTimeStamp",
                    SqlDbType.Timestamp, 8, ParameterDirection.Input, false, byS,
                    byP, "TimeStamp", DataRowVersion.Original, null));

                da.DeleteCommand = DeleteCmd;
            }
            dv.RowStateFilter = DataViewRowState.None;
```

After the Command objects and their Parameter collections are filled in, I'm (finally) ready to execute the DataAdapter Update method. If something goes wrong, I simply pass the exception back to the calling application. In any case, I send the updated DataSet back so the calling application can filter for errors or get the latest values.

```
        da.ContinueUpdateOnError = true;
        Debug.WriteLine("Changes?" + dsChanges.HasChanges().ToString());
        intRowsAffected = da.Update(dsChanges, "InfoRequest");
        Debug.WriteLine("Errors?" + dsChanges.HasErrors.ToString());
    }
    catch ( Exception exg) {...}

        return (dsChanges);

}
```

Creating Custom Exception Handlers

Your Web Service or middle-tier code can use a method return argument to expose public properties or return any object back to the calling application. These method return arguments are effective and efficient ways to expose processed results, operational state, or exception status to the calling program. However, in some cases, you'll need to trip a trappable exception. The documentation suggests that this approach should not be used for ordinary conditions—only "exceptional" situations. Here are a couple of approaches you can take:

- **Do nothing**. In this case when an exception is tripped in the code, it is sent back to the parent—the calling application.

- **Use the throw operator.** This trips an exception in the calling application. throw accepts any Exception object as an argument.

```
    if (SomethingIsWrong == true){
        throw New System.Exception("Something terrible happened");
    }
```

- **Use** `throw` **in your catch block.** The `throw` operator can be used in a try/catch block as well.

```
try{
    ...
catch (Exception exg) {
    ... do something
    throw exg;
}
```

- **Create a custom Exception class.** In special cases, you can create your own Exception object with its own properties and use the `throw` operator to trip the exception. Once you create the custom Exception class, it can be used with the `throw` operator.

```
public class BiblioServiceException : System.Exception {
    public BiblioServiceException(string sMessage):base(sMessage) {
    }
}
```

ADO.NET and SOAP

When I first heard about SOAP, I thought the developers had been hitting the late-night margarita bars again. When they started talking about "SOAP on a ROPE," I knew they were looped. I was wrong—they were just carried away with their newfound standard to replace DCOM. One of the primary (if not the most important) benefits of .NET is the (eventual) elimination of COM components—especially those written by the developer community. COM[7] has never worked particularly well out of process. I'm sure you've heard of DLL hell, but I won't get into the details of that here. Let's just suffice to say that when you try to access a piece of code that resides on your own system, but out of process, or resides on another system visible on the end of a wire, nasty things can happen—nasty things such as slow operations, broken promises, broken interfaces, and miserable developers and their customers.

SOAP is an extension and implementation of XML designed to expose a remote (usually Web-based) class to applications. It can be invoked through XML passed to and through the SOAP interface that exposes the object itself along with its properties, methods (and the method arguments), and its events—all in XML.

---

7. CORBA (a competitor for COM and DCOM) is no better when working out of process.

APPENDIX

Working with the Biblio Sample Database

ALL OF THE EXAMPLES USED in this book are formulated to work against a new test database which I designed to really stress the query engine. I created this database because the current NorthWind and even my larger Biblio databases (used in my earlier books) were simply too small to test against. The new (and improved) Biblio database is considerably larger. The old database was about 50 MB; the new version is over 350 MB with over one million rows. This version was created using SQL Server 2000 so you'll need that version to attach and use it. There are also a couple of small Jet 4.0 databases included. All of these databases are supplied on the companion CD.

The Biblio database has been detached and saved using SQL Server's new sp_detach_db stored procedure, which releases control of the MDF and LDF (data and log) files. These two files must be "reattached" to your SQL Server database to use them. Sorry, there are no Oracle, or DB2 versions of the Biblio sample data. However, I do include a random-data-generator that was used to create the Customer, Order, Item, Address, and Stores tables. With a little work I expect you could get this to work on your target database.

To reattach these files, follow these steps:

1. Copy the two files (newbiblio_data.mdf and newbiblio_data.ldf) from the CD to a convenient place on your hard disk. No, sorry, you can't run this database from the CD. These two files are located in the \Databases directory on the CD.

2. Open SQL Enterprise Manager and drill down to the Databases icon.

3. Make sure you don't already have a Biblio database on your SQL Server. If you do, you have to rename the existing Biblio database (recommended), drop it (get permission first), or rename the new version (not recommended).

4.   Right-click the **Databases** node of your SQL Server Group and choose **All Tasks** and **Attach Database**. Click on the **...** button to browse for the database files that you copied from the CD. SQL Server 2000 will verify the integrity of these files and attach the Biblio database files.

5.   In SQL Enterprise Manager, click on the **Security** tab and add a Login ID for "Admin" with a password "PW". All of the examples use this account to open connections. Grant Admin rights to the Biblio database and any other *test* databases you choose. For security reasons, I would not grant this account access to any production databases.

After the Biblio database is installed, you'll discover it comes with only one UserID, "Admin" with the password "PW". However, you can add yourself (your domain name) as a user (recommended), but if you do, you also need to configure the Biblio database permissions to let you have access to the database. You'll also want to modify the sample applications to use your UserID. No, I do not recommend using the SA UserID.

The CD also contains an SQL script (FixAdminLogin.SQL) in the \Databases directory that can be used from Query Analyzer or ISQL to reset the Login ID Admin to sync up with the database. You'll need to run this script before accessing the database.

Index

Symbols

? parameter marker
  lack of support for by SqlClient .NET
    Data Provider, 85–86
  support for in ADO.NET, 82–83
@ReturnValue parameter, creating and
  adding to stored procedures,
  125–126
+ operator, use of in .NET, 91

A

AcceptRejectRule, ForeignKeyConstraint,
  290
action queries, using Visual Studio to
  generate, 251–258
Add() method, using to construct
  parameters, 115
Add Web Reference dialog, opening,
  333–334
ad hoc queries, executing to perform
  updates, 280
ADOc
  comparing to ADO.NET, 7–9, 142–144
  update strategies, 238–239
ADOc code
  instantiation of objects when
    importing, 18
  leveraging existing in your .NET
    executables, 17–18
ADOc connection objects
  accessing from Visual Basic .NET, 77
  establishing a connection with, 39
ADOc ConnectionString vs. ADO.NET
  ConnectionString, 46
ADOc Field object, compared with
  DataSet, 172
ADOc Fields collection vs. the ADO.NET
  DataColumnCollection, 171
ADOc namespace, instantiating, 76–77
ADOc objects, accessing from .NET
  executables, 18
ADOc properties vs. ADO.NET properties,
  182–183
ADOc Recordset
  vs. the ADO.NET DataReader
    processing loop, 146
  vs. ADO.NET DataTable structure, 170
  vs. the DataTable, 157–196
  importing into an ADO.NET data
    structure, 168–172

ADOc Recordset objects, creating
  DataSets from, 19
ADOc Recordsets, comparing to
  DataTable objects, 169–172
ADO.NET
  adding new DataRows to a DataTable,
    224–225
  vs. ADOc data stream, 36–38
  capturing the SELECT-generated
    rowsets in, 129–132
  command strategies, 79–140
  comparing to ADOc, 7–9, 142–144
  Connection object properties, 53–54
  connection pooling, 71–74
  data access using the DataSet object,
    24
  DataReader strategies, 141–156
  DataSet object hierarchy, 159
  and disconnected data structures,
    20–21
  error management strategies, 301–311
  establishing connections using
    different providers, 39–77
  forms of Find implemented by, 213
  the fundamentals, 12–15
  getting to manage a pessimistic
    locking update, 222
  handling of duplicate DataTable
    columns by, 181
  how it implements constraints,
    285–295
  how it passes data versions to update
    parameters, 264
  how we got here, 2–6
  implementing foreign key constraints,
    289–291
  implementing unique constraints,
    287–289
  introduction to, 1–38
  low-level data stream, 36–38
  .NET Data Providers, 15–20
  a new beginning, 7–9
  vs. other Microsoft data access
    interfaces, 10–11
  possible problems with, 14–15
  reviewing the generated stored
    procedures, 251–254
  and SOAP, 342
  support of Parameter constructors,
    112–114

Apress Titles

ISBN	PRICE	AUTHOR	TITLE
1-893115-73-9	$34.95	Abbott	Voice Enabling Web Applications: VoiceXML and Beyond
1-893115-01-1	$39.95	Appleman	Dan Appleman's Win32 API Puzzle Book and Tutorial for Visual Basic Programmers
1-893115-23-2	$29.95	Appleman	How Computer Programming Works
1-893115-97-6	$39.95	Appleman	Moving to VB. NET: Strategies, Concepts, and Code
1-59059-023-6	$39.95	Baker	Adobe Acrobat 5: The Professional User's Guide
1-893115-09-7	$29.95	Baum	Dave Baum's Definitive Guide to LEGO MINDSTORMS
1-893115-84-4	$29.95	Baum, Gasperi, Hempel, and Villa	Extreme MINDSTORMS: An Advanced Guide to LEGO MINDSTORMS
1-893115-82-8	$59.95	Ben-Gan/Moreau	Advanced Transact-SQL for SQL Server 2000
1-893115-91-7	$39.95	Birmingham/Perry	Software Development on a Leash
1-893115-48-8	$29.95	Bischof	The .NET Languages: A Quick Translation Guide
1-893115-67-4	$49.95	Borge	Managing Enterprise Systems with the Windows Script Host
1-893115-28-3	$44.95	Challa/Laksberg	Essential Guide to Managed Extensions for C++
1-893115-39-9	$44.95	Chand	A Programmer's Guide to ADO.NET in C#
1-893115-44-5	$29.95	Cook	Robot Building for Beginners
1-893115-99-2	$39.95	Cornell/Morrison	Programming VB .NET: A Guide for Experienced Programmers
1-893115-72-0	$39.95	Curtin	Developing Trust: Online Privacy and Security
1-59059-008-2	$29.95	Duncan	The Career Programmer: Guerilla Tactics for an Imperfect World
1-893115-71-2	$39.95	Ferguson	Mobile .NET
1-893115-90-9	$49.95	Finsel	The Handbook for Reluctant Database Administrators
1-59059-024-4	$49.95	Fraser	Real World ASP.NET: Building a Content Management System
1-893115-42-9	$44.95	Foo/Lee	XML Programming Using the Microsoft XML Parser
1-893115-55-0	$34.95	Frenz	Visual Basic and Visual Basic .NET for Scientists and Engineers
1-893115-85-2	$34.95	Gilmore	A Programmer's Introduction to PHP 4.0
1-893115-36-4	$34.95	Goodwill	Apache Jakarta-Tomcat
1-893115-17-8	$59.95	Gross	A Programmer's Introduction to Windows DNA
1-893115-62-3	$39.95	Gunnerson	A Programmer's Introduction to C#, Second Edition
1-59059-009-0	$39.95	Harris/Macdonald	Moving to ASP.NET: Web Development with VB .NET
1-893115-30-5	$49.95	Harkins/Reid	SQL: Access to SQL Server
1-893115-10-0	$34.95	Holub	Taming Java Threads
1-893115-04-6	$34.95	Hyman/Vaddadi	Mike and Phani's Essential C++ Techniques
1-893115-96-8	$59.95	Jorelid	J2EE FrontEnd Technologies: A Programmer's Guide to Servlets, JavaServer Pages, and Enterprise JavaBeans
1-893115-49-6	$39.95	Kilburn	Palm Programming in Basic
1-893115-50-X	$34.95	Knudsen	Wireless Java: Developing with Java 2, Micro Edition
1-893115-79-8	$49.95	Kofler	Definitive Guide to Excel VBA
1-893115-57-7	$39.95	Kofler	MySQL
1-893115-87-9	$39.95	Kurata	Doing Web Development: Client-Side Techniques
1-893115-75-5	$44.95	Kurniawan	Internet Programming with VB

Apress Titles *(continued)*

ISBN	PRICE	AUTHOR	TITLE
1-893115-38-0	$24.95	Lafler	Power AOL: A Survival Guide
1-893115-46-1	$36.95	Lathrop	Linux in Small Business: A Practical User's Guide
1-893115-19-4	$49.95	Macdonald	Serious ADO: Universal Data Access with Visual Basic
1-893115-06-2	$39.95	Marquis/Smith	A Visual Basic 6.0 Programmer's Toolkit
1-893115-22-4	$27.95	McCarter	David McCarter's VB Tips and Techniques
1-893115-76-3	$49.95	Morrison	C++ For VB Programmers
1-893115-80-1	$39.95	Newmarch	A Programmer's Guide to Jini Technology
1-893115-58-5	$49.95	Oellermann	Architecting Web Services
1-893115-81-X	$39.95	Pike	SQL Server: Common Problems, Tested Solutions
1-59059-017-1	$34.95	Rainwater	Herding Cats: A Primer for Programmers Who Lead Programmers
1-59059-025-2	$49.95	Rammer	Advanced .NET Remoting
1-893115-20-8	$34.95	Rischpater	Wireless Web Development
1-893115-93-3	$34.95	Rischpater	Wireless Web Development with PHP and WAP
1-893115-89-5	$59.95	Shemitz	Kylix: The Professional Developer's Guide and Reference
1-893115-40-2	$39.95	Sill	The qmail Handbook
1-893115-24-0	$49.95	Sinclair	From Access to SQL Server
1-893115-94-1	$29.95	Spolsky	User Interface Design for Programmers
1-893115-53-4	$44.95	Sweeney	Visual Basic for Testers
1-59059-002-3	$44.95	Symmonds	Internationalization and Localization Using Microsoft .NET
1-893115-29-1	$44.95	Thomsen	Database Programming with Visual Basic .NET
1-59059-010-4	$54.95	Thomsen	Database Programming with C#
1-893115-65-8	$39.95	Tiffany	Pocket PC Database Development with eMbedded Visual Basic
1-893115-59-3	$59.95	Troelsen	C# and the .NET Platform
1-893115-26-7	$59.95	Troelsen	Visual Basic .NET and the .NET Platform
1-59059-011-2	$39.95	Troelsen	COM and .NET Interoperability
1-893115-54-2	$49.95	Trueblood/Lovett	Data Mining and Statistical Analysis Using SQL
1-893115-16-X	$49.95	Vaughn	ADO Examples and Best Practices
1-893115-68-2	$49.95	Vaughn	ADO.NET and ADO Examples and Best Practices for VB Programmers, Second Edition
1-59059-012-0	$49.95	Vaughn/Blackburn	ADO.NET Examples and Best Practices for C# Programmers
1-893115-83-6	$44.95	Wells	Code Centric: T-SQL Programming with Stored Procedures and Triggers
1-893115-95-X	$49.95	Welschenbach	Cryptography in C and C++
1-893115-05-4	$39.95	Williamson	Writing Cross-Browser Dynamic HTML
1-893115-78-X	$49.95	Zukowski	Definitive Guide to Swing for Java 2, Second Edition
1-893115-92-5	$49.95	Zukowski	Java Collections
1-893115-98-4	$54.95	Zukowski	Learn Java with JBuilder 6

Available at bookstores nationwide or from Springer Verlag New York, Inc. at 1-800-777-4643; fax 1-212-533-3503. Contact us for more information at sales@apress.com.

Apress Titles Publishing SOON!

ISBN	AUTHOR	TITLE
1-59059-022-8	Alapati	Expert Oracle 9i Database Administration
1-59059-015-5	Clark	An Introduction to Object Oriented Programming with Visual Basic .NET
1-59059-000-7	Cornell	Programming C#
1-59059-014-7	Drol	Object-Oriented Flash MX
1-59059-033-3	Fraser	Managed C++ and .NET Development
1-59059-038-4	Gibbons	Java Development to .NET Development
1-59059-030-9	Habibi/Camerlengo/ Patterson	Java 1.4 and the Sun Certified Developer Exam
1-59059-006-6	Hetland	Practical Python
1-59059-003-1	Nakhimovsky/Meyers	XML Programming: Web Applications and Web Services with JSP and ASP
1-59059-001-5	McMahon	Serious ASP.NET
1-59059-021-X	Moore	Karl Moore's Visual Basic .NET: The Tutorials
1-893115-27-5	Morrill	Tuning and Customizing a Linux System
1-59059-020-1	Patzer	JSP Examples and Best Practices
1-59059-028-7	Rischpater	Wireless Web Development, 2nd Edition
1-59059-026-0	Smith	Writing Add-Ins for .NET
1-893115-43-7	Stephenson	Standard VB: An Enterprise Developer's Reference for VB 6 and VB .NET
1-59059-032-5	Thomsen	Database Programming with Visual Basic .NET, 2nd Edition
1-59059-007-4	Thomsen	Building Web Services with VB .NET
1-59059-027-9	Torkelson/Petersen/ Torkelson	Programming the Web with Visual Basic .NET
1-59059-004-X	Valiaveedu	SQL Server 2000 and Business Intelligence in an XML/.NET World

Available at bookstores nationwide or from Springer Verlag New York, Inc. at 1-800-777-4643; fax 1-212-533-3503. Contact us for more information at sales@apress.com.

Apress™

License Agreement (Single-User Products)